Books by Maida Heatter

Maida Heatter's Book of Great Desserts   (1974)

Maida Heatter's Book of Great Cookies   (1977)

Maida Heatter's Book of Great Chocolate Desserts   (1980)

Maida Heatter's New Book of Great Desserts   (1982)

Maida Heatter's Book of Great American Desserts   (1985)

These are Borzoi Books,
published in New York by Alfred A. Knopf.

Maida Heatter's
Book of Great
American Desserts

Maida Heatter's

BOOK OF GREAT AMERICAN DESSERTS

Drawings by Toni Evins

ALFRED A. KNOPF   NEW YORK   1985

THIS IS A BORZOI BOOK
PUBLISHED BY ALFRED A. KNOPF, INC.

Copyright © 1983, 1984, 1985 by Maida Heatter

Illustrations copyright © 1985 by Toni Evins

The recipe for "Barron's Brownies" originally appeared in *Barron's*;
the receipes for "Bull's Eye Cheesecake" and "Chocolate Cheesecake
Brownies" originally appeared in *The New York Times*; and the recipe for
"My Mother's Gingersnaps" originally appeared in *McCall's* magazine.

Library of Congress Cataloging in Publication Data

Heatter, Maida.
Maida Heatter's Book of great American desserts.

Includes index.
1. Desserts.   I. Title.   II. Title: Book of great American desserts.
TX773.H347   1985   641.8'6   84-48657
ISBN 0-394-53809-9

Manufactured in the United States of America
Published September 27, 1985
Second Printing, October 1985

I want to thank my wonderful editor,
Nancy Nicholas. This is our fifth
book together.

Contents

Introduction

Everybody is talking about American food. People are trying to analyze and describe it, to define it, give it a pattern, an age, and borders. Has it been going on a long time or is it something new?

Obviously there is no one kind of American food; there are many kinds. There are recipes that were made when our country was young (apple pie, pecan pie, shoofly pie, cobblers and pandowdies, tea cakes, jam cakes, Indian pudding, things made with cranberries, recipes that use maple syrup, rum, et cetera). And recipes that feature our fabulous fresh fruits and other farm produce because of our progressive farmers and growers and because of our wonderful methods of transportation (jet airplanes transport fresh fruits and vegetables and other perishables from coast to coast in just a few hours). And we have anything and everything chocolate because the whole country loves it and just can't get enough. The same can be said about cheesecakes. And we have many modern creations inspired by nouvelle cuisine, which has had a tremendous influence on our food (lighter and more creative).

That's American? Yes, that's American.

We Americans are loving and tremendously respectful about our old and traditional recipes and have a desire to continue the traditions. And we are daring with new recipes even if we have never heard of them and even if they sound outrageous; we are not shy or bashful. We also have such impassioned romances with many foreign foods that now it is strange to realize that they came to us from other countries. Mainly, we have the freedom and the confidence to pick and choose from the old and the new and the foreign, and to mix them like an artist does with paints on a canvas.

President John F. Kennedy said in his inaugural address: "We are a nation of immigrants." It shows in our cuisine; American recipes reflect the foods from all other countries.

I am incurably fascinated by "old-fashioned" and "Early American" recipes (and also cobbler's benches and spatterware and old quilts and anything Pennsylvania Dutch or primitive), so there are many old recipes in this book and many new ones too.

One thing that might describe these recipes is simplicity—that does not mean quick and easy; it means bare, basic, Early American plainness. And generosity: pies that are deep and cookies that are large and cakes that are "as high as an elephant's eye" and recipes that call for generous amounts of ingredients. Although I made some of the very old recipes with less sugar than they used in the originals, and they taste even better.

This is the greatest country in the world, and we have the best food in the world. No other country produces the quantity of food we do or has the standard of living that we have. (Actually, food is the biggest industry in America.) And now for the first time we also have great American chefs. We should be very proud of many of our young people who are becoming involved with food at the college level and are training for careers in it. (I envy them.) Today being a chef is considered a glamorous position; young people now are proud to say "I am a cook" or "a chef." No other country in the world has the number of modern kitchens with fantastic equipment that we have or the cooking schools and traveling cooking teachers and television shows that teach cooking; therefore, now we have the best home cooks in the world.

Actually, the country is now being bombarded, blitzed, blanketed, with food and everything related to it; the food magazines and cookbooks alone could probably fill the Grand Canyon, the restaurants and grocery stores and take-out stores and pasta shops would cover (as indeed they almost do) the entire state of California, the chocolate truffles would make a mountain as high as Pikes Peak in Colorado, the goat cheese and mesquite and pizzas and jalapeño peppers, laid end-to-end, would stretch from here to the moon, and if all of the ice creams were put in one pile over Central Park it would sink Manhattan. When there is no room in America for more food items, we make room for more. We love it. We eat it up. It is an old story that this is a land of plenty but now more than ever we are wonderfully, deliciously, food crazy—food happy—food nuts.

God bless America.

Maida Heatter

About This Book

I have spent the better part (the best part) of my life cooking, mostly desserts, many American desserts. I have written four other dessert cookbooks. They were not planned as especially American books. But now that I am writing this book of American desserts, I see that what I was doing before was closely related, and many traditional American desserts are in my other books. I am sorry if you look for something here and do not find it; chances are it is in one of my other books. There are too many such recipes for me to repeat them here. And even after writing this one, there are still many wonderful American desserts that I have not written about yet. Maybe next time.

Maida Heatter's Book of Great American Desserts

Ingredients

FLOUR

Many of these recipes call for sifted flour. That means that even if the package is labeled "presifted," you should sift the flour before measuring. If not, since flour packs down while standing, 1 cup of unsifted flour is liable to be a few spoonfuls more than 1 cup of just-sifted flour.

Sift the flour onto a piece of wax paper. Make sure that there is no flour left in the sifter. Then transfer the sifter to another piece of wax paper. Use a metal measuring cup (from a set of graded cups) and lightly spoon the sifted flour into the cup or lift it on a dough scraper and transfer it to the cup—do not pack or press the flour down—and scrape the excess off the top with a dough scraper or any flat-sided implement. If the sifted flour is to be sifted with other ingredients, return it to the sifter, then add the ingredients to be sifted with it, and sift onto the second piece of wax paper. Again, make sure there is nothing left in the sifter.

It is not necessary ever to wash a flour sifter; just shake it out firmly and store it in a plastic bag.

Bleached or unbleached flour can be used in those recipes that call for all-purpose flour.

SUGAR

All sugars should be measured in the graded measuring cups made for measuring dry ingredients.

Brown Sugar: Most brown sugars are made of white granulated sugar to which a dark syrup has been added. Dark brown sugar has a mild molasses, and light brown sugar has a milder, lighter syrup (which may also be molasses). Dark brown has a slightly stronger flavor, but dark and light may be used interchangeably. The label on Grandma's Molasses says, "You can easily make your own brown sugar as you need it by blending together ½ cup of granulated sugar with two tablespoons of unsulphured molasses. The yield is equivalent to ½ cup of brown sugar."

Brown sugar is moist; if it dries out it will harden, so it should be stored airtight. If it has small lumps, they should be strained out. With your fingertips press the sugar through a large, wide strainer set over a large bowl. The Savannah Sugar Refinery is now printing the following directions on its boxes of brown sugar: "If your brown sugar has been left open and becomes hard, place a dampened (not wet) paper towel inside the resealable poly bag and close the package tightly for 12 hours or more. A slice of apple can be used in place of the dampened towel."

Confectioners Sugar: Confectioners sugar and powdered sugar are exactly the same. They are both granulated sugar that has been pulverized and had about 3 percent cornstarch added to keep it powdery. Of the confectioners sugars, 4-x is the least fine and 10-x is the finest. They may be used interchangeably. Confectioners sugar should be strained; you can do several pounds at a time, if you wish. It does not have to be done immediately before using, as flour does. Store it airtight.

If directions say to sprinkle with confectioners sugar, place the sugar in a fine strainer, hold it over the top of the cake or dessert, and tap the strainer lightly with your hand or shake it to shake out the sugar.

Vanilla Confectioners Sugar: This is flavored confectioners sugar that is used to sprinkle over cakes and cookies. It adds a nice mild flavor and a delicious aroma. To make it, fill a jar that has a tight cover with confectioners sugar. Split one or two vanilla beans the long way and bury them in the sugar. Cover tightly and let stand for at least a few days before using. As the sugar is used it may be replaced. The vanilla beans will continue to flavor and perfume the sugar for a month or two.

When you make this, don't bother to strain the sugar beforehand. The vanilla beans give off a small amount of moisture that the sugar absorbs, causing it to become lumpy and making it necessary to strain it just before using.

Crystal Sugar: Crystal sugar, also called pearl sugar, or *Hagelzucker* in German, is generally used to sprinkle over certain cookies and pastries before baking. It is coarser than granulated sugar. It is available at Paprikas Weiss, 1546 Second Avenue, New York, New York 10028; and at H. Roth & Son, 1577 First Avenue, New York, New York 10028. Paprikas Weiss and H. Roth both have catalogs.

BITTER ALMOND EXTRACT

Bitter almond is a flavoring that is stronger than plain almond extract; it has a deliciously and slightly bitter flavor that cuts and mellows desserts that might seem too sweet without it. It is wonderful in chocolate recipes. Or vanilla recipes. Or with peaches or apricots. Whenever I use plain almond extract I add a few drops of bitter almond. I have used it for years but I did not mention it sooner because I did not know a source for it. Now I do.

Bitter almond extract is available from H. Roth & Son, 1577 First Avenue, New York, New York 10028. If you write to them, request a catalog. By the way, at H. Roth they tell me that this extract is made from peach kernels.

ADDING VANILLA EXTRACT

I have read reviews that question the fact that I add vanilla (and other extracts) to the soft butter instead of waiting and adding it last. Since no one has ever said a recipe did not work because of this, I wonder why it matters to some people. However, if you care, here's why I do it.

Many years ago I read an article about cooking by someone who seemed much smarter than I am about food chemistry. The article said that adding the vanilla extract to the butter at the beginning seals in the flavor—something about adding it to the fat before liquid has been added.

I have no idea if this is true or not. I just do it that way in case it is. The results seem to be OK.

WHIPPING CREAM

Plain old-fashioned whipping cream is scarce nowadays unless you have your own cow. Too bad, because the super- or ultra-pasteurized (known as UHT—ultra-high-temperature pasteurized) is not as good, at least I don't think so. The reason dairies make it is that it has a 6-to-8-week shelf life. (They call it a "pull date"; the stores have to pull it off their shelves if it is not sold by the date stamped on the container.) This product is called either "heavy whipping cream" or "heavy cream," depending on the manufacturer. Either one can be used in recipes calling for "whipping cream."

The process of making ultra-pasteurized cream involves heating the cream to 250 degrees for 1 second. It gives the cream a slight caramel flavor (so mild you might not notice it) and makes it more difficult to whip (it will take longer). It is advisable to chill the bowl and beaters in the freezer for about half an hour before whipping. And keep the cream in the refrigerator until you are ready to whip; do not let it stand around in the kitchen—it should be as cold as possible.

It seems to me that baked custards take longer to set if they are made with UHT cream, and ice cream takes longer to churn.

How to Whip Cream: The best way to whip either plain old-fashioned or UHT cream is to place it in a large bowl, set the bowl in a larger bowl of ice and water, and whip with a large, thin-wired, balloon-type whisk. You get more volume that way, and it tastes better.

If that seems like more than you want to fuss with, use an electric mixer or an eggbeater, and chill the bowl and beaters before using them. If the bowl does not revolve by itself, then move the beaters around the bowl to whip all the cream evenly at the same time.

When I whip cream with an electric mixer, I always (and I recommend this to everyone) finish the whipping by hand with a wire whisk; there is less chance of overwhipping. At this stage you can use a smaller whisk than if you are doing it all by hand.

Whipped cream, which can be heavenly, is not quite so delicious if it is whipped until it is really stiff—softer is better.

NO BUTTERMILK? If a recipe calls for buttermilk and you do not have any, here's how to make your own. Warm 1 cup of regular milk (sweet milk) over low heat to room temperature (70 degrees). Place 1 tablespoon of lemon juice in a 1-cup glass measuring cup, then fill to the 1-cup line with the room-temperature milk, stir, and let stand for 10 minutes. (The homemade version will have larger curds than commercial buttermilk has.)

EGGS *Size:* The size of eggs can be very important in certain recipes. In cakes without flour, or with very little, if the egg whites are too large there might be more air beaten into them than the other ingredients can support and the cake might fall. On the other hand, in certain gelatin desserts, or in some mousses or soufflés, if the egg whites are too small there might not be enough air for the dessert to be as light as it should be.

In each recipe, I have indicated the size or choice of sizes that should be used.

To Open Eggs: If directions call for adding whole eggs one at a time, they may all be opened ahead of time into one container and then poured into the other ingredients, approximately one at a time. Do not open eggs directly into the ingredients—you would not know if a piece of shell had been included.

To Separate Eggs: Eggs separate more safely—there is less chance of the yolk breaking—when they are cold. Therefore, if a recipe calls for separated eggs, it is usually the first thing I do when organizing the ingredients so that they are cold from the refrigerator.

The safest way to separate eggs is as follows. Place three small glass custard cups or shallow drinking glasses or bowls in front of you. One container is for the whites and one for the yolks. The third might not be needed, but if you should break the yolk when opening an egg, just drop the whole thing in the third container and save it for some other use.

Tap the side of the egg firmly (but not too hard or you might break the yolk) on the edge of the cup or glass or bowl to crack the shell, with luck, in a rather straight, even line. Then, holding the egg upright and with both hands (so that the halves each make a cup), separate the halves of the shell, letting some of the white run into the cup or glass or bowl. Pour the yolk back and forth from one half of the egg shell to the other, letting all of the white run out. Drop the yolk into the second cup or glass or bowl.

Many professional cooks simply open the egg into the palm of one hand, then hold their fingers, slightly separated, over a bowl. They let the white run through their open fingers, and then slide the left-behind yolk into a second bowl.

As each egg is separated the white should be transferred to another container (that is, in addition to the three—it could be another bowl or glass or it might be the mixing bowl you will beat the whites in), because if you place all of the whites in one container there is a chance that the last egg white might have some yolk in it, which could spoil all of the whites. Generally, a tiny bit of yolk or shell can be removed from the whites with an empty half shell. Or try a piece of paper towel dipped in cold water.

To Beat Egg Whites: The success of many recipes depends on properly beaten whites. After you have learned how, it becomes second nature.

First, the bowl and beaters must be absolutely clean. A little bit of fat (egg yolks are fat) will prevent the whites from incorporating air as they should and from rising properly.

Second, do not overbeat or the whites will become dry and you will not be able to fold them into other ingredients without losing the air you have beaten in.

Third, do not beat them ahead of time. They must be folded in immediately after they are beaten; if they have to wait they separate. (Incidentally, if the whites are being folded into a cake batter, the cake must then be placed in the oven right away.)

You can use an electric mixer, a rotary beater, or a wire whisk (although a wire whisk and a copper bowl are said to give the best results).

If you use an electric mixer or a rotary beater, be careful not to use a bowl that is too large or the whites will be too shallow to get the full benefit of the beaters' action. If the bowl or beaters do not revolve by themselves (as they do in electric mixers on a stand), move the mixer or beater around the bowl to beat all the whites evenly. If you use a mixer on a stand, use a rubber spatula frequently to push the whites from the side of the bowl into the center.

If you use a wire whisk, it should be a large, thin-wired balloon type, at least 4 inches wide at the top. The bowl should be very large, the larger the better, to give you plenty of room for making large circular motions with the whisk. An unlined copper bowl is the best, or you may use glass, china, or stainless steel—but do not beat egg whites in aluminum, which might discolor the whites, or plastic, which is frequently porous and might be greasy from some other use.

A copper bowl should be treated each time before using as follows. Put 1 or 2 teaspoons of salt in the bowl and rub thoroughly with half a lemon, squeezing a bit of the juice and mixing it with the salt. Then rinse with hot water (no soap) and dry. After using a copper bowl, wash it as you would any other, but be sure to treat it before beating egg whites again.

When I beat egg whites with an electric mixer, if they do not have sugar added (sugar makes them more creamy and slightly lessens the chance of overbeating), I always—and I recommend this to everyone—finish the beating with a wire whisk. There is less chance of overbeating, and the whisk seems to give the whites a slightly creamy consistency. At this stage you can use a smaller whisk than the one mentioned above—use any one that seems right for the bowl the whites are in.

People often ask me if I bring whites to room temperature before beating them. If I do, it is a rare occasion and was not planned. They are usually cold when I beat them (because I do not plan ahead and do not have the patience to wait and because I have had equally good results whether cold or at room temperature).

To Freeze Egg Whites or Yolks: Some of the recipes in this book call for yolks and no whites, and some call for only whites. (If you have just a few extra of either left over and do not want to save them for something else, add them to scrambled eggs.)

Leftover egg whites may be kept covered in the refrigerator for a few days or they may be frozen. I freeze them individually (or occasionally two or four together) in ovenproof glass custard cups. When they are frozen, hold one cup upside down under hot running water until the frozen egg white can be removed (but not until it melts). Quickly wrap each frozen egg white individually in plastic wrap and return to the freezer. To use, remove the number you want, unwrap, place them in a cup or bowl, and let stand at room temperature to thaw. Or place them, in a cup or bowl, in a slightly warm oven or in a pan of shallow warm water.

To freeze egg yolks, stir them lightly just to mix, and for each yolk stir in ⅓ teaspoon of granulated sugar or ½ teaspoon of honey. Freeze them in a covered jar, labeling so you will know how many yolks and how much sugar or honey. When thawed, stir to mix well—they will not look exactly the same as before they were frozen (not as smooth), but they will work in recipes.

NUTS

Nuts can turn rancid rather quickly—walnuts and pecans more so than almonds. Always store all nuts airtight in the freezer or refrigerator. In the refrigerator nuts last well for 9 months; in the freezer at zero degrees they will last for 2 years. Bring them to room temperature before using; smell and taste them before you use them (preferably when you buy them)—you will know quickly if they are rancid. If you even suspect that they might be, do not use them; they would ruin a recipe.

To Toast Pecans: Pecans occasionally become limp after they are frozen, so I toast them. Toasted pecans are so great that now I toast all pecans (those that have been frozen and those that have not) before using them, as follows. Place them in a shallow pan in the middle of a preheated 350-degree oven for 15 to 20 minutes, stirring them occasionally, until they are very hot but not until they become darker in color.

To Blanch (or Skin) Almonds: Cover the almonds with boiling water. The skin will loosen almost immediately. Spoon out a few nuts at a time and, one by one, hold them under cold running water and squeeze them between your thumb and forefinger. The nuts will pop out and the skin will remain. Place the peeled almonds on a towel to dry. Then spread them in a shallow baking pan and bake in a preheated 200-degree oven for 30 minutes or so until they are completely dry. Do not let them brown.

If the almonds are to be split, sliced, or slivered, they should remain in the hot water longer to soften; let them stand until the water cools enough for you to touch it comfortably. Then, one at a time, remove the skin from each nut and immediately, while the nut is still soft, place it on a cutting board and cut with a small, sharp paring knife. Then bake to dry them as above. Sliced almonds are those that have been cut into very thin slices; slivered almonds are the fatter, oblong, "julienne"-shaped pieces. Don't expect sliced or slivered almonds that you have cut up yourself to be as even as store-bought ones. (Sometimes I think I like the uneven look better.)

Pistachio Nuts: A light sprinkling of chopped green pistachio nuts is a nice touch. But don't overdo it; less is better than more. Fine pastries might have only about a teaspoon of them sprinkled in the center of the icing on a 9-inch cake.

Buy shelled unsalted green pistachios. They are hard to find, but they keep for a long time in the freezer. Try wholesale nut dealers or specialty nut shops. In New York they are available (by mail too) from Paprikas Weiss, 1546 Second Avenue, New York, New York 10028.

Chop the pistachios coarse or fine on a board using a long, heavy knife. Don't worry about the little pieces of skin that flake off; you can leave them with the nuts (or pick out the large pieces of skin, if you wish).

WHOLESALE NUTS: *I often buy nuts from a wholesale nut company here where it is not necessary to buy huge amounts. Recently I bought a supply of blanched (skinned) hazelnuts, monster cashew nuts, and macadamia nuts, all unsalted and untoasted. I have often used a mixture of them (whole—not cut up) in Brownie recipes; they may be toasted first in a shallow pan in a 350-degree oven for 15 to 20 minutes. Biting into a dark, moist, chocolate Brownie, and finding whole cashews and/or macadamias, et cetera, is fabulous. The nut dealer told me that they will fill mail orders. It is the Barnard Nut Company, 113 N.W. 36th Street, Miami, Florida 33127.*

COFFEE AS A
FLAVORING

Often people ask me about the instruction "use powdered (not granular) instant coffee." If a recipe specifies powdered, it is because the granular would stay in granules and would not dissolve. Spice Islands brand, generally available in specialty food stores, makes powdered instant espresso and also a powdered instant coffee—they both work well in recipes. And Medaglia D'Oro instant espresso, which is powdered and works well, is generally available in large cities.

When a recipe calls for dissolving instant coffee in water, if you leave out the coffee, do not leave out the water.

FRESH GINGER

Do not buy any that is soft and wrinkled—it should be firm and hard (like potatoes). To store: For a few days—or even weeks, if it is firm and fresh—it can just stand at room temperature (like potatoes). For a longer time, it can be stored in the vegetable crisper in the refrigerator—wrapped or unwrapped does not seem to make any difference. Or it can be frozen, wrapped airtight in plastic or foil.

(A chef at a famous San Francisco restaurant told me that he keeps fresh ginger for weeks at room temperature, lying on its side in a shallow dish with about half an inch of water in the dish, and he adds water occasionally as it evaporates. About a month ago, when I had just bought some nice fresh ginger, I put one piece in water, and another alongside it but not in water. Now, a month later, the piece which is not in water looks healthier. The piece that is in water looks barely wrinkled—or is it my imagination? This experiment proves that if it is in good condition when you buy it, ginger is strong and hardy and lasts well almost in spite of what you do to it.)

It is not necessary to peel ginger. It may be grated on a standing metal grater on the side that has small round openings (rather than diamond-shaped openings). It may be grated if it is at room temperature, or refrigerated, or frozen. Either way it is slow work to grate much. But it is quick and easy—it is a breeze—to grate it in a food processor. First slice it crossways into very thin slices, or about 1/8 inch thick. (Although the processor will grate the ginger very well, it will leave fibers in the mixture; slicing it thin before processing reduces the length of fibers. Incidentally, older ginger is more fibrous than young ginger; it is also more gingery and flavorful. But either is wonderful.) Fit the processor with the metal chopping blade. With the motor going, add the slices of ginger one or two at a time through the feed tube, pausing briefly between additions. Stop the machine once or twice to scrape the sides of the bowl with a rubber spatula and then process again for a few seconds.

If you plan to freeze the ginger and then grate it, frozen, in a food processor, it is best to slice it thin before you freeze it. But it is possible, if necessary, to cut up (slice) frozen ginger with a heavy Chinese cleaver, a strong arm, and patience.

It is also possible to grate the ginger (easiest in a processor) and wrap it in measured amounts and freeze it; thaw before using. Or coarsely chop the block of frozen, grated ginger with a heavy cleaver, and drop the pieces through the feed tube of a processor (fitted with the metal chopping blade) with the motor going, and process until it returns to the grated texture. It will be wetter than ginger that has been grated but not frozen, but that does not noticeably affect its use in baking (although sometimes I think that ginger that has been frozen is not as sharp and gingery as it was before it was frozen, but that is hard to judge).

Incidentally, fresh-produce people tell me that Hawaiian ginger is the best.

CHOCOLATE

Callebaut Chocolate: Several years ago the Callebaut Chocolate Company (the chocolate is made in Belgium) sent me some samples and I thought it was absolutely great. But when I tried to buy it I found that it was sold only in huge quantities (will you have one carload or two?). At that time I recommended it to The Four Seasons Restaurant in New York City and the minimum order was more than even they could use.

I am happy to tell you that I just found two sources for it in reasonable amounts—1-pound or 11-pound bars: H. Roth & Son, 1577 First Avenue, New York, New York 10028. And for the other source, just call 1-800-421-9873 and ask for their catalog. (It is S. E. Rykoff & Co. in Los Angeles, California.) When you get their catalog, look for B. DARK CHOCOLATE. That is it, even though the catalog does not mention Callebaut (but if you study the photograph you will see the name imprinted on the chocolate).

Do not order it during very hot weather—it melts. Use it for any recipe that calls for semisweet or bittersweet chocolate (each 17-ounce bar is divided into 8 strips—that makes each strip a generous 2 ounces), or eat it as it is . . . you will love it!

Maillard Chocolate: If you use a lot of Maillard chocolate and would like to buy it wholesale, their address is Box 1158, Bethlehem, Pennsylvania 18106. They have a $150 minimum order. They have a price list. (Tell them I sent you.)

Equipment

ELECTRIC MIXERS

I use an electric mixer on a stand that comes with two different-size bowls and a pair of beaters (rather than one, as some mixers have). Mine is a Sunbeam Mixmaster.

I think it is important, or at least extremely helpful, for many dessert recipes to use a mixer that:
    a. is on a stand;
    b. comes with both a small and a large bowl; and
    c. has space to scrape the sides of the bowl with a rubber spatula while the mixer is going.

I especially recommend that you buy an extra set of bowls and extra beaters—they are generally available at the service center for your mixer.

Incidentally, although I have a hand-held electric mixer, I could live without it. (But if I did not have any other I am sure I would learn to love it.) If you are using a hand-held mixer or an eggbeater, when I say "small bowl of an electric mixer" that means one with a 7-cup capacity, and "large bowl of an electric mixer" means a 16-cup capacity.

THERMOMETERS

Oven Temperature: One of the most important and most overlooked requirements for good results in baking is correct oven temperature. The wrong temperature can cause a cake to fall, to burn, to be underdone, to refuse to rise; it can ruin a soufflé; it can turn cookies that should be wonderfully crisp into pale, limp, soggy things; and it could be the cause of almost any other baking disaster that you might have experienced or heard about.

No matter how new or how good your oven is, *please* double-check the temperature every time you bake. Use a small portable oven thermometer from the hardware store or kitchen shop. Buy the mercury kind—it is best. Light your oven at least 20 minutes ahead of time and place the thermometer on a rack close to the middle of the oven. Give the oven plenty of time to heat and cycle and reheat before you read the thermometer. If it does not register the heat you want, adjust the thermostat up or down until the mercury thermometer registers the correct heat—no matter what the oven setting says.

When you put unbaked cakes or cookies in the oven, they reduce the oven temperature more than you would expect. If you check the temperature on a portable oven thermometer during about the first 10 minutes of baking, don't think that your oven suddenly got sick; give it time to reheat.

Other Thermometers: A friend told me she did not know that her refrigerator was too warm until she served a large chocolate icebox cake at a dinner party and, at the table—with everyone watching—she found that the middle was soft and runny instead of firm as it should have been. And once I didn't know that my freezer wasn't right until the very last minute, when a photographer was here to take pictures of a chocolate dessert; I had waited until he was ready to shoot before I took out of the freezer the big, gorgeous chocolate curls that I had made so carefully and found they had melted and flattened and were no longer curls.

Keep a freezer thermometer in your freezer and a refrigerator thermometer in your refrigerator—and look at them often.

And for many of the recipes in this book you will need a thermometer labeled a "candy-jelly-frosting thermometer," even if you never use it for candy or jelly; it is important to have for making many dessert sauces.

And a frying thermometer is essential for making doughnuts.

Always bend down and read the thermometer at eye level in order to get a correct reading.

CAKE PANS

A New Cake Pan: Fred Bridge of Bridge Kitchenware recently had a new pan made (he said he had it made especially for me). It is a perfectly wonderful pan that makes a gorgeous, tall, and handsome cake.

In my first book there are many recipes that call for a 9-inch tube pan. It was not an unusual pan when I wrote the book; I think that every hardware store carried it. But at just about the same time the book was published, the companies that had manufactured that pan stopped making it.

I cannot tell you how many people wrote to me asking where to buy it. And I cannot tell you how hard my husband and I tried to locate a source for it. Mr. Bridge says that this new pan is for all the requests he has had for "a 9-inch tube pan."

This is not exactly the same as the pan I used originally. My old ones are two-piece; this new one is one-piece. The old ones had an 11-cup capacity; this new one has a 14-cup capacity (filled to overflowing). This new one is heavier, stronger, sturdier, and deeper, and has a much wider tube in the middle. It is available from Bridge Kitchenware, 214 East 52nd Street, New York, New York 10022.

Swirl Tube Pan (a.k.a. Turk's Head mold): Another tube pan that I use very often for many of these recipes is 10 inches in diameter, 4 inches high, has a 1¾-inch-wide tube at the top, a 12-cup capacity, is made in France of heavy tin, and has a beautiful swirl pattern that makes gorgeous cakes. This is also available from Bridge Kitchenware (see above).

My Favorite So-called 9-Inch Loaf Pan: The most popular 8-cup loaf pan measures 9 by 5 by 3 inches. But my favorite shape, available in many kitchen shops, makes a longer and narrower loaf. The pan measures 10¼ by 3¾ (width at the top) by 3⅜ (depth) inches and is made of heavy aluminum (but is not a dark metal). It can be bought at, or ordered by mail from, Bobbi & Carole's Cookshop, 7251 S.W. 57th Court, Miami, Florida 33143.

Miniature Muffin Pans: Once on a car trip from Florida to New York we wandered off the highway in Georgia and found a lovely little kitchen shop. I bought some nonstick miniature muffin pans that are made in Georgia. Each muffin form is 1¾ inches wide and ¾ inch deep; each pan makes 12 muffins. I don't know the name of the shop in Georgia, but my friends at Bobbi & Carole's (see above) have arranged to carry the pans. They will fill mail orders.

Dull/Dark Pans: Bright, shiny surfaces reflect the heat away from the item being baked, preventing the item from browning. Dark, dull metal (black, blue, blue-black, dark brown) and nonstick finishes absorb and hold the heat, encouraging a dark crust on the item being baked. This is especially noticeable when what is being baked is a yeast dough, or a pastry in a quiche or tart pan. These dark pans are becoming more available lately than they used to be. Bridge Kitchenware, 214 East 52nd Street, New York, New York 10022, always has a complete assortment of them.

Tube Pans: In all of these recipes that call for a tube pan, use a one-piece pan unless the recipe specifies a two-piece pan.

COOKIE SHEETS AND ALUMINUM FOIL

I use Wear-Ever cookie sheets that measure 15½ by 12 inches and have only one raised rim, and I line them with aluminum foil (instead of buttering the sheets—the foil keeps the cookies from sticking). The usual extra-large roll of 12-inch foil has 200 feet. If you would like a box of foil that has 1,000 feet, in a strong box with a wonderful cutting edge, you can buy it (and the above cookie sheets) from Bobbi & Carole's Cookshop; see above for address.

DOUBLE BOILERS

Many of the recipes in this book call for a double boiler. You can buy them in hardware stores or kitchen shops. The thing to look for is one in which the upper section is not too deep and is smooth (no ridges). I like the Revere Ware double boilers; they come in two sizes, and I use both.

If necessary, you can create your own by placing a heatproof bowl over a saucepan of shallow hot water. The bowl should be wide enough at the top to rest on the rim of the saucepan, keeping the bowl suspended over (not touching) the water.

ROLLING PINS

If you have many occasions to use a rolling pin (and I hope that you will—with the pies and rolled cookies and doughnuts in this book), you really should have different sizes and different shapes. Sometimes a very long, thick, and heavy pin will be best; for other doughs you will want a smaller, lighter one. The French style, which is extra long (actually, 20 inches long), narrow, and tapered at both ends, is especially good for rolling dough into a round shape, as for a piecrust, while the straight-sided pin is better for an oblong shape.

In the absence of any rolling pin at all, other things will do a fair job. Try a straight-sided bottle, tall jar, or drinking glass.

If you ice many cakes, this is a most important piece of equipment. Not that you can't ice a cake without it; you can, but it will not look the same. You will love the smooth, professional-looking results, and the ease of using a turntable. It works on the same principle as a lazy Susan, and although a lazy Susan can be used in place of a turntable, it usually does not turn as easily.

I put the cake on a plate, and then put the plate on the turntable.

First, put the icing on freely just to cover the cake. Then hold a long, narrow metal spatula in your right hand, with the blade at about a 30-degree angle against the side or the top of the cake. With your left hand slowly rotate the turntable counterclockwise. Hold your right hand still as the cake turns and in a few seconds you will have a smooth, sleek, neat-looking cake. It is fun. And exciting.

I also use the turntable when trimming and then fluting the edge of pie-crust. (You will love using it for this and will wonder how you ever did without it.)

Turntables are available at specialty kitchen shops and at wholesale restaurant and bakery suppliers. They do not have to be expensive. The thing to look for is one that turns very easily. There is no reason a turntable, if it is not abused, should not last a lifetime or two.

PASTRY BAGS

The best pastry bags for many years have been those that are made of canvas and are coated on one side only with plastic. Use them with the plastic coating inside. The small opening generally has to be cut a bit larger to allow the metal tubes (tips) to fit.

They should be washed in hot soapy water, then just set aside to dry. (I usually stand them upright over a glass to dry.)

When filling a pastry bag, always fold down a deep cuff on the outside of the bag. Unless there is someone else to hold it for you, it is generally easiest if you support the bag by placing it in a tall, wide glass or jar. After the bag is filled, unfold the cuff and twist the top closed.

SMALL, NARROW METAL SPATULA

Many of these recipes call for this tool for smoothing the icing around the sides of a cake. Mine is 8 inches long; and it has a 4-inch blade and a 4-inch wooden handle. The blade is ⅝ inch wide and has a rounded top. Although it can bend, it is more firm than flexible. A table knife can sometimes be used in place of this small spatula. Metal spatulas are available in a variety of sizes and shapes at kitchen shops.

Techniques

ABOUT MEASURING

Meticulously precise measurements are essential for good results in baking.

Glass or plastic measuring cups with the measurements marked on the side and the 1-cup line below the top are only for measuring liquids. Do not use them for flour or sugar. With the cup at eye level, fill carefully to exactly the line indicated.

Measuring cups that come in graded sets of four (¼ cup, ⅓ cup, ½ cup, and 1 cup—as well as a new 2-cup size that is pretty handy) are for measuring flour, sugar, and other dry ingredients—and for thick sour cream, and peanut butter. Fill the cup to overflowing and then scrape or cut off the excess with a dough scraper, a metal spatula, or the flat side of a knife.

Standard measuring spoons must be used for correct measurements. They come in sets of four (¼ teaspoon, ½ teaspoon, 1 teaspoon, and 1 tablespoon).

For dry ingredients, fill the spoon to overflowing and then scrape off the excess with a small metal spatula or the flat side of a knife.

<table>
<tr><td>

TO ADD DRY INGRED-
IENTS ALTERNATELY
WITH LIQUID

</td><td>

Begin and end with dry. The procedure is generally to add about one third of the dry, then half of the liquid, a second third of the dry, the rest of the liquid, and then the rest of the dry.

Use the lowest speed on an electric mixer (or it may be done by hand stirring with a rubber or wooden spatula). After each addition mix only until smooth. If your mixer is the type that allows you to scrape the sides with a rubber spatula while the mixer is going, do so to help the mixing along. If the mixer does not allow room, or if it is a hand-held mixer, stop it frequently and scrape the bowl with a rubber spatula; do not beat any more than necessary.

</td></tr>
<tr><td>

ABOUT FOLDING
INGREDIENTS
TOGETHER

</td><td>

Many of the recipes in this book call for folding beaten egg whites and/or whipped cream into another mixture. The whites and/or cream have had air beaten into them, and folding rather than mixing is done in order to retain the air.

This is a very important step and should be done with care. The knack of doing it well comes with practice and concentration. Remember that you want to incorporate the mixtures without losing any air. That means handle as little as possible.

It is important not to beat the whites or whip the cream until they are actually stiff. If you do, you will have to stir and mix rather than fold, thereby losing the air.

Other don't's: Do not let beaten whites stand around or they will become dry and will separate. Do not fold whipped cream into a warm mixture or the heat will deflate the cream. Generally it is best actually to *stir* a bit of the beaten whites or whipped cream into the heavier mixture (to lighten it a bit) before you start to fold in. Then, as a rule, it is best not to add all of the remaining light mixture at once; do the folding in a few additions. The first additions should not be folded thoroughly.

Although many professional chefs use their bare hands for folding, most home cooks are more comfortable using a rubber spatula. Rubber is better than plastic because it is more flexible. Spatulas come in three sizes. The smallest is called a bottle scraper. For most folding the medium size is the one to use. But for folding large amounts in a large bowl, the largest size can be very helpful. The one I mean might measure about 13 to 16 inches from the end of the blade to the end of the handle; the blade will be about 2¾ inches wide and about 4½ inches long.

To fold ingredients together it is best to use a bowl with a rounded bottom, and it is better if the bowl is too large rather than too small.

Hold the rubber spatula, rounded side toward the bottom and over the middle of the bowl, and cut through to the bottom of the bowl. Bring the spatula toward you against the bottom, then up the side and out, over the top, turning your wrist and the blade as you do this so the blade is upside down when it comes out over the top. Return the spatula to its original position, then cut through the middle of the mixture again. After each fold, rotate the bowl slightly in order to incorporate the ingredients as much as possible. Continue only until both mixtures are barely combined.

Occasionally a bit of beaten egg white will rise to the top. If just one or two small pieces rise, instead of folding more, simply smooth over the top gently with the spatula.

If the base mixture has gelatin in it, it should be chilled until it just starts to thicken before beaten egg whites or whipped cream are folded in, or the heavier mixture will sink.

</td></tr>
</table>

When folding, it is ideal to have the gelatin mixture, the whipped cream, and/or the egg whites all the same consistency (although in some cases that is not possible).

TO MEASURE THE CAPACITY OF A CAKE PAN

Fill a large measuring cup with water and pour it into the pan until it just starts to overflow.

If it is a two-piece pan, and the water would run out, fill it with sugar or rice or beans instead of water.

TO BUTTER A FANCY-SHAPED TUBE PAN

If you spread the butter in a fancy tube pan with a piece of crumpled wax paper, it feels clumsy and seems inefficient. If you melt the butter and brush it on, most of the butter runs down to the bottom of the pan. It is best to let some butter stand at room temperature to soften, then use a pastry brush to brush it carefully all over the pan.

ABOUT PREPARING CAKE PANS

In many recipes, after buttering the pan (always with unsalted butter), I dust it with bread crumbs, because there is often less chance of sticking if you use crumbs rather than flour. The crumbs should be fine and dry. They may be homemade (see below), but I always have store-bought ones on hand. If you use bought ones, be sure to buy the ones marked "plain" or "unseasoned."

To prepare a tube pan: When directions call for buttering the pan and then coating it with crumbs, lift the crumbs with your fingers and sprinkle around the tube with your fingers.

In all the recipes in this book, the butter and bread crumbs used to prepare the pan are in addition to those called for in the ingredients.

HOMEMADE BREAD CRUMBS

Use sliced white bread, with or without the crusts. Place the slices in a single layer on cookie sheets in a 225-degree oven and bake until the bread is completely dry and crisp (although if the bread is so stale that it is completely dry, it is not necessary to bake it). Break up the slices coarsely and grind them in a food processor or a blender until the crumbs are rather fine, but not as fine as a powder.

TO WASH STRAWBERRIES

Remove them from their boxes as soon as possible. Place them in a single layer on a tray lined with paper towels and refrigerate until you are ready to wash them. They can be washed many hours before serving or shortly before.

Fill a large bowl with cool water. Place a wide strainer in the bowl, so that the rim of the strainer rests on the rim of the bowl. Place the berries in the strainer, and raise and lower it into the water a few times to rinse the berries. Then lift the strainer and pour the water out of the bowl, and replace the strainer on the rim of the bowl. If you are going to remove the green hulls do it now, and then place the berries in a single layer on a tray covered with paper towels and refrigerate uncovered.

TO WASH BLUEBERRIES

They should be washed ahead of time to allow them to dry. Fill a large bowl with cold water. Place the berries in a wide strainer or a colander and dip it into the water; then let the rim of the strainer rest on the rim of the bowl. Pick out any loose stems or leaves or green berries. Raise the strainer or colander from the water to drain, and repeat as necessary with clean water until the water remains clean (no sand) after the berries are removed. Spread the berries in a single layer on paper towels and let stand, uncovered, to drain and dry.

HOW TO PREPARE ORANGES, GRAPE-FRUITS, AND LEMONS

I use the juice of fresh lemons or oranges in all recipes calling for their juice. In recipes that call for the grated rind of oranges or lemons, the grated rind of fresh fruit has a better flavor than bought dried grated rind.

To Grate the Rind: It is best to use firm, deep-colored, thick-skinned fruit. And it is best if the fruit is cold; the rind is firmer and it grates better. Use a standing metal grater—usually they have four sides, although some are round. Hold the grater up to the light and look at the shapes of the openings from the back, or the inside. You should use the small holes that are round, not diamond-shaped. Place the grater on a piece of wax paper on the work surface. Hold the grater firmly in place with your left hand. With your right hand hold the fruit cupped in your palm at the top of the grater. Move your fingers back a bit so the tips don't get scraped. Now, press the fruit down toward the bottom of the grater. Press firmly, but do not overdo it—all you want is the zest (the thin, colored outside part), so do not work over the same spot on the fruit or you will be grating the white underneath; rotate the fruit in your hand as you press against the grater. It is easy.

Remove the gratings that stick to the inside of the grater with a rubber spatula.

There is no reason ever to hurt yourself grating lemon or orange rind. (Be sure you hold the fruit as described above.)

To Pare the Rind: Use a vegetable peeler with a swivel blade to remove the thin, colored outer rind.

To Peel an Orange, Lemon, or Grapefruit: Place the fruit on a cutting board on its side. With a sharp thin knife cut off the top and bottom. Turn the fruit right side up resting on either end. Hold the fruit with your left hand as you cut down toward the board with a sharp knife in your right hand, curving around the fruit and cutting away a strip of peel—cut right to the fruit itself in order not to leave any of the white underskin. Rotate the fruit a bit and cut away the next strip of peel. Continue all the way around. Then hold the fruit in the palm of your left hand and carefully trim away any remaining white parts.

To Section an Orange, Lemon, or Grapefruit: Work over a bowl to catch the juice. With a small, thin, sharp knife cut down against the inside of the membrane of one section on both sides, releasing the section and leaving the membrane. After removing one or two sections, continue as follows. Cut against the membrane on the left side of a section and then, without removing the knife, turn the blade up against the membrane on the right side of the section. The section will fall out clean. After removing all the sections, squeeze the leftover membrane in your hand to extract any juice. Carefully remove any seeds.

ABOUT DECORATING CAKES

Cake decorating can be just as much a creative art as painting or sculpting. But to me, the pure untouched simplicity of a smooth, shiny chocolate glaze or a topping of barely firm whipped cream is perfection, and adding anything to it would detract from an already perfect work of art. The same goes for an uniced pound cake or loaf cake. Of course there are times when I like to wield a pastry bag and don't ever want to quit. But please don't feel that every cake needs decoration; simplicity is often decoration enough. Anything else might be gilding the lily.

Very often a few small, beautiful fresh flowers are a wonderful decoration. Either place them on the plate alongside the cake or cut the stems short and place a few (or sometimes only one) directly on top of the cake, either resting on the cake or inserted into it.

A red rose in a chocolate cake is especially gorgeous.

HOW TO PREPARE THE PLATE BEFORE YOU ICE THE CAKE

This is done to keep any icing off the plate. It will result in a clean, neat, professional-looking finished product.

Begin by tearing off a 10-inch piece of wax paper. Fold it crossways into four equal strips (fold it in half and then in half again), then cut through the folds with a sharp knife, making four 10 by 3-inch strips. (If the icing is very thick/sticky like a marshmallow or 7-minute icing, I like to use baking pan liner paper instead of wax paper because it is stronger, and I cut the strips a bit longer and a bit wider, but not too large or they will get in the way while I am icing the cake.)

Lay the strips in a square pattern around the rim of a wide, flat cake plate. Then put the cake on the plate and check to be sure that the papers are under the cake all the way around.

After the cake is iced (before the icing hardens), remove the papers by slowly pulling each one out toward a narrow end.

IF YOU PLAN TO TRANSPORT A CAKE

To transport a cake that is iced, here's a trick I learned during the years when I baked desserts at home and my husband took them in a station wagon to his restaurant.

Melt about ½ ounce of semisweet chocolate and place it in the middle of the cake plate. Place the cake directly on the chocolate, which will act as a paste to keep the cake from sliding.

ABOUT WRAPPING COOKIES

Unless I am baking cookies to serve right away, I wrap them in clear cellophane. It gives them an attractive and professional look, keeps them fresh, easy to handle, easy to pack for the freezer, lunch box, or picnic basket, and easy to handle for mailing or to give as a gift.

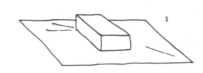

Clear cellophane is hard to find. Try wholesale paper companies, the kind that sell paper napkins, et cetera, to restaurants. Or buy it at, or order it by mail from, Bobbi & Carole's Cookshop, 7251 S.W. 57th Court, Miami, Florida 33143. (It comes on a roll in a box with a cutter edge. If you have a choice of widths, it is easier to handle if it is no more than 20 inches wide.)

If you cannot get cellophane, wax paper or aluminum foil is easier to handle than plastic wrap (which will drive you crazy).

It is easier to cut cellophane with a knife than with scissors. Cut off a long piece, fold it in half crossways, cut through the fold with a long, sharp knife, fold again and cut again, and continue to fold and cut until you have pieces the right width. Then fold and cut in the opposite direction. The final size of the pieces depends on the size of the cookies. If the size is close but a bit too large, do not cut the papers individually (it takes too long). Instead, place the whole pile in front of you and fold one side of the entire pile to the size you want. Place your left hand firmly on the pile, holding the folded side down and at the same time holding the pile so that the papers do not slip out of place. With your right hand cut through the fold with a knife. (If the pile is very large, cut through about one or two dozen pieces at a time.)

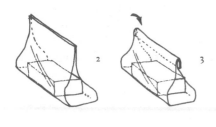

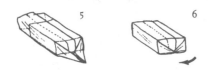

Bar cookies should be wrapped individually. Small drop cookies or thin rolled cookies and some refrigerator cookies may be wrapped two to a package, placed with their bottoms together.

Wrap one cookie as a sample to be sure the papers are the right size.

Spread out as many pieces of cellophane as you have room for (or as many as you have cookies for).

1. Place a cookie in the center of each paper.
2. Bring the two long sides together over the top.

3, 4. Fold over twice so that the second fold brings the cellophane tight against the cookie.

5. Now, instead of just tucking the ends underneath, fold in the corners of each end, making a triangular point.

6. Then fold the triangles down under the cookie.

HOW TO WASH
A PASTRY BRUSH

If you have used the brush for a sugar glaze or preserves, just rinse it under hot running water, separating the bristles a bit with your fingers so the water reaches all of them. If you have used it to butter a pan, it is important to remove every bit of butter or it will become rancid on the brush and I don't know any way ever to get rid of that. First rinse the brush briefly under hot running water. Then rub it well on a cake of soap, rubbing first one side of the bristles and then the other. Rinse well under hot running water, then repeat the soaping and rinsing once or twice more to be sure. To dry, just let it stand bristles up in a dish drainer or a glass.

ABOUT FREEZING
CAKES

I don't think that any baked dessert tastes as good after freezing as when it is fresh. However, if it is frozen for only a short time (a few days or weeks), the difference might be infinitesimal. I have indicated in many recipes that they can be frozen. If it is a big help to you to prepare it ahead, do. But if you have your choice, fresh is best.

If you want to ice a cake first and then freeze it, it may be frozen directly on the cake plate and left on the plate, or, to keep the cake from sticking to the plate, it may be placed on a round of wax paper or baking pan liner paper (cut to fit the bottom of the cake) on the plate, and then removed from the plate and wrapped when it is frozen. Freeze until the icing is firm, then wrap the cake airtight with plastic wrap and, if you wish, rewrap it in foil or in a freezer bag.

Everything should be thawed completely before it is unwrapped. (Foods sweat while thawing. If they thaw while they are still wrapped, the moisture will form on the outside of the wrapping; if they are unwrapped before they thaw, the moisture will form on the food itself—that could spoil the looks of a beautiful smooth glaze or icing.) However, if you have a cake in the freezer and you want some right away, unwrap it, cut it, and serve it. Many cakes are delicious frozen. Just don't let the rest of the cake stand around un-covered—rewrap it immediately.

Label packages—if not, you might wind up with a freezer full of UFOs (Unidentified Frozen Objects).

ABOUT FREEZING
COOKIES

Most cookies freeze quite well (but, like cakes, for a limited time only). It is always extremely handy (I think it is a luxury) to have cookies in the freezer for unexpected company; they usually thaw quickly, and many can be served frozen.

(Almost always, when I need a quick—or not so quick—gift for someone, my first thought is cookies. And if they are in the freezer, individually wrapped in cellophane, all I have to do is plan some attractive packaging for them.)

The same rule about thawing cakes applies to cookies—thaw before unwrapping (if possible).

Any cake or cookie that can be frozen may be thawed and refrozen—even several times. I do it often. I would rather refreeze it immediately than let it stand around and get stale.

I can do a better job if I stand rather than sit.

Cakes and pies should be cut carefully and neatly with a very sharp knife that is long enough. You might not use the whole blade but it gives leverage. Some cakes cut best with a sawing motion—try it. Some cut best with a serrated knife—try that also.

If it is a round cake or a pie, always start cutting each pie-shaped wedge from the exact center. Mark the center with the tip of a knife. Or, to find the center, lightly score the cake or pie in half first in one direction and then in the opposite direction. Then, if you don't trust yourself to cut freehand, mark each quarter lightly with the tip of the knife, marking the outside edge into 2 to 6 portions, depending on the size of the cake or pie and the size of the portions. But always keep your eye on the center so that the slices all radiate out from there.

Talking about size of portions, unless it is for a restaurant—and sometimes even if it is—small portions are better than large.

If it is a loaf cake or a square cake, it may be a big help to use a ruler and toothpicks to mark the portions.

Fruitcakes cut best when they are very cold.

So do pound cakes.

Sponge cakes, angel food cakes, chiffon cakes—all light and airy cakes might cut better with a serrated French bread knife. Try it. Use a sawing motion and do not press down on the cake or you will squash it.

Brownies and many other bar cookies cut best if they are very cold or almost frozen. Work on a cutting surface that is too large rather than too small. Use a very sharp knife. Or try a serrated one.

Occasionally, for certain cakes that stick to the knife, it is best if the knife blade is hot and wet. In the kitchen, work next to the sink and hold the blade under hot running water before each cut. In the dining room, have a tall pitcher of hot water and dip the blade into it.

Sometimes it is best to wipe the blade after each cut.

Mainly, take your time. And if it isn't going well, remember all the options —try a different knife, or a wet blade, or simply wipe the blade.

I once put a cake in the oven and then realized that I had forgotten to use the baking powder the recipe called for. (The cake had beaten egg whites in it, and there was no way I could still add the baking powder.) I learned the hard way that it is necessary to organize all the ingredients listed in a recipe— line them up in the order they are called for—before you actually start to mix. As you use an ingredient, set it aside. That way, nothing should be left on the work surface when you are through. A quick look during and after mixing will let you know if something was left out; if you are lucky, before it is too late.

Pies, Tarts, and Turnovers

Pies

Although pies may not have been created in America, they became an American specialty.

However, many good American cooks have never baked a pie. I am so sorry about all the people who cook and bake and are not intimidated by lengthy or demanding recipes but are afraid to make a pie. Or, for whatever reason, they just never do. They are missing one of the greatest cooking and one of the greatest eating experiences of all.

A plain American pie is a work of art. Every time you make one it is a challenge and when it turns out right you have accomplished something major of which you and your family and friends should be extremely proud. And I would like to add my compliments to the chef.

Pie Pastry

Most, but not all, of this piecrust information is also in two of my other books.

This recipe is for a 9-inch crust. I recommend using an ovenproof glass pie plate.

1 cup sifted all-purpose flour
Scant ½ teaspoon salt
3 tablespoons vegetable shortening (e.g., Crisco), cold and firm

3 tablespoons unsalted butter, cold and firm, cut into very small squares
About 3 tablespoons ice water

(For a 10-inch crust, increase the amounts to 1¼ cups of flour, generous ½ teaspoon of salt, 3¾ tablespoons of vegetable shortening, 3¾ tablespoons of butter, and 3¾ tablespoons of ice water.)

If the room is warm, it is a good idea to chill the mixing bowl and even the flour beforehand. Some pie pros store their flour in the freezer or refrigerator so it will be cold and ready.

Place the flour and salt in a large, wide mixing bowl. Add the shortening and butter. With a pastry blender cut them in until the mixture resembles coarse crumbs. It is all right to leave a few pieces about the size of tiny peas.

Sprinkle 1 tablespoon of the ice water by small drops all over the surface. Stir/mix/toss with a fork. Continue adding the water only until the flour is barely moistened. (Too much water makes the pastry sticky/soggy/tough. Too little makes it hard to roll out without cracks and breaks in the dough.) Do not ever dump a lot of water in any one spot. (I know one cook who uses a laundry-sprinkling container and another who uses a salt shaker to add the water; that way they distribute it in a fine spray all over.) If you add the water too quickly—if you don't stir/mix/toss enough while you are adding it—you might be convinced that you need more water. But maybe you don't; maybe you just need to add the water more slowly and stir/mix more. When adequate water has been added, the mixture will still be lumpy and will not hold together, but with practice you will know by the look of it that it will form a ball when pressed together. I have occasionally had to add a little more water, but very little—1 to 2 teaspoons at the most.

The shortening and butter must not melt (they should remain in little flour-coated flakes), so do not handle now any more than necessary. Turn the mixture out onto a large work surface and, with your hands, just push the mixture together to form a ball. (My mother never touched the dough with her hands at this stage—she turned it out onto a piece of plastic wrap, brought up the sides and corners of the plastic, and squeezed them firmly together at the top, letting the mixture form a ball without actually touching it. Then she flattened it slightly. Now I do it this way too.)

If the dough is too dry to hold together, do not knead it (don't even think about kneading it) but replace it in the bowl, cut it into small pieces with a knife, add a few more drops of water, and then stir again.

However you do it, form it into a ball quickly, flatten it slightly, smooth the edges, wrap in plastic wrap, and refrigerate for at least an hour but preferably overnight. Chilling the dough not only makes it firmer, less sticky, and easier to handle but also allows time for the water to moisten the flour more evenly. If it has been refrigerated overnight let it stand at room temperature 10 to 15 minutes before rolling it out.

Baked Pie Shell

Rolling out the dough is easiest if you work on a pastry cloth. Flour the cloth by rubbing in as much flour as the cloth will absorb, then lightly wipe off any loose excess flour. Rub flour on the rolling pin. (I use a French-style rolling pin that is long and narrow and tapered at both ends. It is too long and too narrow for the stockinette cover that is sold with the pastry cloth; I just reflour it frequently while I use it.)

Place the flattened ball of dough on the cloth. If the dough is very firm, pound/whack it sharply but not too sharply in all directions with the rolling pin to flatten it into a circle about 7 inches in diameter. (Don't pound the dough so hard that it forms deep cracks on the rim.) With your fingers, smooth and pinch together any small cracks at the edges.

Now start to roll, preferably from the center out rather than back and forth and do not turn the dough upside down (it absorbs too much flour and becomes tough). Roll first in one direction and then another, trying to keep the shape round. If the edges crack slightly, pinch them together before the cracks become deep. If the dough cracks anywhere other than on the edges, or if the circle is terribly uneven, do not reroll the dough; simply cut off uneven edges and use the scraps as patches. Moisten the edges of the patch with water, turn the patch upside down, and press it firmly into place.

Reflour the rolling pin as necessary. It should not be necessary to reflour the cloth, but if there is any hint that the dough might stick, reflour it lightly.

Roll the dough into a circle 12 or 13 inches in diameter according to the recipe. It is important that the rolled-out dough be exactly the same thickness all over (a scant ⅛ inch thick) so it will bake evenly.

To transfer the dough to the pie plate, drape it over the rolling pin as follows. Hold the pin over the left side of the dough, raise the left side of the pastry cloth to turn the dough over the rolling pin, roll it up loosely, then move it to the right side of the pie plate and unroll it, centering it evenly. Or fold it in half and lift it over the plate. With your fingers ease the sides down into the plate. Do not stretch the dough or it will shrink during baking.

If you have a cake-decorating turntable place the pie plate on it.

Press the dough into place all over. If your fingernails are in the way, cut a small portion of the dough from an uneven edge, form it into a small ball, flour it lightly, and use it as a tamping tool to press the dough.

With scissors cut the edge of the crust, leaving an even ½- to ¾-inch overhang beyond the outside edge of the pie plate.

Now, to form a hem. I had always believed it was correct to turn the edge of the dough toward the outside and under—back onto itself. Recently I have been turning it toward the inside, and back onto itself. I like it better. So, with floured fingertips, fold the edge to make a hem that extends about ½ inch higher than the rim. Press the hem lightly together between your floured fingertips, pressing it a bit thinner, and making it stand upright.

There are many ways of forming a decorative edge. Here's one. Flour your fingertips. You will be working clockwise around the rim, starting at three o'clock. Place your left forefinger at a right angle across the rim of the dough. (Your left hand will be over the inside of the plate with your finger sticking over to the outside.) With your right hand grip the dough rim, using the thumb and bent-under forefinger. Grip slightly ahead (clockwise) of your left finger, and twist the dough edge toward the center of the plate. Remove both hands and then replace your left forefinger just ahead (clockwise again) of the twist you have just formed. This will be at about four o'clock on the rim. Repeat the twists all around. Check and reshape any uneven spots.

Prick fork holes in the bottom of the pastry ¼ inch apart when baking an empty pie shell.

Place the shell in the freezer for 15 minutes or more until it is frozen firm (this helps prevent shrinking). Wrapped airtight (after it is firm), it may be frozen for months, if you wish.

About 15 or 20 minutes before baking, adjust a rack one-third up from the bottom of the oven and preheat the oven to 450 degrees.

In order to keep the pastry shell in place during baking, cut a 12-inch square of aluminum foil and place it shiny side down in the frozen shell. Press it into place all over. Do not fold the corners of the foil over the rim; let them stand up. Fill the foil at least three-quarters full with dried beans or with pie weights. (I use about 5 cups of a combination of black beans and black-eyed peas that I have been using for the same purpose for about 25 years.)

Bake the frozen shell at 450 degrees for 12 to 13 minutes until it is set and slightly colored on the edges. Remove the pie plate from the oven. Reduce the heat to 400 degrees. Gently, slowly, remove the foil and beans by lifting the four corners of the foil.

Replace the plate in the oven and continue to bake for about 7 or 8 minutes, or longer if necessary. Watch the pie shell almost constantly; if it starts to puff up anywhere, reach into the oven and pierce the puff carefully with a cake tester to release trapped air. Bake until the edges are golden. Do not underbake. A too-pale crust is not as attractive as one with a good color. The bottom will remain paler than the edges. (During baking, if the crust is not browning evenly, reverse the position of the pan.)

Place on a rack and let cool.

NOTES: 1. *The ingredients for the crust may easily be doubled for two shells or for a pie with both a bottom and a top crust.*

2. It is a great luxury to have an unbaked pie shell in the freezer. I try to keep one, frozen in the pie plate, all ready for the oven. When it is frozen I wrap it in plastic wrap or in a freezer bag. Then I have only to line it with foil and fill it with beans or weights when I am ready to bake. (I think a pie shell freezes better unbaked than when already baked.)

TO FORM AN EXTRA-DEEP PIE SHELL

Follow the above directions (rolling the dough ½ inch wider—or 13½ inches) up to folding the hem of the pastry. Fold the hem toward the inside and fold a ¾-inch (rather than a ½-inch) hem. You should have a raised ¾-inch hem standing straight up all around the inner edge of the rim. Form it into a straight, even wall all around. To flute it (keeping it high), leave it upright, lightly flour the thumb and the tip of the index finger of your right hand, and pinch from the outside so the outer edge of the raised wall of pastry forms a horizontal V (or a V that has the point facing the outside). It seems easiest to me to start at the right side (three o'clock) of the plate. Use the index finger of your left hand to support the inside of the crust while you pinch it.

Pinch again 1 inch away from the first. Continue to pinch and form V's all around the outside of the rim 1 inch apart. Then do the same thing on the inside of the rim, this time starting at the left side (nine o'clock) of the plate, pinching between two out-pointing V's on the outside and forming a nice, neat zigzag pattern all around, standing ¾ inch straight up.

PATCHING THE PASTRY

I was making a recipe in which the pastry is baked empty and then a juicy filling is poured in and the pastry is baked again. But while the crust baked empty, it formed a 3- or 4-inch crack right down the middle. If I had poured the filling in, it would have run through the crack, stuck to the pan, and been a disaster. I stood there looking at it, feeling totally helpless.

My husband walked into the room and I didn't think he even saw what had happened, but he did, and without a moment's pause he said, "Patch it with almond paste." It took a few seconds for his brilliant comment to sink in—it was genius. I still cannot understand how he knew so quickly what was probably the only solution possible, and one I have never heard of before.

Since then I have used this sensational trick many times; just a few minutes ago I used it for Date Pecan Pie (see page 38). Whatever would I have done if I had not known about this?

I have used both marzipan and almond paste. The brand I buy is Odense, which is made in Denmark and is generally available at fine food stores all over America. It seems to last forever (either at room temperature or refrigerated), but do not allow it to dry out. After you open it, be sure to wrap it airtight. I use both plastic wrap and aluminum foil.

Cut off a thin slice or break off a small chunk of the marzipan or almond paste, and press it between your fingers to make a thin patch slightly larger than the damaged area. Beat a bit of egg white lightly (only until foamy), then use it as a paste. With your fingertip, brush the white onto one side of the patch and place it, egg white down, over the damage. (I have also used just a bit of water as a paste and it worked, but if you have egg white, I think it might be safer than water.) Flour your fingertips and press gently around the rim of the patch.

Then pour in the filling and no one will ever know, and you will say thank you to Ralph every time you patch pastry this way.

AN ALUMINUM FOIL FRAME

To prevent overbrowning of the edge of a piecrust, make an aluminum foil frame as follows. Cut a 12-inch length of regular aluminum foil (not heavy-duty foil). Fold in half and then in the opposite direction in half again, making a square. Fold once more, making a triangle, the point of which is the middle of the piece of foil. To make a 7-inch hole in the middle, measure 3½ inches from the point of the triangle and cut out a shallow arc from the long side of the triangle to one short side. Open the folded foil frame and lay it over the top of the pie so the edges are covered and the center is exposed to get brown.

(You might want to make two frames and use them both at the same time, placing one over the other so that the points of the second frame are between the points of the first frame.)

After using the frame, reserve it to use over and over again.

Crumb Crusts

Although the crumb mixture can be pressed into place directly in the pie plate, I line the plate with foil first and then remove the foil before filling the crust. This guarantees easy serving—the crust *cannot* stick to the plate. It is a bit more work (or play) but I think well worth it.

For a 9-inch pie plate (I use a glass one), use a 12-inch square of foil. Turn the plate over on a work surface. Place the foil shiny side down over the outside of the plate and, with your hands, press it firmly against the plate all around. Remove the foil. Turn the plate over again and place the shaped foil in the plate. Press the foil firmly into place in the plate with a potholder or a folded towel. Fold the edges of the foil down over the rim of the plate.

Turn the crumb-crust mixture into the foil-lined plate. Using your fingertips, distribute the mixture evenly and loosely over the sides first and then the bottom. Then press the crust firmly and evenly on the sides, pushing it up from the bottom a bit to form a rim slightly (barely) higher than the edge of the pie plate. Be careful that the top of the crust is not too thin. To shape a firm edge, use the fingertips of your right hand against the inside and press down against it with the thumb of your left hand. After pressing the sides and the top edge firmly, press the remaining crumbs evenly and firmly over the bottom. There should be no loose crumbs.

Bake in the middle of a preheated 375-degree oven for 8 minutes. Then cool to room temperature.

Freeze for at least 1 hour, overnight if possible. It *must* be frozen solid.

Remove from the freezer. Raise the edges of the foil and carefully lift the foil (with the crust) from the plate. Gently peel away the foil as follows. Support the bottom of the crust on your left hand and peel away the foil, a bit at a time (do not tear the foil), with your right hand. As you do so, rotate the crust gently on your left hand.

Supporting the bottom of the crust with a small metal spatula or a table knife, ease it back into the plate very gently in order not to crack it. It will not crack or crumble if it has been frozen long enough.

Apple Pie, U. S. A.

This is the traditional, old-fashioned, "American as apple pie" apple pie. Once you have made it, you will glory in the spotlight, be thrilled with pride, and be in apple-pie-in-the-sky heaven.

It is best to put together the pie dough at least an hour before using it, or the day before. (It will be easier to handle cold, and waiting before you use the dough allows for the water to be absorbed more equally.)

Choose the apples carefully. Some are too watery (McIntosh), some are too dry, some have more flavor than others. But there are many varieties that are just right. Granny Smith, Jonathan, Winesap, and Cortland are among the best. (There are others—ask your produce man.)

6 PORTIONS

FILLING

The amount of flour in the filling depends on how juicy the apples are and on how juicy you like your pie. Many people—especially country and farm people, who have probably eaten more pies than most of us—think that any thickening at all is un-American; to those people a good pie has to be eaten from a wide soup bowl with a spoon.

3 tablespoons plus 1 teaspoon unsifted all-purpose
    flour
¾ cup granulated sugar
1 teaspoon cinnamon
¼ teaspoon nutmeg
¼ teaspoon salt

About 3 pounds apples (to make 8 to 9 cups,
    sliced)
1 ounce (¼ stick) unsalted butter, cut into small
    pieces (it is best to cut the butter ahead of
    time and refrigerate it)

TOPPING

Milk   *Additional granulated sugar*

Prepare a double amount of Pie Pastry for a 9-inch pie (see page 21), divide it in half, shape each half into a ball, flour each lightly, flatten slightly, wrap in plastic wrap, and refrigerate for an hour or longer.

If the pastry was refrigerated overnight let it stand at room temperature for 10 to 15 minutes before rolling it out. Place 1 ball of dough on a lightly floured pastry cloth. Pound it lightly with a floured rolling pin. With the rolling pin roll out the dough, keeping the pin, the cloth, and the top of the dough very lightly floured. Roll from the center of the dough out toward the edges. As you start to roll out the dough, watch the rim; if cracks form, pinch them together before they become deep. Keep the shape round and the thickness even. Roll out until you have a circle about 12 inches in diameter.

There are two ways to transfer the circle of dough to the pie plate. One is to fold it in half and place it in the plate. Then unfold it and ease it gently into place in the pan. The other is to roll it up loosely around the rolling pin and unroll it over the plate and then ease it gently into place in the pan. (I think the choice of methods depends on your fingernails; if they are long you will probably prefer rolling the dough on the pin to transfer it.)

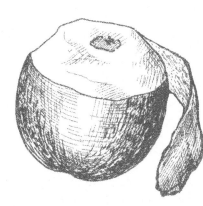

If you have a cake-decorating turntable place the pie plate on it. Trim the edges of the dough with scissors, leaving enough for the dough to lie down flat on the rim of the plate and extend only a scant ¼ inch beyond the outside of the rim.

Place 1 teaspoon of the flour (reserve the remaining 3 tablespoons of flour) in the crust and, with a dry pastry brush, spread it over the bottom.

Refrigerate the pie plate with the bottom crust in place.

Lightly reflour the pastry cloth and roll out the second piece of dough until it is about 12 inches wide (the same as the bottom crust). Slide a flat-rimmed cookie sheet (or anything else that will work) under the pastry cloth and transfer the cloth and dough to the refrigerator.

Adjust a rack one-third up from the bottom of the oven. Preheat the oven to 450 degrees.

In a small bowl mix together the remaining 3 tablespoons of flour with the sugar, cinnamon, nutmeg, and salt and set aside.

With a vegetable parer peel the apples, cut them into quarters, remove the cores, and slice them lengthwise. (Each quarter of a small apple should be cut into 3 slices; each quarter of a large apple should be cut into 4 slices.)

Measure 8 to 9 cups of the apples and place in a large bowl. Add the sugar and flour mixture and toss with your hands to mix thoroughly.

Turn the mixture into the floured bottom crust. Use your fingers to move things around and make an even mound, but do not press down on the apples or you will punch a hole in the crust. Scatter the pieces of butter over the top.

Place a little cup of cold water next to you. With a soft brush or your fingers wet the top of the rim of the bottom crust.

Transfer the top crust (using the same procedure you used for the bottom crust) over the apples, centering it carefully.

Flour your fingertips, and press the rim of the top crust against the wet top rim of the bottom crust. Then, with scissors, trim the top crust, allowing it to extend about ¼ to ½ inch beyond the bottom crust. With your fingertips and a bit of cold water, wet the bottom (the underside) of the rim. Fold the edge of the top crust over and then under the rim of the bottom crust (like tucking in a sheet around a mattress). Press together firmly. Now raise the rim so it stands upright and with your fingers flute a simple zigzag design on the rim (see To Form an Extra-Deep Pie Shell, page 24). Be very careful that the crust does not extend out over the rim of the pan, or it might droop and sag and fall off when the pie is baked.

With a small, sharp knife cut 8 1-inch slits in the top (see illustration) to allow steam and/or juices to escape.

With a pastry brush, brush milk over the top of the crust (except the rim), being careful not to use so much that it runs down in puddles against the rim; if it does, sponge it up with a small piece of paper towel. Sprinkle generously with sugar.

Be prepared to slide a cookie sheet or foil on a rack below to catch juices that might bubble over. If you do not have a rack below you might want to put foil on the floor of the oven, but wait until the pie is almost baked and until it might start to bubble over (which depends on how juicy the apples are) because the cookie sheet or foil might interfere with the baking.

Bake at 450 degrees for 15 minutes. Then open the oven and quickly reach in to cover the rim with an aluminum foil frame (see page 25), folding the points down as quickly as possible.

Lower the oven temperature to 425 degrees and bake for about 45 minutes more (total time is about 1 hour), until the crust is nicely browned and the apples are tender (you can test them with a toothpick through the slits on top).

Cool on a rack. Serve when barely cooled or at room temperature.

Fresh Apricot Pie

This is an old favorite in northern California, but down here in southern Florida it is exciting and unusual. Fresh apricots are a great luxury, mainly because they are available for only a short time (although the season seems to get longer each year). When and if you can get them remember this divine pie. It is extravagantly high and gorgeous, loaded with a generous amount of fruit; juicy/slightly runny, sweet/slightly sour, it is pure, plain, simple—the classic American two-crust pie.

It has become the specialty of the house at our house and it will remain so as long as fresh apricots are available.

Make the pastry ahead (an hour is passable but a day ahead is best), make the pie early in the day for that night (it should have at least 6 hours to cool and chill a bit), and invite someone special.

You will need a 9-inch Pyrex pie plate.

6 TO 8 PORTIONS

PIECRUST

Prepare a double amount of Pie Pastry (see page 21) with this one addition: add 2 teaspoons of granulated sugar along with the salt. Divide the pastry in half, shape each half into a ball, flour the balls lightly, flatten them lightly, wrap in plastic wrap, and refrigerate from an hour to overnight.

FILLING

2½ pounds (22 to 24 medium-size) fresh apricots, just barely ripe (to make 8 to 10 cups pitted halves)

1 tablespoon Amaretto or any other liquor or liqueur, or orange juice

½ teaspoon almond extract
¾ cup granulated sugar
½ cup dark brown sugar, firmly packed
3 tablespoons plus 1 teaspoon "Minute" tapioca

Adjust a rack one-third up from the bottom of the oven and preheat the oven to 500 degrees.

Cut the apricots in half, remove the pits, and place the halves in a wide mixing bowl.

In a small cup combine the Amaretto and almond extract, drizzle it all over the prepared apricots, toss gently with a rubber spatula until completely mixed, and set aside.

In a bowl stir the granulated and brown sugars together until they are thoroughly mixed. Add the tapioca and mix with a rubber spatula, pressing against the ingredients until thoroughly mixed again (this mixing is extremely important; otherwise the pie will have unpleasant lumps of tapioca). Or do this step with your fingers.

Now, this next step must be done slowly and carefully (again, to avoid lumps of tapioca). Very gradually add the sugar mixture to the apricots, adding only a rounded tablespoonful at a time and stirring/folding thoroughly and gently with a rubber spatula after each addition to mix the ingredients without breaking or mashing the fruit. After all of the sugar mixture has been added, let the apricot mixture stand for about 15 minutes, stirring and folding frequently with the rubber spatula. (During this time, the sugars will melt and juices will form and a dark syrup will appear which will begin to soften the tapioca.)

Meanwhile, roll out one piece of the pastry as follows. (If it has been refrigerated overnight it can stand at room temperature for about 10 minutes before being unwrapped.) Flour a pastry cloth and a rolling pin. Place the flattened ball of pastry on the cloth. Press down on the pastry with the rolling pin to flatten it into a circle about 6 inches in diameter. (If cracks form on the edges pinch them together and smooth over them with your fingertip before they become deep.)

Roll the pastry into a 12-inch circle.

If you have a cake-decorating turntable place the pie plate on it.

Either fold the pastry in half and lift it, or drape it over the rolling pin and lift it (whichever feels better to you), and center it carefully over a 9-inch Pyrex pie plate.

Press the sides of the pastry against the plate. With scissors cut the rim, allowing a scant ¼-inch overhang. Place the lined plate in the refrigerator.

Roll out the other half of the dough to the same size as the first half (a 12-inch circle). Then slide a flat cookie sheet under the pastry cloth with the rolled-out dough and transfer the whole thing to the refrigerator.

You will place the apricot halves in the crust to form two rows of fruit, one row toward the rim of the plate and the other row inside—toward the center of the plate.

IMPORTANT: The bottom layer of fruit should be placed cut side up (rounded side down). The pieces of fruit should overlap. Drizzle or spoon on some of the sugar and tapioca syrup that has formed.

After making the two rows (which are the bottom layer of fruit and should fill the crust), make two more rows on top of the bottom rows (this will make a second layer of fruit). IMPORTANT: The second, or top, layer of fruit should be placed cut side down (rounded side up)—the opposite of the first layer. And the pieces should overlap one another again. Drizzle or spoon on some more of the sugar and tapioca syrup.

Any remaining apricot halves should be placed evenly in the center (making that part three rows deep), cut side down—curved side up.

(The reason for all of this "cut side/curved side up/down," et cetera, is that the cut side should always face away from the pastry. I once had the experience that the cut edges of the fruit formed cuts in the bottom of the pastry and allowed juices and syrup to run out.)

With a rubber spatula scrape the bowl clean and distribute every bit of sugar and tapioca syrup evenly over and among the pieces of fruit.

If you have a cake-decorating turntable place the pie plate on it.

Wet the top rim of the bottom crust with a bit of cold water, using a soft brush or your fingertips.

Remove the top crust from the refrigerator and either fold it in half or drape it over the rolling pin, and lift it and place it over the fruit, centering it carefully.

With your fingers press down on the edges of the crusts to seal them together. Then, with scissors, cut the top crust, allowing it to extend a scant ½ inch beyond the bottom crust.

With your fingertips, and a bit of cold water, wet the bottom (the underside) of the rim of the crust.

Dry your hands, flour your fingertips, and fold the edge of the top crust over and under the edge of the bottom crust. Make it an even hem. And with your fingertips press the rim to seal the top and bottom crusts together and also to make the edge a little thinner. Shape the rim (the hem) so it stands upright.

Then flute the edge into a neat design (preferably use the technique described for an extra-deep pie shell—see page 24).

See Note.

TOPPING

Milk   *Granulated sugar*

Brush all over the top—not the rim—with milk. Sprinkle it all generously with granulated sugar.

With a small sharp knife cut 6 or 8 slits in the crust, each about 1 inch long, radiating out from the center, leaving an uncut center about 1 inch in diameter (see illustration, page 28).

If some of the milk has made a puddle in the trench just inside the rim, soak it up with a soft brush or with an edge of paper towel or paper napkin.

Place the pie in the oven and immediately reduce the temperature to 450 degrees. After 10 minutes reduce the temperature again to 375 degrees and continue to bake for 35 or 40 minutes more (total baking time is 45 to 50 minutes) until the crust is nicely colored and the filling just starts to bubble up through the slits in the crust.

During the last few minutes of baking the juices might bubble over the plate; watch for it and be prepared ahead of time either to slide a cookie sheet on a rack below or place aluminum foil on the floor of the oven. (Do not place the cookie sheet or foil in the oven at the beginning of the baking because it might interfere with the bottom of the crust baking properly.)

Cool completely on a rack. Then refrigerate.

Serve the pie cold, plain or with ice cream.

NOTE: *Care beful—if the rim is too heavy (if you have allowed too much overhang when you trimmed the crusts) or if you have shaped it too close to the outside edge of the plate, when it is placed in the oven and it softens from the heat it might fall toward the outside, or even off, the plate.*

Sour Cream Apple Tart

This is an unusual variation on apple pie. It has the advantage of a crust that does not demand the delicate, careful handling of standard piecrust. So tender and flaky and buttery that I could eat it with no filling, this is a cream cheese pastry that can be mixed in an electric mixer; if the mixer continues a bit after it is all done, it does not hurt the delicious pastry one bit. The crust is baked empty, then the apple slices are sautéed in a frying pan and placed in the baked shell. There is a creamy caramel sauce over the apples, and a thick layer of sour cream on top. Gorgeous, dramatically simple looking, and mouth-watering.

If you would like to prepare some of this ahead of time, the unbaked shell can be frozen in the tart pan. (Then be prepared to spend about 1½ hours to finish the tart.)

You will need an 11 by 1-inch two-piece tart pan, preferably made of black or dark blue metal.

8 TO 10 PORTIONS

CREAM CHEESE PASTRY CRUST

This fabulous crust can also be used with other fillings—anything that does not have to be baked in the crust.

It is best to chill the dough for an hour or two before rolling it out or chill it overnight or longer and then let stand at room temperature for 30 to 60 minutes, or as necessary.

4 ounces cream cheese
4 ounces (1 stick) unsalted butter

1 cup sifted all-purpose flour

In the large bowl of an electric mixer beat the cheese and butter until they are softened and incorporated. Then, on low speed, add the flour and beat, frequently scraping the bowl with a rubber spatula, until the ingredients hold together. (This will take several minutes of beating—if they do not want to hold together, turn the mixture out onto a work surface and knead a bit and press together.)

With your hands form the mixture into a smooth ball, flatten it slightly (if you intend to chill this for more than an hour or two, flatten it to about ½-inch thickness), wrap airtight in plastic wrap, and refrigerate.

On a floured pastry cloth with a floured rolling pin roll out the dough into a circle 13 inches, or a bit more, in diameter. Drape the dough over the rolling pin and transfer it to a loose-bottomed 11 by 1-inch tart pan.

Ease it into the pan, do not stretch it, and press it gently into place. Trim the edge with scissors, leaving a generous ½ inch of dough beyond the rim of the pan. It is important to have a high rim with no low spots; if necessary, the dough can be patched to fill in any low spots or cracks (use a drop of water as paste).

To form a narrow hem, roll or fold over the edge of the dough, turning it in toward the middle; let the doubled hem extend about ¼ inch above the rim of the pan.

With pastry pincers form a design around the edge of the dough, or score it lightly every ¼ inch, making lines at an angle with the dull edge of a table knife.

With a fork prick holes all over the bottom of the crust, moving the fork ¾ to 1 inch apart each time.

Place the pan in the freezer for at least 10 to 15 minutes, or longer if you wish. (If it is to remain in the freezer for a longer time, wrap it airtight after it is frozen.)

Before baking, adjust a rack one-third up from the bottom of the oven and preheat the oven to 450 degrees. Line the frozen pastry shell with a 12-inch square of foil shiny side down and fill the foil at least halfway with pie weights or dried beans.

Bake at 450 degrees for 13 minutes, then reduce the temperature to 350 degrees and gently remove the foil and weights from the shell; continue to bake for 7 to 10 minutes more (total baking time is 20 to 23 minutes) until the shell is well browned on the edges and lightly browned on the bottom. Do not underbake.

FILLING

⅓ cup apricot preserves
4 large (about 2 pounds) pie apples—Granny
  Smith (wonderful) or Jonathan

About 2½ ounces (5 tablespoons) unsalted butter
About 2 tablespoons granulated sugar

While the crust is baking, place the preserves (it is not necessary to strain them) in a small pan over moderate heat and stir occasionally to bring to a boil. The preserves should be boiling when the pastry shell comes out of the oven. Brush or spread the hot preserves over the bottom of the baked shell and return the pan to the oven for a minute or two to dry the preserves a bit; set aside.

Peel, quarter, and core the apples. Cut each quarter into 5 lengthwise slices.

Melt about half of the butter in a wide frying pan. Cover the bottom of the pan with some of the apple slices. Sprinkle with just a bit of the sugar. Cook, uncovered, over moderate heat, turning the slices occasionally with two forks until they are tender. Place them on a large plate and set it aside as you continue to sauté all of the slices, using all of the remaining sugar and butter (and a bit more of either or both if necessary). The cooked slices may be piled on top of one another on the plate.

Then, with your fingers, place all of the cooked slices over the preserves in the shell. The way they are placed is not terribly important since they will not show, but you want to have a rather even layer of apples. Here's how I do it.

Start in the middle of the shell and form a rosette (a sunburst? a pinwheel?) of slices overlapping one another right in the middle. Then place slices at right angles to the ones in the middle (these go lengthwise following the line of the rim of the pan), overlapping one another lengthwise. Then you will find that the best way to fill in the remaining space and to use up all of the slices is to form the outside row of apples at a 45-degree angle to the rim (not parallel to the rim and not on a right angle to it). They should all overlap one another deeply. Set aside.

CARAMEL SAUCE

⅔ cup whipping cream   ½ cup granulated sugar

Place the cream in a small pan and cook, uncovered, over medium heat until almost boiling.

At the same time, place the sugar in a frying pan over high heat and stir constantly with a long-handled wooden spatula until the sugar starts to melt and turn brown. Reduce the heat a bit to prevent burning. Continue to stir until the sugar is smooth and a rich caramel color. Remove from the heat, let cool for 1 minute, and then slowly stir the hot cream into the caramelized sugar. Return to the heat and stir again for a minute or so until perfectly smooth.

Let cool for 1 minute and then, with a large spoon, drizzle the caramel sauce over the apples in the crust. Set aside.

SOUR CREAM TOPPING

3 cups sour cream (see Note)   1 teaspoon vanilla extract
1 tablespoon plus 2 teaspoons granulated sugar

Preheat the oven to 350 degrees. Stir the ingredients in a bowl until combined. Pour over the tart. (If there are any low spots along the rim of the crust, do not use all of the sour cream mixture or it will run over.)

With the back of a spoon spread and smooth the sour cream layer carefully. Be careful not to get any of the caramel sauce into the topping; it should be pure white. And be careful to keep the topping just within the rim of the crust; don't let it get on top of it.

Bake for 7 minutes; remove from oven and cool to room temperature.

Refrigerate for at least several hours, or all day. (Do not serve this too soon or the sour cream will be a little runny—although yummy.)

NOTE: *Sour cream keeps well, refrigerated, for a long time. The local dairy says 6 weeks. But after several weeks, although the cream still looks fine, it seems more sour than it was at first. For this particular recipe I recommend that you buy the freshest sour cream available.*

Shoofly Pie

One day I received a mail-order catalog of stunning leather and wool clothes and handmade sweaters from The French Creek Sheep & Wool Company in Elverson, the heart of Pennsylvania Dutch country.

Soon after, on one of our car trips, we drove there. The clothes were spectacular, and Jean and Eric Flaxenburg, who own and run the business (which includes raising their own sheep for the wool), invited us to their charming museumlike home for Shoofly Pie and coffee.

What a way for me to be introduced to one of the oldest and most historic American desserts!

This recipe is from Michelle Swartz, who works at The French Creek Company and is quite famous locally for her wonderful baking. Recipes for this vary from a rather dry crumb cake (great for dunking) to a soupy, runny pie. And then there is this one: soft, tender, moist (but not runny), custardy (but not creamy), and not too sweet.

When our country was very young, word

spread that the people of southeastern Pennsylvania were the best cooks in the colonies. In 1758 the Moravian citizens of Bethlehem built an inn called The Sun Inn. From the beginning it was famous for its food. The great men of the colonies all went there: George Washington (with Martha), Benjamin Franklin, John Hancock—everyone who was anyone ate and slept at The Sun Inn. It is possible that this was the start of basic American cooking.

Shoofly Pie was on the first menu at The Sun Inn.

You need a 10-inch pie plate, preferably Pyrex.

The crust can be made (but not baked) ahead of time and frozen; the crumb mixture for the filling can be made ahead of time. But the molasses mixture should be prepared immediately before baking and the pie should be baked only 2 or 3 hours before serving.

8 TO 10 PORTIONS

PIECRUST *(a ten-inch crust)*

1⅓ cups sifted all-purpose flour
½ teaspoon salt
1 tablespoon granulated sugar
4 ounces (1 stick) unsalted butter, cold and firm,

cut into ½-inch squares (it is best to cut the butter ahead of time and refrigerate it)
1 teaspoon lemon juice
About 3 tablespoons plus 1 teaspoon ice water

Sift together into a wide mixing bowl the flour, salt, and sugar. With a pastry blender cut in the butter until the particles are fine and the mixture resembles coarse meal (some of the particles may be the size of small kernels of corn). Mix the lemon juice with 3 tablespoons plus 1 teaspoon of ice water and very gradually drizzle it over the flour mixture, stirring constantly with a fork (stir even more than you might think necessary). The dry ingredients should all be just barely moistened. If necessary, stir a bit longer, and if the mixture is still too dry stir in a few more drops of water.

Turn the mixture out onto a board or counter top. Handle it very little now. Press it together into a ball; if absolutely necessary you may knead it once or twice, and then form it into a ball. Flatten it into a 5- or 6-inch round, wrap in plastic wrap, and refrigerate for an hour or longer (overnight or a few days is all right too).

Remove the chilled dough from the refrigerator about 10 or 15 minutes before rolling it out; let it stand, wrapped, at room temperature.

Carefully flour a pastry cloth and rolling pin. Place the dough on the floured cloth. (It is considered taboo ever to turn pastry over while you are rolling it out because—the experts say—the dough will absorb too much flour and will become tough. But if you are careful and if you don't use too much flour on the cloth, I think it is all right to turn the dough over once while you are rolling it out. It might handle better if you do.)

Carefully roll the dough into a 14-inch circle.

Drape the dough over the rolling pin and carefully transfer it to the pie plate, centering it as well as you can. If you have a cake-decorating turntable place the pie plate on it. Trim and flute the edge (see page 24); it is not necessary to make an extra-deep crust.

Place the lined pie plate in the freezer or refrigerator. (If you are going to freeze it for any more than an hour or so, wrap it airtight in plastic wrap after it is frozen solid.)

FILLING

1 cup unsifted flour
⅔ cup dark brown sugar, firmly packed
2 ounces (½ stick) unsalted butter cut into ½-inch squares

1 egg graded "large"
1 cup molasses (see Note)
¾ cup very hot water
1 teaspoon baking soda

Adjust an oven rack one-third up from the bottom and preheat the oven to 450 degrees.

Stir the flour and sugar together in a wide bowl to mix. Add the butter and rub the ingredients together with your fingertips to make coarse crumbs. (There is not enough butter to absorb all of the dry ingredients, therefore some of the flour and sugar will remain powdery—and some of the butter may remain obvious and only partially mixed with the dry ingredients. That is as it should be.)

In the small bowl of an electric mixer beat the egg just to mix. On low speed beat in the molasses. Pour the hot water into a 1-cup glass measuring cup; add the baking soda and stir to dissolve. On low speed gradually add the water mixture to the molasses mixture, beating until incorporated.

Stir half of the crumb mixture (1 cup) into the molasses mixture and without waiting pour it into the chilled crust (which may be frozen). Sprinkle the remaining crumb mixture evenly on top and place in the oven (most of the top crumb mixture will sink into the filling during baking). IMMEDIATELY REDUCE THE OVEN TEMPERATURE TO 350 DEGREES.

Bake for about 30 minutes or until the filling is set and does not quiver when the pie plate is shaken gently from side to side. Do not over-bake. (And do not be disappointed when you see that the fluted rim of the crust has shrunk and settled itself onto the edge of the filling—it happens.)

Cool to room temperature. Serve at room temperature, or even slightly warm. It is more tender/delicate/delicious than if it is refrigerated.

Serve plain or with softly whipped cream. (For 1 cup of cream add ½ teaspoon vanilla extract or 1 tablespoon brandy and 2 tablespoons granulated sugar.)

NOTE: *You can use any dark or light molasses; however, I have recently discovered Plantation Brand Barbados Unsulphured Molasses, which I buy in health food stores, and it has a delicious, mild flavor. In Pennsylvania Dutch country they use Turkey Table Syrup.*

Blackberry Pie

We drove through the spectacular redwood forest called the Avenue of the Giants in northern California where the trees are so tremendous that in two locations the road goes right through the middle of tree trunks. Just on the outskirts of the forest we saw a billboard that read PRIZE-WINNING HOME-MADE BLACKBERRY PIE. *The sign was for a small restaurant in a private home. I'd never had blackberry pie before. The thick layer of deep magenta filling was somewhat soft and juicy and just the merest bit runny, slightly and wonderfully tart with a flavor reminiscent of raspberries—but different. They had used wild blackberries that grow profusely in that area. The topping was a buttery, brown sugar,*

spicy, crumbly crumb mixture. I'll never forget it.

Just recently, frozen dry-packed blackberries have become available throughout most of the country. This pie, made with the frozen berries, is similar to and as good as the redwood forest pie. (Nancy Nicholas, my editor, lives near a blackberry patch. She made this with fresh berries. "Sublime," she said.)

The prebaked crust and the crumb topping can be prepared ahead of time and refrigerated or frozen, if you wish. Putting the filling together takes only minutes. It is best to bake the pie only a few hours before serving.

6 TO 8 PORTIONS

CRUMB TOPPING

½ cup unsifted all-purpose flour
½ cup dark brown sugar, firmly packed
1 teaspoon cinnamon

¼ teaspoon nutmeg
3 ounces (¾ stick) unsalted butter, cold and firm, cut into small pieces

In a wide bowl stir the flour, sugar, cinnamon, and nutmeg to mix thoroughly. Cut in the butter with a pastry blender until the mixture makes coarse crumbs. There may be some small pieces of butter still visible; that's fine. If necessary, rub the ingredients a bit between your hands to incorporate the dry ingredients. Refrigerate, freeze, or use right away.

1 9-inch <u>baked</u> extra-deep pie shell (see page 22)
⅔ cup granulated sugar
2 tablespoons "Minute" tapioca
1 1-pound box (4 cups) frozen dry-packed
    blackberries (individually frozen)

1 tart cooking apple (to make 1 cup, diced)
2 tablespoons lemon juice

Adjust a rack one-third up from the bottom of the oven and preheat the oven to 350 degrees.

Have the prebaked crust ready. Since this filling becomes very juicy as it bakes and since the juices would run out of any places they could get through (which would make the bottom crust stick to the plate), please hold the empty crust (in the glass plate) up to the light and examine it carefully for any little holes or even any too-thin spots. If there are any and if you have a bit of almond paste or marzipan, please cover the holes or thin spots (see Patching the Pastry, page 24). Or, since the pastry is going to be baked again, you can make patches with any little leftover scraps that were cut off the sides of the unbaked crust while you trimmed and shaped it. They can be pasted on with a bit of lightly beaten egg white or with a bit of water.

In a wide bowl combine the sugar and tapioca, add the frozen berries, stir gently with a rubber spatula, and let stand for 15 minutes, stirring occasionally. Meanwhile, peel, quarter, and core the apple and cut it into ¼- to ⅓-inch cubes. Stir it into the berry mixture. Sprinkle the lemon juice over the fruit and gently stir together.

Spread the berry mixture in a smooth layer in the crust. Slowly and carefully sprinkle the crumb topping evenly over the berry mixture.

To prevent the rim of the pie from overbrowning, cover it with an aluminum foil frame (see page 25) and fold down the corners of the foil loosely over the crust.

Bake at 350 degrees for 1 hour. Then remove the foil frame, raise the heat to 450 degrees, and continue to bake for 8 to 10 minutes more—only until the filling begins to bubble up around the edges. (Watch it frequently and do not let it bubble over.)

Remove from the oven. At this point the filling will be thin and soupy, but when it cools it will become firm and will slice nicely.

Serve at room temperature, plain or with vanilla ice cream or slightly sweetened vanilla-flavored whipped cream.

NOTE: *It is especially important that the crust be high and not have any low spots or the filling will bubble over.*

Date Pecan Pie

On a recent trip by car from California to Florida we drove through Palm Springs and Indio, California, which is where dates grow. We stopped at a stand to drink date-shakes (see Note) and to buy dates to take home. I realized that all the dates I had ever eaten were, literally, dried and dry. In Indio even the dried dates are so fresh that they are as soft and moist as a fresh juicy plum. Eating them is a thrill; I couldn't stop.

This is the way they make pecan pie in Indio, and it has to be the world's best. Even with super-market dates, we still say the pie is the best. The dates are barely distinguishable in the pie but they add an incredible chewy, caramel quality.

When you shop for dates, buy the softest ones you can find. If they are dry and hard when you begin, they will stay that way. Do not use the cut-up, sugared dates.

The pie will be thick, gooey, very chewy/crunchy/yummy—wonderful. It should be served cold to be at its best.

8 TO 10 PORTIONS

1 9-inch <u>baked</u> extra-deep pie shell (see page 22)
8 ounces (1 cup, packed) pitted dates
4 ounces (1 stick) unsalted butter
4 eggs graded "large"
1 cup granulated sugar

1 tablespoon all-purpose flour
⅛ teaspoon salt
1 teaspoon vanilla extract
1 cup light corn syrup
6 ounces (1½ cups) pecan halves

Adjust a rack one-third up from the bottom of the oven and preheat the oven to 350 degrees.

Have the prebaked pie shell ready.

With scissors or a knife cut the dates into medium-size pieces, cutting each date into about 6 pieces, and set aside.

Melt the butter in a small pan over low heat.

Meanwhile, in the small bowl of an electric mixer beat the eggs for a minute or two until they are very foamy. Add the sugar, flour, salt, and vanilla and beat to mix well. Beat in the melted butter (either warm or cooled) and the corn syrup. Remove the bowl from the mixer. Stir in the dates.

Using a slotted spoon, remove the dates, letting most but not all of the liquids run off them, and place them in an even layer in the prepared pie shell. (Reserve the liquids.)

Sprinkle the pecans evenly over the dates. Slowly and carefully pour the reserved liquids over the nuts, covering them all, even though they will rise to the top.

Bake for 45 minutes. The pie will be well browned although the center will still be shaky and soft. Do not bake longer—the center will become firm as it cools and still firmer when it is refrigerated.

Cool on a rack and then refrigerate for a few hours. If you do not have time for that, place the pie in the freezer for 30 minutes or a bit longer. Any way you do it, get it really cold or the filling might be a little too runny and not so chewy (although it will still taste fabulous).

Use a strong, heavy, sharp knife for cutting the pie. If the pie resists the knife and feels tough, that means it is just right—and will feel perfect in your mouth.

Everyone seems to agree that as wonderful as this is plain, it is better still with whipped cream or vanilla ice cream.

2 cups whipping cream

3 tablespoons maple syrup or honey

3 tablespoons rum or bourbon

In a chilled bowl, with chilled beaters, whip the above ingredients only until the cream holds a soft shape, not until it is stiff/dry. If you whip the cream ahead of time refrigerate it and then, if it has separated a bit, whisk it lightly with a wire whisk just before serving. Pass the cream separately or spoon it onto the individual plates alongside the pie.

NOTE: *If you would like to order dates directly from a date grower in Indio, write for a catalog from Jensen's, 80-653 Highway 111, Indio, California 92201, or from Shields Date Gardens, 80-225 Highway 111, Indio, California 92201.*

Frozen Peanut Butter Pie

This is served frozen; it may be made many days or even a week or two ahead. It is something like chocolate peanut butter ice cream. The crust is made with chocolate cookies and salted peanuts; the filling has milk chocolate, cream cheese,

peanut butter, and whipped cream. It never freezes too hard to serve easily.

This is adapted from a non-chocolate pie that is served at Mary Mac's Tearoom in Atlanta.

8 PORTIONS

CRUMB CRUST

6 ounces (24 wafers) chocolate wafers (to make 1¼ cups crumbs)

¼ cup salted peanuts

3 ounces (¾ stick) unsalted butter

See Crumb Crusts (page 25); line a 9-inch pie plate with foil.

Make crumbs of the cookies; break them coarse and crumble in a food processor or a blender until fine. Set aside in a bowl. In the processor or blender grind the nuts until fine. Add the nuts to the crumbs. Melt the butter and add it to the nut and crumb mixture, stir to mix thoroughly.

See Crumb Crusts to shape and bake the crust, but bake this one at 350 degrees for 7 minutes, and follow the Crumb Crust directions to cool, freeze, and then remove the foil from the crust.

FILLING

8 ounces milk chocolate

8 ounces cream cheese (at room temperature)

½ cup smooth peanut butter

¾ cup milk

1 cup confectioners sugar, strained or sifted

1 cup whipping cream

Break up the chocolate and place it in the top of a small double boiler over shallow warm water on low heat. Cover the pot with a folded paper towel (to absorb steam) and with the pot cover. Let stand until almost melted, then uncover and stir until completely melted and smooth.

Meanwhile, in the large bowl of an electric mixer beat the cream cheese and peanut butter until soft and perfectly smooth. Beat in the chocolate. On low speed gradually beat in the milk, scraping the sides of the bowl as necessary. Beat in the sugar. Remove the bowl from the mixer.

In the small bowl of an electric mixer with clean beaters whip the cream until it holds a shape.

Add the whipped cream all at once to the peanut butter mixture and fold together gently only until just incorporated.

Pour as much of the filling into the crust as it will hold comfortably. Let the remaining filling stand at room temperature. Place the filled crust in the freezer for about 10 minutes. Then pour on about half of the reserved filling. Freeze again for about 10 minutes. Then add all of the remaining filling to the pie, and return it to the freezer.

Freeze until the top is firm and then cover airtight with plastic wrap. Store in the freezer.

Transfer to the refrigerator for 10 to 15 minutes before serving.

Savannah Banana Pie

This has a crumb crust made of Amaretti (Italian macaroons), a layer of sliced bananas, a layer of divine caramel (which is nothing but baked condensed milk), whipped cream, and butter-crunch candy. It is soft/chewy/creamy and crisp/brittle/crunchy—all wonderful. The combination of flavors and textures is out of this world.

This has several parts to it—all easy and fun—but they do take time; start this the day ahead or about 8 hours before serving.

This recipe is adapted from one in Savannah Style, *a cookbook by the Junior League of Savannah, Georgia (Kingsport Press, 1980).*

8 PORTIONS

MACAROON CRUST

This is an irresistibly delicious crust that you can use with any other cooked filling.

8 ounces Amaretti (see Notes), to make a generous 1½ cups crumbs

3 ounces (¾ stick) unsalted butter, melted

Adjust a rack to the middle of the oven and preheat the oven to 375 degrees. Prepare a 9-inch pie plate for a crumb crust by lining it with aluminum foil (see Crumb Crusts, page 25).

To crumb the macaroons, I place them, still in their tissue paper wrappings, on a firm surface, pound them briefly with my hand or with a cleaver just to break them up, then unwrap and process them in a food processor until they become crumbs. Add the melted butter and process to mix. (Or crumb them any other way and mix them with the butter.)

Turn the mixture into the foil-lined pie plate and press it into place.

Bake for 10 minutes. Cool, then freeze for at least an hour until completely firm. Remove the foil and set aside. See Crumb Crusts on how to remove the foil from the plate.

1 14-ounce can sweetened condensed milk   *3 to 4 ripe but not overripe bananas*

Adjust a rack to the middle of the oven and preheat the oven to 425 degrees.

Pour the condensed milk into an 8- or 9-inch Pyrex pie plate. Cover it airtight with aluminum foil, pressing the edges over the rim of the plate to seal. Place the plate in a large, shallow pan. Pour hot water about ½ inch deep into the large pan and bake for 1 hour and 20 to 30 minutes. The condensed milk will bake to a rich caramel color. During baking, add more water to the large pan if necessary. Remove the pie plate from the larger pan, then remove the foil covering and set the caramel aside to cool completely.

From 4 to 8 hours before serving, peel the bananas and cut them crosswise into ¼-inch slices. Do the cutting over the crust and let the slices fall into the crust. Flatten the layer of bananas a bit.

With a teaspoon place small spoonfuls of the cooled caramelized milk all over the bananas (if you place too much in any one spot you will not have enough to go around). Then, with the back of the spoon, smooth the top a bit to cover the bananas completely.

Refrigerate from 4 to 8 hours.

WHIPPED CREAM TOPPING

About 3 ounces Almond Roca (see Notes)   *½ teaspoon vanilla extract*
1½ cups whipping cream   *1 or 2 drops (only) almond extract*
2 tablespoons confectioners sugar

Unwrap the candy and on a cutting board cut down on the candy bars with a small, sharp knife to slice the candy thin. Set it aside.

In a small chilled bowl, with chilled beaters, whip the cream with the sugar and vanilla and almond extracts only until the cream holds a definite shape but not until it is really stiff. (To prevent overwhipping I whip with the electric mixer until the cream holds a soft shape and then finish the whipping with a wire whisk.)

Place the cream by tablespoonfuls in a circle around the rim of the pie—do not cover the middle of the filling.

Sprinkle the candy over the whipped cream.

Refrigerate and serve very cold.

NOTES: 1. *Amaretti, Italian macaroons, are now in almost every "gourmet" store and in many not so "gourmet," as well as in many of the over-abundance of mail-order catalogs that have recently flooded our country. The brand I buy is Amaretti di Saronno, Lazzaroni & Company, made with apricot kernels, not almonds. They can be bought at, or ordered by mail from, Manganaro Foods, 488 Ninth Avenue, New York, New York 10018.*

2. Almond Roca is a wonderful buttercrunch candy with a crisp center and a chocolate coating made by Brown & Haley in Tacoma, Washington 98401. It comes in a pink tin can and is usually available at any fine food store. English toffee candies can be substituted. Or Heath Bars.

Marbleized Chiffon Pie

This is a very old recipe that the Hershey company used to print on the labels of large bars of milk chocolate. Why did they stop? The filling is similar to a Bavarian mixture, but just before it is turned into the crust it is mixed (only slightly) with melted milk chocolate (giving a marbleized effect). The original recipe calls for a graham cracker crust, but you can use any kind of a crumb crust. This recipe now calls for a peanut butter cookie crumb crust. The cookies are quick and easy to make and they add tremendously to the deliciousness of the pie. This crust can be used for any other pie that you would prepare in a crumb crust.

The combinations of light/airy/fluffy with crisp/crunchy/chewy, and milk chocolate with peanut butter and whipped cream are sensational. It is a fabulous pie.

8 PORTIONS

PEANUT BUTTER COOKIE CRUMB CRUST

10 ounces Peanut Butter Icebox Cookies (see page 316), to make 2 cups crumbs

3 ounces (¾ stick) unsalted butter, melted

Adjust a rack to the middle of the oven and preheat the oven to 325 degrees. (This crust is baked at a lower temperature than most crumb crusts.)

Break up the cookies and crumb them in a food processor fitted with the metal chopping blade, or (in several batches) in a blender, or pound them with a rolling pin between two large pieces of wax paper. In a bowl mix the crumbs and butter. Then follow the directions for a 9-inch Crumb Crust (see page 25), but bake this crust for 10 minutes at 325 degrees and then open the oven door and let the crust cool in the oven.

MARBLEIZED CHIFFON FILLING

8 ounces milk chocolate
¼ cup cold tap water
1 envelope unflavored gelatin
⅔ cup milk
2 eggs graded "large," separated

5 tablespoons granulated sugar
½ teaspoon vanilla extract
1 cup whipping cream
Pinch of salt

Break up the chocolate and place it in the top of a double boiler over warm water on low heat. Cover the top of the pot with a folded paper towel (to absorb steam), then with the pot cover, and let cook very slowly until the chocolate is melted. Then uncover, remove from the hot water, and set aside to cool to room temperature, stirring occasionally with a rubber spatula.

Place the cold tap water in a small custard cup, sprinkle the gelatin over the top, and let stand.

Place the milk in the top of a small double boiler over warm water on moderate heat and let cook, uncovered, until scalded (or until there is a lightly wrinkled skin on the top of the milk).

Meanwhile, place the yolks in a small bowl and beat them with a whisk until well mixed. (Place the bowl on a folded towel to prevent slipping.) While beating with the whisk, gradually add 3 tablespoons of the sugar (reserve the remaining 2 tablespoons of sugar). Whisk briskly until pale.

Gradually add the hot scalded milk to the egg yolk mixture, whisking constantly. Then return the mixture to the top of the small double boiler over warm water on moderate heat. Cook, scraping the bottom and sides with a rubber spatula, until slightly thickened. (When it is just right, it will register 180 degrees on a candy thermometer.)

Remove the top of the double boiler. Add the softened gelatin, stir until melted, add the vanilla, and transfer to a rather large mixing bowl. Let stand for a few minutes.

Meanwhile, in a chilled bowl, with chilled beaters, whip the cream until it holds a shape but not until it is really stiff. Set aside.

In a small bowl, with clean beaters, whip the egg whites with the salt until the whites hold a soft shape. Gradually add the remaining 2 tablespoons of sugar, and beat only until the whites just barely hold a firm shape but not until they are stiff or dry. Set aside.

Place the bowl of milk and egg yolk mixture into a larger bowl of ice and water. Stir and scrape the bottom and sides constantly until the mixture cools, chills, and then just barely begins to thicken. Do not let it actually set. Remove from the ice and water.

In three or four small additions, fold half of the chilled mixture into the whipped cream and the other half into the beaten egg whites.

In the large bowl that the milk and egg yolk mixture chilled in, fold together the whipped cream mixture and the egg white mixture.

Add the room-temperature melted chocolate. Fold together (with a large rubber spatula) very briefly (only two or three foldings) until the mixtures are roughly marbleized. Do not overdo it. (When you serve the pie you will see that the chocolate and filling have formed a fascinating layered effect.)

Pour as much of the marbleized mixture into the crust as it will hold. Place in the freezer or refrigerator for only a few minutes to harden slightly, then pour the remaining marbleized mixture on the top.

Refrigerate for at least 3 to 4 hours.

WHIPPED CREAM TOPPING

1 cup whipping cream
2 tablespoons confectioners or granulated sugar

½ teaspoon vanilla extract
Optional: milk chocolate

In a chilled bowl, with chilled beaters, whip the cream with the sugar and vanilla until it holds a shape.

Either spread the cream to cover the top of the pie or put it in a pastry bag fitted with a star tube and press out in a design over the top of the pie.

If you like, sprinkle the top generously with coarsely grated milk chocolate or with milk chocolate curls made with a vegetable parer.

Use a rather long, heavy knife to cut portions.

Salted Almond Chocolate Pie

When a new taste sensation hits the nation it doesn't take long to spread from coast to coast. All over the country people are discovering the taste appeal of chocolate that is both sweet and salty. It's new, it's tantalizing, it's delicious.

This has a crisp crumb crust made of chocolate wafer cookies (I use Nabisco). The soft and gooey milk chocolate filling has marshmallows and coarsely chopped, chunky, roasted salted almonds. It is served frozen, at which point it is similar to ice cream (when the pieces of marshmallow in the filling are frozen they become wonderfully deliciously chewy).

The crust can be made ahead of time and stored in the freezer, if you wish. The filling is quick and easy. The pie should be frozen for at least 3 hours before serving—although it can wait in the freezer for days.

6 TO 8 PORTIONS

CHOCOLATE WAFER CRUMB CRUST

6 ounces bought chocolate wafer cookies (to make 1½ cups crumbs)

3 ounces (¾ stick) unsalted butter, melted

Adjust a rack one-third up from the bottom of the oven and preheat the oven to 300 degrees. Line a 9-inch pie plate with aluminum foil (see Crumb Crusts, page 25).

Coarsely break up the chocolate wafers and spin them in a food processor—or pound them in a bag—to make crumbs. Mix the crumbs with the melted butter and turn into the lined pie plate; press into shape. Bake for 15 minutes. (This chocolate crumb crust should be baked longer and slower than the usual crumb crust; it will become especially dry, crisp, and crunchy.) Then turn off the heat, open the oven door, and let the crust stand in the oven to cool off slowly.

When it is cool, place the crust in the freezer for at least an hour and then remove the foil lining. Refrigerate until ready to fill. See Crumb Crusts for directions on how to shape the crust, bake, cool, and freeze it, and how to remove the foil from the plate.

SALTED ALMOND CHOCOLATE FILLING

This is a new version of an old favorite called Chocolate Mallow.

20 marshmallows
8 ounces milk chocolate
½ cup light cream
⅓ cup roasted salted almonds (in the nut section

of most supermarkets; I buy Blue Diamond brand)
1 cup whipping cream

With wet scissors (dipped into cold water) cut 16 of the marshmallows into quarters (reserve the remaining 4 marshmallows). Place cut marshmallows in the top of a large double boiler. Break up the chocolate and add it, then add the light cream. Place over hot water on medium heat. Cover and cook, stirring occasionally, until the marshmallows and chocolate are melted.

Meanwhile, with wet scissors, cut the remaining 4 marshmallows into pieces about ½ inch in size. Set them aside.

Cut the nuts very coarse; they should not be fine. I use a small rounded wooden chopping bowl with a round-bladed knife. Or you can chop them on a board with a heavy French chef's knife. (Cutting each nut into 4 or so pieces is about right, but they should be uneven, with some larger pieces.) Set the nuts aside.

In a small chilled bowl, with chilled beaters, whip the cream until it just holds a shape. Refrigerate the whipped cream until you are ready for it.

When the chocolate mixture is melted and smooth, remove it from the hot water and set it aside, stirring occasionally until completely cool. (To save time place the top of the double boiler into a bowl of ice and water and stir constantly until cool.) The cooled chocolate mixture will be quite stiff. Gradually, in about four additions, fold the whipped cream and the cut-up marshmallows into the cooled chocolate mixture. Do not fold any more than necessary: it is all right if some of the cream is not completely incorporated.

Turn the mixture into the crust. Smooth the top. Freeze for at least 3 hours.

Unless you plan to freeze the pie for days, do not cover it, because wrapping might stick. If you are freezing for longer, place the pie in a box.

Chocolate Mousse Pie

This is from the Wine Cellar restaurant in Charleston, South Carolina. It has a crumb crust made of chocolate wafers and a dense rum-flavored chocolate mousse filling. Whipped cream and chocolate curls or grated chocolate are on top.

The crust can be made ahead of time and frozen, if you wish. The filling should be refrigerated overnight after it is in the crust. The whipped cream can be fixed at the last minute or a few hours before serving.

8 PORTIONS

CRUST

1 8½-ounce package chocolate wafer cookies (Oreo sandwich cookies can be substituted, filling and all) to make 1½ cups crumbs

1 teaspoon powdered (not granular) instant coffee or espresso
3 ounces (¾ stick) unsalted butter

Adjust a rack one-third up from the bottom of the oven and preheat the oven to 375 degrees. Line a 9-inch pie plate with aluminum foil (see Crumb Crusts, page 25).

Coarsely break up all but 9 of the cookies (you will not use them for this recipe) and place them in a food processor fitted with the metal chopping blade. Add the coffee and process until you have even crumbs. (The cookies can be crushed by placing them, with the coffee, in a double or triple plastic bag and rolling over them with a rolling pin.) Place the crumbs in a mixing bowl.

Melt the butter and stir it into the crumbs with a rubber spatula.

Turn the mixture into the prepared pie plate. See Crumb Crusts for directions on how to shape the crust, bake, cool, and freeze it, and how to remove the foil from the plate.

CHOCOLATE MOUSSE FILLING

6 ounces semisweet chocolate (see Note)   3 tablespoons dark rum
3 eggs graded "large"   1 cup whipping cream

Break up the chocolate and place it in the top of a large double boiler over hot water on moderate heat. Cover with a folded paper towel (to absorb steam) and the pot cover. Let cook until the chocolate is almost all melted. Then uncover and stir until smooth. Remove the top of the double boiler and set it aside to cool.

Separate 2 of the eggs; set aside the whites. In a rather small bowl place 1 egg and the 2 egg yolks. Beat or whisk until mixed. Mix in the rum and set aside.

In a small chilled bowl, with chilled beaters, whip the cream until it just holds a point when the beaters are raised. Set aside.

In a clean small bowl, with clean beaters, beat the 2 egg whites until they hold a firm shape when the beaters are raised but not until they are stiff/dry. Set aside.

Add the egg and rum mixture to the chocolate and mix briskly with a small wire whisk until smooth.

Very gradually at first, fold about half of the chocolate mixture into the beaten whites. Then, in a larger bowl, fold together the remaining chocolate and the whites.

Now, very gradually at first, fold about half of the chocolate mixture into the whipped cream. Then fold the whipped cream into the remaining chocolate mixture. Do not handle any more than necessary during any of this folding together.

Pour the mousse into the prepared crust, smooth the top with the back of a spoon, and refrigerate, uncovered, overnight.

WHIPPED CREAM

1½ cups whipping cream   2 tablespoons rum
3 tablespoons confectioners or granulated sugar   ½ teaspoon vanilla extract

In a chilled bowl, with chilled beaters, whip the ingredients until the cream is stiff enough to hold its shape. It should be firm enough not to run when the pie is served, but a bit too soft is always nicer than a bit too stiff.

Place the cream evenly by large spoonfuls over the filling, and then smooth the top. Leave it smooth or form peaks with the bottom of a large spoon.

TOPPING

Milk chocolate curls or grated semisweet chocolate

Work directly over the pie or over a length of wax paper. Form milk chocolate curls with a vegetable parer or grate semisweet chocolate with a cheese grater. If you have worked over paper, lift the paper to funnel the curls or grated chocolate onto the pie.

Refrigerate for a few hours, if you wish, or serve immediately.

NOTE: *I generally reach for Tobler Tradition or Lindt Excellence when a recipe calls for semisweet chocolate. Lately I have also been using a lot of Poulain. However, a neighbor of ours recently made this pie with semisweet chocolate morsels and it was delicious.*

Individual Maple Pecan Tarts

Crisp, buttery crusts with a semifirm, chewy maple syrup filling that is loaded with pecans. Divine.

The crusts can be shaped in the pans ahead of time and frozen, if you wish. The filling is quick and easy to mix, but it can be done a day ahead and refrigerated if that fits your schedule better. These are best when they are fresh but it is fine to bake them even in the morning for that evening.

You need special pans for making these. Kitchen shops call the pans either individual quiche or tartlet pans. They are made of black metal, they have loose bottoms and fluted rims, and they measure 4¾ inches (across the top) by 11/16 inch (in depth—inside). They are made in France and can be bought at, or ordered by mail from, Bobbi & Carole's Cookshop, 7251 S.W. 57th Court, Miami, Florida 33143. (If you never use these pans for anything but this one recipe, I think you will agree that it is worth having them.)

6 INDIVIDUAL PIES

PASTRY

This can be mixed in a food processor, or otherwise. Shaping these pastry shells takes time and patience but is great fun.

1¾ cups plus 2 tablespoons sifted all-purpose flour
¼ teaspoon salt
3 tablespoons granulated sugar
4 ounces (1 stick) unsalted butter, cold and firm,
    cut into small squares

3 egg yolks from eggs graded "large"
1 tablespoon plus 1½ teaspoons ice water

Place the flour, salt, and sugar in the bowl of a food processor fitted with the metal chopping blade. Turn the machine on and off two or three times just to mix the ingredients. Add the butter and let the machine run for about 5 seconds until the mixture resembles coarse meal.

(It is not necessary to mix the yolks.) With the machine running add the yolks and water through the feed tube and process just until the mixture forms a ball.

To make the pastry without a processor, mound the flour on a large work surface. Make a well in the center and place all the remaining ingredients in the well. With the fingertips of your right hand work the center ingredients together. Gradually incorporate the flour, using a dough scraper or a wide metal spatula in your left hand to help move the flour toward the center. When all the flour has been absorbed, knead briefly until the dough holds together, and finish by "breaking" the pastry as follows. Form it into a ball; then, starting at the side of the dough farthest from you and using the heel of your hand, push off small pieces (about 2 tablespoons), pushing the dough against the work surface and away from

you. Continue until all the dough has been pushed off. Re-form the dough and "break" it off again.

Whichever way you have mixed the dough, now form it into a perfectly even fat sausage shape with flat ends, wrap it in plastic wrap, and refrigerate for a few hours or overnight.

When you are ready to roll out the dough, cut it into 6 equal pieces (they must be exactly the same size). The dough will be too firm to roll immediately. Let it stand for a few minutes. Flour a pastry cloth and a rolling pin.

Place a piece of the firm dough on the cloth and press down on it with the rolling pin to soften it a bit, then roll it into a circle 6 inches wide. This dough may be turned over once or twice during rolling, if you wish, to keep both sides lightly floured and to prevent sticking. The cloth and rolling pin should be lightly refloured as necessary.

After rolling out a circle of dough, use anything round and 6 inches in diameter as a pattern (I use a 6-inch flan ring), place it on the dough and with a small, sharp knife cut around the rim to form a perfect circle. Then fit the dough into the individual pans. A slightly more complicated method, but one that also works, is to fit the round of dough into one of the individual pans, press it into place, and then with scissors trim the edge evenly, leaving ¼ to ½ inch of the pastry above the rim of the pan.

With your fingers gently turn in the edge of the pastry to form a narrow hem; the folded edge of the hem should be a bit higher than the top of the pan (with no low spots or the filling will run over). The top of the rim will crack slightly when the dough is folded; it is OK. Press the double thickness of pastry firmly together against the inside of the pan. (If your fingernails are in the way, bend a finger and use the bent finger joint to press with—or use two bent finger joints together.)

With pastry pincers, or with tines of a fork, make a neat, ridged design on the rim.

Place the lined pans in the freezer or refrigerator to become firm.

FILLING

2 eggs graded "large"
⅔ cup maple syrup
⅔ cup light brown sugar, firmly packed
¾ teaspoon vanilla extract

1½ tablespoons unsalted butter, melted
2 teaspoons dark rum
7 ounces (2 cups) pecans, toasted (see To Toast
    Pecans, page 7) halves or large pieces

In the small bowl of an electric mixer beat the eggs to mix. On low speed, beating only to mix, add the maple syrup, sugar, vanilla, melted butter, and the rum.

When you are ready to bake, adjust a rack one-third up from the bottom of the oven and preheat the oven to 350 degrees.

Place the individual pans lined with pastry on a jelly-roll pan or a cookie sheet.

Divide the pecans among the pans, placing them casually, but preferably with rounded sides up if you are using nut halves (instead of pieces). You can just estimate, or measure ⅓ cup of pecans for each pan.

Transfer the filling to a pitcher that is easy to pour from and pour the filling evenly into the pans, pouring in a slow stream to wet the tops of the nuts. Do not fill the pie shells completely at first—if you use too much filling in one shell, there might not be enough to go around. The filling should almost—but not quite—reach to the tops of the crusts.

Bake for 30 minutes, reversing the position of the jelly-roll pan or cookie sheet front to back once after about 20 minutes to ensure even browning. After 30 minutes the rims should be golden brown.

Remove from the oven and let stand for about 15 minutes. If some filling ran out of a tart, that tart should be removed from its pan as soon as possible; if you wait the filling hardens and it becomes more difficult.

To remove the tarts from the pans, place a pan on a small, narrow jar or other object; the sides should slip down easily, but they might need a little help from you. Then use a wide metal spatula to transfer the tart from the bottom of the pan to a rack to cool.

Many people like to serve whipped cream with pecan pie (especially in Texas, where the pecan is the state nut, and they eat a great many pecan pies). And many people think it is best with ice cream (at Spago, in Beverly Hills, California, they serve individual pecan pies—this size and shape—with a scoop of caramel ice cream on top; see page 339). I think it depends on the occasion and the menu. But the tarts absolutely plain, with nothing, are perfect.

Rancho Santa Fe Lemon Tart

A tender and crisp crust and a wondrously creamy lemon filling covered with an apricot glaze and looks like a million dollars. It is easy but because the dough is rolled quite thin it takes a light touch and TLC.

You will need an 11 by 1-inch loose-bottom quiche or tart pan made of black metal because black metal browns the crust better than shiny metal does.

12 PORTIONS

PASTRY

It is best to make the pastry ahead of time; it should be refrigerated for 2 to 24 hours before it is rolled out. It can also be frozen, but if it is, refrigerate it overnight (to thaw) before using.

1 egg yolk
1 tablespoon ice water
1 tablespoon plus 1 teaspoon whipping cream
½ teaspoon vanilla extract
¼ teaspoon almond extract

1½ cups sifted all-purpose flour
¼ teaspoon salt
1½ tablespoons granulated sugar
4 ounces (1 stick) unsalted butter, cold and firm,
    cut into 8 to 10 pieces

The pastry can be made in a food processor or by hand. Either way, start by combining the yolk, ice water, whipping cream, and the vanilla and almond extracts in a small container (preferably with a spout if you are going to use a food processor). Refrigerate.

In a processor: Fit the bowl with the metal chopping blade, place the flour, salt, and sugar in the bowl, turn the machine on/off once, add the butter and process on/off about 10 or 12 times (for a total of 10 or 12 seconds) only until the mixture resembles coarse crumbs. With the machine running, quickly pour the cold egg yolk mixture through the feed tube and then process on/off only until the dough barely begins to hold together and just leaves the sides of the bowl (but not until it forms a ball).

By hand: Place the dry ingredients in a wide mixing bowl, add the butter, and with a pastry blender cut it in until the mixture resembles coarse crumbs. Then with a fork stir in the cold egg yolk mixture.

Whichever way you have mixed the ingredients, now turn the dough out onto a work surface and press it together to form a ball, then place it on plastic wrap and pat into a 6-inch circle. Wrap in plastic wrap and refrigerate for 2 hours or more.

When you are ready to shape the crust, have an 11 by 1-inch black metal quiche pan at hand. Place the round of dough on a floured pastry cloth. With a floured rolling pin roll out the dough carefully (it will become quite thin) to form a circle about 14 inches in diameter. (Reflour the rolling pin occasionally while you are working with it and spread a tiny bit of flour over the top of the dough once or twice to prevent sticking.)

Hold the rolling pin across the dough (from twelve o'clock to six o'clock) and raise the left side of the pastry cloth to lift about half of the dough and flip it over the rolling pin. Using the rolling pin, carry the dough over to the quiche pan, center it as well as you can, then lower and unroll it over the pan. Remove the rolling pin and with your fingers ease the sides of the dough down into the pan. (If necessary, the dough can be patched; you can cut some off one part, dampen the top edge of the patch with a bit of water, turn it upside down [because the top probably has less flour on it and will therefore stick better], and place it over another part. Press the edges securely to seal.)

Trim the edge with scissors, leaving a ½-inch overhang. Fold ¼ inch of the overhang in toward the center of the circle to make a narrow hem extending about ¼ inch above the rim. Press gently to make it neat and smooth. Then, with pastry pincers make a design on the rim or, with the dull side of a knife blade, score the rim gently with little lines on a slant, about ¼ inch apart.

Prick fork holes in the bottom of this pastry about ½ inch apart.

Refrigerate or freeze the pastry shell for at least 30 minutes (or longer) before baking.

To bake, adjust a rack to the middle of the oven and preheat the oven to 400 degrees.

Line the chilled pastry shell with a 12-inch square of foil shiny side down. Fill the foil with dried beans or pie weights and bake for 20 minutes. Remove the foil and beans or weights and continue to bake for about 5 minutes more until the bottom of the shell just begins to color slightly.

Remove the shell from the oven and reduce the oven temperature to 250 degrees. (If there are any cracks or holes in the bottom of the pastry shell, see Patching the Pastry, page 24.)

Let the shell stand to cool while you prepare the filling.

LEMON FILLING

1½ cups whipping cream
7 egg yolks from eggs graded "large"
1 tablespoon cornstarch

¾ cup granulated sugar
⅔ cup lemon juice (see Note)

Place the cream in a saucepan over moderate heat, stirring occasionally, until the cream just comes to a boil.

Meanwhile, in a wide bowl beat the yolks lightly with a wire whisk, just to mix. In a small bowl stir the cornstarch and sugar together and then gradually whisk them into the yolks, just to mix. Gradually whisk in the lemon juice. When the cream comes to a boil add it gradually, whisking to mix but not enough to make the mixture foamy.

Pour about 2 cups of the filling into a small, wide pitcher (a plastic 2-cup measuring cup, for instance). Pour the remaining filling into the pastry shell, carefully place the shell in the oven, then reach into the oven and slowly pour the 2 cups of filling from the pitcher (this prevents spilling).

Bake for 1 hour at 250 degrees. The filling will still appear slightly soft but it will firm as it cools.

Remove from the oven and let stand until completely cool.

APRICOT GLAZE

½ cup apricot preserves

1 tablespoon Cognac

Heat the preserves in a small pan to soften. Strain to remove any coarse pieces. Return to the pan and stir in the Cognac.

When the tart has cooled completely heat the glaze until it comes to a boil. Pour the hot glaze gently over the tart and tilt the pan to run the glaze all over the top. It must touch the crust all around; if necessary, use a brush very gently.

Refrigerate.

Remove the sides of the pan and, using a flat-rimmed cookie sheet as a spatula, transfer the tart gently and carefully to a wide, flat serving plate.

Whipped cream is optional.

OPTIONAL WHIPPED CREAM

2 cups whipping cream
¼ cup confectioners sugar

1 teaspoon vanilla extract
Optional: fresh cherries or berries

In a chilled bowl, with chilled beaters, whip the cream with the sugar and vanilla only until the cream holds a soft shape, not until it is stiff.

Serve the cream separately, spooning or pouring it alongside each portion.

This does not need a thing but if you just happen to have some fresh black cherries with long stems or fresh strawberries with bright green hulls or fresh blackberries or raspberries, arrange a circle of them around the top of the pie.

NOTE: *The amount of lemon juice can be increased to ¾ cup if you love a sour lemon taste; I consider ⅔ cup a happy medium.*

Blueberry Custard Tart

This has a buttery, cookielike crust and a creamy custard filling full of fresh blueberries. A wonderful summer dessert. The crust can be prepared in the pan way ahead of time and frozen, if you wish. The filling is quick and easy.

The crust can be partially baked early in the day or just before using. But the final baking— with the filling—should be done about 4 hours before serving, if possible.

You will need an 11 by 1-inch loose-bottomed quiche or tart pan, preferably black or blue-black metal, rather than shiny silver colored; the dark color makes the crust brown.

8 PORTIONS

PASTRY

1 cup unsifted all-purpose flour
2 tablespoons granulated sugar
¼ teaspoon salt
4 ounces (1 stick) unsalted butter, cold and firm, cut into small pieces (it is best to cut the butter ahead of time and refrigerate it)
1 egg graded "large"

This can be put together in a processor, a mixer, or by hand.

In a processor: Fit the bowl with the metal chopping blade. Place the flour, sugar, salt, and butter in the bowl. Process on/off for 10 seconds (10 1-second pulses) until the mixture resembles coarse crumbs. Add the egg and process briefly (about 15 seconds) until the ingredients are all moistened and the mixture just holds together.

In an electric mixer: The same procedure can be followed, using the large bowl of the mixer and low speed. Use a rubber spatula to keep pushing the ingredients into the beaters.

By hand: Place the dry ingredients in a bowl. Add the butter and cut it in with a pastry blender until the mixture resembles coarse crumbs. Beat the egg lightly to mix, add it and stir well with a fork until the ingredients just begin to hold together.

Whichever way you have arrived at this stage, now turn the mixture out onto a board. Push it together with your hands, knead it—with the heel of your hand only—a few times until the dough is very smooth. Form it into a ball, flatten it slightly, cover it loosely, and let rest for about 20 minutes.

It is not necessary to chill this dough before using it. However, if you make it way ahead of time and freeze it, place it in the refrigerator overnight to thaw. If it is very firm when you use it, pound it gently with a rolling pin until it is soft enough to be rolled out.

On a floured pastry cloth with a floured rolling pin roll out the dough until it forms a circle about 13½ to 14 inches in diameter. The dough will become very thin; it is important to keep it the same thickness all over.

Place the rolling pin over one edge of the dough, roll up one side of the dough onto the rolling pin, lift it, and unroll the dough over the tart pan, centering it carefully. Quickly ease the dough on the sides down into the pan, making the sides a little thicker. If you have a cake-decorating turntable place the pan on it. Then, with scissors, trim the edges, leaving an even ½ to ¾-inch border standing up over the rim of the pan. If the

52

pastry is not wide enough in some places and too wide in others, trim the excess and use it where you need it. Wet the edges of the patch with a bit of water, turn it upside down, and press it securely where you need it.

Now fold in a narrow hem—about ¼ inch wide—folding toward the middle (not toward the outside) and leaving the rim of the pastry raised a bit above the edge of the pan. With pastry pincers form a design on the rim or, with the dull side of a knife blade, form shallow ridges on an angle to decorate it.

(Prick fork holes about ½ inch apart in the bottom of the pastry.)

Place the quiche pan lined with the dough in the freezer for at least 15 to 20 minutes, or as much longer as you wish. (If you freeze it longer, wrap it airtight after it becomes firm. It can be baked frozen.)

To bake, adjust a rack one-third up from the bottom of the oven and preheat the oven to 400 degrees.

Center a 12-inch square of foil shiny side down over the frozen shell, press the foil into place in the shell, and fill it with dried beans or pie weights. Bake for 15 minutes, remove the shell from the oven, and slowly and gently remove the foil (with the beans or weights) by raising all four corners at once.

Return the shell to the oven and continue to bake for 5 to 10 minutes more until it is dry and the bottom barely begins to color.

Remove the shell from the oven and let cool for about 10 minutes. Meanwhile, lower the oven temperature to 325 degrees and prepare the filling.

BLUEBERRY CUSTARD

2 cups fresh blueberries
¼ cup granulated sugar
¼ teaspoon cinnamon
¼ teaspoon nutmeg

2 eggs graded "large" plus 2 additional egg yolks
1 teaspoon vanilla extract
1 cup whipping cream

Wash and thoroughly dry the berries (see To Wash Blueberries, page 14). Set aside.

Sift or strain together the sugar, cinnamon, and nutmeg. In a large bowl beat the eggs and yolks lightly just to mix. Stir in the dry ingredients, vanilla, and cream.

Place the blueberries evenly in a layer in the prepared pastry shell. Gently and slowly pour part of the cream mixture over the berries. Do not fill the shell all the way or it might spill on the way to the oven. With the back of a large spoon tap any berries that are on top of the custard just to wet the tops a bit.

Place the pan in the oven, then reach in and pour in the remaining custard. (If there are any low spots on the rim of the pastry, the custard would run over; watch it carefully and if necessary do not use the full amount.)

Bake for about 35 minutes until the custard no longer shakes if you tap the pan, and until a small, sharp knife gently inserted into the middle of the custard comes out clean. (The knife test leaves a scar; use it only if you are not sure otherwise.)

Let the tart cool to room temperature.

Remove the sides of the pan by placing the pan on a shallow custard cup; the sides will slip down.

I always prefer to remove desserts from the bottom of a quiche pan or springform rather than serve on the bottom. In this case removing the tart is a bit touchy because it is so wide, so tender, and so fragile; however, it can be done. But you decide. If the tart looks gorgeous and you do not want to chance hurting it, do not attempt to transfer it. (Just place it on a folded napkin on a wide, flat serving plate.) But if you do decide to transfer it, here's how. Do it now, after the tart has reached room temperature and before it is refrigerated. (When it is refrigerated it might stick to the bottom because of the butter in the pastry.) Use a flat-sided cookie sheet as a spatula. Gently ease it under the tart, holding your left hand at the opposite side of the tart to help it up onto the cookie sheet. Transfer over a flat plate or a board you will serve it on. Now move your left hand to the side of the tart that is closest to you and very gently—without any real pressure—ease the tart off the sheet onto the plate or board.

Refrigerate the tart for 1 to 3 hours before serving.

OPTIONAL DECORATION: *Place a row of fresh strawberries on the filling around the circumference of the tart. Or form a circle of small rosettes of whipped cream around the circumference.*

Prune and Apricot Turnovers

These were a specialty of my mother's. All the years I lived at home it was a special treat for me if my mother let me decorate the turnovers. But she was artistic and creative and she liked decorating them herself, so usually we each did half. And we tried to outdo each other.

Although these are wonderfully delicious, the first things I think of when I think "turnovers" are fun—and gorgeous. If you do craft work of any kind

you will love making these; it can become a hobby.

The pastry is flaky, the filling is sweet and tart and almost-but-not-quite runny.

The prunes and apricots should be soaked overnight before they are stewed. Then the prune and apricot filling and the pastry should both be refrigerated for several hours or overnight before they are used.

9 OR 10 LARGE TURNOVERS

PRUNE AND APRICOT FILLING

6 ounces (1 cup) dried pitted prunes
6 ounces (1 cup) dried apricots
1½ cups water

½ cup granulated sugar
½ teaspoon salt

In a covered 2-quart container or saucepan soak the prunes and apricots in the water overnight.

The next day bring the combined ingredients to a boil, uncovered, over moderate heat. Reduce the heat, allowing the mixture to simmer slowly. Cook the fruit only until it is tender and until the water is almost completely absorbed or evaporated but do not mash the fruit or allow it to disintegrate. This needs almost constant stirring to prevent burning, but in order not to break up the fruit any more than necessary, stir only gently, with a wooden spatula. And do not really stir; all you are trying to do is keep the fruit on the bottom from burning, so just push the spatula around the bottom slowly, as necessary. After about 5 minutes of simmering add the sugar and salt and continue to simmer and stir until there is only a little liquid remaining but do not cook until too dry. Total cooking time (including the first 5 minutes) is about 20 minutes. The mixture will continue to thicken as it cools.

Then cool and refrigerate.

PASTRY

Make a double recipe of Pie Pastry for a 9-inch pie (see page 21). On a lightly floured surface knead gently only two or three times until the ingredients just barely hold together, wrap, and refrigerate overnight or for several hours.

When you are ready to bake, adjust two racks to divide the oven into thirds and preheat the oven to 425 degrees. Line two cookie sheets with aluminum foil shiny side up. Prepare the egg wash.

EGG WASH (glaze)

1 egg yolk   1 teaspoon water

In a small cup stir the yolk and water together. Strain through a fine strainer. Set aside.

Lightly flour a pastry cloth and a rolling pin. Cut the pastry in half, return one piece to the refrigerator, and place the other piece on the pastry cloth.

With a floured rolling pin gently pound the firm pastry until it is soft enough to roll. Roll it out until it is ⅛ inch thick, reflouring the pin as necessary and sprinkling and then spreading a bit of flour over the surface of the dough occasionally if necessary; it is generally not necessary to reflour the pastry cloth while rolling if it has been well floured.

The rolled-out dough will be cut with a 5-inch round cookie cutter. That's a large one, and hard to find (see Note). Or it can be cut with a knife into 5-inch squares. If you are going to cut it into squares you should plan ahead and roll out the dough into a 5- or 10-inch width. Cut out the rounds or squares. Reserve remaining scraps but do not press or knead them together; just place them on top of each other and reroll and recut. Reroll the scraps only once (the pastry would not be flaky after further rerolling); reserve them to make cut-out decorations for the tops of the turnovers. You should have 9 or 10 rounds or squares.

Place the rounds or squares on wax paper or foil.

Divide the filling among the rounds or squares, placing it to one side of center but not too close to the edge. Use a rounded tablespoon of the filling for each turnover. (You will have a few spoonfuls of leftover filling; it is a delicious spread for toast or crackers.)

Place a small cup of cold water next to your work area.

Fold over one turnover at a time. With a soft brush wet a border about ½ inch wide around one half of the round or square (the squares can be folded to make rectangles or triangles). Fold the dry half of the pastry over the wet border and press the borders together gently. Place the folded turnovers on the foil-lined cookie sheets.

With the backs of the tines of a fork, floured if necessary, press around the borders to seal the edges together and to make a ridged design.

Shape all of the turnovers.

Now roll out the remaining pastry scraps; it is best to roll this a bit thinner than the dough for the turnovers themselves. Cut out designs using small cookie cutters, truffle cutters, the tip of a knife or scissors. Use cold water as a paste to fasten the design on; just brush or finger a bit of water where you want it on the turnover before applying the design.

Then, with a soft brush, brush the egg wash gently all over the top, including the design and the rim. But do not use so much that it runs down on the sides; it would make the turnovers stick. Two thin coats are best (if you allow the wash to form puddles on the turnovers they will not brown evenly).

With a four-pronged fork pierce the top once, avoiding the design, to allow steam to escape.

(At this point these can be frozen to bake later on. Let them stand until the egg wash dries. Then place the cookie sheet in the freezer. When the turnovers are frozen, peel the foil away from the backs of the turnovers and wrap each individually in plastic wrap. When you are ready to bake, unwrap, place on foil-lined sheets, and put into the preheated oven frozen. They seem to bake in the same time even if they are frozen.)

Bake for about 30 minutes, reversing the sheets top to bottom and front to back as necessary to ensure even browning. Bake until nicely browned; do not underbake. (If you bake only one sheet at a time bake it in the middle of the oven: one sheet takes less time.)

Cool the turnovers on a rack. However, if you can arrange to serve these warm, by all means do so.

If the turnovers are frozen after they are baked, they can quickly be thawed and reheated, unwrapped, in a 350-degree oven.

VARIATIONS: *My mother never added anything to the filling so this is the way I think it should be. But I have at times added a few coarsely chopped walnuts and it was wonderful. Also, when I added 2 to 3 tablespoons Cognac to the cooked and cooled filling, I thought that was the best.*

NOTE: *Fred Bridge says he will have 5-inch round cutters by the time this book is published. Bridge Kitchenware, 214 East 52nd Street, New York, New York 10022.*

Layer Cakes

There are a few wonderful and delicious layer cakes that are not American (Dobos torte, for one) but only Americans know about real, no-holds-barred, six to seven inches high, three or four layers, layer cakes with a capital L. Layer cakes are a totally American institution.

**ICING TALL
LAYER CAKES**

The most important thing to remember and concentrate on when icing a tall layer cake is that the sides must be straight up and down; it is very easy to form a cake that looks like the leaning tower of Pisa. The only advice I know to keep a cake straight is to be conscious of it and to work carefully. (Or, as the taxi driver said when a young man carrying a violin while walking on Times Square asked, "How do I get to Carnegie Hall?," "Practice, boy, practice.")

And stand back and look at it from a distance so you can really see it, and study it.

Another important part is the rim of the top layer. Somehow that is where hollows want to appear. The best solution I know for that is to reserve some of the icing and apply it with a pastry bag fitted with a star-shaped tube, forming a border of rosettes on the top right around the rim. That will camouflage any hollows or uneven spots and will give the cake a finished and professional look. Just one word: Those rosettes are always more attractive if they are not too large; otherwise they overwhelm the cake and give it a heavy and coarse look.

American Chocolate Layer Cake

I remember a heart-wrenching disappointment when I was very young. I had been told that I was going to have a piece of chocolate layer cake; my anticipation was overwhelming. But when it came I was thrown into despair. It was a white cake— a white cake with chocolate icing.

I learned early that that's what Americans call a chocolate layer cake.

THIS IS IT, *the most stupendous of all chocolate layer cakes (over 5 inches high). It is enough for a very large party, or a small army.*

It has four layers of rich butter cake, two of which have optional chunky walnut pieces throughout. The icing is a dark chocolate sour cream concoction that is miraculous; it is thick/smooth/shiny, and it doesn't care if you use it right away or after lunch, it doesn't care if you work over it again and again.

What's more, both the cake and the icing are easy and foolproof.

(You need five cake racks for removing four layers from the pans.)

20 OR MORE PORTIONS

4 cups sifted all-purpose flour
4 teaspoons double-acting baking powder
¼ teaspoon baking soda
½ teaspoon salt
1 pound (4 sticks) unsalted butter
1½ teaspoons vanilla extract

½ teaspoon almond extract
2 cups granulated sugar
6 eggs graded "large"
¾ cup milk
Optional: 6 ounces (1½ cups) walnuts, cut or
        broken into medium-size pieces

Adjust two racks to divide the oven into thirds and preheat the oven to 350 degrees. Butter four 9-inch round layer cake pans, line them with baking pan liner paper or wax paper cut to fit, butter the paper, dust the pans all over with fine dry bread crumbs, tilt the pans from side to side to coat them evenly, and then turn them upside down over paper and tap them to shake out loose crumbs. Set the pans aside.

Sift together the flour, baking powder, baking soda, and salt, and set aside.

In the large bowl of an electric mixer beat the butter until soft. Add the vanilla and almond extracts and then the sugar and beat to mix. Add the eggs one or two at a time, and beat until incorporated after each addition. On low speed add the sifted dry ingredients in three additions alternating with the milk in two additions.

Remove the bowl from the mixer. You will have a generous 8 cups of batter. Place a generous 2 cups in two of the prepared pans. Stir the optional nuts into the remaining batter and place half of it (a generous 2 cups) in each of the two remaining pans.

With the underside of a large spoon spread the batter to the sides of the pans. To encourage the cakes to rise with flat tops (without domes) spread the batter more thickly around the edges and slightly thinner in the middle of the pans.

Place two of the pans on each oven rack, staggering them so that the pans on the lower rack are not directly below those above.

Bake for 25 to 28 minutes. (I have made this cake many times and have never found it necessary to change the positions of the pans during baking; somehow they always bake evenly, even though that is unusual for my oven.) Bake until the tops just barely spring back when they are gently pressed with a fingertip, and the sides of the cakes just barely begin to come away from the sides of the pans. Do not overbake or the cake will be dry.

As soon as the cakes are done remove them from the oven, cover each one with a rack and turn the pan and rack over, remove the pan—if the paper lining does not come off by itself leave it on—cover with another rack, and invert again, leaving the cakes right side up to cool.

When they have cooled, cover each one with a rack and turn over briefly to remove the paper linings. Then turn right side up again. Brush each cake with a pastry brush to remove loose crumbs on the sides.

Prepare a large flat cake plate by lining it with four strips of wax paper (see illustration, page 16). Place 1 cake on the plate, checking to be sure that it touches the papers all around. If you have a cake-decorating turntable, place the cake plate on it.

Let stand, and make the icing. Or, if you wish, the icing may be made while the cakes are baking.

CHOCOLATE SOUR CREAM ICING

This doesn't run and it doesn't harden; you can apply it smoothly or in swirls—it works like a charm with a pastry bag.

16 ounces milk chocolate
12 ounces semisweet chocolate (I use 1-ounce
squares of Hershey or Nestlé; use any
semisweet you like)

Pinch of salt
1 teaspoon vanilla extract
1 pint (2 cups) sour cream

Break up the chocolates and place them in the top of a large double boiler over shallow warm water on low heat. Cover the pot with a folded paper towel (to absorb steam) and with the pot cover. Let cook until almost completely melted, then uncover and stir with a wooden spatula until completely melted.

Transfer to the large bowl of an electric mixer. Add the salt, vanilla, and sour cream and beat on low speed until as smooth as satin (this is spectacular looking).

Let stand at room temperature for about an hour or so until cool and slightly thickened.

If you have a cake-decorating turntable and are experienced at using it you will probably want to smooth the icing on the top and sides; without a turntable you will probably want to form the icing into swirls. If you plan to smooth it, you will probably also want to form a circle of rosettes around the top rim. If so, remove and reserve about ⅔ cup of the icing.

Whether you plan to smooth the icing or swirl it, do not use too much between the layers or you will not have enough to go around (in spite of the fact that this looks like enough icing for a dozen cakes).

With a long, narrow metal spatula spread a scant ¼-inch layer of icing over the cake, making it a bit thicker at the rim to fill in the space. Place the next layer on (if you have used nuts, alternate the nut layers with the plain ones) right side up, and ice the same as you did the first. Place the third layer on, right side up (align the layers carefully), ice, and then place the fourth layer on, right side up (all four layers are right side up).

Cover the sides of the cake with the icing, and then the top. Make sure it is all straight and even. Then smooth or swirl. Carefully remove the paper strips by slowly pulling each one out toward a narrow end.

If you have smoothed the icing and if you would like to decorate the rim (I do), fit a 12-inch pastry bag with a #7 star-shaped tube. Fold down the sides of the bag toward the outside to make a 2- or 3-inch hem, transfer the reserved icing to the pastry bag, unfold the hem, and twist the top of the bag closed.

If you are working on a counter top transfer the cake and the turntable to a table; it is easier to use a pastry bag for decorating the top of a cake if you are working above it rather than alongside it—especially a cake this high. Form a row of rather large rosettes (about the size of Hershey's Kisses) just touching one another on top of the cake around the rim.

Now, how about that? I salute you.

Serve this on wide plates.

Star-Spangled Banana Cake

I made 3 of these for a big New Year's Eve party. After icing each cake I wrapped a shiny yellow ribbon around its middle, made big fluffy bows, inserted tiny yellow and white silk flowers in each bow, and taped a little "Happy New Year" sign onto one of the streamers of each bow. (I inserted a long bamboo skewer deep into the cake right under each bow to support its weight.)

The secret is to make the whole thing, ribbon, bow, and bouquet, ahead of time, using a cake pan as a dummy. Cut the ribbon at the side of the pan opposite the bow, then just "dress" the cake by taping the ribbon together at the back of the cake.

The cakes were beautiful, but they are equally delicious and equally attractive without these decorations.

This is a big, bold, beautiful four-layered Southern banana-nut cake, 6 inches high, with a mountain of fluffy white icing and a shower of coconut. This is for occasions: birthdays, New Year's Eve, or for the cover of a magazine. It is not difficult to make, there is nothing tricky, but stacking the four layers with the abundance of icing takes courage.

20 PORTIONS

BANANA LAYERS

3 cups sifted all-purpose flour
2 teaspoons double-acting baking powder
½ teaspoon salt
6 ounces (1½ sticks) unsalted butter
1 teaspoon vanilla extract
¼ teaspoon almond extract
2 cups granulated sugar

3 eggs graded "large"
About 5 large fully ripened bananas (to make 2½ cups, mashed)
1 teaspoon baking soda
6 ounces (1½ cups) pecans, chopped fine (not ground)
½ cup buttermilk

Adjust two racks to divide the oven into thirds and preheat the oven to 350 degrees. Prepare four 9-inch round layer cake pans as follows. Butter the bottoms and sides, line the bottoms with rounds of baking pan liner paper or wax paper cut to fit, then butter the paper, dust with fine dry bread crumbs, then invert over paper and lightly tap out excess crumbs. Set the pans aside.

Sift together the flour, baking powder, and salt and set aside.

In the large bowl of an electric mixer beat the butter until it is soft. Beat in the vanilla and almond extracts and the sugar, beating only to combine well. Add the eggs one at a time, beating thoroughly after each addition. (The mixture might appear curdled—it is OK.)

Coarsely mash the bananas on a wide plate with a fork (they should not be liquefied or puréed). Place them in a bowl and mix in the baking soda. Stir the bananas and then the nuts into the creamed butter mixture.

On low speed add half of the sifted dry ingredients, then the buttermilk, and finally the remaining dry ingredients, beating only until mixed after each addition.

Divide the batter among the pans. Smooth the tops. The layers will be very thin.

Place two pans on each rack; do not place pans directly over or under others.

Bake for 28 to 30 minutes until the tops spring back when pressed gently with a fingertip and the layers barely begin to come away from the sides of the pans.

Cover each layer with a rack, invert pan and rack, remove pan and paper lining, cover with another rack, and turn the layers over again, leaving them right side up to cool.

With a dry pastry brush, brush the sides of the cooled layers to remove loose crumbs.

Before icing the cake place four 12 by 4-inch strips of baking pan liner paper or wax paper in a square pattern around the sides of a large cake platter (see illustration, page 16). Place one layer on the platter right side up and check to be sure that the papers touch the cake all around. (See Variation below.)

If you have a cake-decorating turntable, place the platter on it.

SOUTHERN FLUFFY WHITE ICING

You will need an electric mixer with a 4-quart bowl.

3 cups granulated sugar
⅓ cup light corn syrup (e.g., Karo)
¾ cup boiling water
¾ cup egg whites (from 6 eggs graded "large"; they may be whites that were frozen and then thawed)

Pinch of salt
1 teaspoon vanilla extract
¼ teaspoon almond extract
7 ounces (2⅔ cups, loosely packed) moist shredded coconut

Place the sugar, corn syrup, and boiling water in a 2½- to 3-quart saucepan over moderate heat. Stir frequently with a wooden spatula until the sugar is dissolved. When the mixture comes to a full boil, remove it from the heat and set it aside briefly.

In the large bowl of an electric mixer beat the egg whites with the salt until the whites stand up straight when the beaters are raised.

Transfer the hot syrup to a pitcher that is easy to pour from and, beating at high speed, pour the hot syrup in a thin threadlike stream into the whites, holding the pitcher about 12 inches above the mixer bowl. Pour slowly and scrape the sides of the bowl occasionally with a rubber spatula to keep the entire mass well mixed. It will look as though the bowl will not hold all of the icing; it will, but you must watch it carefully and reduce the speed if necessary to prevent the icing from overflowing.

After all the syrup has been beaten in, add the vanilla and almond extracts and continue to beat (at high speed, if possible) for about 15 more minutes until the icing is very stiff and holds a straight peak when the beaters are raised. Remove the bowl from the mixer.

Spread a generous layer of the icing about 1 inch thick over the first layer of cake. Then place the second cake layer over the icing, also right side up. Cover it with another inch-thick layer of icing. Continue layering the cakes and the icing.

Spread a thick layer of the icing around the sides and then spread all the remaining icing (it will be a thick layer) over the top.

With a long, narrow metal spatula smooth the sides and then the top (be sure the sides are straight and the top is flat).

Place the coconut on a large piece of paper right up against the cake platter. Take a handful of the coconut in the palm of your hand, then turn your hand to place the coconut on the side of the cake. Some of the coconut will stick to the cake and some will fall to the platter; with your fingers transfer the fallen coconut to the pile of coconut on the paper. Pick up another handful and continue to coat the sides with the coconut. If there are spots on the sides near the bottom where there is no coconut just fold the paper strips up against the cake and the coconut that has fallen to the strips will stick to the sides of the cake. Then sprinkle all the remaining coconut over the top of the cake.

Remove the paper strips gently by pulling each one out toward a narrow end.

Let the cake stand at room temperature.

To serve, have dinner plates ready—cake plates are too small for this. Use a long, sharp knife and have a deep pitcher of very hot water to dip the knife into before each cut so you can cut with a hot, wet blade. Or if you prefer to serve on smaller plates, serve the two top layers first (making 10 two-layer portions) and then the two bottom layers (10 more portions).

VARIATION: *Sprinkle a generous amount of light rum onto each layer when it is in place on the plate, just before icing it. If you do use the rum, use enough so you really taste it.*

Pecan Sweet Potato Cake

Hallelujah! An old-fashioned Southern spectacular production, a majestic, regal-looking, three-layer sweetheart, 6 inches high, light/moist/spicy/chunky/nutty, with a generous amount of marshmallow filling and icing and a coating of shredded coconut over all. It is made with shredded raw (uncooked) sweet potatoes—most unusual and most delicious.

The cake can be made ahead of time and frozen, if you wish, but wait until the day of the party to ice it.

10 TO 12 PORTIONS

2¼ cups sifted all-purpose flour
1 tablespoon double-acting baking powder
¼ teaspoon salt
1 teaspoon ground ginger
1 teaspoon nutmeg
2 cups granulated sugar
1½ cups tasteless salad oil
4 eggs graded "large," separated
¼ cup boiling water
1 teaspoon vanilla extract

1 pound (about 1½ large) raw sweet potatoes or yams (to make 2 cups, tightly packed, when shredded)
6 ounces (1½ cups) toasted pecans (see page 7), broken into large pieces
⅓ cup apricot preserves (to be used when icing the cake)
7 ounces (2⅔ cups, loosely packed) shredded coconut (to be used when icing the cake)

Adjust a rack to the middle of the oven and preheat the oven to 350 degrees. Butter three 8-inch round layer cake pans, line them with baking pan liner paper or wax paper cut to fit, then butter the paper, dust all over with fine dry bread crumbs, invert the pans over paper and tap gently to shake out excess, and set aside.

Sift together the flour, baking powder, salt, ginger, and nutmeg and set aside. In the large bowl of an electric mixer beat the sugar and oil just to mix; add the egg yolks and beat to mix. Then add the boiling water and the vanilla, scraping down the sides of the bowl and beating until smoothly mixed. Remove the bowl from the mixer and set aside.

To prepare the sweet potatoes, peel them with a vegetable parer and then grate them on the fine grater of a food processor or with a hand-held grater set over a piece of aluminum foil—use the side of the grater that has small round—not diamond-shaped—openings (to see the shape of the openings hold the grater up and look at the holes through the back). Measure 2 cups, tightly packed.

Stir the potatoes and then the pecans into the batter.

In the small bowl of an electric mixer (with clean beaters) beat the whites until they hold a straight shape when the beaters are raised but not until they are stiff/dry.

Without being too thorough, fold about one third of the whites into the batter, then fold in the remaining whites, handling as little as necessary until just incorporated.

Divide the batter among the prepared pans and smooth the tops.

Bake the three pans on the same oven rack for 30 to 35 minutes until the cakes barely begin to come away from the sides of the pans. (These layers might not spring back when pressed with a fingertip, even though they will be done.)

Cool in the pans for 2 to 3 minutes. Then cover each pan with a rack, turn the pan and rack over, remove the pan and paper lining, cover with another rack, and turn over again, leaving the layers right side up to cool.

When you are ready to ice the cake, place four 12 by 4-inch strips of baking pan liner paper or wax paper in a square pattern around the sides of a large cake plate (see illustration, page 16). There will be such a thick layer of icing that it does not matter if the layers are placed right side up or upside down (I place them all right side up). Place one layer on the plate, checking to see that it touches the papers all around. If you have a cake-decorating turntable, place the cake plate on it.

Stir the apricot preserves in a small saucepan over moderate heat to melt. Then press them through a strainer. With a teaspoon or a pastry brush, spread the first cake layer with one third of the preserves. Reserve remaining preserves.

MARSHMALLOW ICING
You will need a candy thermometer.

1½ cups granulated sugar
⅔ teaspoon cream of tartar
⅔ cup water
⅛ teaspoon salt
⅔ cup egg whites (from 4 to 5 eggs graded "large";

they may be whites that were frozen and then thawed)
1 teaspoon vanilla extract
¼ teaspoon almond extract

Place the sugar, cream of tartar, and water in a 6-cup saucepan (preferably one that is tall and narrow—in a wide one the mixture will be too shallow to reach the bulb of a thermometer). With a wooden spatula stir over moderate heat until the mixture begins to boil. Cover airtight and let boil for 3 minutes. (This keeps the steam in the pot and dissolves any sugar crystals that cling to the sides. However, if you still see any granules when you remove the cover, dip a pastry brush in cold water and use it to wipe the sides.)

Uncover and insert a candy thermometer. Raise the heat to high and let boil without stirring until the thermometer registers 242 degrees.

Shortly before the sugar syrup is done (or when the thermometer registers about 236 degrees—soft-ball stage), add the salt to the egg whites in the large bowl of an electric mixer and beat until the whites are stiff. (If the sugar syrup is not ready, turn the beater to the lowest speed and let it beat slowly until the syrup is ready. Or you can let the whites stand, but no longer than necessary.)

When the syrup reaches 242 degrees (medium-ball stage), turn the mixer to high speed and gradually add the syrup in a thin stream (it may be easiest if you pour the syrup into a pitcher and add it from the pitcher). Then continue to beat at high speed, scraping the bowl occasionally with a rubber spatula, for about 5 minutes or until the icing is quite thick and stiff. Add the vanilla and almond extracts a minute or two before the icing is stiff enough. If necessary, beat some more. The icing may still be warm when it is used.

Spread the first cake layer with the icing about ½ inch thick. Place the second layer over it and spread with one third of the melted apricot preserves, and then cover it with a layer of the icing, again ½ inch thick. Cover with the third cake layer and the remaining preserves.

Now, it is best to ice the sides first. Use a long, narrow metal spatula to ice the sides thinly at first, and then build it up until it is about ½ inch thick, or thicker. Smooth the sides. Use the remaining icing on the top. Spread it smooth. After the sides and the top are smooth and even, then, with the back of a teaspoon or with the spatula, form swirls and peaks evenly on the top of the cake.

To coat the sides with the coconut, first spread out the coconut on a length of foil or wax paper next to the cake plate. Take a handful of the coconut in the palm of your hand and turn your hand to place the coconut on the sides of the cake, starting at the top and working your way down. When much of the coconut falls onto the plate, remove it with your fingers and replace it either on the cake or on the pile of coconut on the paper. Then use a long, narrow metal spatula to pick up coconut that has fallen to the plate and turn it onto the sides of the cake. Finally, fold the paper strips around the bottom up against the cake, and the coconut that has fallen to the strips will stick to the base of the cake. Last, sprinkle all the remaining coconut over the top.

Remove the paper strips by pulling each one slowly and gently toward a narrow end.

Since this cake is so high, use a long-bladed knife to cut it and dinner plates to serve it on; it will fall off the edges of smaller plates.

Prune and Walnut Layer Cake

This beauty consists of three layers of moist and rich, prune and nut, buttermilk and sour cream cake, mildly spiced, and generously filled and covered with a fantastic and extravagant chocolate–cream cheese–buttercream mousse. Prune cakes of all kinds were made on the farms and in the cities many years ago; this one is an old favorite—it is wonderful.

24 PORTIONS

Generous 1½ cups stewed pitted prunes, tightly packed (see Notes)
3 cups minus 2 tablespoons sifted all-purpose flour
1 teaspoon baking soda
½ teaspoon double-acting baking powder
½ teaspoon salt
1 teaspoon cinnamon
1 teaspoon nutmeg
1 teaspoon cloves
2 tablespoons unsweetened cocoa powder (preferably Dutch-process)

8 ounces (2 sticks) unsalted butter
1 teaspoon vanilla extract
1¾ cups granulated sugar
3 eggs graded "large" or "extra-large," separated
½ cup buttermilk
½ cup sour cream
8 ounces (generous 2 cups) walnuts, cut or broken into medium-size pieces

Adjust two racks to divide the oven into thirds and preheat the oven to 350 degrees. Butter three 9-inch round layer cake pans, line them with rounds of baking pan liner paper or wax paper cut to fit, then butter the paper, dust all over with fine dry bread crumbs, and invert over paper and tap out excess crumbs. Set aside.

Coarsely chop the prunes (I chop them on a board with a large French chef's knife—or you can cut them with scissors) and place them in a wide strainer or a colander over a bowl to drain, but not to dry completely (they add moisture to the cake).

Sift together the flour, baking soda, baking powder, salt, cinnamon, nutmeg, cloves, and cocoa and set aside.

In the large bowl of an electric mixer beat the butter until soft. Add the vanilla and 1½ cups of the sugar (reserve the remaining ¼ cup of sugar) and beat to mix. Add the egg yolks and beat until incorporated. On low speed add the sifted dry ingredients in three additions, alternating with the buttermilk and then the sour cream, scraping the bowl with a rubber spatula and beating until smooth after each addition. Remove the bowl from the mixer and stir in the prunes and nuts. Set aside.

In the small bowl of an electric mixer (with clean beaters) beat the egg whites until they hold a soft point. Reduce the speed slightly and gradually add the remaining ¼ cup of sugar. Then beat again briefly at high speed only until the whites just barely hold a straight point when the beaters are raised.

In two additions fold the whites into the batter. Divide the batter among the pans and smooth the tops.

Bake for 35 to 40 minutes until the cakes just begin to come away from the sides of the pans, and until the tops spring back when they are pressed lightly with a fingertip in the middle. Do not overbake. Toward the end of the baking, if the cakes are not browning evenly, exchange the positions of the pans.

Let stand for 2 to 3 minutes and then cover each pan with a rack, turn the pan and rack over, remove the pan and paper lining, cover the cake with another rack, and turn it over again, leaving the cakes right side up to cool on racks.

Before icing the cake, prepare a wide, flat cake plate by placing four 12 by 4-inch strips of baking pan liner paper or wax paper in a square pattern around the sides of the plate (see illustration, page 16). Place one cake layer on the plate upside down (all three layers will be upside down). Check to see that it touches the papers all around. If you have a cake-decorating turntable, place the cake plate on it.

CHOCOLATE–CREAM CHEESE–MOUSSE ICING

14 to 16 ounces semisweet chocolate (see Notes)
8 ounces cream cheese, preferably at room
    temperature
8 ounces (2 sticks) unsalted butter
1 teaspoon vanilla extract

½ cup plus 2 tablespoons granulated sugar
2 eggs graded "large," separated
1 cup whipping cream
Pinch of salt

Break up the chocolate and place it in the top of a large double boiler over warm water on low heat. Cover with a folded paper towel (to absorb steam) and the pot cover and heat until almost completely melted. Then uncover and stir until completely melted. Remove the top of the double boiler and set aside briefly.

In the large bowl of an electric mixer beat the cream cheese and butter with the vanilla and ½ cup of the sugar (reserve the remaining 2 tablespoons of sugar) until well mixed. Add the melted chocolate (which should still be warm to help dissolve the granules of sugar) and beat well until the sugar is dissolved. Beat in the 2 egg yolks (reserve the whites), beating at high speed until the mixture is as smooth as honey and has lightened slightly in color. Set aside.

In a small chilled bowl, with chilled beaters, whip the cream until it is very firm or as firm as you can make it without taking any chance that it might turn to butter. (The safest way to do this is to use the mixer only until the cream holds a soft shape. Then finish the whipping with a whisk. That way you have better control of what is happening and there is less chance of overbeating.) Set aside.

In a clean small bowl, with clean beaters, beat the egg whites with the salt until the whites hold a soft shape. Reduce the speed to moderate and gradually add the remaining 2 tablespoons of sugar. Increase the speed again and continue to beat briefly only until the whites hold a straight shape when the beaters are raised, but not until they are stiff/dry. Set aside.

Without being too thorough, fold the whipped cream in two additions into the chocolate mixture, then add the beaten whites and continue to fold gently only until the mixtures are blended—do not handle any more than necessary.

With a long, narrow metal spatula spread a layer of the icing a generous ½ inch thick over the bottom layer of cake. Place the second layer of cake upside down over the icing. Spread that with another generous ½-inch-thick layer of icing. Cover with the top layer of cake (also upside down).

Spread a rather thick layer of the icing all around the sides, and then over the top. If you wish, reserve about ¾ cup of the icing for decorating the cake. (To do this, place the icing in a small pastry bag fitted with a #4 or medium-size star-shaped tube. Form a row of small rosettes just touching one another around the top rim of the cake.)

DECORATION

2 to 3 ounces milk chocolate
Unsweetened cocoa powder (preferably Dutch-
　　process)

Confectioners sugar

With a vegetable parer form small curls of milk chocolate, allowing them to fall onto a piece of wax paper. With a large spoon or wide spatula gently transfer the curls to the top of the cake, placing them within the ring of rosettes, or, if you have not made rosettes, cover the top of the cake all the way to the edges. Make it a generous layer of chocolate curls.

Then sprinkle the top of the cake with unsweetened cocoa powder through a fine strainer held over the cake. And then, using a clean fine strainer, cover with a layer of confectioners sugar.

CAUTION: *Do not tilt the cake plate until the icing has been refrigerated or the layers will slide out of place. Take my word for it and hold the plate very carefully.*

Remove the strips of baking pan liner paper or wax paper by pulling each one out slowly toward a narrow end.

Refrigerate for at least several hours before serving. The cake should be very cold when it is served. Serve small portions.

NOTES: *1. If you want to stew the prunes yourself, you will need a 12-ounce box of dried pitted prunes or 1 pound of prunes with pits. If you buy them already stewed, you will need a 1-pound 9-ounce jar.*

2. I have made this with 14 ounces (2 7-ounce bars) of Poulain chocolate and also with 16 ounces (4 4-ounce bars) of Maillard's Eagle Sweet chocolate, and it was wonderful both ways.

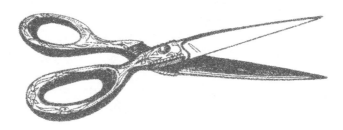

Boston Cream Pie

Long ago there was a famous American dessert called "pudding-cake pie." When the great Parker House Hotel opened in Boston, in 1855, they added a chocolate icing to the dessert and renamed it Boston Cream Pie. It immediately became, and has remained, one of America's most loved desserts. It is a plain white two-layer sponge cake (moist and tender) with a vanilla pastry cream filling (like a vanilla pudding, creamy and delicate) and a thin layer of dark semisweet chocolate glaze on top: an addictive combination.

It is so very simple and easy looking that you might think it should be easy to make, but simple-looking and plain things are often more difficult than elaborate things. Making this cake involves great care with folding in beaten whites and yolks and sifted dry ingredients and melted butter. And the filling calls for patience in making the custard carefully and slowly so you don't wind up with scrambled eggs.

But then—joy! It is a great accomplishment. My congratulations to you.

There are many recipes for Boston Cream Pie. This is the best I've ever had. We originally ate it in Boston; the recipe is adapted from one in the revised edition of The Boston Globe Cookbook (Globe Pequot Press, 1981).

I don't know why this cake is called a pie.

8 PORTIONS

VANILLA PASTRY CREAM

Unless you want to make the cake ahead of time and freeze it, make this first in order to chill it well before using.

2 eggs graded "large"
¼ cup plus 1 tablespoon sifted all-purpose flour
¼ teaspoon salt
⅔ cup granulated sugar
2 cups milk

1 teaspoon vanilla extract
¼ teaspoon almond extract
1 ounce (¼ stick) unsalted butter, cut into small pieces

In a small bowl beat the eggs lightly just to mix; set aside. Mix the flour, salt, and sugar in a heavy 2-quart saucepan. Gradually stir in the milk, then cook, stirring constantly, over medium-low heat until the mixture comes to a boil and starts to thicken. Continue to stir and boil gently for a minute or two. The mixture should become as thick as a medium white sauce—or about like vichyssoise.

Remove the pan from the heat. With a ladle add about ½ cup of the hot mixture to the eggs and stir well to mix. Repeat, adding ½ cup at a time, until you have added about half of the hot mixture to the eggs. Then, very slowly, stirring constantly, stir the egg mixture into the remaining hot milk mixture.

Place the pan over low heat and cook, still stirring constantly, for 2 minutes. Remove from the heat. Mix in the vanilla and almond extracts and the butter.

Immediately (to stop the cooking) pour the mixture into a bowl. Cut a round of wax paper to fit on top of the pastry cream (touching it), and place the paper directly on the cream. This will prevent a skin from forming.

Now, either let this stand until cool and then refrigerate for at least an hour, or save time by placing the bowl in a larger bowl of ice and water to cool quickly, and then refrigerate for at least an hour.

BOSTON SPONGE CAKE

1 cup sifted all-purpose flour
1 teaspoon double-acting baking powder
3 eggs graded "large," separated
¼ teaspoon salt
⅔ cup granulated sugar

1 teaspoon vanilla extract
1 tablespoon lemon juice
2 tablespoons cold tap water
3 tablespoons unsalted butter, melted

Adjust a rack to the middle of the oven and preheat the oven to 350 degrees. Butter a 9 by 1½-inch round cake pan, line the bottom with a round of baking pan liner paper or wax paper cut to fit, then butter the paper, and dust all over with fine dry bread crumbs. Invert the pan over paper and tap lightly to shake out excess crumbs. Set the pan aside.

Sift together the flour and baking powder and set aside.

Beat the egg whites and the salt in the small bowl of an electric mixer until the whites hold a soft shape. Reduce the speed to moderate and gradually add ⅓ cup of the sugar (reserve the remaining ⅓ cup of sugar). Then increase the speed again and continue to beat very briefly only until the whites just hold a point when the beaters are raised or when some of the whites are lifted on a rubber spatula, but do not beat until the whites are stiff or dry.

Transfer the beaten whites to the large bowl of the mixer. Scrape the beaters with your finger to remove most of the whites and scrape the bowl with a rubber spatula. (It is not necessary to wash the bowl or beaters.) Set aside.

Place the yolks in the small bowl of the mixer. Beat briefly, then gradually add the remaining ⅓ cup of sugar and continue to beat at high speed until the mixture is very light—almost white. Beat in the vanilla and lemon juice; then on low speed add the cold tap water, scraping the bowl as necessary and beating only until the mixture is smooth.

In about four additions fold the yolks into the whites (do not handle any more than necessary . . . do not be too thorough, especially with the first few additions).

Place the dry ingredients in a sifter and hold the sifter over the bowl, sifting with one hand and folding with the other. The dry ingredients should be added in four or five additions. (Do not handle any more than necessary.)

The melted butter may be slightly warm or it may have cooled to room temperature but it must still be liquid. Add it all at once to the batter and fold gently only until barely (but not absolutely) incorporated.

Turn the batter into the prepared pan and smooth the top.

Bake for about 30 minutes until the top springs back when pressed gently with a fingertip.

Remove from the oven. With a small, sharp knife cut around the rim of the cake to release it. Let stand in the pan for 5 minutes. Then cover the pan with a rack, turn the pan and the rack over, remove the cake pan—do not remove the paper lining, which should be clinging to the cake—cover the cake with another rack and turn over again, leaving the cake right side up to cool.

The next step is to cut the cake into two thin layers. I think it is easiest and safest if you first chill the cake in the freezer for about 30 minutes or longer. Place the cold cake upside down on a flat cake plate. Remove the paper lining from the cake. If you have a cake-decorating turntable, place the cake plate on it. Use a long, thin, sharp knife (I use a ham slicer—or you might like to use a serrated knife) and carefully cut the cake into two thin layers.

Carefully remove and set aside the top layer.

Turn the chilled pastry cream onto the bottom layer of the cake. With a long, narrow metal spatula spread the pastry cream to ½ inch from the edges of the cake. (If it goes any closer to the edges the weight of the top layer might spread it out too far.)

Cover with the top layer. Now refrigerate the cake while you make the glaze.

CHOCOLATE GLAZE

¼ cup whipping cream   4 ounces semisweet chocolate, chopped coarse

Place the cream in a small, heavy saucepan over moderate heat until it begins to bubble. Add the chocolate, stir briefly until partly melted, then remove the pan from the heat and continue to stir until completely melted. Transfer the glaze to a small bowl and let stand for about 10 minutes, stirring occasionally.

Pour the glaze onto the cake; then, with a long, narrow metal spatula, smooth it just to the edge of the cake. Try to avoid having the glaze run down the sides of the cake, but if a bit does, leave it.

Refrigerate and serve cold.

Kentucky Cake

This was a famous Southern cake over 100 years ago. Versions of it were also called Union Cake. It is a large two-layer cake, each layer mixed and baked separately; one layer dark and spicy, the other white and lemony. It is filled and iced with a thick coating of marshmallowlike 7-minute icing.

Fancy and gorgeous, it makes a scrumptious birthday cake or Christmas cake. The layers can be made way ahead and frozen, if you wish; the cake should be iced the day it is served.

10 TO 12 PORTIONS

DARK LAYER

⅓ cup dark raisins
1 cup sifted all-purpose flour
¼ teaspoon salt
⅓ teaspoon baking soda
½ teaspoon cinnamon
⅛ teaspoon cloves
¼ teaspoon nutmeg
¼ teaspoon mace
¼ teaspoon allspice

¼ teaspoon dry mustard
3 ounces (¾ stick) unsalted butter
⅓ cup dark brown sugar, firmly packed
2 eggs graded "large," separated (reserve the whites for the white layer)
⅓ cup buttermilk
⅓ cup dark or light molasses
Optional: 1 tablespoon bourbon (to be used when icing the cake)

Adjust a rack one-third up from the bottom of the oven and preheat the oven to 375 degrees. Since you will eventually make two layers of cake, why not prepare both pans now? Butter two 9-inch round layer cake pans, line the bottoms with rounds of baking pan liner paper or wax paper cut to fit, then butter the paper, dust with fine dry bread crumbs, and invert over paper and shake out excess crumbs. Set the pans aside.

Cut the raisins coarsely by placing them on a board and cutting down on them with a long, heavy French chef's knife. Put them in a small bowl, add about 1 tablespoon of the flour, and toss to separate and coat the pieces thoroughly.

Sift the remaining flour with the salt, baking soda, cinnamon, cloves, nutmeg, mace, allspice, and mustard and set aside. In the small bowl of an electric mixer beat the butter until soft, then beat in the sugar. Add the yolks and beat until incorporated. On low speed gradually add the buttermilk and molasses, and then the sifted dry ingredients (the mixture will appear slightly curdled—it is all right). Remove the bowl from the mixer.

Stir in the floured raisins (along with any loose flour in the bowl).

Turn into the prepared pan, smooth the top, and bake for 25 to 30 minutes until the top of the cake springs back when it is pressed gently with a fingertip and the cake begins to come away from the sides of the pan.

Let stand for a minute or two, cover with a rack, turn the pan and the rack over, remove the pan and the paper lining, cover the cake with another rack, and turn over again, leaving the cake right side up on the rack to cool.

With a dry pastry brush, brush away loose crumbs from the sides of the cool cake.

WHITE LAYER

1 cup sifted all-purpose flour
⅛ teaspoon salt
1 teaspoon double-acting baking powder
3 ounces (¾ stick) unsalted butter
½ teaspoon vanilla extract
1 teaspoon lemon extract

⅔ cup granulated sugar
⅓ cup milk
Finely grated rind of 1 large lemon
2 egg whites (reserved from making the dark layer)
Optional: 1 tablespoon bourbon (to be used when
    icing the cake)

Adjust a rack one-third up from the bottom of the oven and preheat the oven to 375 degrees.

Sift the flour with the salt and baking powder and set aside.

In the small bowl of an electric mixer beat the butter until soft; beat in the vanilla and lemon extracts and the sugar. On low speed add about one third of the sifted dry ingredients and then gradually add all of the milk (the mixture will probably appear curdled after adding the milk—it is OK). Still on low speed add the remaining dry ingredients and beat only until smooth.

Remove the bowl from the mixer and stir in the grated lemon rind.

In a clean small bowl, with clean beaters, beat the whites only until they hold a straight shape when the beaters are raised but not until they are stiff/dry. Then, in several additions, small at first, fold the whites into the batter, handling as little as possible (the first few additions should not be thorough).

Turn into the prepared pan and smooth the top.

Bake for 25 minutes until the top of the cake springs back when pressed lightly with a fingertip and the sides of the cake begin to come away from the pan.

Let stand for a minute or two, cover with a rack, turn the pan and rack over, remove the pan and the paper lining, cover with another rack and turn over again, leaving the cake right side up to cool on the rack.

With a dry pastry brush, brush away loose crumbs from the sides of the cool cake.

To ice the cake, place four 12 by 4-inch strips of baking pan liner paper or wax paper in a square pattern around the sides of a large cake platter (see illustration, page 16) and place the dark layer upside down on the plate, making sure it is touching the paper all around. If you have a cake-decorating turntable, place the cake platter on it.

Pour the optional bourbon into a small cup and, with a pastry brush, brush it over the layer. (Or hold your thumb over the top of the bottle, turn the bottle upside down, and allow the bourbon out only very slowly; just drizzle it onto the cake.)

7-MINUTE ICING

½ cup egg whites (from about 4 eggs graded "large"; they may be whites that were frozen and then thawed)
1½ cups granulated sugar
¼ cup plus 1 tablespoon cold water

1 teaspoon cream of tartar
⅛ teaspoon salt
1 teaspoon vanilla extract
½ teaspoon lemon extract

To make this amount of icing it is best to use a double boiler that has at least a 10-cup capacity. If yours has less, create your own large one. Use a metal or heavy pottery bowl with a slightly rounded bottom and a saucepan only slightly narrower than the bowl, in which to place the water. The bowl should rest on the rim of the saucepan. The water in the saucepan should not be deep enough to touch the bowl.

Place all of the ingredients except the extracts in the bowl over water on moderate heat.

With a portable electric mixer start to beat at high speed immediately; cook and beat for about 5 minutes (it used to take 7 minutes before electric mixers), or until the mixture stands in straight peaks when the beaters are raised.

Instantly transfer the mixture to the large bowl of an electric mixer (unless that is what you cooked it in, in which case replace it on the mixer stand) and continue to beat, scraping down the sides occasionally with a rubber spatula. Add the vanilla and lemon extracts and beat for a few minutes until the icing is quite stiff. Use immediately.

Spread a smooth layer of the icing about ¾ inch thick over the dark layer.

Place the white layer over the icing right side up (bottoms together), brush or sprinkle on the optional bourbon, and spread a thick layer of the icing around the sides of the cake. Then place all of the remaining icing on the top. With a long, narrow metal spatula smooth the sides and top. Then, with the back of a teaspoon, form even rows of peaks right next to one another on the top and then on the sides.

Remove the paper strips by pulling each one out slowly toward a narrow end.

When serving the cake it will be a help to dip the knife in a deep pitcher of hot water before each cut and, if necessary, to wipe the blade after each cut.

Cakes Made with Fruits or Vegetables

Sauerkraut Chocolate Cake

America is a young country, and Americans are not steeped in the traditions of centuries. We are bold and creative and we have the daring of youth. I tip my hat to whoever dared to try putting sauerkraut into a cake and discovered that they had made a delicious, moist, and fudgy cake. They must have had a bumper crop of cabbage, and *they must have made more sauerkraut than they could eat.*

No one will ever know about the sauerkraut unless you tell them, and even then they will think you are kidding.

10 TO 12 PORTIONS

⅔ cup drained sauerkraut, firmly packed
2¼ cups sifted all-purpose flour
¼ teaspoon salt
1 teaspoon double-acting baking powder
1 teaspoon baking soda
½ cup unsweetened cocoa powder (preferably Dutch-process)

5⅓ ounces (10⅔ tablespoons) unsalted butter
1 teaspoon vanilla extract
1½ cups granulated sugar
3 eggs graded "large"
1 cup cold tap water or prepared strong coffee, cooled (see Note)

Adjust a rack to the middle of the oven and preheat the oven to 350 degrees. Butter two 9-inch round layer cake pans, line the bottoms with baking pan liner paper or wax paper cut to fit, then butter the paper, dust all over with fine dry bread crumbs, and invert over paper and tap out excess crumbs. Set aside.

Place the sauerkraut in a large bowl, add cold water to cover, with your hands work the water all through the sauerkraut to rinse it lightly, drain in a strainer, and then squeeze the sauerkraut a bit in your hands to remove most of the water that remains (but don't overdo it or you will make the cake dry). It is all right if the sauerkraut still smells like sauerkraut—the cake will not taste, or smell, like it.

Now, to chop the sauerkraut. If you have a round wooden chopping bowl with a chopping knife that has a curved blade, use it now. (There are many times when I find this old-fashioned kitchen tool the only thing that seems right.) Or, in a food processor fitted with the metal chopping blade, chop for only 10 to 15 seconds. Or place the sauerkraut on a large chopping board and chop it with a large French chef's knife. It should be rather fine. Set the sauerkraut aside.

Sift together the flour, salt, baking powder, baking soda, and cocoa and set aside.

In the large bowl of an electric mixer beat the butter until soft. Beat in the vanilla and sugar, then the eggs one at a time. On low speed add the sifted dry ingredients in three additions alternating with the water or coffee in two additions. Beat until smooth. Remove the bowl from the mixer and stir in the sauerkraut.

Place half of the mixture in each of the prepared pans and smooth the tops.

Bake for about 30 minutes until the tops of the cakes just barely spring back when pressed lightly with a fingertip. Do not overbake.

Let the layers stand in the pans for a few minutes. Then cover each pan with a rack, turn the pan and rack over, remove the pan and the paper lining, cover with another rack and turn over again, leaving the layer right side up.

This cake might stick to the rack. Therefore, after about 5 minutes, cover each layer with a rack and turn over again only briefly to loosen the bottom and make sure it is not sticking, then replace it right side up to finish cooling.

To ice the cake, place four 10 by 3-inch strips of baking pan liner paper or wax paper in a square pattern around the sides of a large cake plate (see illustration, page 16). Place one cake layer on the plate upside down and check to be sure that it is touching the papers all around. If you have a cake-decorating turntable, place the cake plate on it.

ICING

16 ounces (1 pound) milk chocolate	1 cup sour cream

Break up the chocolate and place it in the top of a large double boiler over warm water on low heat. Cover and let cook slowly only until partly melted. Then uncover and stir until completely melted. Transfer the chocolate to the small bowl of an electric mixer.

Add the sour cream and beat until smooth. Use immediately.

Spread about one third of the icing over the layer on the plate. Cover the frosted layer with the other layer right side up (bottoms together in the middle). Pour the remaining icing over the cake. With a long, narrow metal spatula smooth the icing over the top, allowing a bit to run down on the sides. Then, with a small, narrow metal spatula, smooth the icing over the sides.

Remove the paper strips under the cake by pulling each one gently toward a narrow end.

Refrigerate and serve cold.

To serve, be prepared with a pitcher of very hot water to dip the knife into; the hot, wet blade will prevent sticking.

NOTE: *Dissolve 1 tablespoon of instant coffee in a few spoons of hot water in a 1-cup glass measuring cup; then fill the cup with cold water to the 1-cup line.*

Red Beet Cake

This chocolate cake made with beets is a county fair prizewinner from Twin Falls, Idaho. Fairs have been showcases of Americana and a part of our heritage since the early 1800s. Farmers see the latest equipment, animals are paraded and bought and sold, incredible examples of farm produce (such as 100-pound pumpkins) are displayed, kids eat cotton candy and ride Ferris wheels, and farm wives from coast to coast have a chance to swap recipes and to show off their cooking and baking skills. Recipes that win blue ribbons at fairs are sought after as rare treasures. Many of the recipes, such as this one, were created especially to use up some of the plentiful farm crops.

This is made with beets, but if you do not tell, no one will ever suspect. It is a coal-black cake—moist, tender, delicious—somewhat like a wonderful devil's food cake. The chocolate icing is a thick, fluffy mixture the color of coffee with cream; it stays soft and fluffy and does not form a crust.

1¼ to 1½ cups puréed cooked beets (see Notes)
1¾ cups sifted all-purpose flour
1½ teaspoons baking soda
¼ teaspoon salt
3 ounces unsweetened chocolate

3 eggs graded "large"
1½ cups granulated sugar
1 cup tasteless salad oil
1 teaspoon vanilla extract

Adjust a rack to the middle of the oven and preheat the oven to 350 degrees. Butter the bottom and sides of a 13 by 9 by 2-inch cake pan. Dust the bottom of the pan well with fine dry bread crumbs. Set aside.

Prepare the beets and set them aside.

Sift together the flour, baking soda, and salt and set aside.

Place the chocolate in the top of a small double boiler over warm water on moderate heat, cover the pot with a folded paper towel (to absorb steam) and then with the pot cover, and let stand until almost melted. Then uncover and stir until completely melted. Remove the top of the double boiler and set aside to cool slightly.

In the large bowl of an electric mixer beat the eggs just to mix. Then beat in the sugar, oil, vanilla, melted chocolate (which may still be warm), the beets, and the sifted dry ingredients, beating only until incorporated after each addition.

Turn into the prepared pan, smooth the top, and bake for 35 minutes until the top springs back when pressed gently with a fingertip, a toothpick inserted in the middle comes out clean, and the cake just begins to come away from the sides of the pan.

Either let the cake cool completely in the pan (if you are going to ice it in the pan—see Notes) or let it cool for 20 minutes, then cover with a large oblong board or serving tray, hold the board or tray and the pan firmly together, and turn them both over. Remove the pan and let the cake cool.

FLUFFY CHOCOLATE ICING

2 ounces unsweetened chocolate
6 ounces (1½ sticks) unsalted butter
1 cup granulated sugar
1 teaspoon vanilla extract

Pinch of salt
¼ cup sifted all-purpose flour
1 cup milk

Place the chocolate in the top of a small double boiler over warm water on moderate heat. Cover the pot with a folded paper towel (to absorb steam) and with the pot cover. Let stand for a few minutes until partly melted, then uncover and stir until completely melted and smooth. Set aside to cool.

Place the butter in the small bowl of an electric mixer and beat until soft. Add the sugar and beat at high speed for about 5 minutes. Beat in the vanilla and the salt.

Meanwhile, in a small, heavy saucepan, beat the flour and about ¼ cup of the milk with a small wire whisk until smooth. Gradually beat in the remaining milk. Place over moderate heat and stir constantly with a rubber spatula until the mixture comes to a low boil. Reduce the heat a bit and let simmer, still stirring and scraping the bottom and sides of the pan, for 2 minutes. Remove from the heat, place the bottom of the saucepan briefly in a bowl of ice and water, and continue to stir gently and scrape the pan, until the mixture cools. (Do not stop the gentle stirring or the mixture might form lumps; if so, beat it briskly with a small wire whisk.)

Add the melted chocolate to the sugar and butter mixture, beat a bit to incorporate, and then gradually add the thickened milk mixture, beating only as necessary to incorporate.

Pour the icing over the cake and spread it smoothly over the top (do not cover the sides) and either leave it smooth or, with the bottom of a teaspoon, form swirls and peaks.

Refrigerate the cake either just long enough for the icing to set, or longer. It may be served cold or at room temperature (however, if it is practical to serve it cold, do).

NOTES: 1. *You can use fresh beets, either boiled or baked to order, or left-overs, or canned beets. They should be well drained and then processed in a food processor fitted with the metal chopping blade until they look like baby food (turn the processor on/off a few times and scrape down the sides of the bowl once or twice—do not overprocess), or they can be sliced and mashed with a fork on a large plate and then worked through a food mill. A 1-pound can of cooked beets, when drained and puréed, will measure about 1¼ cups.*

2. There are many times when it is more practical to bake a cake in a square or oblong pan and ice it right in the pan, especially if you are taking it somewhere. This cake can be left in the pan, iced in the pan, and served directly from the pan.

Sweet Potato Pound Cake

This can be made with fresh or canned sweet potatoes or yams. It is a big, beautiful cake; plain, rich, dense, fine textured, moist, delicious, with a fascinating coating of ground salted peanuts. This is wonderful any time but seems especially at home on a Thanksgiving table. Or at Halloween. But don't wait.

ABOUT 16 PORTIONS

⅔ cup salted peanuts
2½ cups mashed, cooked sweet potatoes (see Note)
3 cups sifted all-purpose flour
2 teaspoons double-acting baking powder
1 teaspoon baking soda
1 teaspoon cinnamon

¾ teaspoon nutmeg
¼ teaspoon salt
8 ounces (2 sticks) unsalted butter
1 teaspoon vanilla extract
1 cup granulated sugar
1 cup light brown sugar, firmly packed
4 eggs graded "large"

Adjust a rack one-third up from the bottom of the oven and preheat the oven to 350 degrees. Butter a 10-inch Bundt pan (or any other tube pan with a design and a 12–14-cup capacity), even if it has a nonstick finish. Place the peanuts in the bowl of a food processor fitted with the metal chopping blade and process them for about 5 seconds until they are fine but uneven; or chop/grind them any other way. Place the peanuts in the buttered pan (use your fingertips to sprinkle them on the center tube), rotate and tilt the pan to coat all parts of it, then invert the pan over paper for excess nuts to fall out; do not tap the pan—you want as heavy a coating of nuts as will hold. About half of the nuts that fall onto the paper should be sprinkled back over the bottom of the pan to make a heavy layer; the remaining nuts should be set aside to be sprinkled over the top of the cake.

If you are using canned sweet potatoes or yams, pour them into a strainer to drain off all the syrup. In a food processor fitted with the metal chopping blade process half of the sweet potatoes at a time; it will be necessary to stop the machine frequently and scrape the sides of the bowl with a rubber spatula. Do not add any liquid; the sweet potatoes should be dry. Or they can be mashed in a large bowl with a potato masher. They must be perfectly smooth. Set aside.

Sift together the flour, baking powder, baking soda, cinnamon, nutmeg, and salt and set aside.

In a large bowl of an electric mixer beat the butter until soft. Add the vanilla and both sugars and beat until mixed. Beat in the eggs one at a time (the mixture will appear curdled but it will be all right). Add the mashed potatoes and beat to mix. Then, on low speed, add the sifted dry ingredients and beat until incorporated, scraping the bowl as necessary with a rubber spatula.

Turn the batter into the prepared pan. Smooth the top. Sprinkle with the reserved chopped peanuts.

Bake for 1 hour and 15 minutes until a cake tester comes out dry and clean.

Let the cake stand in the pan for 15 minutes. Then remove it to the serving plate or to a rack as follows. To remove it to the serving plate just cover the pan with the plate, hold them together and turn them both over, and remove the pan. But to transfer the cake to a rack first, cover the top of the cake pan with a 12-inch square of aluminum foil, fold down the sides, cover with a rack, hold them together and turn everything over, and remove the pan (this keeps the loose nuts from flying around). Let stand until cool and then transfer to a serving plate or board.

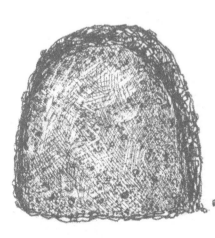

NOTE: *If you use canned sweet potatoes or yams, you will need 2 17-ounce cans (which will just make a scant 2½ cups when mashed but it is enough), or 1 40-ounce (2 pounds, 8 ounces) can (which will be a little bit more than you need—measure and use only 2½ cups).*

To use fresh sweet potatoes either bake or steam them in a vegetable steamer; do not boil them in water (they should be dry).

Long Island Potato Cake

This has mashed potatoes, which add to its moistness without affecting the flavor. It is coal-black, semisweet dense chocolate—with a generous amount of prunes and nuts.

You can cut the recipe in half and make only one loaf, if you wish.

2 SMALL LOAVES

¾ pound raw potatoes (to make 1 cup, mashed—see Note)
8 ounces dried pitted prunes, soft and moist (to make 1 cup, firmly packed)
2 cups sifted all-purpose flour
1 tablespoon double-acting baking powder
1 teaspoon cinnamon
1 teaspoon powdered (not granular) instant coffee or espresso
¾ teaspoon salt

½ teaspoon nutmeg
¾ cup unsweetened cocoa powder (preferably Dutch-process)
4 ounces (1 stick) unsalted butter
1 teaspoon vanilla extract
1½ cups granulated sugar
4 eggs graded "large"
½ cup milk
6 ounces (1½ cups) walnuts, broken into large pieces

Adjust a rack one-third up from the bottom of the oven and preheat the oven to 300 degrees. Butter two 8 by 4 by 2½-inch loaf pans (each with a scant 5-cup capacity), dust them with fine dry bread crumbs, invert them over a piece of paper and tap lightly to shake out excess. Set aside.

Peel the potatoes, cut into quarters or eighths, place in a saucepan with about an inch of water over moderate heat, and cook, partially covered, until tender when tested with a toothpick. Drain and mash in a food mill or processor or potato ricer to make 1 cup mashed potatoes. Set aside.

Meanwhile, with scissors, cut the prunes into pieces the size of large raisins (or small olives) and set aside.

Sift together the flour, baking powder, cinnamon, powdered coffee, salt, nutmeg, and cocoa. Set aside.

In the large bowl of an electric mixer beat the butter until it is soft. Beat in the vanilla and sugar, then add the eggs one at a time, beating until incorporated after each addition.

Add the potatoes (which may be warm or cool) and beat until smooth. Then, on low speed, add half of the sifted dry ingredients, then the milk, and then the remaining dry ingredients, beating until smooth after each addition.

Remove the bowl from the mixer, stir in the prunes (be sure to stir them well enough to separate all the pieces), and finally stir in the nuts.

Place half of the mixture in each pan, smooth the tops, and then with the bottom of a teaspoon form a trench down the length of each loaf; the trench should be about 1 inch deep and about 1 inch wide, and it should stop about 1 inch from each narrow end of the pan. (The trench prevents the cake from rising too high in the middle; it will make a beautifully shaped loaf with a nicely rounded top.)

Bake for 1 hour and about 25 minutes until a cake tester inserted gently in the middle comes out clean—do not overbake.

Cool in the pans for 10 minutes.

Then place a potholder or a folded towel over the top of a loaf and with a potholder under the pan turn the loaf out into the palm of your right hand, remove the pan, cover the loaf with a rack, and turn the loaf and the rack over, leaving the loaf right side up to cool. Remove the other loaf from its pan.

Wrap the cooled loaves in plastic wrap or foil and refrigerate overnight or for a few days, or place in the freezer for about an hour before serving.

NOTE: *If you prefer, you can use dry instant mashed potatoes prepared with only water or water and milk (no salt or butter). To measure the mashed potatoes use a metal cup made for measuring dry ingredients.*

Carrot Cake

Carrot cakes seem to be popular in every part of our country. With all the traveling we do, I am constantly made aware of them. They are served not only at tearooms, coffee shops, and luncheonettes, but on airplanes, at a Long Island chicken farm, where the farmer's daughter makes them, at a chili joint in New Mexico, where Pedro makes them, and also at a swanky place with chandeliers and thick carpets, and caviar on the menu (The Four Seasons Clift Hotel in San Francisco). Some carrot cakes are better than others, but as Will Rogers said (he was talking about men—not

cakes), I have never met one I didn't like.

This one is a three-layer beauty, a humdinger, it's "the bee's knees." This has more carrots than most, and the smooth and buttery cream cheese icing has less sugar than most.

Make this for a big occasion, for many people, for a happy party. And make it ahead of time (see below). Serve the cake cold.

This is foolproof and easy, but not quick.

12 TO 20 PORTIONS

5 ounces (1 cup) dark raisins
1 pound carrots (to make 4 cups shredded, firmly packed)
2 cups minus 2 tablespoons sifted all-purpose flour
2 teaspoons double-acting baking powder
1 teaspoon baking soda
1 teaspoon salt
2 teaspoons cinnamon

1 tablespoon unsweetened cocoa powder
4 eggs graded "large" or "extra-large"
2 teaspoons vanilla extract
1 cup granulated sugar
1 cup dark brown sugar, firmly packed
1¼ cups corn oil
5½ ounces (generous 1½ cups) walnuts, cut into medium-small pieces

Adjust two racks to divide the oven into thirds, and preheat the oven to 350 degrees. Butter three round 9-inch layer cake pans, line them with baking pan liner paper or wax paper cut to fit, butter the paper, dust all over with fine dry bread crumbs, invert over paper and tap out excess crumbs, then set aside.

To steam the raisins, place them in a vegetable steamer or a strainer over shallow water in a saucepan. Cover the pan, place on high heat, and let the water boil for about 10 minutes. Then uncover and set aside.

It is not necessary to peel the carrots; just cut off the ends, wash them well with a vegetable brush, and drain or dry them. They may be grated on a standing metal grater or in a food processor. Or they may be grated

on a fine, medium, or coarse grater; I have used all these methods and found very little difference in the cakes—no one was better than the others. Measure and set aside.

Sift together the flour, baking powder, baking soda, salt, cinnamon, and cocoa, and set aside.

In the large bowl of an electric mixer (or in any other large bowl, with an egg beater or a wire whisk) beat the eggs to mix. Beat in the vanilla, both sugars, and the oil. Then, on low speed, add the dry ingredients and mix only until incorporated. Stir in the carrots, the raisins, and the nuts.

Divide among the prepared pans. The solid ingredients have a tendency to mound in the center of the pans; use the bottom of a teaspoon to distribute them evenly in the pans.

Place two layers on one rack and one layer in the center of the other rack—no pan should be directly above another. Bake for 35 to 40 minutes until the tops just spring back when gently pressed with a fingertip and the cakes begin to come away from the sides of the pans. If the cakes are not baking evenly you may reverse the pans, front to back and top to bottom, after about 20 minutes, but I don't find it necessary with this recipe.

Remove from the oven. Let stand for 2 or 3 minutes, cover each pan with a rack, turn pan and rack over, remove pan (do not remove the paper linings—they keep the cake moist—but if they come off by themselves it is OK), cover with another rack and turn over again, leaving the cakes right side up to cool.

When cool, brush loose crumbs off the sides of the cakes.

Before you fill and ice the layers they should be frozen for at least an hour or so until they are firm enough to handle (or they might crack from handling), or freeze for as much longer as you wish. I like to freeze them overnight or longer and ice them a day or two before serving. If you do freeze them for an extended time, wrap them after they become firm. (If the layers have been frozen for a long time do not thaw them before icing.)

CREAM CHEESE ICING

16 ounces cream cheese (at room temperature)   1 teaspoon vanilla extract
4 ounces unsalted butter (at room temperature)   2 cups sifted or strained confectioners sugar

In the large bowl of an electric mixer beat the cheese and butter until soft and smooth. On low speed beat in the vanilla and sugar, and then on high speed beat for a few moments until smooth.

Prepare a large flat cake plate by lining it with four strips of wax paper (see page 16). If you have a cake-decorating turntable place the cake plate on it.

If the paper linings are still on the bottoms of the cakes they should be removed now.

Place one cold and firm cake layer upside down on the plate, checking to be sure that the paper strips touch the cake all around.

Spread a thin layer (⅔ cup) of the icing evenly over the cake. Cover with the second layer, also upside down. Spread another thin layer (⅔ cup) of the icing over the second layer. Cover with the third layer, also upside down (all three layers should be upside down). Now use as much of the icing as you need to cover the sides of the cake, and then the top. You can work over this icing again and again. If you are using a turntable, take your time, work carefully, and with a long, narrow metal spatula smooth the icing around the sides and then on the top. Without a turntable you will probably be better off swirling the icing a bit, but it is a thin layer of icing and cannot be swirled deeply.

Remove the paper strips by slowly pulling each one out toward a narrow end.

If you decorate the cake with the following optional decoration do it immediately before the icing dries.

OPTIONAL DECORATION

12 to 20 walnut or pecan halves or 12 to 20
marzipan carrots (see below)

The cake can be left plain, or it can be decorated with a circle of nut halves or marzipan carrots around the top rim. If you use the carrots place them pointed end in, green end out. The carrots or the nuts should be pressed slightly into the icing to keep them in place. (Or you can place a few fresh flowers either right on top or alongside just before serving.)

Refrigerate the cake for a few hours or for a day or two. Serve it very cold, right from the refrigerator. Cut small portions; it is rich.

MARZIPAN CARROTS (24 1¾-inch carrots)

Marzipan fruits and vegetables are generally eaten as candy; they make gorgeous cake decorations. If you plan to use these to decorate the Carrot Cake, make them before you ice the cake—they can be made days, weeks (or more), ahead of time if you wish. The icing must not dry out or form a crust before you place the carrots on the cake, or they will not stay in place when you serve the cake.

This is such fun that once you make them you might become addicted and never quit.

12 unsalted green pistachio nuts (see Notes)   Orange paste or liquid food coloring (or red and
3½ ounces (⅓ cup) almond paste or marzipan   yellow—see page 88)
   (see Notes)

Let's start with the stems. In a small saucepan of boiling water boil the pistachio nuts for 45 seconds. Quickly remove one, hold under running water and peel the skin. If the skin comes off easily, drain the others immediately (extra boiling bleaches them), but if necessary boil a few seconds longer. Drain and peel them all. While the nuts are soft from the boiling, with a small sharp knife cut them the long way into quarters (unless they are very large, in which case you can cut them into sixths). They will not all be green, and they will not be green inside; use the greenest. Set aside.

Now, the carrots. Place the almond paste or marzipan on a smooth work surface (not wood, because the food coloring will stain it) and flatten it a bit with your hand. If you have orange food coloring place a dab of it on the almond paste or marzipan (use as much as you need to make the paste a rich carrot color). If you are using red and yellow liquid coloring (they make orange), mix 4 drops of each in a small saucer. Pour it on top of the almond paste or marzipan (use a bit of the almond paste to wipe out the saucer). With the heel of your hand knead the color into the almond paste or marzipan. If necessary use a dough scraper to remove the mixture from the work surface. Knead until the color is smooth.

Wash and dry your hands. If the mixture is a bit sticky, powder your hands lightly with confectioners sugar. Form the mixture into a ball and then, with your hands, roll it into a 12-inch sausage shape.

Cut into ½-inch lengths. Roll the pieces between your hands into carrot shapes about 1¾ inches long.

Then, to score them with uneven lines that go around (like real carrots), place one on the work surface. Use the dull side of a small paring knife, or a not-too-sharp table knife. Rest the edge of the knife across the carrot and roll the carrot back and forth with the knife pressing very gently, to make a line around the carrot. (Actually, the line should not go all the way around—it should stop a little short of being a complete circle. The lines should not all be the same length and they should not all start/stop at the same place around the carrot.) Score lines about ⅛ inch apart from each other all over the carrots.

Now, with a toothpick, make one or two small holes in the wide end of the carrot and insert one or two strips (they may look more like wedges) of the pistachio nuts.

Is that adorable? So cute you could eat it.

If you do not plan to use these soon (within a few hours) cover a dish or tray with plastic wrap, place the carrots on it, and then cover airtight with more plastic wrap. They can wait at room temperature for many weeks.

NOTES: *1. See page 7 on buying pistachios. In place of pistachios you may use slivered (julienned) almonds. Using a brush, paint them with green food coloring before inserting them into the carrots.*

2. Although this recipe uses very few pistachios, they seem to last for years in the freezer. And if you have them you will find many other uses for them. (A few, chopped fine, sprinkled on whipped cream or chocolate icing add an elegant touch. And mixed with other nuts in Brownies they are gorgeous.)

3. Almond paste or marzipan is generally available at better food stores across the country. Odense brand, made in Denmark, seems to be the most popular; it is very good. (The ingredients listed on the almond paste are almonds, sugar, and liquid glucose. On marzipan they are almonds, sugar, liquid glucose, and sorbitol. So they are very similar.)

4. Store leftover almond paste or marzipan tightly wrapped in plastic wrap and aluminum foil or it might dry out and form a crust.

Ginger Carrot Cake

Only a few years ago if you wanted fresh ginger in this country you had to go to a Chinatown in one of a few large cities. But now, as a result of America's love affair with Chinese food, you can find fresh ginger in almost every large produce market.

This cake is similar to a pound cake, with more body and chewiness supplied by the whole wheat flour and grated carrots. It is a marvelous coffee or tea cake, a new and unusual recipe.

12 TO 16 PORTIONS

2¼ ounces (⅔ cup) walnuts (for coating the pan)
2 ounces (¼ cup) preserved ginger in syrup
2 ounces (a piece about 3 inches long and 1 to 1½ inches wide) fresh ginger (see Fresh Ginger, page 8)
¾ pound carrots (to make 3 cups shredded, firmly packed)
2 cups sifted all-purpose flour

1 cup sifted all-purpose whole wheat flour
2 teaspoons double-acting baking powder
¼ teaspoon salt
5 eggs graded "large"
1 teaspoon vanilla extract
2 cups granulated sugar
1 cup tasteless salad oil
1 cup milk

Adjust a rack one-third up from the bottom of the oven and preheat the oven to 350 degrees. Generously butter a tube pan with at least a 12-cup capacity (butter the pan whether it is nonstick or not). I especially like this in the 12-cup "swirl-design" tube pan (see page 10), which does not have a nonstick finish.

Chop the walnuts fine in a food processor fitted with the metal chopping blade; process on/off quickly 10 to 12 times (10 to 12 seconds). Or chop the nuts fine any other way. Turn them into the buttered pan. Over paper, tap and turn the pan to coat it all with the nuts (use your fingers to sprinkle the nuts on the tube), then invert the pan over the paper to allow loose nuts to fall out (but do not tap the pan or you will tap out too many nuts). Reserve the loose nuts that fall onto the paper, and set the pan aside.

With a small, sharp paring knife slice the preserved ginger very thin. You should have ¼ cup of sliced ginger, firmly packed, along with any syrup that clings to the ginger. Set aside.

Grate the fresh ginger fine and set it aside.

It is not necessary to peel the carrots; wash them well and trim both ends. Grate them fine, medium, or coarse, either in a food processor or on a standing metal grater. Set aside.

Sift together both the flours, baking powder, and salt and set aside.

Place the eggs in the large bowl of an electric mixer and beat well at high speed for a few minutes. Add the vanilla and sugar and beat until well mixed. Then add the oil and the milk and beat well. On low speed gradually add the sifted dry ingredients, beating only until mixed.

Remove the bowl from the mixer and stir in the reserved chopped nuts, the sliced preserved ginger, the grated fresh ginger, and the grated fresh carrots. (If you add the carrots while you are still using the mixer, they will form lumps on the blades and it will be difficult to smooth them out.)

The batter will be thin; turn it into the prepared pan.

Bake for 1 hour and 5 to 10 minutes until a cake tester inserted gently into the middle of the cake comes out clean and the top of the cake springs back when it is pressed lightly with a fingertip.

Cool in the pan for 15 minutes. Then cover with a rack, hold the rack and the pan together, and turn them over. Remove the pan. If you have used a pan with a fancy design, leave the cake upside down. If you have used a pan with a flat bottom you might prefer to serve the cake right side up; if so, cover it with another rack and gently turn the rack and the cake over again.

Cool completely. I like to chill this for an hour or so in the freezer, or longer in the refrigerator, before slicing. Cut into thin slices.

Tomato Soup Cake

A can of Campbell's Tomato Soup is such a symbolic bit of Americana that prints of it hang in the country's best museums. But who ever thought of putting it into a cake?

This is a date and nut spice cake baked in a square pan, covered with a sensational new bitter-sweet chocolate icing. If you don't tell what's in the cake no one will guess. They will think it is gingerbread even though it has no ginger or molasses. You could call it a soup-to-nuts cake.

16 SQUARES

2 cups sifted all-purpose flour
¼ teaspoon salt
1 teaspoon baking soda
2 teaspoons double-acting baking powder
1½ teaspoons cinnamon
¾ teaspoon nutmeg
¼ teaspoon cloves
1 tablespoon unsweetened cocoa powder
    (preferably Dutch-process)

4 ounces (1 stick) unsalted butter
1 teaspoon vanilla extract
1 cup granulated sugar
2 eggs graded "large"
1 10¾-ounce can tomato soup (undiluted)
4 ounces (½ cup, packed) pitted dates, cut into
    medium-size pieces (easiest to cut with
    scissors)
4 ounces (1 cup) walnut halves or pieces

Adjust a rack one-third up from the bottom of the oven and preheat the oven to 375 degrees. Butter a 9-inch square cake pan. Dust it over with fine dry bread crumbs, then invert the pan over paper and tap lightly to shake out excess crumbs; set aside.

Sift together the flour, salt, baking soda, baking powder, cinnamon, nutmeg, cloves, and cocoa and set aside.

In the large bowl of an electric mixer beat the butter until it is soft. Add the vanilla and sugar and beat to mix. Add the eggs one at a time and beat until incorporated after each addition. On low speed add half of the sifted dry ingredients, scraping the bowl and beating until incorporated. Then beat in the tomato soup. Finally add the remaining dry ingredients and beat until smooth.

Remove the bowl from the mixer and stir in the dates and nuts.

Turn into the prepared pan and smooth the top.

Bake for about 40 minutes until a toothpick inserted in the middle comes out clean.

Remove from the oven. Either let the cake cool completely in the pan (if you are going to ice it in the pan—see Note) or let stand for about 20 minutes, then cover with a rack, turn the pan and rack over, remove the pan, cover with a serving plate or a board and turn again, leaving the cake right side up to cool completely. Then prepare the icing.

BITTERSWEET CHOCOLATE ICING

If you prefer a sweeter flavor you can substitute semisweet chocolate for all or part of the unsweetened chocolate.

½ cup whipping cream

3 ounces unsweetened chocolate, chopped coarse

5 ounces milk chocolate, chopped or broken coarse

Place the cream in a small saucepan over moderate heat and let it cook, uncovered, until there is a slightly wrinkled skin on the top or small bubbles around the edge.

Add the unsweetened chocolate and stir until it is almost all melted. Then add the milk chocolate, reduce the heat to low, and stir until completely melted.

Transfer the mixture to the small bowl of an electric mixer. Beat at medium-high speed for a minute or two until the mixture becomes beautifully smooth/shiny/thick. Then, without waiting, pour it onto the cake and quickly spread it over the top only with a long, narrow metal spatula. If you wish, form wide ridges in the icing, using the tip of the spatula.

NOTE: *Like the Red Beet Cake (see page 80), this can be baked and iced in the pan and served directly from the pan.*

Prune and Apricot Pound Cake

A brown sugar buttery cake with a crunchy toasted almond coating, it is made with both cream cheese and butter, both prunes and apricots, and both walnuts and almonds. Delicious and beautiful, it may be served for almost any occasion. Or make it for a gift; since this is such a very unusual recipe (yet easy to make), a loaf of the cake—and the recipe—make a special gift.

You can cut the recipe in half and make only one cake, if you wish.

2 SMALL LOAVES

2 ounces (½ cup) blanched almonds (for coating the pans)

8 ounces (1 cup, tightly packed) dried pitted prunes, soft and moist

6 ounces (⅔ cup, tightly packed) dried apricots, soft and moist

2 cups sifted all-purpose flour

2 teaspoons double-acting baking powder

½ teaspoon salt

8 ounces cream cheese

8 ounces (2 sticks) unsalted butter

1¼ cups light brown sugar, firmly packed

4 eggs graded "large"

Finely grated rind of 1 large lemon

Finely grated rind of 1 deep-colored orange

3½ ounces (1 cup) walnut halves or large pieces

Adjust a rack one-third up from the bottom of the oven and preheat the oven to 350 degrees. Butter two 8½ by 4½ by 2¾-inch loaf pans, each with a 6-cup capacity (see Note). Crisp the almonds by placing them in a shallow pan in the preheated oven for about 10 minutes only until they are hot but not until they have colored. To chop the almonds, place them in the bowl of a food processor fitted with the metal chopping blade and process for 20 to 25 seconds, turning the processor on/off a few times, until the almonds are chopped fine but uneven (do not overprocess); or chop them any other way.

Place all of the chopped almonds in one of the buttered pans. Over a piece of wax paper tilt the pan from side to side to coat all of the surfaces. Then invert the pan over the wax paper; do not tap the pan, just allow loose almonds to fall out onto the paper. Pour all of the almonds from the wax paper into the second pan and repeat the directions to coat all its surfaces, and then allow the loose almonds to fall out onto the wax paper. With your fingers sprinkle just a few of the remaining chopped almonds over the bottoms of the pans to make a generous coating. (Reserve the remaining chopped almonds to sprinkle over the tops of the loaves.) Set aside.

With scissors cut the prunes and apricots into uneven slices or pieces ¼ to ½ inch wide and set them aside.

Sift together the flour, baking powder, and salt and set aside.

In the large bowl of an electric mixer beat the cream cheese with the butter until soft and smooth. Beat in the brown sugar. Then add the eggs one at a time, beating until incorporated after each addition. On low speed gradually add the sifted dry ingredients, scraping the bowl with a rubber spatula as necessary and beating only until the mixture is smooth. Beat in the prunes and apricots. Remove the bowl from the mixer.

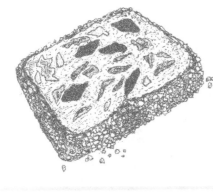

With a heavy wooden spatula stir in the grated rinds, and then the walnuts.

Place half of the mixture in each of the pans. Smooth the tops.

Sprinkle the reserved chopped almonds all over the tops.

Bake for 1 hour, then cover the top loosely with foil to prevent over-browning, and continue to bake for an additional 20 to 30 minutes until a cake tester gently inserted in the middle comes out dry (total baking time is 1 hour and 20 to 30 minutes).

Cool the loaves in the pans for 20 minutes.

Then cover the top of one of the pans with foil and fold it down around the sides (to prevent any loose nuts from flying around), cover the foil with a potholder, turn the pan over into the palm of your right hand, remove the pan, cover the loaf with a cake rack and turn the loaf and the rack over again, leaving the loaf right side up on the rack. Remove the foil. Repeat with the other loaf. Let stand until cool.

Wrap the loaves in plastic wrap and let stand for several hours or overnight, or refrigerate for an hour or so. All pound cakes should rest a bit before they are served.

NOTE: *I have also made this in slightly smaller pans; they measured 8 by 4 by 2½ inches, and they had a scant 5-cup capacity. They worked fine and* the loaves were lovely. In these smaller pans the batter will fill the pans almost to the top, but it will not run over during baking—don't worry. In the smaller pans the loaves should be loosely covered with aluminum foil after only about 30 minutes of baking but the total baking time remains about the same.

VARIATION—RAISIN POUND CAKE: *Follow the above recipe, using 5 ounces (1 cup) dark raisins and 5 ounces (1 cup) light raisins in place of the prunes and apricots. (You will love it.)*

Savannah Fig Cake

This is an old and famous Southern recipe for a wonderful cake that is light, tender, delicate, almost as moist as a pudding, and easy to make. It is baked in a fancy tube pan and is topped with a divine butterscotch icing. It keeps well, and can be made a day ahead.

10 TO 12 PORTIONS

1 17-ounce can kadota figs in syrup (I use California-grown Oregon brand)
7 ounces (2 cups) walnuts
2 cups sifted all-purpose flour
1 teaspoon baking soda
½ teaspoon salt
1 teaspoon cinnamon

1 teaspoon allspice
3 eggs graded "large"
1 teaspoon vanilla extract
1 cup buttermilk
1 cup tasteless salad oil
1 cup granulated sugar
½ cup light brown sugar, firmly packed

Before anything else, place the figs in a wide strainer set over a wide bowl and let stand to drain (you will not use the drained syrup for this recipe).

Adjust a rack one-third up from the bottom of the oven and preheat the oven to 350 degrees. You will need a tube pan with a design and about an 11-cup capacity, about 9 inches in diameter, preferably (but not necessarily) with a nonstick finish. Butter the pan (even if it has a nonstick finish). Place ¾ cup of the nuts (reserve the remaining 1¼ cups nuts) in the bowl of a food processor fitted with the metal chopping blade and process for 7 seconds, or chop very fine any other way. Place the finely chopped nuts in the buttered pan and tilt the pan from side to side to coat it all with the nuts; any loose nuts that remain in the pan may be left there to form a nice nutty coating on the top of the cake. Set the pan aside.

Process the remaining 1¼ cups of nuts for 5 seconds; they should be a bit coarser than those for coating the pan. Or chop them into medium-size pieces any other way. Set them aside.

Sift together the flour, baking soda, salt, cinnamon, and allspice. Set aside.

In the large bowl of an electric mixer beat the eggs to mix, then add the vanilla, buttermilk, oil, and both sugars, and beat to mix. On low speed add the sifted dry ingredients, scraping the bowl as necessary with a rubber spatula and beating only until mixed. Remove the bowl from the mixer.

With a small knife, cut the drained figs roughly into quarters.

With a rubber spatula fold the reserved nuts and the figs into the batter. Turn the mixture into the prepared pan and smooth the top.

Bake for 50 to 60 minutes until a cake tester inserted gently into the middle of the cake comes out clean and the top of the cake springs back when it is pressed lightly with a fingertip.

Let cool in the pan for 10 or 15 minutes. Then cover with a cake plate and, holding the pan and the plate firmly together, turn them both over. Remove the pan. Let the cake stand until cool.

BUTTERSCOTCH CARAMEL ICING

This Early American icing is remarkable. It has a caramel and butterscotch flavor, is as smooth and creamy as honey, and although it is poured onto the cake, it sets quickly so it stops running but remains deliciously soft— it will not become hard or granular. I find this foolproof, even though it will remind you a bit of classic fudge, which is definitely not.

You will need a candy thermometer and a heavy saucepan with a 2-quart capacity. Butter the sides of the pan; it discourages sugar granules from clinging to the sides.

½ cup buttermilk
1 cup granulated sugar
6 ounces (1½ sticks) unsalted butter

½ teaspoon baking soda
1 tablespoon light corn syrup
1 teaspoon vanilla extract

Place the buttermilk, sugar, butter, baking soda, and corn syrup in a heavy 2-quart saucepan over low-medium heat. As the butter and sugar begin to melt, stir occasionally with a wooden spatula and if necessary wash down the sides a few times with a pastry brush dipped in water to remove any undissolved sugar granules.

When the mixture boils, reduce the heat to low, stir occasionally to be sure that it does not burn on the bottom (which it wants to do if you leave it alone too long or if the heat is too high). Do not raise the heat. The mixture will foam up high to the top of the pan when it starts to boil, but after a while it will settle down to a lower level. Insert a candy thermometer. Continue to scrape the bottom occasionally. The temperature will reach 220 degrees rather quickly, but then it will take a long time to go higher. As the mixture boils, it will gradually turn golden. And when the temperature goes over 220 degrees, the color will darken to a rich caramel. Continue to cook until the temperature reaches 238 degrees. Be patient. Or, if you must, raise the heat to low-medium, scraping the bottom and stirring constantly.

When the icing reaches 238 degrees remove it from the heat. Pour it into the small bowl of an electric mixer and add the vanilla. Place the bowl into the large bowl of the mixer. Fill the space in the large bowl about halfway up with ice and cold water. Adjust the mixer stand to the setting for the small bowl and beat at high speed for several minutes until the mixture lightens slightly in color (it should become about the color of coffee with cream) and thickens slightly. It should be a consistency so that when you pour it over the cake it will run down the sides a bit, but not so thin that it runs off the cake onto the plate.

Very gradually pour the icing in a ribbonlike stream onto the top of the cake. Pour it slowly, around and around, pouring it over itself several times. Do not pour very much onto one spot at one time or it will run down onto the plate. It should not be necessary to smooth or spread this. When it is perfect, the sides of the cake should be only partly covered with the icing. Very little, if any, should actually run down onto the plate.

Apricot Strip

It occurred to me one day to use apricots instead of figs for a new version of Fig Newtons. The filling developed into a wonderful conserve that remains slightly more gooey than the original fig filling. Therefore, serve these on a plate with a fork. They are wunderbar! *They can be made weeks ahead; they freeze perfectly.*

The conserve and the dough should both be refrigerated overnight or longer, if you wish. Shaping these is a bit tricky—it takes patience—

but they are well worth the effort.

You will need a large cookie sheet with three flat sides to use as a spatula for transferring the roll of filled pastry both before it is baked and then again after (unless you have something else that will serve the same purpose). I also use that kind of cookie sheet for baking these, although rims would not be in the way for baking.

12 TO 18 GENEROUS PORTIONS

APRICOT CONSERVE (5 *cups*)

The apricots should be soaked overnight, so plan accordingly.

12 ounces dried apricots
1½ cups water
1 large navel orange
3 ounces (⅔ cup, packed) light raisins
1 cup granulated sugar

1 15- or 16-ounce can (2 cups) crushed pineapple, packed in its own juice (no sugar)
3½ ounces (1 cup) walnuts, cut into medium-size pieces

Place the apricots in a wide, heavy saucepan (or you can soak them in a bowl and transfer them to the saucepan for cooking). Add the water. Cover and let stand overnight, stirring once or twice when the apricots on the bottom have absorbed water and those on top are above the water. After the fruit has softened, press down on it occasionally with a fork or spoon to keep all of it wet.

The next day grate the orange-colored rind of the orange (see page 15) and add it to the apricots. Then peel the orange—cut away every bit of white, and, working over a bowl to catch the juice, with a small, sharp knife cut down against the membrane of each section, releasing the sections. Squeeze the remaining membrane in the palm of your hand to squeeze any remaining juice. Add the orange sections and the juice to the apricots. Then add the raisins, sugar, and pineapple (including its juice).

Place the saucepan over moderate heat. Bring to a boil, stirring once or twice to avoid burning. Reduce the heat and simmer, covered, for 10 minutes—again stirring once or twice.

Then uncover, stir frequently with a wooden spatula, and cook until all the moisture has evaporated. As the mixture thickens, lower the heat to prevent burning. The conserve should be as thick as you can get it without letting it burn. (If the mixture is dry but the apricots seem to need more cooking, cover the saucepan briefly.) Total cooking time is about 1 to 1¼ hours.

Cooking and stirring will break up the apricots and the orange sections and turn the mixture into a divine jam. While the fruit is cooking, cut it with the edge of the spatula, pressing it against the sides of the saucepan. After all the cooking and stirring the fruit should remain slightly chunky; the consistency will be about like cooked oatmeal, although it will thicken a bit more when refrigerated.

When the conserve is done, remove from the heat to cool. Then stir in the nuts. Transfer to a covered container and refrigerate.

(Incidentally, this is a great spread for toast.)

DOUGH

1 cup sifted all-purpose flour
2 cups unsifted all-purpose whole wheat flour
1 teaspoon double-acting baking powder
½ teaspoon baking soda
½ teaspoon salt

4 ounces (1 stick) unsalted butter
½ cup light brown sugar, firmly packed
½ cup honey
1 egg graded "large"

Sift together the sifted all-purpose flour, the unsifted whole wheat flour, the baking powder, baking soda, and the salt. Set aside.

In the large bowl of an electric mixer beat the butter until soft. Beat in the sugar, honey, and the egg. On low speed gradually add the sifted dry ingredients, scraping the bowl as necessary with a rubber spatula and beating until they are incorporated and the dough is smooth.

Turn the mixture out onto a work surface. With your hands form the dough into about a 6-inch square 1½ or 2 inches thick. (If the dough is too sticky to handle, place it on a long piece of plastic wrap, fold the four sides of the plastic over the dough and, with your hands, press against the plastic wrap to shape the dough into a square.)

Wrap in plastic wrap and refrigerate.

The next day (or a few days later), when you are ready to bake, adjust a rack to the top position in the oven and preheat the oven to 400 degrees. Line a 12 by 15½-inch cookie sheet with aluminum foil shiny side up. Set aside.

Remove the block of dough from the refrigerator and cut it in half, forming two oblongs about 3 by 6 inches. Return one piece to the refrigerator until you are ready for it.

Flour a pastry cloth and a rolling pin. If the dough is too firm to roll, place it on the cloth and pound it lightly with the pin to soften it a bit; keep the shape oblong.

Roll out the dough slowly and carefully until it is 15 inches long and 6 inches wide, keeping the shape as neat as possible.

Now, picture the finished product: the filling will be placed in a strip down the middle and the two long sides will be folded over the filling, overlapping one another. In order not to have that overlapping section too thick, roll the edges of the two long sides a little thinner, making the oblong 7 to 7½ inches wide (slightly thinner along the long edges).

Use 2 cups of the filling for each strip of dough. Measure carefully. Do not use more than 2 cups because the dough will not cover more. (You will not use the remaining conserve for this recipe.) Using two teaspoons, one for picking up with and one for pushing off with, spoon 2 cups of the filling neatly down the middle of the dough, lengthwise, forming a band of filling that is a generous 1 inch deep and a generous 2 inches wide; stop the filling ½ inch from the narrow ends. With the bottom of a spoon, smooth the filling lightly to level it, but do not flatten it and do not make it any wider.

If the long sides are not exactly straight and even, just push the ruler against them to straighten them. (However, if they are very uneven they should be cut straight and patched if necessary.)

Use the pastry cloth to help fold one long side up over the filling. With a pastry brush, brush water in a ½-inch border along the edge. Then, using the other half of the pastry cloth, fold the other half of the dough up and over the wet edge. Press lightly to seal. The edges should overlap by about ½ inch.

Use the pastry cloth again to help roll the whole thing over so the seam is on the bottom. Use a flat-sided cookie sheet as a spatula and transfer the roll gently and carefully to the foil-lined cookie sheet, placing the roll either lengthwise down the middle or on an angle, seam down.

With your hands, perfect the shape of the roll, making it straight, smooth, and even. Press down gently on the two narrow ends to seal them. There will be small surface cracks in the pastry—it is all right.

Bake for 15 to 18 minutes until the pastry is golden brown all over, reversing the sheet front to back as necessary to ensure even browning.

Remove from the oven and let stand on the cookie sheet for about 15 minutes. Then use a flat-sided cookie sheet as a spatula to transfer the roll to a rack to cool . . . HANDLE WITH CARE!!!

Shape and bake the second roll.

Place the cooled rolls in the refrigerator or freezer until cold and firm before slicing. (I find that the strips cut more neatly with a serrated knife than they do with a straight-edged knife. Try both.)

Cut straight across or on an angle. Cut into 12 to 18 dessert-size bars (6 to 9 from each strip), or they can be cut narrower, if you wish.

The strips can be served either cold or at room temperature, either plain or with ice cream.

Banana Black Cake

There are many old Southern recipes called Black Cake. Usually it is a dark and heavy cake made with candied fruit. This one is different: a date-nut, jam and banana cake, huge (almost 7 pounds —over 3½ inches high); it keeps well and can be made several days ahead. It is dense, chewy, moist, mildly spiced, and not too sweet.

This cake might have been made long ago in one of the magnificent old plantation homes on the shore of the James River in Virginia. It might have been served on an elaborate sterling silver tray. Served, possibly, to George and Martha Washington, perhaps with a cut-crystal cup of rich and creamy eggnog.

25 PORTIONS

10 ounces (3 cups) walnuts
10 ounces (1½ cups, firmly packed) pitted dates, soft and moist
2¼ cups sifted all-purpose flour
1 cup unsifted all-purpose whole wheat flour
¼ cup unsweetened cocoa powder (preferably Dutch-process)
1 teaspoon nutmeg
1 teaspoon allspice
½ teaspoon salt
½ teaspoon cloves
½ teaspoon ground ginger
1 teaspoon cinnamon

8 ounces (2 sticks) unsalted butter
2 teaspoons vanilla extract
1 cup granulated sugar
1 cup light brown sugar, firmly packed
4 eggs graded "large"
1 1-pound jar (1½ cups) seedless blackberry jam
5 medium-size fully ripened bananas (to make 2 cups, mashed)
2 teaspoons baking soda
⅓ cup buttermilk
5 ounces (1 cup) dark raisins
Optional: confectioners sugar (to sprinkle over the cake)

Adjust two racks, one (for the cake) one-third up from the bottom of the oven; another (for a shallow pan of water) at the lowest position. Preheat the oven to 300 degrees. Butter a plain (no-design) 10 by 4-inch tube pan (with an 18- to 20-cup capacity), preferably (but not necessarily) with a nonstick finish; butter the pan even if it has a nonstick finish. Line the bottom with a round of baking pan liner paper cut to fit. Butter the paper. Set aside briefly.

To coat the pan with nuts, chop ⅔ cup of the walnuts fine (reserve the remaining 2⅓ cups) either in a food processor fitted with the metal chopping blade (process for 7 seconds) or any other way (they must be fine). Turn the nuts into the buttered and lined pan and tilt the pan in all directions to coat it all over (use your fingers to sprinkle the nuts on the tube). Loose nuts should be distributed evenly on the bottom of the pan to make a heavy layer on what will be the top of the cake. Set the pan aside.

Chop the remaining 2⅓ cups of nuts less fine; they should be cut into medium-size pieces. Either process them on/off 5 times (5 seconds) or cut them any other way. Set the nuts aside.

Cut the dates into medium-size pieces, cutting each date into 4 or 5 pieces. (If the pieces stick together, place them in a bowl and toss with about a tablespoon of the granulated sugar, to coat and separate them.) Set the dates aside.

Sift together the white flour, whole wheat flour, cocoa, nutmeg, allspice, salt, cloves, ginger, and cinnamon and set aside.

In the large bowl of an electric mixer beat the butter until soft. Beat in the vanilla and both sugars. Then add the eggs one at a time, beating after each addition until it is incorporated. (The mixture will probably appear curdled—it is OK.) Beat in the blackberry jam.

Peel the bananas and place them on a wide, flat plate. Mash them coarse with a fork. Measure 2 cups and beat this into the batter.

In a 1-cup measuring cup stir the baking soda into the buttermilk until the baking soda dissolves. Add to the batter and beat well, scraping the sides of the bowl as necessary with a rubber spatula.

On low speed gradually add the sifted dry ingredients, beating until incorporated. Remove the bowl from the mixer.

With a heavy wooden spatula stir in the prepared dates, the nuts, and the raisins.

Turn the mixture into the prepared pan and smooth the top. Cover the top of the pan with a piece of aluminum foil large enough to fold the sides down (heavy-duty foil is best for this).

Place the covered pan in the oven.

Place a shallow pan of hot water on the lowest rack (to keep steam in the oven).

Bake for 1 hour, then remove the aluminum foil and continue to bake for another 1½ hours (total baking time is 2½ hours) until a cake tester inserted gently in the cake, all the way to the bottom, comes out clean. (During baking the top will crack; it is all right.)

Let the cake stand in the pan for about 20 minutes.

Now, care beful! This cake is so heavy that turning it out of the pan is tricky. First—again—cover the pan with foil large enough to fold down the sides (to keep any loose chopped nuts from flying around) or work over the sink. Cover the cake pan with a rack. Hold the pan and the rack firmly together and—here goes—turn them both over. The cake will immediately fall out of the pan onto the rack; don't be surprised when it does.

Let stand until cool. Chill the cake until cold and firm, then wrap it airtight in a large plastic bag. Refrigerate overnight or for a few days, if you wish.

If you wish, sprinkle the top of the cold cake with confectioners sugar.

Cut the cake while it is cold into thin thin slices.

Serve plain or with vanilla ice cream.

Date-Nut Extra

This is a most unusual loaf. It is a date-nut bread-cake, an applesauce cake, a banana cake and a spice cake, all in one. You have a treat in store. Moist, not too sweet, wonderful with tea or coffee.

This makes a large loaf (slightly over 3 pounds). You need a pan with a 10-cup capacity. I use a heavy-weight metal loaf pan that measures 10 by 5 by 3 inches. However, in place of a large loaf pan, you can use two smaller loaf pans, or a tube or Bundt pan with a 10-cup capacity. (In two smaller loaf pans, or even in a tube pan, it might take a little less baking time; test carefully and do not underbake.)

A 10-INCH LOAF

7 ounces (2 cups) walnuts
8 ounces (1 cup, firmly packed) pitted dates
1 cup sifted all-purpose flour
1 cup sifted all-purpose whole wheat flour
1 teaspoon double-acting baking powder
¾ teaspoon baking soda
1 teaspoon cinnamon
½ teaspoon nutmeg
½ teaspoon ground ginger
¼ teaspoon salt
¼ teaspoon allspice
¼ teaspoon cloves
¼ teaspoon mace
4 ounces (1 stick) unsalted butter
1 cup light brown sugar, firmly packed
2 eggs graded "large"
1 cup unsweetened applesauce (I use Mott's Natural Style)
2 medium-small fully ripened bananas (to make ¾ cup, mashed)

Adjust a rack one-third up from the bottom of the oven and preheat the oven to 350 degrees. Butter a 10-cup loaf pan (see above) and set it aside.

Chop ½ cup of the walnuts very fine (reserve the remaining 1½ cups) either on a board with a long, heavy chef's knife or in a food processor fitted with the metal chopping blade. (In a processor, turn the motor on/off 7 times to chop the nuts fine enough, but not too fine.)

Place the chopped nuts in the buttered loaf pan. Hold the pan over a piece of paper and tilt and turn the pan in all directions to coat it heavily with the nuts. Allow excess nuts to fall out onto the paper.

Now break the reserved 1½ cups of walnuts into large pieces, add the excess chopped nuts, and set aside.

With scissors cut the dates into medium-size pieces, cutting each date into 4 or 5 pieces, and set aside.

Sift together the white flour, the whole wheat flour, the baking powder, baking soda, cinnamon, nutmeg, ginger, salt, allspice, cloves, and mace and set aside.

In the large bowl of an electric mixer beat the butter until soft. Beat in the sugar, and then the eggs one at a time. Add the applesauce and beat to mix (it will cause the mixture to look curdled—it is all right). On a flat plate with a fork mash the bananas coarse (they should not be liquefied in a food processor). Measure ¾ cup and add to the batter; mix well.

On low speed gradually add the sifted dry ingredients, scraping the bowl with a rubber spatula and beating only until mixed.

Remove the bowl from the mixer and stir in the reserved walnuts and the dates.

Turn into the prepared pan and smooth the top. Then, if you have used a loaf pan, form a slight trench with the bottom of a teaspoon down the length of the top surface (it will prevent the cake from rising too high).

Bake for 1¼ hours until a cake tester inserted gently in the middle of the cake comes out clean and dry. Remove from the oven. Let stand for 10 to 15 minutes. (During baking the cake will form a crack on top— it is OK.)

If you have used a loaf pan, place a folded towel or a large potholder on the palm of your right hand. With your left hand turn the pan gently over onto the folded towel or potholder and lift off the loaf pan. Cover the loaf with a rack and turn the rack and the loaf over, leaving the cake right side up to cool. To remove the cake from a tube or Bundt pan, cover it with a rack, turn both over, remove the pan, and leave the cake upside down.

Let stand until cool. Or, if you want it sooner, use a serrated French bread knife to cut with. It is delicious still warm.

East Blue Hill Blueberry Coffee Cake

This simple cake is made in an 8-inch square cake pan then cut into squares and served from the pan, preferably while it is still warm. It is quick and easy, a Down East, state of Maine cake. You will love to serve it for breakfast or brunch or any time you would serve a coffee cake. Or serve it with ice cream for a dinner dessert— wonderful.

8 OR 9 PORTIONS

6 ounces (1½ cups) fresh blueberries
1½ cups sifted all-purpose flour
2 teaspoons double-acting baking powder
½ teaspoon cinnamon
¼ teaspoon nutmeg
¼ teaspoon salt
2 ounces (½ stick) unsalted butter

1 teaspoon vanilla extract
¾ cup plus 3 tablespoons granulated sugar
1 egg
⅔ cup milk
Finely grated rind of 1 large lemon
Optional: Crystal sugar (see page 4) or
    additional granulated sugar

Adjust a rack one-third up from the bottom of the oven and preheat the oven to 350 degrees. Butter an 8-inch square cake pan and dust it all over with fine dry bread crumbs or with toasted or untoasted wheat germ, invert the pan over paper and tap lightly to shake out excess. Set aside.

Wash the berries (see To Wash Blueberries, page 14) and let drain.

Sift together the flour, baking powder, cinnamon, nutmeg, and salt and set aside. In the small bowl of an electric mixer beat the butter until it is soft. Beat in the vanilla and ¾ cup of the granulated sugar (reserve the remaining 3 tablespoons). Beat in the egg. Then, on low speed, add half of the sifted dry ingredients, then the milk, and then the remaining dry ingredients, beating only until incorporated. Remove the bowl from the mixer and stir in the grated rind. Turn into the prepared pan and smooth the top.

In a bowl toss the berries gently with the remaining 3 tablespoons of granulated sugar. Spoon the berries and sugar evenly over the top of the cake.

Bake for 45 or 50 minutes until the top is lightly browned and the cake barely begins to come away from the sides of the pan.

If you wish, after the cake is baked sprinkle it lightly with crystal sugar or granulated sugar and place under a preheated broiler for only a minute or so (watch it carefully) to darken and glaze the top a bit more.

Cool slightly in the pan. Then cut into squares and serve warm.

Blueberry Surprise Cake

Light, tender, delicate, moist, delicious, quick and easy—a one-layer sour cream cake with fresh blueberries hidden inside. This is a lovely coffee cake for breakfast or brunch either while it is still warm or after it has cooled.

8 TO 10 PORTIONS

BLUEBERRY SURPRISE

1 cup fresh blueberries
3 tablespoons granulated sugar
1 teaspoon cinnamon
¼ teaspoon nutmeg

1 teaspoon lemon juice (before squeezing the
    juice, grate the rind and reserve to use in the
    cake)

Wash and dry the berries (see To Wash Blueberries, page 14). Then, in a bowl, combine the sugar, cinnamon, and nutmeg. Stir in the berries gently. Drizzle on the lemon juice. Let stand.

CAKE

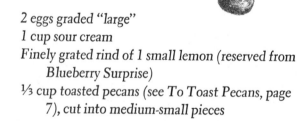

2 cups sifted all-purpose flour
2 teaspoons double-acting baking powder
¼ teaspoon salt
8 ounces (2 sticks) unsalted butter
1 teaspoon vanilla extract
1⅓ cups granulated sugar

2 eggs graded "large"
1 cup sour cream
Finely grated rind of 1 small lemon (reserved from
    Blueberry Surprise)
⅓ cup toasted pecans (see To Toast Pecans, page
    7), cut into medium-small pieces

Adjust a rack one-third up from the bottom of the oven and preheat the oven to 350 degrees. Butter a 9 by 3-inch springform pan and dust all over with fine dry bread crumbs. Invert the pan over paper and tap lightly to shake out excess crumbs. Set aside.

Sift together the flour, baking powder, and salt and set aside. In the large bowl of an electric mixer beat the butter until it is soft. Beat in the vanilla and sugar. Then add the eggs and beat until incorporated. Add the sour cream and, scraping the bowl as necessary with a rubber spatula, beat only until incorporated. On low speed add the sifted dry ingredients and beat only until smooth.

Remove the bowl from the mixer and stir in the grated rind.

Turn half of the mixture into the prepared pan, smooth the top, and then spoon on the blueberry mixture, keeping it ½ to 1 inch away from the sides of the pan.

Stir the pecans into the remaining batter and spoon it over the batter in the pan. Spread it smooth.

Bake for 1 hour and 20 to 30 minutes until the top of the cake springs back when it is pressed lightly with a fingertip.

Let the cake stand in the pan for about 15 minutes. Meanwhile, prepare the glaze.

GLAZE

1 cup confectioners sugar

1 tablespoon lemon juice

A few drops boiling water

In a bowl beat the sugar and lemon juice with just a few drops of boiling water as necessary to make it semi-liquid; the mixture should be thick—just barely thin enough to pour (if necessary, adjust with more sugar or drops of water).

Release and remove the sides of the springform pan. Cover the cake with a rack, turn the cake and the rack over, remove the bottom of the cake pan, cover the cake with a cake plate and very carefully turn the cake and the plate over again, leaving the cake right side up.

Stir the glaze and drizzle it over the warm cake, letting some of it run down the sides.

When you cut the cake you will see that the weight of the berries has not allowed the bottom half of the cake to rise—you will barely see the bottom half—but the top half more than makes up for it; it is wonderfully light and all in all a joy.

Cranberry Upside-Down Cake

If you like the tart flavor of cranberries you will be wild about this; I do and I am. It is a single layer of lovely, moist white cake covered with a generous topping of fresh cranberries that is brushed with red currant jelly after baking. It is shiny cranberry-red gorgeous. This is traditionally served with a generous ladleful of whipped cream, but I have added a different cream (ricotta cheese). Although this is all quick and easy I would be happy to serve it at a Thanksgiving dinner. This can be a luncheon or dinner dessert, or a brunch coffee cake, or a treat to serve with tea or coffee in the afternoon.

You need fresh cranberries for this.

8 PORTIONS

12 ounces (4 cups) fresh cranberries
5 ounces (1¼ sticks) unsalted butter, at room temperature
1 cup plus 2 tablespoons granulated sugar
1¼ cups sifted all-purpose flour
1½ teaspoons double-acting baking powder
¼ teaspoon salt

1 egg graded "large"
1 teaspoon vanilla extract
⅔ cup milk
Finely grated rind of 1 large deep-colored orange
⅓ cup red currant jelly (to be used after the cake is baked)

Adjust a rack one-quarter up from the bottom of the oven and preheat the oven to 350 degrees. You will need a 9 by 1½-inch round layer cake pan (it should not be shallower).

Wash the cranberries briefly in cold water, discard loose stems, drain, and then spread the berries on a towel to dry a bit.

Use 4 tablespoons (½ stick) of the butter (reserve the remaining ¾ stick of butter)—it must be soft but not melted. Spread a bit of it on the sides of the pan and then, with the bottom of a spoon, spread the remainder (of the 4 tablespoons) over the bottom of the pan. Sprinkle ½ cup plus 2 tablespoons of the sugar (reserve the remaining ½ cup) over the butter. Sprinkle the berries over the sugar. They will almost fill the pan—it is OK. Set the pan aside.

Sift together the flour, baking powder, and salt with the remaining ½ cup of sugar and set aside.

In the small bowl of an electric mixer beat the remaining ¾ stick of butter until soft. Beat in the egg and vanilla. Then, on the lowest speed, add the sifted dry ingredients in three additions alternately with the milk in two additions, mixing only until just combined (the mixture might appear slightly curdled—it is OK). Remove the bowl from the mixer, stir in the grated rind, and pour over the berries.

Smooth the top. The pan will be full—OK.

Bake for 1 hour; the top will become quite brown during baking.

Cool the cake in the pan on a rack for 20 minutes. After 10 minutes cut around the sides with a small, sharp knife to release the cake.

Meanwhile, place the jelly in a small pan over moderate heat; stir occasionally until the jelly melts and comes to a boil. Set aside briefly.

After the 20 minutes are up, cut around the sides of the cake again. Then cover with a flat cake plate, hold the pan and the plate firmly together, and turn them both over. Remove the pan.

Pour the melted jelly onto the cake and with the bottom of a spoon spread it to cover the top completely (right up to the edges—if a bit runs over the sides it is OK, but not too much).

Let stand until completely cool. Serve the cake at room temperature. If you serve this by itself it is really quite tart, but with something bland and creamy and icy cold it is divine. You could serve vanilla ice cream or whipped cream (with a bit of sugar and vanilla), or, if you have a food processor, serve Ricotta Cream (see page 360). To serve 6 to 8 portions of the cake, use 2 15-ounce containers of ricotta cheese. Be sure that the Ricotta Cream is very very cold (even place it in the freezer for 15 to 20 minutes before serving), and place a mound of it on each plate next to the cake.

Chocolate Cakes*

A recent scientific study conducted at the University of Delaware has concluded that chocolate reduces stress and depression. I knew it all the time.

Chocolate Festival Cake

I made this up when the Hershey company held their First Annual Chocolate Festival in Hershey, Pennsylvania, in 1982. I wanted a cake that was as American as a Hershey bar. I demonstrated it before a large audience and then served it to everyone there. Although it is a very large cake, that day I cut it into extra-thin slices and was able to serve many more than 24 portions. I don't know for sure if the audience was impressed by my dexterity in being able to serve so many people from one cake or if the applause was for the cake itself; however, the cake and I got a standing ovation.

It is dark-dark chocolate, a cross between a pound cake and a fudge cake, made with peanut butter, bananas, and both chocolate and cocoa. It is firm but moist, rich and dense, not too sweet, and easy to make. It is thickly covered with a swirly chocolate and peanut butter icing.

24 PORTIONS

4 ounces semisweet chocolate
3 cups sifted all-purpose flour
1 tablespoon double-acting baking powder
2 teaspoons baking soda
1 teaspoon salt
8 ounces (2 sticks) unsalted butter
1 cup smooth peanut butter
1 tablespoon vanilla extract
1 pound (2¼ cups, packed) dark brown sugar
1 cup (about 2) finely mashed fully ripened
     bananas (see Note)
6 eggs graded "large"
1 cup strained unsweetened cocoa powder
     (preferably Dutch-process)
1¼ cups milk

Adjust a rack one-third up from the bottom of the oven and preheat the oven to 350 degrees. You will need a 10 by 4-inch tube pan with an 18-cup capacity; it can be nonstick or not and it can be a one-piece pan or one with detachable sides. Butter the pan (even if it is nonstick), line the bottom with a round of baking pan liner paper or wax paper cut to fit, then butter the paper, dust all over with fine dry bread crumbs, invert the pan over paper and tap out excess crumbs. Set aside.

Place the chocolate in the top of a small double boiler over warm water on moderately low heat, cover the pot with a folded paper towel (to absorb steam) and with the pot cover. Let cook until the chocolate is almost melted, then uncover and stir until completely melted. Remove the top of the double boiler and set aside to cool.

Sift together the flour, baking powder, baking soda, and salt and set aside.

In the large bowl of an electric mixer beat the butter until soft. Beat in the peanut butter and vanilla, then the sugar, scraping the bowl as necessary with a rubber spatula. Next, mix in the melted chocolate, then the mashed bananas, and then the eggs one at a time, beating until incorporated after each addition. On lowest speed add the cocoa, still scraping the bowl as necessary, and beat until smooth.

On low speed gradually add half of the milk, then half of the sifted dry ingredients, then the remaining milk, and finally the remaining dry ingredients, beating until smooth after each addition.

Turn the mixture into the prepared pan. Briskly rotate the pan a bit, first in one direction, then the other, to smooth the top.

Bake for 1 hour, then cover the top loosely with foil to prevent over-browning, and continue to bake for an additional 25 to 30 minutes until a cake tester gently inserted into the cake—in several places, all the way to the bottom—comes out clean (total baking time is 1 hour and 25 to 30 minutes). The top of the cake will crack during baking—it is OK.

Cool in the pan for 20 minutes. Then cover with a rack, turn the pan and the rack over, remove the pan and the paper lining, and let the cake cool upside down on the rack.

When the cake is completely cool, place four 10 by 3-inch strips of wax paper or baking pan liner paper in a square pattern on a large flat cake plate (see illustration, page 16). Transfer the cake to the plate and check to be sure that the papers are touching the cake all around.

If you have a cake-decorating turntable, place the cake plate on it.

CHOCOLATE–PEANUT BUTTER ICING

16 ounces milk chocolate, broken up
2 ounces unsweetened chocolate, chopped coarse
4 ounces (1 stick) unsalted butter, cut into ½-inch pieces

1 egg
12 ounces (1½ cups) smooth peanut butter

Place both chocolates in the top of a large double boiler over warm water on rather low heat. Cover for a few minutes, then uncover and stir frequently until melted and smooth.

Remove the top of the double boiler. Add the butter a few pieces at a time, stirring with a wooden spatula until smooth.

In the large bowl of an electric mixer beat the egg just to mix, then add the peanut butter and the chocolate mixture (which can be warm or cool) and beat until very smooth. As this mixture cools it will thicken; you might want to chill it quickly by putting it in the freezer or by placing the bowl in a larger bowl of ice and water. Or just let it stand awhile. When it is thick enough to hold its shape, beat it again for a moment.

This is a lot of icing and it makes a thick layer. Spread it first on the sides and then on the top of the cake. With a long, narrow metal spatula smooth the sides first and then the top. Then, form peaks and swirls all over the sides and top as follows. Dip a teaspoon into water (hot or cold), shake it off, and with the bottom of the wet spoon form little curls and swirls in the icing. Continue to wet the spoon every time you move it to form another swirl (the wet spoon gives the icing a smooth finish).

Remove the paper strips by pulling each one out slowly toward a narrow end.

NOTE: *The bananas must be fully ripened, with brown/black spots on the skin, to have the best flavor for baking with. Mash them on a large, flat plate with a fork. (In a processor they become too liquid.)*

Big Daddy's Cake

A big, gorgeous cake baked in a large Bundt pan, topped with a dark, thick chocolate glaze that runs down the sides unevenly. When you cut into the cake you will find a moist, tender white cake, studded with pecans, and containing a tunnel of soft and gooey chocolate sauce. Most delicious. And a total mystery, to me at least. The white batter is poured into the pan, then topped with a chocolate sauce. During baking they change places; the chocolate sauce goes down to the bottom of the white batter, without leaving a trace of chocolate on the white. Ah, sweet mystery . . .

If you can serve this before the icing and the surprise chocolate tunnel inside become firm it is best. I have made this cake late in the morning and after dinner the icing and the chocolate tunnel were still properly soft and moist. Longer than that they became firm.

12 PORTIONS

7 ounces (2 cups) toasted pecans (see page 7)
4 cups sifted all-purpose flour
2 teaspoons double-acting baking powder
1 teaspoon salt
6 ounces semisweet chocolate (I use Maillard's Eagle Sweet)
3 tablespoons hot water or strong coffee (2 to 3 teaspoons instant coffee in 3 tablespoons water)

3 tablespoons whipping cream
12 ounces (3 sticks) unsalted butter
1½ teaspoons vanilla extract
¼ teaspoon almond extract
2¼ cups granulated sugar
6 eggs graded "large"
1¼ cups milk

Adjust a rack one-third up from the bottom of the oven and preheat the oven to 350 degrees. Generously butter a 10-inch Bundt pan or any other fancy tube pan with a 14-cup capacity (butter it even if it has a nonstick finish).

Coarsely break up half the pecans and set them aside to sprinkle on the batter just before baking. Chop the remaining cup of pecans fine. (I do it on a large board with a long, heavy French chef's knife—the pieces will be uneven but aim for pieces about the size of rice.)

Place the finely chopped pecans in the buttered pan, turn the pan and shake it from side to side to coat it completely with the nuts. Invert the pan over paper and allow loose nuts to fall out. Then, with your fingers, sprinkle those loose nuts into the bottom of the pan and set aside.

Sift together the flour, baking powder, and salt and set aside.

Break up or chop the chocolate coarse and place it in the top of a small double boiler over hot water on moderate heat. Add the water or coffee. Cover the pan and cook until the chocolate is melted. Remove the top of the double boiler from the heat, stir briskly with a small wire whisk until smooth, add the whipping cream and whisk again until smooth. Set aside.

Beat the butter in the large bowl of an electric mixer until soft and smooth, then beat in the vanilla and almond extracts and the sugar and continue to beat for about 2 minutes. Then add the eggs one at a time, scraping the bowl as necessary, and beating until thoroughly incorporated after each addition. On low speed gradually add the sifted dry ingredients in three additions alternately with the milk in two additions. (After adding the milk, and even after adding the dry ingredients, the mixture will appear curdled—it is OK.)

Turn the batter into the prepared pan and smooth the top. With the bottom of a large spoon form a trench around the middle of the top of the cake (about ½ inch deep and 1½ inches wide).

Stir the prepared chocolate mixture and spoon it into the trench, keeping away from the sides of the pan.

With your fingertips sprinkle the reserved coarsely broken pecans all over the top of the batter (they should touch the sides of the pan).

Bake for 50 to 55 minutes, then cover the top of the pan loosely with foil to prevent overbrowning. Continue to bake for 15 to 20 more minutes (total baking time is 1 hour and 5 to 15 minutes) until a cake tester inserted gently in the middle of the cake comes out clean. (During baking the top will form a deep crack—it is all right.)

Let the cake cool in the pan for 20 minutes. Then cover it with a wide, flat cake plate and, holding the pan and the plate firmly together, turn them both over. Be careful while doing this—the cake is very heavy. Get a good secure grip on the cake pan with a potholder; the other hand should be over the middle of the plate with your fingers spread apart for support. Remove the pan.

Let the cake stand until cool, and then make the glaze.

BIG DADDY'S GLAZE

6 ounces semisweet chocolate (I use Maillard's Eagle Sweet)   2 teaspoons solid vegetable shortening (e.g., Crisco)

Break up or chop the chocolate coarse and place it with the shortening in the top of a small double boiler, uncovered, over hot water on moderate heat. Stir occasionally until melted and smooth.

Pour the glaze over the top of the cake. Then smooth the top a bit, allowing a small amount of the glaze to run down into the grooves of the cake.

Let stand at room temperature and serve at room temperature.

Chocolate Sponge Cake

A lady told me that the best sponge cake she ever made is the one in Craig Claiborne's New York Times Cook Book *(Harper & Brothers, 1961). But, she said, she wished it was chocolate and asked me how she could change it to a chocolate cake. I took a guess, without knowing the recipe, and suggested that she try to substitute cocoa for ¼ cup of the flour. Then I decided to try it myself. This is it.*

As the lady said, "You just put everything in the mixer and that is all there is to it (well, almost), and it is so light it feels as though it might fly away."

You need an electric mixer on a stand for all the beating.

10 TO 12 PORTIONS

¾ cup sifted cake flour
½ teaspoon salt
1 teaspoon cinnamon
2 teaspoons powdered (not granular) instant coffee
   or espresso

¼ cup unsweetened cocoa powder (preferably
   Dutch-process)
6 eggs graded "large"
2 teaspoons vanilla extract
1 cup granulated sugar

Adjust a rack one-third up from the bottom of the oven and preheat the oven to 325 degrees. You will need a 10 by 4-inch angel-food tube pan with a loose rim—the bottom and tube being in one piece. It must not be a nonstick pan. Do not butter or line the pan. Place it in the sink (which is where you will need it) until you are ready for it.

Sift together the flour, salt, cinnamon, powdered instant coffee, and cocoa. Then resift together six more times. Set aside.

Place the eggs and vanilla in the small bowl of an electric mixer and beat at high speed for a few minutes until the eggs rise to the top of the bowl. Transfer the eggs to the large bowl of the mixer and continue to beat at high speed for about 15 minutes until the eggs have thickened to the consistency of soft whipped cream.

Then, while still beating at high speed, very slowly add the sugar 1 tablespoon at a time. It should take 3 minutes to add the sugar.

Now, on lowest speed, add the dry ingredients 1 heaping tablespoon at a time. While adding the dry ingredients it is helpful to scrape the bowl gently a few times with a rubber spatula. Do not beat any longer than necessary now, or you will deflate the eggs.

Quickly run cold water into the cake pan in the sink, then pour it out, leaving the pan wet and cold. Gently pour the cake batter into the pan, pouring first on one side of the tube and then on the other. (The batter will reach only halfway to the top of the pan.)

Bake for 50 to 55 minutes until the top just barely springs back when it is pressed gently with a fingertip. (This cake is so extraordinarily light that you might not see it spring back.) The top of the cake will be flat and it will have risen to about 1 inch below the top of the pan.

Remove the cake from the oven and immediately, gently, turn the pan over and let stand upside down until the cake is completely cool.

(When I know I want to freeze this whole, I freeze it in the pan, before cutting it loose.)

Use a sharp knife that has a firm 6- or 7-inch blade; slide the blade in around the edge of the cake, pressing it against the pan (away from the cake). Slowly and carefully cut all around the cake, using a short up and down sawing motion and always pressing against the pan.

Then raise the pan from the counter and push the bottom up to release the sides; then lift out the tube. Next, with the pan upright, cut the bottom of the cake away from the bottom of the pan, still pressing the blade against the pan. Finally cut around the center tube.

Cover the cake with a serving plate, turn the cake and the plate over, remove the bottom of the pan, and leave the cake as it is, upside down.

I like the simplicity of this just plain, but it is also very nice with a bit of confectioners sugar sprinkled through a fine strainer over the top, then surrounded with a ring of large fresh strawberries with the stems and hulls left on.

Use a serrated French bread knife and a sawing motion to cut this; do not press down on it or it will squash.

Kansas City Chocolate Dream

Variations of this recipe pop up in many areas of the country under many different names: Chocolate Upside-Down Cake, Chocolate Sauce Pudding, Chocolate Pudding Cake, Hot Fudge Sauce Cake, to name a few. In most cases, whatever the name, you will have a square pan of chocolate cake floating in a rather thin, dark chocolate syrup; both the cake and the syrup are spooned out together and served like a pudding with a sauce.

This Missouri recipe is similar, but is something else. It is a small, shallow square upside-down cake which, when it is turned onto a cake plate, covers itself with a thick layer of dark chocolate topping that resembles nothing I can think of. The topping is as dark and shiny as black patent leather, as tender and semifirm as a pot de crème, and as mocha-chocolate flavored as you might weave dreams about.

The topping and the cake are baked together. Sensationally quick/easy/foolproof. This is wonderful just as soon as it has barely cooled, or it can wait hours, or it can be frozen.

8 OR 9 PORTIONS

CAKE

1 cup sifted all-purpose flour
2 teaspoons double-acting baking powder
¼ teaspoon salt
2 tablespoons unsweetened cocoa powder (preferably Dutch-process)

⅔ cup granulated sugar
¾ cup milk
1 teaspoon vanilla extract
1 ounce (¼ stick) unsalted butter, melted
½ cup walnuts, broken into medium-size pieces

Adjust a rack one-third up from the bottom of the oven and preheat the oven to 350 degrees. Butter a shallow 8-inch square cake pan and set aside.

Sift together into the small bowl of an electric mixer the flour, baking powder, salt, cocoa, and sugar. Add the milk, vanilla, and melted butter and beat until smooth and slightly pale in color. Remove the bowl from the mixer. Stir in the nuts. Turn into the buttered pan and smooth the top. Let stand.

TOPPING

⅓ cup granulated sugar
6 tablespoons unsweetened cocoa powder (preferably Dutch-process)

½ cup dark brown sugar, firmly packed
2 teaspoons granular instant coffee
1 cup water

In a small, heavy saucepan combine all the ingredients. Stir over rather high heat until the sugars melt and the mixture comes to a full boil.

Gently ladle the boiling hot mixture all over the cake batter.

Bake for 40 minutes until a toothpick inserted gently into the cake comes out clean. (During baking the topping will sink to the bottom.) Set aside to cool in the pan.

When the cake has cooled cover with a square or oblong serving plate or a cutting board. Holding them firmly together, turn the pan and the plate over. If the cake does not slide out of the pan easily (and it probably will not), hold the plate and the pan firmly together upside down and tap them on the work surface. Now the cake will come out, and it will be covered with the topping, some of which will still be in the pan; use a rubber spatula to remove it all and put it on the cake. Smooth the top gently or pull the topping up into uneven peaks.

Serve immediately or let stand all day or freeze. (If you freeze this do not cover with plastic wrap; the topping never does freeze hard and plastic wrap will stick to it. Just cover the whole thing with an inverted box deep enough so it doesn't touch the cake.) Freezing diminishes the flavor of all foods, especially this. Although this can be served frozen, it has more flavor if it is brought to room temperature.

This cake does not need a thing but a plate and fork; however, if you are serving it for a birthday party or some other festivity, ice cream is wonderful with it.

Williams-Sonoma Chocolate Cake

Offhand, I can't think of any great chocolate recipes that include wine in the ingredients. Cognac, rum, bourbon, even Scotch whisky, and most liqueurs, but not wine. Some foods scream out "Where's the wine?" but chocolate does not.

Recently, in San Francisco Wes Halbruner, the book buyer for Williams-Sonoma, gave me this wonderful chocolate recipe that uses port wine. (I was told to use Ficklin brand, however. . . .) It is an extraordinary cake, a taste thrill, a rare treat.

Wes said I should use Callebaut chocolate (which surely is divine), however, I have made this with other delicious semisweet chocolates as well and the cake was always wonderful.

The recipe, as I received it, said that the cake must be served hot, right from the oven. Hot is fantastic, but I love it at any temperature—even frozen.

Serve it plain. Or with whipped cream and fresh raspberries or strawberries.

8 PORTIONS

4 ounces (1 stick) unsalted butter
½ cup port wine
4 ounces semisweet chocolate
1 cup granulated sugar

3 eggs graded "large," separated
¾ cup sifted all-purpose flour
⅛ teaspoon salt

Adjust a rack to the center of the oven and preheat the oven to 325 degrees. Butter a 10-inch springform pan (which may be from 2 to 3 inches deep), line the bottom with baking pan liner paper or wax paper cut to fit, butter the paper, dust all over with flour, and then invert the pan and tap out excess. Set aside.

Place the butter, port, and chocolate in a small, heavy pan over rather low heat and stir occasionally until the butter and chocolate are melted.

Meanwhile, remove and reserve 2 tablespoons of the sugar. Add the remaining sugar to the egg yolks in the small bowl of an electric mixer;

beat at high speed for a few minutes until very pale. On low speed gradually add the warm melted chocolate mixture (I suggest that you pour the mixture into a pitcher first to make it easier to add) and beat until smooth. Then beat in the flour. Remove the bowl from the mixer.

This may be prepared hours ahead to this point; if so, cover this bowl and the bowl of whites and let stand at room temperature.

In a clean small bowl with clean beaters beat the egg whites and the salt until the whites hold a soft shape. Gradually add the reserved 2 tablespoons of sugar and beat until the whites hold a definite shape when the beaters are raised, but not until they are stiff/dry.

Fold about one third of the chocolate mixture into the beaten whites. Then transfer both the remaining chocolate mixture and the egg white mixture to a larger bowl and fold them together gently only until just incorporated. Do not handle any more than necessary.

Pour the mixture into the prepared pan.

Bake for 30 minutes.

Remove from the oven and let stand for 5 minutes. Then, gently, cut around the sides of the cake with a table knife to release it from the pan, and then release and remove the sides of the pan.

Cover the cake with a rack and turn the rack and cake over. Remove the bottom of the pan and the paper lining. Cover the cake with a flat serving plate and turn rack, cake, and plate over again, leaving the cake right side up. The cake will be only 1 inch high.

Serve as soon as possible (or later).

Cowtown Chocolate Cake

Many Texans call Dallas "Cowtown," a name that came about when Dallas was the center of the cattle industry. This cake was famous years ago at a Dallas coffee shop. It is an extremely choco- *late two-layer cake with an equally chocolate semisoft icing that stays semisoft.*

12 PORTIONS

1½ cups sifted all-purpose flour
¼ cup unsweetened cocoa powder
    (preferably Dutch-process)
1 teaspoon baking soda
½ teaspoon salt
1 teaspoon powdered (not granular) instant
    coffee or espresso

5 ounces unsweetened chocolate
4 ounces (1 stick) unsalted butter
1 teaspoon vanilla extract
1 cup light brown sugar, firmly packed
1 cup granulated sugar
3 eggs graded "large," separated
1¼ cups buttermilk

Adjust a rack to the middle of the oven and preheat the oven to 350 degrees. Butter two 9-inch round layer cake pans, line them with rounds of baking pan liner paper or wax paper cut to fit, then butter the paper, and dust the pans all over with fine dry bread crumbs. Invert the pans over paper and tap lightly to shake out excess. Set the pans aside.

Sift together the flour, cocoa, baking soda, salt, and powdered coffee or espresso. Resift the ingredients one more time and set them aside.

Place the chocolate in the top of a small double boiler over warm water on moderate heat. Cover the pan with a folded paper towel (to absorb steam) and the pot cover. Let cook until the chocolate is almost completely melted. Then uncover and stir with a rubber spatula until it is completely melted and smooth. Remove the top of the double boiler and set aside.

In the large bowl of an electric mixer beat the butter until it is soft. Beat in the vanilla and brown sugar.

Remove and reserve 3 tablespoons of the granulated sugar; beat the remaining granulated sugar into the butter mixture. Add the yolks and beat well. Then add the melted chocolate (which may be slightly warm or cool) and beat until smooth.

On low speed add the sifted dry ingredients in three additions alternately with the buttermilk in two additions, scraping the bowl as necessary with a rubber spatula and beating only until smooth after each addition. Remove the bowl from the mixer and set aside.

In the small bowl of the electric mixer (with clean beaters) beat the egg whites until they hold a soft shape. Reduce the speed to moderate and gradually add the reserved 3 tablespoons of granulated sugar. Increase the speed again and continue to beat only until the whites hold a point when the beaters are raised but not until they are stiff/dry.

The chocolate mixture will be quite thick; add about one quarter of the whites and fold the two together, or stir a bit if necessary to incorporate. Then add the remaining beaten whites and fold until completely incorporated.

Place half of the batter in each of the cake pans and smooth the tops.

Bake for about 35 minutes until the tops of the cakes barely spring back when pressed gently with a fingertip and the cakes just begin to come away from the sides of the pans.

Remove from the oven and cut gently around the sides of the cakes with a small, sharp knife to release. Let stand for 5 minutes.

Cover each cake with a rack, turn cake pan and rack over, remove cake pan and paper lining, cover with another rack, and turn over again, leaving the cakes right side up to cool.

When you are ready to ice the cake, place four 10 by 3-inch strips of baking pan liner paper or wax paper in a square pattern on a large flat cake plate (see illustration, page 16). Place one layer on the plate upside down, checking to be sure that the papers touch the cake all around. If you have a cake-decorating turntable, place the cake plate on it.

ICING

1 cup whipping cream
1 cup granulated sugar
4½ ounces unsweetened chocolate

Pinch of salt
4 ounces (1 stick) unsalted butter, cut into slices
1 teaspoon vanilla extract

Stir the cream and sugar in a 2½- to 3-quart heavy saucepan over moderate heat until the mixture comes to a boil. Reduce the heat and let the mixture simmer for 6 minutes, stirring occasionally. Remove the pan from the heat, add the chocolate and stir until it is melted, then add the salt, butter, and vanilla and stir until the butter is melted and the mixture is smooth.

Place the pan in a large bowl of ice and water and scrape the bottom continuously for a few minutes with a rubber spatula until the mixture is cool and slightly thickened. Transfer the mixture to the small bowl of an electric mixer and beat at high speed for a few minutes until the color becomes slightly lighter and the icing is thick enough to hold its shape.

Spread a layer of the icing about ¼ inch thick over the layer on the plate. Place the other layer on it, right side up (bottoms together). Spread the remaining icing thinly on the sides of the cake, and more thickly on the top. With a small, narrow metal spatula smooth the sides, and then with a long, narrow metal spatula smooth the top.

Now, to form a pattern on the top, with the tip of the metal spatula make a straight row of little peaks just touching each other down the middle of the cake. Then repeat, making rows of peaks just touching each other (and the rows just touching) to cover the top of the cake completely.

Remove the paper strips by pulling each one out toward a narrow end.

Frozen Fudge Cake

I was with a group of well-known food people. We were talking about chocolate. The enthusiasm was unanimous when we spoke about eating chocolate that is frozen. Each had several favorites, mainly certain candy bars, that they said were extra delicious when frozen (Snickers, Mars, Milky Way, Hershey's Golden Almond Bar). I spoke more about certain baked goods; many things I had put in the freezer so I wouldn't eat them (Brownies and chocolate chip cookies, most chocolate cakes that are made without flour, and rich fruit cakes). We all agreed that even if it is difficult to cut or bite into some of these frozen sweets, that is part of the excitement and taste thrill.

This flourless cake is a recipe that Jane Salz- *fass Freiman sent to me. She got it from The Commissary restaurant in Philadelphia when she was on tour for her cookbook, The Art of Food Processor Cooking (Contemporary Books, Inc., 1980). The Commissary calls it Mocha Fudge Cake. It is meant to be served refrigerated but I say* SERVE IT FROZEN. *Jane says it is "like a giant whipped cream–frosted truffle—absolutely divine." Frozen, the taste is tantalizing, something like an extra-dense and extra-solid chocolate ice cream.*

Make this days or even weeks ahead, if you wish. You will need a 10 by 3-inch springform pan. This takes long, slow baking.

16 PORTIONS

18 ounces semisweet chocolate, chopped coarse or broken up (see Note)
2¼ cups granulated sugar
1 pound (4 sticks) unsalted butter, cut up

1 scant tablespoon granular instant coffee
1 cup boiling water
9 eggs graded "large"

Adjust a rack one-third up from the bottom of the oven and preheat the oven to 250 degrees. Butter the bottom and sides of a 10 by 3-inch spring-form pan. Line the bottom of the pan with a round of baking pan liner paper cut to fit. Butter the paper. Dust the pan and paper with un-sweetened cocoa powder, invert the pan over paper and tap to remove excess cocoa, and set the pan aside.

Place the chocolate, sugar, and butter in a heavy 3-quart saucepan. Dissolve the coffee in the water and pour into the saucepan. Stir occasionally over moderately low heat until everything is melted and smooth.

Pour the mixture into a very large bowl. If the mixture is not smooth beat it briskly with a large, heavy wire whisk. If it is still not smooth, strain it, then return it to the large bowl.

In a small bowl beat the eggs briefly only until they are slightly foamy. Then gradually pour the eggs into the warm chocolate mixture, stirring constantly with a large wire whisk.

Pour the mixture into the prepared cake pan and bake for 2 hours. (It is advisable to keep a portable mercury thermometer in the oven while this cake bakes; the temperature should not rise above 250 degrees.) During baking the edges of the cake will rise above the rim of the pan; the center will be lower.

After 2 hours, turn off the oven, open the oven door, and let the cake stand for 30 minutes. As the cake cools it will sink back to its original height and will be flat on top. Remove the pan from the oven and let stand until cool.

When the cake is cool, release and remove the sides of the pan. Then cover the cake with a board or a cookie sheet, carefully turn the cake and the board or cookie sheet over, remove the bottom of the cake pan and the paper lining, cover the cake with a flat cake plate and very carefully turn the cake and the plate over again, leaving the cake right side up.

Place the cake in the freezer. When the cake is frozen, wrap it well with plastic wrap.

(If you would like to freeze this cake or any cake, *not* on a cake plate, here's how. When you remove the cake from the cake pan and while it is upside down, cover it with a round of baking pan liner paper or wax paper cut to fit. Cover the paper with a cake plate or anything flat and turn the cake and the plate over. Place in the freezer. Now, when the cake is frozen, you can easily lift it—because of the paper lining—to wrap it in plastic wrap and return it to the freezer, not on a cake plate.)

Do you know the temperature in your freezer? I have two freezers, each one with a thermometer in it. The large freezer is extra cold—20 degrees below. The freezer top of the refrigerator is from 0 to 5 degrees above. When I store this cake in the colder freezer it is too hard to slice easily, therefore I transfer it to the refrigerator (not the freezer part) for about 45 minutes before serving. But when it is in the freezer where the temperature is from 0 to 5 degrees above it can be served directly and is not too hard to slice.

Therefore, check the temperature of your freezer and proceed accordingly. Or, if you do not have a freezer thermometer, check the firmness of the cake by inserting the tip of a small, sharp knife into the middle of the cake.

WHIPPED CREAM

2 cups whipping cream
⅓ cup confectioners sugar

¾ teaspoon vanilla extract
2 tablespoons Cognac or rum

In a chilled bowl, with chilled beaters, whip the ingredients until the cream is just firm enough to be used as an icing. Just before serving spread the cream over the top and sides of the cake. Or spread about two thirds of it on the cake and use the remainder with a pastry bag and a star tip to pipe rosettes on the top.

Or, if you do not plan to serve all or even most of the cake at one time, it is best not to put the whipped cream on the cake before serving; serve the cake and the cream separately. Then you can easily refreeze any leftover cake.

NOTE: *I have made this with Maillard's Eagle Sweet chocolate and with Lindt Excellence. Use any semisweet or bittersweet or extra-bittersweet chocolate.*

Dione's Chocolate Roll

The first cooking programs I remember on American television were done by Dione Lucas. She was a sensational cook, showman, and teacher. When she opened an omelet restaurant in New York City called The Egg Basket, I think I was one of the first customers. The restaurant had a counter, at the end of which Dione Lucas prepared omelets for everyone to watch. I had the first stool, and I had the time of my life. She was a magician with omelets.

The restaurant served only one dessert, Dione Lucas's famous Chocolate Roll.

Some time later I considered myself ex-

tremely lucky to be able to attend cooking classes at Ms. Lucas's cooking school in the basement of a brownstone in New York City. There were about seven people in each class, and everyone cooked—all at once. We were allowed to choose whatever we wanted to cook. I chose this at my first class.

You will need a 12 by 18-inch (across the top) jelly-roll pan. That is larger than the usual hardware store size. It is available from Bridge Kitchenware, 214 East 52nd Street, New York, New York 10022.

10 PORTIONS

8 ounces semisweet chocolate (I use Maillard's Eagle Sweet; Ms. Lucas used some other)
⅓ cup boiling water
8 eggs graded "large," separated
1 cup granulated sugar

Pinch of salt
¼ cup unsweetened cocoa powder (preferably Dutch-process, to be used after the cake is baked)
Additional cocoa powder, if necessary

Adjust a rack to the middle of the oven and preheat the oven to 350 degrees. Now you must line a 12 by 18 by 1-inch jelly-roll pan with aluminum foil. Heavy-duty foil, which is wide enough for this, is too stiff. Regular lighter-weight foil is not wide enough; therefore you have to use two lengths. Tear off two 21-inch lengths of regular foil. Turn the pan upside down. Place one length of foil over the pan, shiny side against the pan, placing it off to one side so that when it is pressed into place there will be about ½ inch of foil extending above the rim of one long side, and the two short sides, of the pan. Place the second length of foil so that it partly covers the first and will extend above the other long side of the pan. With your hands fold down the sides and corners of the foil, shaping it to fit the pan. Remove the foil. Turn the pan right side up. Place the shaped foil in the pan, and press it into place.

To butter the foil, place a piece of butter in the pan and set the pan in the oven to melt the butter, then spread it with a pastry brush or with a piece of crumpled wax paper over the bottom and sides. Set aside.

Break up the chocolate and place it and the boiling water in the top of a double boiler over warm water on moderate heat and cover until the chocolate is almost melted. Then stir until completely melted and smooth. Remove the top of the double boiler. If the mixture is not completely smooth, beat it with a beater or an electric mixer, and then let stand to cool until tepid or room temperature.

Place the egg yolks in the small bowl of an electric mixer and add ¾ cup of the sugar (reserve the remaining ¼ cup of sugar). Beat at high speed for 5 minutes until almost white.

In a larger bowl fold together the cooled chocolate and the yolk mixture until smoothly colored. Set aside.

Place the egg whites and the salt in the clean large bowl of the electric mixer. With clean beaters, beat until the whites hold a soft shape. Reduce the speed to moderate and gradually add the remaining ¼ cup of sugar. Increase the speed to high again and continue to beat only until the whites just barely hold a straight point when the beaters are raised, but not until they are stiff/dry.

With a large rubber spatula fold about one third of the whites into the chocolate mixture without being thorough. Fold in another third, just briefly. Then add the remaining whites and carefully fold together until no whites show. (It was at this point that Ms. Lucas took the spatula from my hand and said, "When there are just one or two areas of white, and they rise to the top of the chocolate, smooth over them gently with the spatula, like this—instead of folding too much.")

Turn into the prepared pan. In order not to handle this any more than necessary, it is best to place it in large mounds all over the pan— instead of in one mound. Gently smooth it into the corners and level the top.

Bake for 17 minutes.

Meanwhile, wet a large linen or smooth cotton towel with cold water and wring it out.

When the cake is removed from the oven it should remain in the pan for 20 minutes, covered with the damp towel. And, to keep the steam and moisture in the cake, the damp towel should be covered with one or two layers of dry linen or cotton towel, or with foil or plastic wrap.

After 20 minutes, remove the towels from the top of the cake.

Through a fine strainer held over the top, strain the ¼ cup of cocoa all over the cake, including the edges.

Cover the cake with two overlapping lengths of wax paper and cover the wax paper with a large cookie sheet (or a tray or board or what have you). Holding the pan and the cookie sheet firmly together, turn them over. Remove the pan. Slowly remove the foil (it will come off easily).

Cover the cake with plastic wrap or wax paper to prevent drying out and let the cake cool completely while you prepare the whipped cream.

WHIPPED CREAM FILLING

Whipped cream for filling a cake roll should be just as stiff as is possible without curdling. Chilling the bowl and the beaters helps it to whip stiffly with less chance of trouble.

(Dione Lucas had her own way of doing it. She placed the cream in a large bowl, and that into a larger bowl partly filled with ice and water. And she beat with a large balloon whisk. Sometime in my youth I must have whipped too long, making butter instead of whipped cream. That must be why I have always been gun-shy of overwhipping. During that first class with Dione Lucas, I whipped the cream in a bowl set over ice and I whipped with the balloon whisk as I was told. Every time my whisking slowed down, because I thought the cream was stiff enough, no matter where she was in the room and no matter what she was doing [fluting mushrooms or decorating a ballotine] she called out, "More—it's not stiff enough." I did what she said. It became the stiffest whipped cream I had ever made and it was not butter. The ice-cold bowl seemed to have something to do with it.)

1½ cups whipping cream   1 teaspoon vanilla extract
3 tablespoons confectioners sugar

In a chilled bowl, with chilled beaters or a large whisk, whip the cream with the sugar and vanilla until the cream is firm.

Uncover the cake and place the cream by large spoonfuls over it. With a long, narrow metal spatula spread the cream evenly up to the edge on three sides of the cake; stop the cream about 1 inch short of one long side.

Using the wax paper to help, roll the cake the long way toward the long side that has the 1-inch border.

As you finish rolling the cake, the final turn should deposit the cake seam down onto a chocolate roll board or any long, narrow serving platter.

There will be a few cracks on the surface of the cake—it is to be expected. If you wish, you can sift additional cocoa over the cracks to hide them a bit.

Refrigerate, and serve cold.

Other Cakes

Oreo Cookie Cake

A Washington-based reporter from USA Today called me to say she was doing a story on bought chocolate cookies and asked if I ever buy any. (Yes, I do. Especially Afrikas from specialty food stores, and chocolate-covered graham crackers.) During our conversation she told me that Oreo cookies are the most popular commercial cookies in the world: more Oreo cookies are sold than any other. (I would have guessed chocolate chip cookies.)

The conversation inspired me to add Oreo cookies to a white sour cream cake I had been making just before the phone rang. As a matter of fact, as you will see, part of the batter was in the pan already when the phone rang. And when I baked it, it was so good I wrote the recipe that way.

See if anyone can guess before you tell them what this cake is. No one could when I served it. It is similar to a pound cake but more moist, it has a divine flavor, a delicious crust—and Oreo cookies.

16 PORTIONS

14 or 15 Oreo sandwich cookies
2¾ cups sifted all-purpose flour
½ teaspoon salt
1 teaspoon baking soda
8 ounces (2 sticks) unsalted butter
1 teaspoon vanilla extract

¼ teaspoon almond extract
1½ cups granulated sugar
3 eggs graded "large"
1 cup sour cream
Optional: confectioners sugar

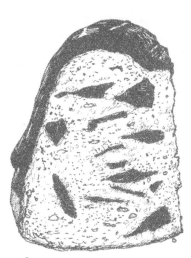

Adjust a rack one-third up from the bottom of the oven and preheat the oven to 350 degrees. You need a tube pan with a 10- to 12-cup capacity, preferably one with a rounded bottom and a fancy design (this is especially beautiful made in the swirl-patterned pan with a 12-cup capacity, see page 10). Butter the pan well (even if it has a nonstick finish) and dust all over with fine dry bread crumbs, invert it over paper, and tap out excess crumbs. Set the pan aside.

Place the cookies on a cutting board. With a sharp, heavy knife cut them one at a time into quarters; at least, that should be what you have in mind—actually, they will crumble and only a few will remain in quarters. Set aside.

Sift together the flour, salt, and baking soda and set aside.

In the large bowl of an electric mixer beat the butter until soft. Add the vanilla and almond extracts and the granulated sugar and beat to mix well. Then add the eggs one at a time, beating until thoroughly incorporated after each addition. On low speed add the dry ingredients in three additions alternately with the sour cream in two additions, scraping the bowl as necessary with a rubber spatula and beating only until incorporated after each addition.

Place about 1½ cups of the mixture by heaping teaspoonfuls in the bottom of the pan. Smooth with the bottom of a teaspoon and then, with the bottom of the spoon, form a rather shallow trench in the mixture.

Now add the cut-up Oreo cookies to the remaining batter and fold them in very gently, folding as little as possible just to mix them with the batter.

With a teaspoon place the mixture by heaping spoonfuls into the pan over the plain batter. And, with the bottom of the spoon, smooth the top. This is going to be the bottom of the cake, but the cake doesn't know that and it rises in a round dome shape. To prevent that a bit, spread the batter slightly up on the sides of the pan, leaving a depression in the middle. It will not help completely, but it can't hurt.

Bake for 1 hour until a cake tester inserted gently into the cake comes out clean and dry. When done, the top will feel slightly springy to the touch. During baking the cake will form a crack around its surface and the crack will remain pale—that is as it should be.

Cool in the pan for 15 minutes. Then cover the pan with a rack and turn the pan and rack over. Remove the pan. Let the cake cool.

The cake can be served as it is, plain (plain, but moist and wonderful) or with confectioners sugar sprinkled through a fine strainer over the top, or with the following gorgeous, thick, dark chocolate, candylike glaze just poured unevenly over the top. To glaze, place the cake on a rack over a large piece of wax paper or aluminum foil.

GLAZE

6 ounces semisweet chocolate (I have used Poulain and Maillard's chocolates for this—both delicious)

2 ounces (½ stick) unsalted butter
About 1 tablespoon whipping cream

Break up the chocolate and place it in the top of a small double boiler over warm water on low heat. Cover with a folded paper towel (to absorb steam) and with the pot cover and let cook until barely melted. Then remove the top of the double boiler and stir the chocolate until completely smooth.

Cut the butter into small pieces and add it to the chocolate, stirring until melted and smooth. Then stir in the cream very gradually (different chocolates use different amounts of cream); the mixture should be thick, just barely thin enough to flow slowly and heavily.

Pour the glaze around and around over the top of the cake, letting it run down unevenly in places.

Let the cake stand until set and then transfer to a cake plate.

Miami Beach Sour Cream Cake

This is an outstanding "plain" cake, one of the very best I ever ate. It has a gorgeous golden, honey-colored almond crust, a mild almond and lemon buttery flavor, and a fine-grained sensational texture that is truly magical.

12 TO 16 PORTIONS

About ⅔ cup blanched almonds (to prepare the pan)
3 cups twice-sifted cake flour (see Notes)
¼ teaspoon baking soda
¼ teaspoon salt
3½ ounces (⅓ cup) almond paste or marzipan

8 ounces (2 sticks) unsalted butter
½ teaspoon almond extract
2⅓ cups granulated sugar
6 eggs graded "large" or "extra-large," separated
1 cup sour cream
Finely grated rind of 1 large lemon

Adjust a rack one-third up from the bottom of the oven and preheat the oven to 300 degrees. Butter a 10 by 4- or 4¼-inch tube pan (that is, a straight-sided pan, like an angel-food pan, with a 16-cup capacity); butter the pan even if it has a nonstick finish.

Grind the almonds in a food processor by turning the machine on/off quickly a few times, and then letting it run for about 30 seconds until most of the nuts are rather fine, with a few still in small pieces. Or grind the nuts in any nut grinder. They do not have to be completely powdered.

Turn the ground nuts into the buttered pan. Hold the pan over paper and rotate the pan so that the nuts coat the entire buttered surface. To make the nuts stick to the center tube you must pick them up with your fingers and sprinkle them onto the tube. Loose nuts that do not stick to the pan may just be sprinkled onto the bottom of the pan. Set the pan aside.

Sift the flour twice more with the baking soda and salt (see Notes) and set aside.

In the large bowl of an electric mixer beat the almond paste or marzipan with the butter until soft and smooth. Beat in the almond extract. Then add the sugar and beat until thoroughly mixed. Add the yolks and beat, scraping the bowl with a rubber spatula, until thoroughly mixed.

On low speed beat in ½ cup of the sour cream, then half of the sifted dry ingredients, the remaining ½ cup of sour cream, and the remaining dry ingredients, scraping the bowl and beating only until mixed.

Remove the bowl from the mixer and stir in the grated lemon rind.

In a small bowl (with clean beaters) beat the egg whites until they hold a definite shape when the beaters are raised, but not until the whites are stiff or dry. (Since these whites are not beaten with any sugar added to them—which would help to keep them creamy [see Notes]—it is especially important not to overbeat them or they will be too dry to fold in properly.)

With a large rubber spatula stir a few tablespoons of the whites into the batter and then, in about three additions, fold in the remaining whites, without being thorough about the folding until the end.

Turn the mixture into the prepared pan.

To level the top, briskly rotate the pan a bit first in one direction, then the other. The pan will be only half filled—it is OK.

Bake for 1½ hours. During baking the cake will rise to ½ inch or 1 inch below the top of the pan. When the cake is done, a cake tester inserted gently into the cake will come out clean and the top will spring back if it is pressed gently with a fingertip. (There will be a shallow crack around the circumference of the cake—it is all right.)

Remove from the oven and let stand for 20 minutes, during which time the cake will sink down about an inch—that's all right too.

Cover with a rack, turn the pan and rack over, remove the pan, cover with another rack and turn over again, leaving the cake right side up to cool completely.

Transfer the cooled cake to a cake plate. You could sprinkle confectioners sugar on the top, but I think that this is too good to need or want anything at all.

NOTES: 1. *To make sure we understand each other, the flour for this cake must be cake flour, and it should be sifted twice before it is measured. Then it should be sifted twice again after it is measured, with the baking soda and salt.*

2. *I tried this recipe with some of the sugar beaten into the egg whites and I tried it the way the recipe is written, with the egg whites beaten without any of the sugar. It was not easy for me to decide, but after due and serious consideration I came to the conclusion that the cake is better this way.*

VARIATION: *The wife of the mayor of Miami Beach asked me if I would create a cake specifically for Miami Beach. That was a great challenge, because people who live here in Miami Beach know a good cake when they taste one, and they expect the best.*

I had just been working on the recipe for Miami Beach Sour Cream Cake. I thought of all the people I know here, and I came to the conclusion that they would approve. But to make it especially appropriate, I changed it slightly to an orange cake.

MIAMI BEACH ORANGE CAKE: *Follow the above recipe with these additions.*

Grate the rind of 1 large or 2 medium-size deep-colored oranges fine. Stir the rind into the cake mixture along with the grated lemon rind; that is, just before you beat the egg whites.

While the cake is baking, prepare this Orange Glaze.

ORANGE GLAZE

¾ cup orange juice   ¼ cup granulated sugar

In a small saucepan mix about ¼ cup of the juice with the sugar and stir over moderate heat until the sugar is dissolved. Add the warm mixture to the remaining ½ cup of juice.

When you remove the cake from the oven, let it stand for about 5 minutes. Then slowly spoon the glaze over the cake. After the glaze is all applied, let the cake stand for 15 to 20 minutes. Then cover with a large flat cake pan and carefully turn the plate and the pan over. Remove the pan, leaving the cake upside down. Do not try to move the cake; it is too moist.

Old-Fashioned Coconut Cake

This is a pretty little black and white coconut cake; the shallow top part of the cake is dark chocolate, and you will wish for more of it.

You will need a fancy tube pan with a 10- to 12-cup capacity; the cake looks lovely in the 12-cup swirl pan (see page 10).

(see page 10).

12 PORTIONS

1¼ cups sifted all-purpose flour
1¼ cups sifted cake flour
1 teaspoon double-acting baking powder
¼ teaspoon salt
8 ounces (2 sticks) unsalted butter
1 tablespoon vanilla extract
1 teaspoon coconut extract
¼ teaspoon almond extract

1 1-pound box (3¼ cups, packed) confectioners sugar (it can be unsifted)
4 eggs graded "large"
1 cup whipping cream
2 tablespoons unsweetened cocoa powder (preferably Dutch-process)
3½ ounces (1 cup, firmly packed) shredded coconut (it can be sweetened or unsweetened)

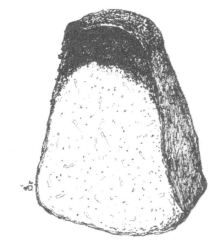

Adjust a rack one-third up from the bottom of the oven and preheat the oven to 350 degrees. Butter a 10- to 12-cup fancy tube pan (even if it has a nonstick finish), dust the pan all over with fine dry bread crumbs (use your fingers to crumb the tube), tilt the pan from side to side over paper, and then invert it and tap out excess crumbs. Set aside.

Sift together both of the flours with the baking powder and salt and set aside.

In the large bowl of an electric mixer beat the butter to soften. Add the vanilla, coconut, and almond extracts and the sugar and beat to mix, scraping the bowl as necessary with a rubber spatula. Add the eggs one at a time, beating well after each addition. On low speed add the sifted dry ingredients in three additions alternately with the cream in two additions.

Remove the bowl from the mixer. Transfer 1 cup of the batter to a small bowl. Add the cocoa to the small bowl and stir well to mix. Add the coconut to the remaining batter and stir to mix.

Place teaspoonfuls of the chocolate mixture just touching one another in the bottom of the pan. Do not spread to smooth. Then pour in the coconut mixture. Smooth the top. The cake wants to rise high in the middle, around the tube, and will be served upside down; therefore use the bottom of a large spoon to spread the dough out toward the rim of the pan, making it higher around the rim and lower around the tube. (This will not make the top as flat as you might like, but it will help a bit.)

Bake for 1 hour and about 25 minutes until a cake tester inserted gently in the cake comes out clean.

Let the cake cool in the pan for 15 to 20 minutes. Then cover the pan with a rack, turn the pan and the rack over, and remove the pan. Unless the pan does not want to be removed, in which case simply bang the pan and the rack together against a hard surface until the cake slips out.

Let the cake stand until it is completely cool and then for several hours more before serving.

Key West Rum Cake

This is from the southern tip of Florida, where it is called Pirate's Cake. It is similar to a pound cake but the top is dark, semisweet, candylike chocolate and the bottom, which is light colored, is flavored with almond and loaded with pecans. The entire cake is drenched with a powerful rum syrup. The combination of flavors is sensational, and when you cut into the cake you will be surprised and delighted to see what the chocolate mixture did. Also, it keeps well. (We took one of these, just wrapped in plastic, on a car trip from Florida to New York during a heat wave. Four days after we left home we brought it to a luncheon at a friend's house. It was divine.) This is an old recipe that many old-time local cooks treasure as a secret.

You will need a tube pan with a 13- or 14-cup capacity it is gorgeous in the "New Cake Pan" (see page 10) with a 10–14-cup capacity and no design or you can use any other with a design.

10 TO 12 PORTIONS

2 cups sifted all-purpose flour
2 teaspoons double-acting baking powder
¼ teaspoon salt
2 ounces semisweet chocolate
1 ounce unsweetened chocolate
8 ounces (2 sticks) unsalted butter
1 teaspoon vanilla extract

½ teaspoon almond extract
1½ cups granulated sugar
4 eggs graded "large"
¼ teaspoon baking soda
7 ounces (2 cups) toasted pecans (see To Toast Pecans, page 7), broken into medium-size pieces

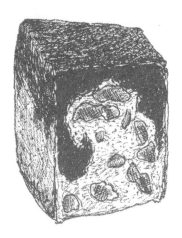

Adjust a rack one-third up from the bottom of the oven and preheat the oven to 350 degrees. Butter a tube pan with a 10- to 14-cup capacity and dust all over with fine dry bread crumbs (use your fingers to crumb the tube), invert the pan over paper and tap lightly to shake out excess crumbs. Set aside.

Sift together the flour, baking powder, and salt and set aside.

Place both of the chocolates in the top of a small double boiler over warm water on moderate heat. Cover the pot with a folded paper towel (to absorb steam) and with the pot cover. Let stand over the heat until the chocolate is almost all melted, then stir until completely melted. Remove the top of the double boiler and set aside.

In the large bowl of an electric mixer beat the butter until soft. Beat in the vanilla and almond extracts and then the sugar. Add the eggs one at a time, beating until thoroughly incorporated after each addition. Then, on low speed, gradually add the sifted dry ingredients, scraping the bowl as necessary with a rubber spatula and beating only until incorporated.

With your finger scrape the beaters and then replace them, unwashed, in the mixer. Remove the bowl from the mixer. Remove 1 cup of the batter and place it in the small bowl of the mixer. Add the baking soda and the melted chocolate and beat until mixed.

Use a teaspoon (a regular teaspoon—not a measuring spoon) to place the chocolate batter in the bottom of the pan. With the bottom of the spoon spread it to make a rather smooth layer.

Now mix the pecans into the remaining cake batter and place it, with a teaspoon or a tablespoon, evenly over the chocolate layer. Smooth the top.

Bake for 1 hour until a cake tester inserted gently into the middle of the cake comes out clean.

While the cake is baking, prepare the syrup.

RUM SYRUP

½ cup water
⅔ cup granulated sugar

⅔ cup light rum (I use Bacardi Silver Label)
1 tablespoon lime juice

Stir the water and sugar in a small saucepan over moderate heat until the mixture comes to a boil. Let boil without stirring for 5 minutes. Remove from the heat and let stand until almost completely cool. Then stir in the rum and lime juice.

When the cake is done let it cool in the pan for 15 minutes. Spoon or brush the syrup over the hot cake until it all is absorbed.

Then, while the cake is still hot, place a flat cake plate over the pan and, holding the plate and pan firmly together, turn them over. Now remove the pan and let the cake cool.

Do not try to cut the slices too thin—they will crumble.

Walnut Cake

This fabulous "plain" cake has a luxurious flavor and an irresistible crunchy and nutty crust. The pan is coated with butter and ground nuts which, with long, slow baking, become deliciously crusty. The cake is loaded with ground nuts, which keep it moist and rich. It is wonderful for any occasion,

or make it as a delicious gift for someone very special.

It is easiest to prepare the nuts in a food processor.

12 PORTIONS

9 ounces (2½ cups) walnuts
2 cups sifted all-purpose flour
1 teaspoon double-acting baking powder
½ teaspoon salt
½ teaspoon mace or nutmeg
8 ounces (2 sticks) unsalted butter

1 teaspoon vanilla extract
¼ teaspoon almond extract
1 tablespoon plus 2 teaspoons brandy
2 cups granulated sugar
5 eggs graded "large"

Adjust a rack one-third up from the bottom of the oven and preheat the oven to 325 degrees. You will need a tube pan that has at least a 9-cup capacity—I have used one with a swirl pattern (see page 10) and also a Bundt pan (this can be made in a slightly larger pan and still look nice). Butter the pan well, even if it has a nonstick finish; it must be heavily buttered (best done with soft butter—not cold and firm, and not melted). Set aside for a moment.

Place 1 cup of the nuts (reserve the remaining 1½ cups of nuts) in the bowl of a food processor fitted with the metal chopping blade. Process on/off quickly 8 to 10 times, or for 8 to 10 seconds. Some of the nuts·will be ground, some will remain in small pieces—that is correct.

Turn the nuts into the buttered pan (do not wash the processor now). Over a piece of paper tilt the pan in all directions to coat it generously with the nuts. The only way to get the nuts onto the center tube is to sprinkle them on with your fingertips. Then, over the paper, invert the pan for a moment—do not tap the pan—to allow a spoonful or two of the loose nuts to fall onto the paper. If more than that should fall out of the pan pick up the excess with your fingertips and sprinkle them back over the bottom of the pan. Set the pan aside. (Reserve the spoonful or two of ground nuts to sprinkle over the top of the cake when it is in the pan.)

Place the remaining 1½ cups of nuts in the processor bowl and process on/off 5 or 6 times (5 or 6 seconds). The nuts should have a few slightly larger pieces than those that were used for coating the pan. Set the nuts aside.

Sift together the flour, baking powder, salt, and mace or nutmeg. Set aside.

In the large bowl of an electric mixer beat the butter until soft. Beat in the vanilla and almond extracts and the brandy.

Add the sugar and beat for about a minute. (Occasionally, when someone has trouble with a recipe like this, which is similar to a classic pound cake, we have found that the trouble was caused by overbeating. Do not beat until the sugar liquefies.)

Then add the eggs one at a time, scraping the bowl with a rubber spatula as necessary and beating until incorporated after each addition. Beat for about a minute after the last addition. On low speed gradually add the sifted dry ingredients and beat only until smoothly incorporated.

Remove the bowl from the mixer and stir in the reserved 1½ cups of ground nuts.

Turn the batter into the prepared pan and smooth the top. With your fingertips sprinkle the reserved 1 or 2 spoonfuls of ground nuts over the top of the cake.

Bake for about 1¾ hours until a cake tester inserted gently in the middle of the cake comes out clean. The top of the cake forms a crack during baking—it is all right.

Let the cake stand in the pan for 20 to 30 minutes. Then cover it with a cake plate. Hold the pan and plate firmly together and turn them over, then lift off the pan; if it does not slip right off, bang both the pan and the plate together against the counter top—but be gentle.

Let the cake stand until cool. Then chill it in the freezer or refrigerator before slicing. After the cake has been chilled it can wait at room temperature, can be stored in the refrigerator, or can be frozen.

When this is cold it slices beautifully with any really sharp knife, but if it is to be sliced at room temperature, use a serrated French bread knife.

Walnut Rum-Raisin Cake

The early New England sailors were given a ration of rum every day, a custom carried over to the New World from England. Rum was a popular drink as well as a popular ingredient in baking and dessert making.

This pretty cake made in a tube pan is loaded with rum-soaked raisins, and then generously basted with a tropical rum sauce. It is moist, keeps well, is easy to make, and especially delicious.

Soak the raisins at least overnight before making the cake.

12 PORTIONS

5 ounces (1 cup) light or dark raisins or a mixture of both
⅓ cup dark rum (I use Myers's, from Kingston, Jamaica)
8½ ounces (2¼ cups) walnuts (see Note)
2½ cups sifted all-purpose flour
2 teaspoons double-acting baking powder
1 teaspoon baking soda
¼ teaspoon salt

¼ teaspoon nutmeg
8 ounces (2 sticks) unsalted butter
1 teaspoon vanilla extract
1 cup granulated sugar
2 eggs graded "large"
1 cup buttermilk
Finely grated rind of 2 lemons
Finely grated rind of 2 oranges
Optional: confectioners sugar

Soak the raisins with the rum in a covered jar overnight, turning the jar occasionally (if the jar might leak, place it in a small bowl).

Adjust a rack one-third up from the bottom of the oven and preheat the oven to 350 degrees. Butter a fancy tube pan (even if it is a nonstick pan) with at least a 9-cup capacity.

Place ¾ cup of the walnuts (reserve the remaining 1½ cups of walnuts) in the bowl of a food processor fitted with the metal chopping blade and process on/off 10 to 12 times (10 to 12 seconds) until the nuts are chopped medium-fine. Or chop them any other way. To coat the pan place the chopped nuts into the buttered pan and turn the pan from side to side to cover it all with the nuts. Sprinkle the nuts with your fingers onto the tube of the pan. Excess or loose nuts may remain in the bottom of the pan. Set aside.

Place the remaining 1½ cups of walnuts in the food processor bowl and process on/off 6 to 8 times (6 to 8 seconds) until the nuts are chopped to medium-size pieces. Or chop them any other way. Set aside.

Sift together the flour, baking powder, baking soda, salt, and nutmeg. Set aside.

In the large bowl of an electric mixer beat the butter until it is soft. Add the vanilla and sugar and beat to mix. Then beat in the eggs. On low speed add the sifted dry ingredients in three additions alternately with the buttermilk in two additions.

Remove the bowl from the mixer, and stir in the lemon rind, orange rind and the rum-soaked raisins along with any rum that has not been absorbed. Stir the reserved nuts into the batter.

Turn into the prepared pan and smooth the top.

Bake for 55 to 60 minutes until a cake tester inserted gently in the middle comes out clean.

Let the cake stand in the pan for about 10 minutes. Meanwhile, prepare the Rum Sauce.

½ cup granulated sugar
¼ cup water
¼ cup orange juice

3 tablespoons lemon or lime juice
¼ cup dark rum

In a small saucepan over moderate heat stir the sugar and water until the mixture comes to a boil. Let boil without stirring for 2 minutes. Remove from the heat. Cool for a few minutes. Stir in the orange and lemon or lime juices, and then the rum.

Now, to remove the cake from the pan, cover it with a cake plate. Holding the cake plate and the pan firmly together, turn them over and remove the cake pan.

With a wide pastry brush, brush the warm sauce all over the warm cake; the cake will easily absorb all the sauce. Let cool.

If you wish, sprinkle confectioners sugar through a fine strainer over the top before serving.

NOTE: *After this recipe was printed in* The New York Times *I received a lovely letter from a lady whose husband is allergic to walnuts. She substituted almonds and said, "I can't believe it would taste better with walnuts! It's a wonderful cake—and perfect for the holidays."*

Marbleized Spice Cake

Marble cakes intrigue me, visually as well as otherwise. This is one of the most visual—and delicious. But you need a special pan, which, until recently, I could not find. Now that Mr. Fred Bridge has his "New Cake Pan" (see page 10) we can all make this old Southern beauty, which is truly a glorious sight to behold. It is a spice cake.

You will make two batters: a dark one with molasses, yogurt, cocoa, and spices, and a light one with vanilla and almond.

This recipe is adapted from one in Just Desserts *by Helen McCully (Ivan Obolensky, Inc., 1961).*

12 TO 16 PORTIONS

DARK BATTER

2 cups sifted cake flour
1 teaspoon baking soda
1 teaspoon cinnamon
½ teaspoon nutmeg
½ teaspoon ground ginger
¼ teaspoon salt
1 tablespoon unsweetened cocoa powder
  (preferably Dutch-process)

1 teaspoon powdered (not granular) instant coffee or espresso
4 ounces (1 stick) unsalted butter
1 cup dark brown sugar, firmly packed
4 egg yolks from eggs graded "large" (you will use the whites in the light batter)
½ cup dark molasses
1 cup unflavored yogurt (I use Dannon)

Adjust a rack one-third up from the bottom of the oven and preheat the oven to 350 degrees. You need a tube pan with a 14-cup capacity; the new cake pan that I mention above measures 9½ inches in diameter and 3¾ inches in depth and has a wider tube in the middle than most tube pans. Butter the pan and then dust it all over with fine dry bread crumbs; to

coat the center tube with crumbs it is necessary to sprinkle them on with your fingertips. Invert the pan over paper and tap to shake out excess. Set the pan aside.

Sift together the flour, baking soda, cinnamon, nutmeg, ginger, salt, cocoa, and coffee or espresso and set aside. In the large bowl of an electric mixer beat the butter until soft, add the sugar and beat to mix, then add the yolks all at once with the molasses. Beat until smooth and slightly lighter in color. On low speed add the sifted dry ingredients in three additions alternately with the yogurt in two additions. Beat, scraping the bowl with a rubber spatula as necessary, until the ingredients are smooth. Set aside, or, if you do not have another large bowl for the mixer and another set of beaters, transfer the mixture to any other bowl and then set aside.

LIGHT BATTER

2½ cups sifted cake flour
2 teaspoons double-acting baking powder
¼ teaspoon salt
4 ounces (1 stick) unsalted butter
1 teaspoon vanilla extract

¼ teaspoon almond extract
1 cup granulated sugar
¾ cup milk
4 egg whites (left from using the yolks in the
    dark batter)

Sift together the flour, baking powder, and salt and set aside. In the large bowl of an electric mixer beat the butter until soft. Add both extracts and ¾ cup of the sugar (reserve the remaining ¼ cup) and beat until thoroughly mixed. On low speed add the sifted dry ingredients in three additions alternately with the milk in two additions. Beat, scraping the bowl with a rubber spatula as necessary, until the ingredients are smooth. Set aside.

In the small bowl of an electric mixer (with clean beaters) beat the egg whites until they hold a soft shape. Reduce the speed to moderate and gradually add the remaining ¼ cup of sugar. Increase the speed again and beat briefly only until the whites hold a definite shape.

With a rubber spatula fold the egg whites, in three additions (do not fold thoroughly until the end), into the batter.

Now comes the fun: putting the two batters into the pan in a pattern. Here's how. Use two large serving spoons, one for each batter. Start with the dark batter. Place 4 or 5 spoonfuls in the bottom of the pan, leaving a space between each of the dark mounds (for some of the light cake). Then place a spoonful of the light batter in each space and place a spoonful of the light over each mound of dark. Continue alternating the batters.

Rotate the pan briefly and briskly, first in one direction, then the other, to smooth the top.

Bake for about 1 hour until a cake tester inserted gently to the bottom comes out clean. Cool the cake in the pan for 10 minutes. Then cover with a rack, turn the pan and the rack over, remove the pan—(gorgeous?)—and let stand until cool.

NOTE: *We love this plain, as is, with nothing. But we also love it with ice cream and chocolate sauce; a sensational party dessert.*

Other Cakes 133

Mocha Chip Chiffon Cake

The original chiffon cake was flavored with orange juice and orange rind. I have heard of chiffon cakes in a variety of flavors. But this one is brand new, inspired by the success of mocha chip ice cream.

This is not too sweet, with a fascinating coffee flavor and bits of semisweet chocolate all through it.

It is lovely with tea or coffee, or along with ice cream and/or fruit for a fancy dessert.

3 ounces semisweet chocolate (see Note)
2 cups sifted all-purpose flour
1¾ cups granulated sugar
1 tablespoon powdered (not granular) instant
    coffee or espresso
1 tablespoon double-acting baking powder
½ teaspoon salt
½ cup tasteless salad oil

7 eggs graded "large," separated
½ cup Kahlua or Tia Maria or any coffee-flavored
    liqueur
¼ cup cold tap water
2 teaspoons vanilla extract
½ teaspoon cream of tartar
Optional: confectioners sugar

Adjust a rack one-third up from the bottom of the oven and preheat the oven to 325 degrees. You will need a 10 by 4-inch tube pan (angel-food cake pan); it must not be a nonstick pan, and it must be the kind that is made in two pieces—the bottom and tube in one piece and the sides in a separate piece. Do not butter the pan.

On a board, with a heavy knife, cut the chocolate into small pieces. Aim for pieces about ¼ inch in diameter, although some pieces will be larger and some will be smaller and some will be crumbs; do not leave any pieces larger than ¼ inch because this is a very light cake and larger pieces might sink to the bottom. Set aside.

Into a large mixing bowl sift together the flour, 1¼ cups of the sugar, the powdered instant coffee or espresso, the baking powder, and the salt.

With a rubber spatula make a wide well in the middle of the dry ingredients. Add, in the following order, without mixing, the oil, egg yolks (reserve the egg whites), coffee liqueur, water, and vanilla. With a large or medium-size strong wire whisk beat the ingredients until smooth. Remove the whisk and with a rubber spatula stir/fold in the chopped chocolate. Set aside.

In the large bowl of an electric mixer beat the egg whites until foamy, add the cream of tartar, and beat at high speed until the whites hold a soft shape. Reduce the speed to moderate and gradually add the remaining ½ cup of sugar. Then, on high speed again, beat until the whites hold a straight and stiff peak when the beaters are withdrawn. For this recipe the whites should be stiffer than for most; when the whites are firm beat for 1 minute more to be sure. That should make them just right; more beating than that might make them too dry.

If you have a large-size rubber spatula use it now; if not, the regular size is the next best thing. In three additions fold about three quarters of the yolk mixture into the whites, without being too thorough (without being even a bit thorough). Then fold the whites into the remaining yolk mixture, this time being thorough enough to just barely incorporate the mixtures.

Gently pour the batter into the cake pan and gently smooth the top if necessary.

Bake for 1 hour and 10 to 15 minutes until the top springs back when pressed gently with a fingertip. The top will crack during baking—it is OK.

Immediately turn the pan over and "hang" it upside down over the neck of a narrow bottle. (Even if your pan has a raised tube in the middle or three little feet on the sides, they probably will not raise the cake enough to keep it off the counter top.)

When the cake is completely cool remove it from the pan as follows. You will need a sharp knife with a firm blade about 6 inches long. Insert the knife between the cake and the rim of the pan, all the way to the bottom, pressing the blade firmly against the rim in order not to cut into the cake. With short up and down motions saw all around the cake, continuing to press the blade against the pan. Then cut around the tube (if possible, use a knife with a narrower blade here).

Remove the sides of the pan by pushing up on the bottom of the pan. Then, carefully, cut the bottom of the cake away from the pan, still pressing against the pan.

Cover the cake with a wide, flat cake plate, turn the cake and the plate over, and lift off the bottom of the pan, leaving the cake upside down.

Sprinkle the optional confectioners sugar over the cake through a fine strainer, although the dramatic height of this cake (almost 5½ inches) is beauty enough.

Use a serrated bread knife and a sawing motion to slice the cake without squashing it.

NOTE: *I have used Tobler Tradition and Tobler Extra-Bittersweet. Use any good chocolate, preferably semisweet or bittersweet, and preferably a chocolate that is a thin bar rather than a thick one; it will be easier to cut up.*

The Farmer's Daughter's Cake

An 8-inch square, single-layer white cake—light and tender but with body—covered with an old-fashioned chocolate icing. Since this is made with whipping cream (and no butter), my guess is that the recipe was perfected on a dairy farm where they had plenty of real heavy cream. But it works with the kind of cream available for sale in stores today.

This is so easy it is hard to believe.

9 SQUARES

2 cups sifted all-purpose flour
2 teaspoons double-acting baking powder
¼ teaspoon salt
2 eggs graded "large"

1 teaspoon vanilla extract
¼ teaspoon almond extract
1 cup granulated sugar
1 cup whipping cream (not whipped)

Adjust a rack to the middle of the oven and preheat the oven to 350 degrees. Butter an 8 by 8 by 2-inch square cake pan, dust all over lightly with fine dry bread crumbs, invert it over paper, and tap lightly to shake out excess crumbs. Set aside.

Sift together the flour, baking powder, and salt and set aside.

In the small bowl of an electric mixer beat the eggs to mix, beat in the vanilla and almond extracts and the sugar to mix. Then beat in the cream and finally, on low speed, add the sifted dry ingredients and beat only until smooth.

Pour into the prepared pan and if necessary smooth the top.

Bake for 35 to 40 minutes until the cake just begins to come away from the sides of the pan and until a toothpick inserted gently in the middle comes out clean. (The cake will rise with a domed top but will flatten as it cools; the top might or might not form a crack during baking—if it does it is all right.)

Remove from the oven and let stand for 5 minutes, then cut around the sides carefully to release, and let stand for 5 minutes more.

Cover with a rack, turn the pan and rack over, remove the pan, and let the cake stand upside down to cool. When cool, transfer the cake bottom side up to a cake plate or a cutting board. There is a chance that more icing might run down on the sides than you want; therefore, protect the plate by sliding a 12 by 2- to 3-inch piece of baking pan liner paper or aluminum foil under each side of the cake.

The icing can be made up to the beating stage while the cake is baking, or while it is cooling.

OLD-FASHIONED CHOCOLATE ICING

Gorgeous—dark and delicious and very easy.

4 ounces unsweetened chocolate
½ cup cold milk
1⅓ cups granulated sugar

2 egg yolks
1 tablespoon plus 1 teaspoon unsalted butter
1 teaspoon vanilla extract

Place the chocolate, milk, and sugar in a small, heavy saucepan over moderate heat. Stir until the chocolate is melted and the sugar is dissolved (this does not have to boil). Remove from the heat and let stand for a minute.

In a small bowl stir the yolks lightly with a small wire whisk just to mix. Very gradually stir in about half of the warm chocolate mixture, and then add the yolks to the remaining warm chocolate mixture.

Cook over low heat, stirring, for 1 minute. (The mixture might not look smooth now, but if you did not add the warm chocolate mixture to the yolks too quickly, it will be OK.)

Transfer to the small bowl of an electric mixer and stir in the butter and vanilla. Let stand until cool. (Up to this point the icing can be made while the cake is baking or cooling if you wish.)

Then beat the icing at high speed for about 10 to 15 minutes (reduce the speed as necessary if the icing splashes) until the mixture is smooth/shiny/very slightly paler in color, and as thick as a heavy syrup.

If you pour the icing all at once now onto the cake, too much of it will run down the sides. Pour about half of it onto the cake. Let stand for a minute or so, then pour a bit of the icing onto the middle and toward the corners of the cake. Wait another minute or so. Now you can probably pour the remaining icing over the top, and probably only very little will run down the sides (which is the way it should be), but if it still seems too runny, pour more gradually. It is not necessary to smooth the top.

Let the cake stand for a few hours for the icing to set. The icing will become dry to the touch but it will remain deliciously soft.

Slowly pull each piece of paper or foil out toward a narrow end.

Ginger Ginger Cake

This is not even remotely like "gingerbread." It is a moist sour cream cake made gingery with generous amounts of both fresh and candied ginger. The texture is somewhat like a pound cake but more moist than most. During baking part of the candied ginger will settle to the bottom of the cake, which will become the top when it is turned out of the pan, and it will have a deliciously chewy and candylike texture. I made this for a friend who is crazy about candied ginger; he said the longer he kept it the better it got.

This has no salt; it doesn't need it.

16 TO 24 SLICES

3 cups sifted all-purpose flour
¼ teaspoon baking soda
6 ounces (about ¾ cup) candied ginger
3 to 4 ounces (a piece 3 to 4 inches long and about 1 inch thick) fresh ginger (see Fresh Ginger, page 8)

8 ounces (2 sticks) unsalted butter
2¾ cups granulated sugar
6 eggs graded "large," separated
1 cup sour cream

Adjust a rack one-third up from the bottom of the oven and preheat the oven to 350 degrees. Butter a 10 by 4¼-inch angel-food tube pan (it may be a one-piece nonstick pan) with an 18-cup capacity; butter the pan even if it has a nonstick finish. Dust it all over with fine dry bread crumbs, invert it over paper and shake out excess crumbs, and set the pan aside.

Sift together the flour and baking soda and set aside.

Cut the candied ginger into ¼- to ⅓-inch pieces and set aside.

Grate the fresh ginger and set aside.

In the large bowl of an electric mixer beat the butter until it is soft. Gradually beat in the grated fresh ginger and 2¼ cups of the sugar (reserve the remaining ½ cup). Then beat in the egg yolks.

On low speed gradually add the sifted dry ingredients in two additions alternately with the sour cream in one addition. Remove the bowl from the mixer.

Stir in half of the diced candied ginger (reserve the remaining diced candied ginger). Set aside.

In the small bowl of the electric mixer (with clean beaters) beat the egg whites until they hold a soft shape. Reduce the speed to moderate and gradually add the remaining ½ cup of sugar. Then increase the speed again and beat only until the whites hold a peak when the beaters are withdrawn.

In three additions fold the whites into the batter; with the first two additions fold only partially—do not be too thorough—and with the last addition do not fold more than necessary to incorporate the whites.

Turn into the prepared pan and smooth the top. Sprinkle the reserved candied ginger on top.

Bake for about 1½ hours until a cake tester inserted gently into the cake comes out clean. (The cake will not rise to the top of the pan.)

Let the cake cool in the pan for 10 to 15 minutes. (The cake will sink about an inch as it cools.) Then cover the pan with a cake plate and, holding the pan and the plate firmly together, turn them over and remove the pan and let the cake cool.

White Pepper and Ginger Lemon Cake

This is a brand-new version of an Early American buttermilk cake (white pepper and fresh ginger are "hot" now) similar to a pound cake but so rich and moist it is almost a pudding with a fascinating combination of dynamite flavors. Beautiful, delicious, unusual, and so easy it is a piece of cake.

8 TO 10 PORTIONS

Finely grated rind of 2 large lemons
2 tablespoons lemon juice
½ ounce (a piece about ½ inch long and 1 inch wide) fresh ginger (see Fresh Ginger, page 8)
3 cups sifted all-purpose flour
¾ teaspoon baking soda
¾ teaspoon double-acting baking powder

½ teaspoon salt
2 teaspoons moderately packed, finely ground white pepper (preferably freshly ground)
8 ounces (2 sticks) unsalted butter
1¾ cups granulated sugar
3 eggs graded "large" or "extra-large"
1 cup buttermilk

Adjust a rack one-third up from the bottom of the oven and preheat the oven to 325 degrees. Butter a 10- to 12-cup tube pan with a design (butter the pan even if it has a nonstick finish), dust it with fine dry bread crumbs (be sure to butter and crumb the center tube—sprinkle the crumbs on the tube with your fingers), then invert it over paper, tap to shake out excess crumbs, and set aside.

In a small cup mix the rind and juice.

Grate the fresh ginger and add it to the lemon juice mixture.

Sift together the flour, baking soda, baking powder, salt, and pepper, and set aside.

In the large bowl of an electric mixer beat the butter until soft. Add the sugar and beat for about a minute. Then add the eggs one at a time, beating until incorporated after each addition.

On low speed add the sifted dry ingredients in three additions alternately with the buttermilk in two additions. Remove from the mixer and stir in the lemon and ginger mixture.

Turn into the prepared pan. Smooth the top by briskly rotating the pan first in one direction, then the other (the batter will be rather heavy).

Bake for 1 hour and 15 to 20 minutes until a cake tester inserted gently in the middle comes out clean and dry. (If you have used a 12-cup pan the cake will not rise to the top of the pan—it is all right.)

Let the cake stand in the pan for 5 to 10 minutes. Cover with a rack, turn the pan and rack over, remove the pan, and place the cake on the rack over a large piece of aluminum foil (to catch drippings of the glaze).

LEMON GLAZE
This should be mixed as soon as the cake is put in the oven.

⅓ cup lemon juice   ½ cup granulated sugar

Stir the juice and sugar together and let stand while the cake is baking.

When the cake is removed from the pan, stir the glaze and, with a pastry brush, brush it all over the cake (including the hole in the middle). The cake will easily absorb it all. If some of the glaze drips onto the foil, transfer the rack and pour the glaze that dripped back over the cake.

Let stand until cool.

With two wide metal spatulas, or using a flat-sided cookie sheet as a spatula, transfer to a serving plate. This is even better if it ages for a day or two—the spicy hotness cools a bit as it ages—covered with plastic wrap.

Serve in thin slices.

NOTE: *From 1 to 10, Ralph rates this a 4 for hotness; I give it a 7. It can be made more or less hot with more or less pepper and ginger.*

Sweet Breads

Banana Carrot Loaf

Banana cakes and carrot cakes are two American favorites; this combines both in one delicious, slightly spicy loaf that perfumes the house while baking and drives everyone crazy with desire. This is homey and old-fashioned, and yet it is brand new.

5 ounces (1 cup) light raisins
About 3 medium-size carrots (to make 1 packed cup, grated)
2 cups sifted all-purpose flour
1 tablespoon unsweetened cocoa powder (preferably Dutch-process)
1 teaspoon baking soda
1 teaspoon cinnamon

¼ teaspoon nutmeg
½ teaspoon salt
2 eggs graded "large" or "extra-large"
1 cup dark brown sugar, firmly packed
¾ cup tasteless salad oil
About 2 large fully ripened bananas (to make 1 cup, mashed)

Adjust a rack one-third up from the bottom of the oven and preheat the oven to 350 degrees. Butter a 9 by 5 by 3-inch loaf pan (8-cup capacity) and dust it with fine dry bread crumbs or with toasted wheat germ; invert the pan over paper and tap lightly to shake out excess crumbs. Set aside.

Steam the raisins as follows. Place them in a strainer or a colander over shallow hot water in a saucepan over moderate heat, cover, and let the water boil for about 5 minutes. Then remove the strainer or colander and set aside.

Wash the carrots with a brush or vegetable sponge (it is not necessary to peel them) and grate them on a fine, medium, or coarse grater. On a four-sided standing metal grater use the side that has small round—not diamond-shaped—openings (look at the shape of the openings from the inside or underside of the grater). You need 1 cup, packed. Set aside.

Sift together the flour, cocoa, baking soda, cinnamon, nutmeg, and salt and set aside.

In the large bowl of an electric mixer beat the eggs just to mix. Beat in the sugar and oil.

Peel the bananas and mash them on a wide, flat plate with a table fork; they should be coarsely mashed and slightly lumpy. (Do not use a processor or blender, which might mash them too much.)

Beat the bananas, raisins, and carrots into the egg mixture. Then on low speed add the sifted dry ingredients and beat, scraping the bowl with a rubber spatula, until thoroughly mixed.

Turn the mixture into the prepared pan and smooth the top. Bake for about 1 hour and 10 minutes until a cake tester inserted gently into the middle of the loaf, all the way to the bottom, comes out clean. Toward the end of the baking time, if the top of the loaf becomes too dark, cover it loosely with foil. During baking the top of the loaf will form a wide crack—that is OK.

Cool the loaf in the pan for 10 or 15 minutes. Then cover the pan with a rack, hold the pan and rack together and turn them over, remove the pan, cover with another rack, and gently and carefully turn both racks over again, leaving the loaf right side up to cool on the rack.

Peanut Banana Bread

Years ago my husband owned a restaurant in Miami Beach. During that time the Republican party held their convention in Miami Beach to nominate a candidate for the presidency. I thought it would be a good idea, in order to get some publicity for the restaurant, to serve elephant meat omelets (the symbol of the Republican party being an elephant). We found that we could buy canned elephant meat at Bloomingdale's. To get some ideas about how to serve the omelet, I called the Explorers Club in Washington, D.C., and Treetop, William Holden's restaurant in Kenya. I spoke to the chef at each restaurant; they loved the idea. After much discussion and consideration we de-

cided that the omelet would be rolled around the elephant meat (which resembled beef stew), on each side there would be half a sautéed banana, and over the top a generous handful of coarsely chopped peanuts. (It was a huge success; the publicity was tremendous.)

Since then I never see bananas without thinking of peanuts and elephant meat, and I never see peanuts without thinking of bananas and elephant meat.

This delicious banana bread has peanuts (but no elephant meat)—and is gorgeous.

1 9-INCH LOAF

1¾ cups sifted all-purpose flour
1 teaspoon double-acting baking powder
1 teaspoon baking soda
4 ounces (1 stick) unsalted butter
1 cup dark brown sugar, firmly packed
3 eggs graded "large"

3 large fully ripened bananas (to make 1½ cups, mashed)
⅓ cup sour cream
4 ounces (1 cup) salted peanuts
½ cup light raisins

Adjust a rack one-third up from the bottom of the oven and preheat the oven to 325 degrees. Butter a 9 by 5 by 3-inch loaf pan (with an 8-cup capacity) and dust it with fine dry bread crumbs; invert it over paper and tap to shake out excess crumbs. Set aside.

Sift together the flour, baking powder, and baking soda and set aside.

In the large bowl of an electric mixer beat the butter until it is soft, then beat in the sugar, then the eggs one at a time.

Peel the bananas and mash them coarse on a large, flat plate with a table fork; do not mash them smooth. Add the mashed bananas and the sour cream to the batter and beat to mix.

On low speed gradually beat in the sifted dry ingredients, beating only until just incorporated.

Place the peanuts in the bowl of a food processor fitted with the metal chopping blade and process on/off 2 or 3 times (for 2 or 3 seconds) to chop them coarse (or chop them on a board with a long, heavy knife). Mix the peanuts and raisins into the batter.

Turn into the prepared pan and smooth the top.

Bake for about 1 hour and 15 minutes until a cake tester inserted gently in the middle comes out clean.

Cool in the pan for 10 or 15 minutes. Then cover with a rack. Hold the pan and rack firmly together and turn both over. Remove the pan. With your hands carefully and gently turn the loaf right side up and let stand to cool. Then wrap and refrigerate until serving time.

This makes divine toast but it is better toasted under the broiler than in the toaster. Toasted or not, eat it plain, or with cream cheese and jelly.

Pecan, Peanut Butter, Banana Bread

Dark, moist, sweet, wheaty, nutty, even adorable. This very old recipe is said to have been used by George Washington's family. There was a lady named Corrie M. Hill from Montgomery, Alabama, who was one of the most famous hostesses *in her day, and Mrs. Hill's great-great-grandfather was George Washington's uncle. This banana bread was one of Corrie Hill's specialties.*

2 SMALL LOAVES

1 cup sifted all-purpose flour
1 cup sifted all-purpose whole wheat flour
1 teaspoon baking soda
½ teaspoon salt
¼ teaspoon nutmeg
3 ounces (¾ stick) unsalted butter
½ cup smooth peanut butter

1 cup dark brown sugar, firmly packed
2 eggs graded "large" or "extra-large"
2 to 3 large fully ripened bananas (to make 1 cup, mashed)
6 ounces (1½ cups) pecan halves or large pieces, toasted (see To Toast Pecans, page 7)

Adjust a rack one-third up from the bottom of the oven and preheat the oven to 375 degrees. Butter two small loaf pans, each with a 4- to 5-cup capacity (the pans may measure about 8 by 4 by 2½ inches). Dust them all over with toasted wheat germ or fine dry bread crumbs or uncooked oatmeal, invert over paper, and tap to shake out excess. Set aside.

Sift together both the flours, the baking soda, salt, and nutmeg and set aside. In the large bowl of an electric mixer beat the butter until softened. Add the peanut butter and beat to mix. Beat in the sugar, and then the eggs one at a time.

Peel the bananas and mash with a fork on a large plate; do not use a blender or processor, because the bananas should not be liquefied—they may remain coarse and uneven with a few slightly larger pieces.

Beat the bananas into the mixture. Then, on low speed, add the sifted dry ingredients and beat only until incorporated. Remove the bowl from the mixer and stir in the pecans.

Pour half of the batter into each of the prepared pans and smooth the tops.

Bake at 375 degrees for 15 minutes and then reduce the temperature to 350 degrees and bake for about 35 to 40 minutes more (total baking time is about 50 to 55 minutes). Test by inserting a cake tester to the bottom of each loaf; bake until the tester comes out dry. The loaves will not fill the pans to the top; it is OK—they are not supposed to. During baking the tops of the loaves will crack, and the cracks will remain paler than the rest.

Let the loaves cool in the pans for 5 to 10 minutes, then turn each loaf out onto a folded towel in your hand and place the loaves on a rack to cool.

Blueberry Applesauce Loaf

Cake? Coffee cake? Sweet bread? All three. Two golden-brown loaves with crisp, nutty crusts and soft, moist slices loaded with juicy, purple blueberries and pecan halves that do not sink. Make this in the summer during blueberry season and plan to serve it while it is very fresh.

6 ounces (1½ cups) pecan halves or large pieces, toasted (see To Toast Pecans, page 7)
2 cups fresh blueberries
2 cups sifted all-purpose flour
1 cup sifted all-purpose whole wheat flour
1 tablespoon double-acting baking powder
½ teaspoon baking soda
½ teaspoon salt

½ teaspoon mace
2 eggs graded "large" or "extra-large"
¼ cup tasteless salad oil
1 cup plus 2 tablespoons granulated sugar
1 cup unsweetened applesauce (Mott's Natural Style has no sugar and no preservatives)
2 teaspoons lemon juice

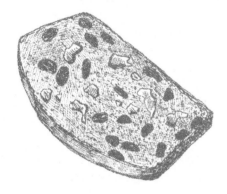

Adjust a rack to the middle of the oven and preheat the oven to 350 degrees. Generously butter two loaf pans that measure about 8 by 4 by 2¼ inches (each with a 4- to 5-cup capacity). To coat the pan with chopped nuts, grind ¾ cup of the pecans (reserve the remaining ¾ cup of pecans) in a food processor or a nut grinder until they are quite fine (but not until they become buttery). Sprinkle the ground or chopped nuts in the buttered pans. Tilt the pans from side to side, then invert them over paper but do not tap to shake out excess nuts. The pans should be heavily coated. Any loose nuts that fall out should be reserved to sprinkle on top of the loaves before baking. Set the pans and the reserved ground nuts aside.

Wash the berries (see To Wash Blueberries, page 14) and let them drain.

Remove and reserve 1 tablespoon of the all-purpose flour. Sift together the remaining all-purpose flour, the whole wheat flour, baking powder, baking soda, salt, and mace and set aside.

In the large bowl of an electric mixer beat the eggs just to mix. Beat in the salad oil and 1 cup of the sugar (reserve the remaining 2 tablespoons of sugar). Mix in the applesauce and lemon juice. On low speed add the sifted dry ingredients and beat only until smoothly mixed. Remove the bowl from the mixer.

Stir in the remaining ¾ cup of pecan halves or pieces.

Place the washed and dried blueberries in a wide bowl. Add the reserved tablespoon of all-purpose flour and toss gently with a rubber spatula to flour the berries without squashing them.

Gently fold the floured berries into the batter with a rubber spatula. Barely mix and be careful not to squash the berries.

Place half of the mixture in each pan and gently smooth the tops. Sprinkle the tops with any reserved ground nuts. Then sprinkle the tops with the remaining 2 tablespoons of sugar.

Bake for 50 to 55 minutes until a cake tester inserted gently into the loaves comes out clean and the loaves begin to come away slightly from the sides of the pans. During baking the tops of the loaves will crack—it is OK.

Cool the loaves in the pans for 10 to 15 minutes. Then carefully cut around the sides to release. Place a folded towel or a potholder on the palm of your hand. Turn a pan over onto the towel or potholder, carefully lift off the pan, and then carefully place the loaf right side up on a rack to cool. Repeat with the other loaf.

Let the loaves stand until they reach room temperature before serving. You can speed up the process in the freezer, if you wish.

A serrated tomato-slicing knife cuts these loaves beautifully.

If you do not plan to serve a loaf while it is really very fresh it is best to freeze it; if it stands at room temperature or even in the refrigerator the moisture from the berries makes the loaf soggy.

Hollywood Honey Cake

No butter, no eggs, no sugar; a delicious and nutritious loaf with whole wheat flour, raisins, and nuts. Not too sweet. Serve it as a plain cake, or use it for cheese sandwiches, or toast it and serve with butter or cream cheese (toasted, plain and dry, is my favorite way). Toasted, it becomes very chewy and crunchy. This takes long and slow baking. It keeps wonderfully—it even seems to get better. Easy to make.

1 9-INCH LOAF

3½ ounces (¾ cup) dark raisins
3½ ounces (1 cup) walnuts
1 cup sifted all-purpose flour
2 cups unsifted all-purpose whole wheat flour
Scant 1 teaspoon salt

¾ teaspoon baking soda
2½ teaspoons double-acting baking powder
1½ cups milk
½ cup honey

Adjust a rack one-third up from the bottom of the oven and preheat the oven to 275 degrees. Butter a 9 by 5 by 3-inch loaf pan (butter the pan even if it has a nonstick finish). Even though it is a larger pan than necessary, I especially like this in a 9¼ by 5¼ by 2⅞-inch pan with a nonstick finish made by Westbend. Set the pan aside.

Steam the raisins by placing them in a vegetable steamer or in a a strainer over shallow water on moderate heat; cover and let the water boil for about 5 minutes. Then uncover and let stand off the heat.

Break the walnuts into medium-size pieces and set aside.

Sift together into the large bowl of an electric mixer both of the flours with the salt, baking soda, and baking powder. Add the milk and honey and beat on low speed until smooth. Remove from the mixer.

Stir in the raisins and nuts.

Turn into the prepared pan, smooth the top, and bake for 1 hour and 20 minutes until the top springs back when pressed lightly with a fingertip, the loaf begins to come away from the sides, and a cake tester inserted gently in the center of the loaf comes out clean and dry.

Cool in the pan for about 10 minutes. Then cover the pan with a potholder or a folded towel and turn it over into the palm of your hand. Remove the pan, cover the cake with a rack and turn over again, leaving the cake right side up to cool completely.

Scones

Scones, lightly sweetened biscuits, came to America with the first settlers from England. Recently, in bakeries and in tearooms, in South Carolina, in New England, and in California, we ate scones. I was surprised to see them, because the main thing about scones is to eat them immediately as they come out of the oven—difficult to do in a bakery or tearoom. But no one seemed to mind, and I was told that they are extremely popular now. If you have had scones hours after they were baked and you liked them, wait until you taste these as soon as they are baked.

The only secret for making good scones is that the mixing should be as quick as possible; there should be a minimum of handling. They are divine for breakfast. Or tea. Or with a fruit salad *luncheon. They are elegant and homey at the same time.*

Although these can literally be put together in just a few minutes, much of the recipe can be done ahead of time. The eggs and milk can be mixed and refrigerated overnight; the butter can be cut into the sifted dry ingredients and that mixture can be refrigerated overnight. Then, before baking, the two mixtures can be quickly stirred together even before the oven has time to heat (give the oven a head start).

These scones are dropped, not rolled; they are more tender than scones that have enough flour to be rolled out.

12 SCONES

1 egg plus 1 egg yolk
½ cup milk
2 cups sifted all-purpose flour
2 teaspoons double-acting baking powder
½ teaspoon salt
¼ cup granulated sugar

3 ounces (¾ stick) unsalted butter, cold and firm, cut into ½-inch squares (it is best to cut the butter ahead of time and refrigerate it)
¼ cup currants
Additional granulated sugar (to sprinkle over the tops)

Adjust a rack to the middle of the oven and preheat the oven to 450 degrees. Line a cookie sheet or a jelly-roll pan with baking pan liner paper, or use it unlined and unbuttered (scones stick to foil).

In a small bowl beat the egg and the yolk just to mix. Mix in the milk and set aside.

Sift together into a wide bowl the flour, baking powder, salt, and sugar. Add the butter and, with a pastry blender, cut until the mixture resembles coarse meal; some of the butter particles may be the size of dried split peas (or thereabouts). Stir in the currants. Form a well in the middle.

Add the egg mixture all at once to the well and with a fork stir quickly only until the dry ingredients are barely moistened. Do not stir one bit more than necessary. The mixture will be quite moist.

Using a rounded tablespoon of the batter for each scone, drop the mounds of batter at least 1 inch apart (12 scones will fit on one 15½ by 12-inch sheet), and sprinkle the tops lightly with a bit of additional sugar.

Bake for 15 minutes, reversing the sheet front to back once during baking to ensure even browning. Bake only until the scones are lightly (and unevenly) golden.

Serve immediately. Delicious plain, but traditionally served with butter and preserves or marmalade.

If you have some left over, even from the day before, split and toast them under the broiler, then butter them, return them to the broiler for a few seconds to melt the butter (watch them carefully), and serve. (Actually, these are so good toasted that you might plan to make them a day ahead on purpose.)

VARIATIONS: *A few spoonfuls of chopped walnuts and/or candied ginger may be stirred in along with, or instead of, the currants. You can use ¾ cup of whole wheat flour in place of ¾ cup of the white flour—then they're called Brown Tea Scones.*

Yeast Pastries

ABOUT USING YEAST　All of these yeast recipes are written for active dry yeast that comes in ¼-ounce envelopes (there are 2 teaspoons of yeast in each envelope), three envelopes fastened together. The expiration date is printed on the back; be sure to check it.

Dissolving: The water that the yeast is dissolved in should be from 105 to 115 degrees when tested with a thermometer—I use a candy thermometer. To test it without a thermometer, sprinkle a bit of it on the inside of your wrist; it should feel comfortably warm.

Rising: Alice Waters says in her *Chez Panisse Menu Cookbook* (Random House, 1982): "All bread-baking operations, including rising, are best carried out at 70 to 80 degrees . . . as long as the dough and the room temperature are above 65 to 70 degrees the yeast will perform."

I like Alice's casual approach. Yeast is really strong and will adjust to different temperatures (within reason). At a lower temperature it will rise more slowly, but it will rise. At a higher temperature it will rise faster. Yeast begins to activate at about 50 degrees and it dies at a temperature above 115 degrees. Many bakers say that slow rising is best.

In Florida, where the temperature seems to hover around 80 degrees for most of the year, I put the bowl of dough to rise in the mailbox.

However, if you have to create the right temperature, here's how to do it in your oven. Place a large, shallow pan of hot water on the bottom rack of the oven and turn on the oven light—I mean the light bulb—not the heat (it adds a bit of warmth). Place a room thermometer on a rack above the hot water. Watch the room thermometer; you will be able to maintain a steady temperature by adding additional hot water or by opening the oven door when necessary.

Once the yeast has started to grow and the dough has started to rise, the dough itself gives off heat. Therefore it is not always necessary to use the pan of water during the entire rising time.

If you want to delay the rising process at any stage, place the dough, during its rising, in the refrigerator. The cold will slow down the rising. Then, when it is placed in a warm temperature again, it will resume rising (after it reaches room temperature).

If a yeast dough has been shaped and has been rising in the oven, it may be removed from the oven and may stand at room temperature while the oven is heating to the temperature specified for baking. (Before you turn the oven on don't forget to remove the room thermometer.)

Kneading: Flour the dough lightly and shape it into a ball. Place it on a large, lightly floured board or roomy work surface. Push the heel of your right hand down into the dough and push hard, pushing away from you. Then, with your left hand, fold the farther edge of the dough toward you and over the center, and at the same time give the dough a quarter turn to the right. Repeat pushing, folding, and turning the dough with a smooth rhythm. Keep extra flour handy as you knead; if the dough becomes sticky, flour it and the work surface as necessary. And keep a dough scraper handy to use if the dough sticks to the work surface.

Cream Cheese Coffee Cake

This delicious delicious cake is made from a rich and tender, slightly sweetened yeast dough, filled with a generous amount of cream cheese filling similar to a cheesecake, and topped with dark, shiny strips of dough arranged to resemble a braid. It looks spectacular, it tastes sensational, it is a challenge—exciting, fun, gratifying—you will love it.

Actual preparation and baking time are little, but the dough is a slow riser; it takes 2 to 2½ hours to rise in a bowl before it is shaped and 1 hour to rise after it is shaped before it is baked.

The dough can be mixed in a food processor or it can be stirred by hand to mix.

10 TO 12 PORTIONS

3 ounces (¾ stick) unsalted butter
⅔ cup warm water (105 to 115 degrees)
1 tablespoon plus ½ cup granulated sugar
2 envelopes active dry yeast

About 3 cups unsifted bread flour or unsifted unbleached all-purpose flour
½ teaspoon salt
1 egg

Butter a 10- to 12-cup bowl for the dough to rise in; set aside.

To mix the dough in a food processor, cut the butter into small pieces and in a small pan over very low heat melt it slowly and then set it aside to cool but not to harden.

Meanwhile, measure the warm water in a 2-cup glass measuring cup, stir in 1 tablespoon of the sugar (reserve the remaining ½ cup of sugar), sprinkle on the yeast, stir with a knife to mix, and set aside for 5 to 10 minutes until the yeast rises to about the 1-cup line.

Place 3 cups of the flour, the salt, and the remaining ½ cup of sugar in the processor bowl fitted with a metal chopping blade. Process on/off once or twice to mix.

In a 1-cup glass or plastic measuring cup (or anything small that has a spout) stir the egg into the melted butter to mix. Then, start the processor again and, while it is going, add the egg and butter mixture and the yeast mixture (which may be stirred a bit to deflate—to make it easier to pour—if you wish). Process until the ingredients form a ball and then continue to process for 1 minute. (I have made this recipe many times with different flours, and 3 cups of flour was always the right amount. However, if the mixture is too sticky to handle, add a bit more flour 1 teaspoon at a time; if it is too dry, add a bit more water 1 teaspoon at a time.)

Flour a large work area lightly and knead the dough for 1 minute. Then place it in the buttered bowl, cover with plastic wrap, and place the bowl in a draft-free spot to rise (see Rising, page 153).

To mix the dough by hand, read the above directions and adapt them as follows. Melt and cool the butter, mix the yeast with the warm water and 1 tablespoon of the sugar, and let rise. Then in a large bowl mix the egg, melted butter, and the yeast mixture and gradually stir in as much of the remaining flour as you can. Place the balance of the flour on a large work surface, turn the dough out onto the flour, and knead until incorporated. Then knead for about 5 minutes until smooth and elastic. Place in the buttered bowl, cover, and let rise.

The dough should rise until more than doubled in volume. In my kitchen 2 hours is the time it takes when I have used unbleached all-purpose flour, and 2½ hours when I have used bread flour.

CREAM CHEESE FILLING

1 tablespoon water
1 tablespoon granulated sugar
½ cup light raisins
1 tablespoon dark rum
16 ounces cream cheese, at room temperature
½ cup confectioners sugar

1 egg yolk
½ teaspoon vanilla extract
Finely grated rind of 1 deep-colored orange or 1
  very large lemon
⅓ cup apricot preserves (to be used later)

Stir the water and granulated sugar in a very small saucepan or frying pan over moderate heat. Bring to a boil, add the raisins, stir for 15 seconds, add the rum and stir for 15 more seconds. Remove from the heat and set aside, stirring occasionally until cool. (There will be no liquid remaining, or almost none.)

In the small bowl of an electric mixer beat the cheese until it is soft and smooth. Add the confectioners sugar, yolk, and vanilla and continue to beat until completely mixed. Remove the bowl from the mixer and stir in the grated rind and the prepared raisins (along with any remaining rum syrup even if it is a minute amount). Set aside.

When the dough has risen, punch it down, fold in the sides, and press on them to deflate. Turn the dough out onto a large, lightly floured work surface, knead it once or twice, form it into a square or oblong, cover loosely with plastic wrap, and let stand for 15 minutes.

This cake will be shaped and baked on a 15½ by 12½-inch cookie sheet. You will now line part of the cookie sheet with foil, which will line the section the cake is on and will also form little retainers at the two narrow ends of the cake, which is where the cheese filling might run out. Tear off a piece of aluminum foil about 4 inches longer than the cookie sheet. Fold the foil in half lengthwise, shiny side out. Butter the full length of one side of the folded foil and place the foil, buttered side up, in the middle of the sheet, lengthwise, with about 2 inches of overhang at each end. Set aside.

With a lightly floured rolling pin roll the dough out until it is the size of the cookie sheet. This dough is elastic and it will resist you; just let it rest occasionally for a few minutes and then roll it again. Gently pull out the corners of the dough from time to time to keep it oblong, but if the shape turns out uneven you will be able to fix it (push the sides in or pull them out) with your fingers after it is on the cookie sheet.

Place the rolling pin along the narrow end of the dough and loosely roll the dough up around the pin to transfer it to the cookie sheet. Then unroll it onto the sheet (on top of the foil). Adjust the shape with your fingers to make it even and rather squared off on the corners.

In a small bowl stir the preserves to soften and spread them over the dough, staying about 2 inches away from the edges (it will be a very thin layer of preserves).

With a spoon place the cheese filling in a strip 4 inches wide down the middle of the dough, staying about 1½ inches away from the two narrow ends. Smooth the strip a bit but do not make it any wider than 4 inches.

With a ruler and the point of a small knife, mark 1-inch lengths along the long sides of the dough, then with a sharp knife cut through the dough at the marks, making cuts at right angles to the filling. Start the cuts a scant 1 inch away from the filling and cut through the outside border of the dough.

Now, to form an interwoven braid design on the top. Place the sheet in front of you with a short side of the sheet nearest to you. Start at the farther end and bring each one of the strips up and over the filling, placing it at a slight downward angle. Cross first one side and then the other. Each strip seals and holds down the one before it. When you get to the last two strips stretch them out gently to make them long enough to tuck under the sides of the cake. Wet their undersides with water to hold them in place and, with your fingers or a pastry brush, also dab a little water between the top and bottom of the dough at the end of the cake and press them together to seal. Finally, at each end of the cake, fold the over-hanging foil in half to strengthen it. This will make the overhang about 1 inch. Then lift up the end of the foil and press it against the cake, pinching it together at both sides to keep it in place.

Cover the cake loosely with plastic wrap and set aside to rise (see Rising, page 153) for 1 hour. (The cake will rise more in the oven.)

About 20 minutes before baking, adjust a rack one-third up from the bottom of the oven and preheat the oven to 350 degrees. Prepare the egg wash.

EGG WASH

1 egg yolk   Scant 1 tablespoon milk

Stir the yolk and milk to mix and pour through a fine strainer into a small cup.

Shortly before baking, brush the wash all over the top and sides of the cake, using a soft brush. Repeat, making two layers of the wash. Try not to allow the wash to run down onto the pan; use a paper napkin to soak up any that might run down.

Bake the cake for 28 to 30 minutes until the top is beautifully browned, reversing the sheet front to back once after about 20 minutes if the cake is not browning evenly.

Cool the cake on the pan for about 10 minutes. Then, using a flat-sided cookie sheet as a large spatula, transfer the cake to a rack to cool.

If there are leftovers this can be refrigerated for a day or two and it will still be just as delicious. Or it can be frozen. The cake can be served cold or at room temperature.

Doughnuts

These doughnuts are light, moist, delicate, with a mahogany-colored crust and a shiny, almost transparent glaze all over.

This is a yeast dough made with mashed potatoes (a.k.a. spudnuts). After the dough rises, it is refrigerated for 2 to 24 hours. Then it is rolled out and cut into doughnut shapes. At that point you have a choice: either let the doughnuts rise for about 1½ hours and fry them, or refrigerate the doughnuts to be fried later in the day or the following day, or freeze the doughnuts for up to a week before frying. With all these options it is easy to serve doughnuts while they are still hot when they are at their best. You can serve them fresh for breakfast (if you get up enough ahead of time).

Doughnuts are an American institution; making them in your own kitchen is a real thrill.

My large doughnut cutter measures 3½ inches in diameter and the hole in the middle is ¾ inch. It is available at Bridge Kitchenware, 214 East 52nd Street, New York, New York 10022.

You will need a deep-frying thermometer and, if possible, a household thermometer to take the room temperature.

24 TO 48 DOUGHNUTS, DEPENDING
ON THE SIZE OF THE CUTTER

¾ pound fresh white potatoes (to make 1 cup, mashed)
About 1½ cups tap water
¼ cup warm water (105 to 115 degrees)
¾ cup granulated sugar
1 envelope active dry yeast
1 teaspoon salt
About 6½ cups unsifted all-purpose flour or bread flour

4 ounces (1 stick) unsalted butter, at room temperature, cut into small pieces
2 eggs graded "large"
¾ teaspoon nutmeg
1 teaspoon vanilla extract
Fat for deep frying (I use a 3-pound can of solid Crisco)

Generously butter a 4- to 6-quart bowl for the dough to rise in; set it aside.

Peel the potatoes, cut them into quarters or eighths, place them in a saucepan, add about 1½ cups tap water, cover, place over high heat until the water comes to a boil, and then reduce the heat and let simmer, partially covered, until the potatoes are tender when tested with a toothpick. Remove from the heat.

Meanwhile, place the ¼ cup warm water in a 1-cup glass measuring cup. Add 1 teaspoon of the sugar (reserve the remaining sugar) and the yeast. Stir a bit with a knife and let stand for about 10 minutes to rise.

Measure 1 cup of the warm potato water, pour it into the large bowl of an electric mixer, add the remaining sugar, the salt, and 1 cup of the flour (reserve the remaining flour). Beat well.

After the yeast mixture has risen an inch or two, beat it into the dough.

Drain the potatoes and mash them smoothly in a food processor or in the small bowl of an electric mixer or in a food mill. Measure 1 cup of the mashed potatoes (which should still be warm) and add it to the yeast mixture along with the butter, eggs, nutmeg, and vanilla. Beat until the butter is smoothly incorporated and the ingredients are thoroughly mixed. Then, gradually, on low speed, add the remaining flour ½ cupful at a time.

When the mixture begins to thicken so much that it crawls up on the beaters, remove the bowl from the mixer and, with a heavy wooden spoon or spatula, stir in more of the flour, adding only as much as can be stirred in.

Any remaining flour should be set aside on the farther corner of a large board or work surface. Smooth a bit of it onto the middle of the work space. Turn the dough out onto the floured space. Start to knead the dough, adding the remaining flour (or more) as necessary to make a dough that you can knead. But do not add any more than you really must have. Knead for about 5 minutes until the dough is smooth, rubbery, and feels alive.

Form the dough into a ball, place it in the buttered bowl, turn the dough around to butter all sides of it, cover the bowl with plastic wrap, and place it in a warm, draft-free spot to rise until it is double in volume (see Rising, page 153).

Make a fist and punch down the risen dough, then fold in the sides and press down to deflate. Replace the dough in the bowl, cover airtight, and refrigerate for 2 to 24 hours.

Turn the dough out onto a floured pastry cloth, cut it in half, and work with one half at a time, reserving the other half in the bowl in the refrigerator.

With a floured rolling pin roll the dough out on a lightly floured pastry cloth until it is about ⅓ inch thick. (If the dough is rubbery and resists being rolled out, just let it rest for 5 to 10 minutes and then roll it again; repeat as necessary.)

With a floured doughnut cutter or with two floured round cookie cutters (one for the doughnut and one for the hole) cut out the doughnuts, starting at the outside edge of the dough and cutting right next to each other in order not to have any more leftover scraps than necessary. (See Note.)

Roll and cut the remaining half of the dough.

Reserve the little rounds that made the holes in the doughnuts; fry those just as they are when you fry the doughnuts. Reserve all the other scraps, knead them together a bit, let rest briefly, then roll and cut.

Now, to fry the doughnuts without refrigerating or freezing (for frying at a future time), place them on cookie sheets lined with lightly oiled aluminum foil in a warm, draft-free spot to rise, uncovered, for about 1½ hours (see Rising, page 153). To refrigerate the doughnuts to be fried several hours later, or the following day, place them on cookie sheets lined with lightly oiled aluminum foil, cover them with plastic wrap, and refrigerate. To freeze them before frying, place them on the lightly oiled foil-lined sheets in the freezer until firm. Then wrap them airtight—individually, in plastic wrap—and return to the freezer.

Before frying either refrigerated or frozen doughnuts, bring them to room temperature, wrapped, then unwrap and place them on lightly oiled foil-lined sheets in a warm, draft-free spot for 1 to 1½ hours until double in size.

To fry the doughnuts, you will need a wide, rather shallow pan (about 10 by 3 inches is a good size). About 30 minutes before frying, place the fat (or oil, if you wish) in the pan (it should be about 1½ inches deep) and heat slowly to 365 degrees.

Have ready two long forks or flat wire whisks for turning the doughnuts and for removing them from the fat. And have a wide metal spatula (pancake turner) ready to transfer the doughnuts to the fat. Have large brown paper bags ready for draining the doughnuts.

While the fat is heating, prepare the glaze.

GLAZE

1 pound (3¼ cups packed) confectioners sugar	¼ teaspoon almond extract
1 teaspoon vanilla extract	About ¾ cup milk

Place the sugar and flavorings in the small bowl of an electric mixer and gradually add the milk while beating. Add enough milk to make a thick but pourable mixture that forms a wide ribbon when poured. Cover and let stand.

Place a large rack over aluminum foil to glaze the doughnuts.

When everything is ready, dip the wide metal spatula into the hot fat to coat it and then gently slide it under a doughnut, pressing down against the foil (and away from the doughnut). Transfer to the hot fat and hold it briefly until the doughnut slides off.

Immediately add another doughnut to the fat. (After you have made a few you can fry three or four at a time, but do just two at a time at first.)

Keep the thermometer in the fat and adjust the heat as necessary to maintain a 365-degree temperature. Fry the doughnuts for 2 minutes on one side, then turn them over gently with the two flat whisks or forks (without piercing the doughnuts) and fry on the other side for 2 minutes. They will become beautifully dark brown and extravagantly high and gorgeous, and they will probably have a pale streak around their middles.

With the flat whisks or a wide fork lift a fried doughnut from the fat and place it on a brown paper bag to drain a bit (for less than a minute).

Quickly transfer it to the large rack set over foil and with a wide pastry brush generously brush the glaze all over the top and sides of the hot doughnut, then turn it over and glaze the other side. Repeat with remaining doughnuts. Let them stand on the rack briefly until the glaze dries.

Serve immediately or let stand and serve later, but the fresher the better. "Get 'em while they're hot," if possible.

NOTE: *Many experts say that you should press the cutter down firmly and then lift it up without wiggling it (the theory being that if you wiggle it, it squashes the sides together and the doughnuts will not rise properly). My cutters do not cut completely through without a wiggle or two—so I wiggle. But try it without wiggling.*

Cinnamon Buns

Arlene Train of Albany, Oregon, sent this sensational recipe to me with a note saying, "They are wonderfully light and delicious and they disappear quickly." I don't think she would believe just how quickly. My husband lost all control with these. He ate more than I will tell. I hadn't planned it that way but it was his dinner. Then he had to go to bed. A few hours later he asked for more.

These are the largest, lightest, old-fashioned, country-style, sweet yeast rolls. Yeast loves potatoes. When yeast dough is made with potatoes, as this is, it becomes especially alive and fat and happy.

These are not really an after-dinner dessert; serve them as a coffee cake, or a sweet bread.

12 VERY LARGE BUNS

1 cup mashed potatoes (see Notes)
1 cup milk
½ cup plus 1 tablespoon granulated sugar
½ teaspoon salt
2 ounces (½ stick) unsalted butter, cut up
¼ cup warm water (105 to 115 degrees—see Notes)

1 envelope active dry yeast
1 egg graded "large" or "extra-large"
1 teaspoon vanilla extract
About 4¼ cups unsifted all-purpose flour or
     bread flour
Additional flour

Generously butter a 4- to 6-quart bowl for the dough to rise in; set it aside.

Place the mashed potatoes (which may be warm or cool) in a saucepan and, stirring constantly, add the milk very gradually. Stir in ½ cup of the sugar (reserve the remaining 1 tablespoon of sugar), and the salt and butter. Place over low heat and stir occasionally until the mixture is warm (105 to 115 degrees). It is not necessary for the butter to have melted completely.

Meanwhile, in a 1-cup glass measuring cup, stir the warm water with the remaining tablespoon of sugar, sprinkle on the yeast, stir briefly with a knife, and set aside for about 10 minutes until the mixture rises to about the ¾-cup line.

In a small bowl beat the egg to mix and add the vanilla.

When the potato and milk mixture is warm enough, transfer it to the large bowl of an electric mixer. Beat in the yeast mixture and the egg. On low speed gradually add about 3 cups of the flour. Beat on low speed for a minute or two. Remove the bowl from the mixer. The dough will be wet and sticky now. With a heavy wooden spatula gradually stir in the remaining 1¼ cups of flour.

Flour a large work surface. Turn the dough out onto the floured surface. The dough will probably still be too sticky to knead. If it is, add a bit of additional flour and, with a dough scraper or a wide metal spatula, turn the dough over and over with the additional flour—adding still a bit more if necessary—until you can handle the dough. Then knead it for 5 minutes, again adding additional flour if necessary. (You might have to add a total of ½ to ¾ cup additional flour. But potato dough has a tendency to remain a bit sticky even when it has enough flour so do not use more than you must.) After about 5 minutes of active kneading, the dough should be smooth and feel alive.

Place the dough in the buttered bowl, turn it around in the bowl to butter all sides, cover the bowl with plastic wrap and place it in a warm, draft-free spot to rise for 1 to 1½ hours (see Rising, page 153) until the dough is at least double in volume.

Then make a fist, punch down the middle of the dough, and fold in and press down the sides of the dough to deflate it all.

Turn the dough out onto a lightly floured surface, cover it loosely with plastic wrap, and let stand for about 10 minutes.

Meanwhile, butter a 15½ by 10½ by 1-inch jelly-roll pan.

With a long, heavy floured rolling pin, roll out the dough into about an 18-inch square. The dough will be rubbery and will resist you. Just let it stand occasionally for a few minutes and then roll it again. After a few tries it will do what you want.

FILLING

2 tablespoons granulated sugar
1½ teaspoons cinnamon
¼ teaspoon nutmeg

1 ounce (¼ stick) unsalted butter, melted
5 ounces (1 cup) dark raisins, steamed (see Notes)

In a small bowl mix the sugar with the cinnamon and nutmeg. With a wide pastry brush, or with the palm of your hand, spread the butter all over the surface of the rolled-out dough. With a large spoon, sprinkle the cinnamon-sugar on the dough, then sprinkle on the raisins.

With your hands roll the dough up like a jelly roll. The roll of dough should be the same thickness all over; shape it as necessary.

Place the roll seam down in front of you. With a ruler and toothpicks mark the dough into 12 even pieces. With a sharp, heavy knife cut the pieces; use a sawing motion.

Place the pieces cut side down (and up) in the prepared pan, making 3 rows with 4 buns in each row.

Cover loosely with a lightweight towel and set to rise again for about 1 hour. During rising the buns will rise and grow into each other.

(If the dough is rising in the oven, remove it about 20 minutes before the baking time and let stand, covered, at room temperature in a draft-free spot.)

Adjust a rack one-third up from the bottom of the oven and preheat the oven to 375 degrees.

Bake the buns for about 20 minutes, reversing the pan front to back once after about 12 minutes of baking, until the buns are nicely but lightly browned. (Do not overbake or the buns will dry out.)

Remove from the oven and let stand for about 5 minutes. Meanwhile, prepare the glaze.

GLAZE

1 tablespoon unsalted butter, at room temperature
¾ to 1 cup confectioners sugar
Pinch of salt

½ teaspoon vanilla extract
A few drops almond extract
About 2 tablespoons light cream

In the small bowl of an electric mixer beat all of the ingredients together until the mixture is smooth. It should be thick, barely thin enough to pour —adjust the cream and/or sugar as necessary.

Drip the glaze in a rather narrow stream every which way all over the warm buns.

Let stand until completely cool. (I think they are even better a few hours later.)

Just before serving, cut the rolls apart with a small, sharp knife and with a wide metal spatula remove them from the pan.

NOTES: 1. *The mashed potatoes can be made with instant dry mashed potatoes or fresh potatoes. It takes about ¾ pound fresh potatoes to make 1 cup mashed. Peel, cut into chunks, place in a small saucepan with water, boil, partially covered, until tender, drain, and then mash the potatoes. If you are using fresh potatoes save the water they boiled in and use some of it for dissolving the yeast (first heat it as necessary); since yeast loves potatoes so much, this will make it extra happy.*

2. *To steam the raisins, place them in a vegetable steamer or a strainer over shallow water in a saucepan. Cover, place over moderate heat, and let the water boil for about 5 minutes until the raisins are soft and moist. Then uncover and set the raisins aside until you are ready for them.*

CINNAMON BUN
FRENCH TOAST

If any of the above Cinnamon Buns have lasted long enough to become stale, they make divine French toast. Cut each bun straight down into 3 wide slices. For each 2 portions use 2 buns, 1 egg, and ¼ cup of milk. Beat together the egg and milk, transfer to a shallow baking dish, add the slices, and let stand for about 30 minutes, turning the slices very carefully to keep them from falling apart. Then fry them in a wide frying pan in clarified butter (see page 219). Turn them over gently, using a wide metal spatula in one hand and a fork in the other hand. Fry over moderate heat until golden brown (do not try to fry the top sides of the slices). Serve with warm maple syrup, or with marmalade.

Old Grand-Dad Sticky Buns

Light and airy, sticky and gooey, shiny, nutty, divine—they are great fun to make and they look sensational. When you make these you might decide to open a bakery, and if you carry these, the bakery will be a huge success.

It is best to use nonstick muffin pans; they are not expensive—hardware stores and supermarkets have them. You need two pans, each for 12 standard-size muffins (buns).

24 BUNS

½ cup warm water (105 to 115 degrees)
2 tablespoons granulated sugar
1 envelope active dry yeast
1 cup milk
About 4 cups unsifted all-purpose flour or
    bread flour
½ teaspoon salt
1 egg yolk

2 cups light brown sugar, firmly packed
½ cup plus a few teaspoons of additional bourbon
4 ounces (generous 1 cup) large pecan halves,
    toasted (see To Toast Pecans, page 7)
2 ounces (½ stick) unsalted butter, at room
    temperature (it must be soft)
2 teaspoons cinnamon

Butter a large bowl for the dough to rise in; set it aside.

Stir the water and granulated sugar together in a 1-cup glass measuring cup, add the yeast, stir briefly with a knife, and set aside for about 10 minutes until foamy.

Place the milk in a small pan over low heat and warm it to 105 to 115 degrees.

This dough can be made in a food processor or by hand.

To make it in a processor, fit the bowl with the metal chopping blade. Place about 3 cups of the flour in the processor bowl. Add the salt. Turn the motor on and, through the feed tube, add the egg yolk, gradually add the warm milk, and then the yeast mixture (which will have risen up near the top of the cup—incidentally, you can stir and deflate it before you add it to the flour mixture or you can pour it in just as it is). Process until the mixture forms a ball and comes away from the sides of the bowl, then continue to process for about 45 seconds more.

To mix this by hand, place about 3 cups of the flour in a large mixing bowl, add the salt, egg yolk, warm milk, and the yeast mixture, and beat well with a heavy wooden spatula (or with an electric mixer).

Whichever way you have mixed the ingredients, now place the remaining flour on a large work surface. Turn the dough out near the flour and knead, adding only as much of the flour as you need to be able to handle the dough. You probably will not use all of it.

If you prepared the dough in a processor it needs only about 1 minute of kneading; otherwise, it needs about 5 minutes of kneading.

When the dough becomes smooth and feels alive, form it into a ball and place it in the buttered bowl, turn the dough around in the bowl to butter all sides of it, cover the bowl with plastic wrap, and set it to rise in a draft-free spot where the temperature is about 80 to 85 degrees (see Rising, page 153). The dough should rise until it doubles in volume; it will take about 45 to 60 minutes.

Meanwhile, prepare the muffin pans. Butter the pans generously (use additional butter to the ½ stick called for). Place a rounded tablespoonful of the light brown sugar in each pan (that should use up about half of the sugar—reserve the balance). Place a teaspoon of bourbon in each pan to wet the sugar. Place 3 pecan halves in each pan, rounded sides down. Set the pans aside.

When the dough has risen, make a fist, punch down the middle of the dough, fold over the sides and press them in, and then turn the dough out onto a lightly floured surface. Knead it just two or three times, cover it loosely with plastic wrap, and let stand for about 10 minutes.

Cut the dough in half, set aside and cover one piece, and place the other piece on the lightly floured surface. Flour a rolling pin and roll the dough out into a rectangle 10 by 12 inches. As you roll the dough, occasionally use your fingers and gently pull out the corners of the dough to make a rectangle with squared corners.

With a narrow metal spatula or the bottom of a spoon spread 1 ounce of the soft butter over the dough. With your fingers sprinkle half of the remaining brown sugar over the butter. Then sprinkle lightly with a few teaspoons of the additional bourbon. Then, through a fine strainer, sprinkle

1 teaspoon of the cinnamon (reserve the remaining teaspoon of cinnamon for the other pan) all over the surface.

Roll the dough up tightly like a jelly roll, starting at a 12-inch side. With a ruler and the tip of a small, sharp knife mark the roll into 12 equal pieces.

When you cut this roll into pieces, the dough will want to stick to the knife, causing the slices to squash (which really will not matter a bit). But to avoid some of the sticking and squashing, spray the knife blade with Pam before making the first cut (and possibly one more time after making several additional cuts). Cut into 12 pieces.

Flatten each piece slightly, cut side up (and down), either by pressing it between your hands or by pressing it against the work surface with your fingertips.

Place the pieces cut side up (and down) in the prepared muffin forms. Cover the pan loosely with plastic wrap and place in a draft-free spot, preferably where the temperature is about 80 degrees, and let stand to double in volume.

Prepare the second panful, and let it rise too. It will take about 35 minutes, more or less, for the buns to rise.

Before baking, adjust a rack one-third up from the bottom of the oven and place a large piece of aluminum foil on the rack below to catch any syrup that might bubble over. Or, if your oven does not have another rack below, place the foil on the floor of the oven. Preheat the oven to 375 degrees.

Bake these only one pan at a time; first bake the ones you shaped first—the others can wait. Bake for about 25 minutes until the buns are beautifully browned (they will rise magically during baking).

As soon as you remove a pan from the oven, immediately cover it with a cookie sheet and turn the pan and the sheet over; hold the pan upside down for a moment, to allow the syrup to run out onto the sheet, then remove the pan and with two wide metal spatulas (or what have you) pick up any nuts that fell off, place them on the buns, and scrape up any syrup that runs onto the cookie sheet and replace it on top of the buns.

When the syrup stops running, use the spatulas to transfer the buns to a dish or tray.

Let the buns cool for about 20 minutes, or completely, before serving.

Aren't they gorgeous? And delicious?

Leftovers may be frozen. Place them on a foil-covered tray, freeze the buns, and then cover airtight with plastic wrap. Thaw before uncovering.

Carol's Crescents

Carol Whiteside is a charming young lady who loves to bake so much that she fulfilled a popular American dream: she went into a dessert business from her home, in Lawrenceville, New Jersey. She specializes in a variety of popular chocolate chip cookies (Carol's are thick and chewy—very different from the usual because they contain ground nuts), lemon cake (East 62nd Street Lemon Cake, to be exact, on page 115 of my first book), and these crescents.

Traditionally these are also called nut horns, or rugelach. Variations of these (with yeast, without yeast, with cream cheese, without cream cheese) came to America from Europe generations ago with many of our ancestors. They are popular now with home cooks and with bakery cooks and at classy take-out food stores all over the country.

They are delicate, crisp, flaky, cinnamon-nutty, bite-size pastries; wonderful with tea or coffee, or along with a fruit or ice cream dessert. Or to wrap as a gift. They take time and patience and are a creative pastime.

The dough must be refrigerated overnight before it is shaped and baked.

80 CRESCENTS

DOUGH

8 ounces (2 sticks) unsalted butter
1 tablespoon granulated sugar
1 envelope active dry yeast
3 egg yolks
1 teaspoon vanilla extract

¼ teaspoon almond extract
1 teaspoon salt
1 cup sour cream
3 cups unsifted all-purpose flour

In a 10- or 12-cup heavy saucepan over low heat melt the butter. Remove from the heat. Stir in the sugar. Cool to lukewarm (105 to 115 degrees). Then sprinkle on the yeast and stir briefly with a knife. Let stand for 5 minutes. Add the yolks, vanilla and almond extracts, salt, and sour cream, and stir with a wire whisk until smooth. Add the flour and stir with a wooden spatula until incorporated.

Now, process half of the dough at a time in a food processor with the metal chopping blade (or process it all at once in the large-size processor) for 45 seconds, or just stir and beat it well by hand for a few minutes.

Place the dough in a buttered bowl (the dough will rise only very little, therefore it is only necessary for the bowl to be slightly larger than the volume of dough), cover with plastic wrap, and refrigerate overnight.

Any time before shaping the dough, prepare the filling.

FILLING

4 ounces (generous 1 cup) walnuts
1 cup granulated sugar

3½ teaspoons cinnamon
6 ounces (1¼ cups) currants

The walnuts must be chopped until very fine; they should not be ground. It is best to chop them on a large board using a long, heavy French chef's knife. Some of the pieces will be larger than others; the large pieces should not be larger than grains of rice.

In a bowl stir the chopped nuts with the sugar and cinnamon. Set aside.

To plump the currants, cover them with boiling water, let stand for

3 to 4 minutes, strain, and then spread them out on paper towels to dry. Pat the tops a bit with paper towels and set aside. (Do not add the currants to the nut mixture.)

When you are ready to bake, adjust one rack to the middle of the oven (for one sheet) or adjust two racks to divide the oven into thirds (for two sheets). Preheat the oven to 350 degrees. Line cookie sheets with baking pan liner paper or with aluminum foil shiny side up (the paper is better but the foil will do).

With a strong, heavy metal spoon, or with a wooden spatula, remove the dough from the bowl and place it on a counter top or work surface (it will be sticky and stiff and difficult to transfer). With your hands, press it together, knead it for a few moments, and form it into a fat sausage. Mark and then cut the sausage shape into 5 equal pieces. Wrap them individually in plastic wrap or wax paper and refrigerate.

Place about one fifth of the sugar-cinnamon-nut mixture on an unfloured pastry cloth. Unwrap 1 piece of the dough and place it on the sugar mixture. Press down on the dough with the palm of your hand to flatten the dough, turn it over and press with your hand again to coat both the top and the bottom of the round of dough thoroughly with the sugar mixture.

Then, with a rolling pin, roll out the dough until it is a very thin round 11 or 12 inches in diameter. The dough may be turned over a few times to keep both sides well sugared. While rolling, if a crack forms at the edge, pinch it together before it becomes too large.

Sprinkle one fifth of the currants on the round of dough, placing them more heavily around the outside of the dough than at the center.

With a very long, sharp, heavy knife cut the dough into 16 pie-shaped wedges. (Use the full length of the blade and cut straight down; first cut into quarters and then cut each quarter into 4 wedges—cutting all the way across the round each time.)

With your fingers roll each wedge from the outside toward the point. Place the rolls 1 inch apart, point down, on the lined sheets. (Some of the currants should peep out at the edges.)

Cover the sheet loosely with plastic wrap and let stand at room temperature for 10 to 15 minutes before baking. Do not look for these to rise.

You can bake either one or two sheets at a time. If you have only one sheet in the oven, reverse it front to back once during baking to ensure even browning. If you have two sheets in the oven, reverse them top to bottom and front to back as necessary to ensure even browning. Bake for 20 to 25 minutes until the crescents are lightly colored all over; they should not be too pale. (They will rise only slightly during baking.)

If you have used baking pan liner paper, the crescents can be lifted off as soon as they come out of the oven; if you have used foil, the crescents should stand on the foil for a few minutes until they can be lifted off easily. Cool the crescents on racks.

Repeat the directions to shape and bake the remaining dough.

These are best when they are very fresh, but they can be frozen.

Zwieback

The name is German for "twice baked." It originated as a way of using up stale rolls. But in Miami Beach it is so popular that bakeries make fresh rolls specifically for Zwieback, and they can't make it fast enough. It is indeed twice baked to make very hard, dry, brittle, crisp, crunchy, only slightly sweetened crackers. Wonderful with tea or coffee or just to have around for a nibble any time.

YIELD 72—96 CRACKERS

¼ cup warm water (105 to 115 degrees)
½ cup granulated sugar
1 envelope active dry yeast
1 cup milk
2 ounces (½ stick) unsalted butter, at room temperature, cut into small pieces

About 4 cups unsifted all-purpose flour or bread flour
1 teaspoon salt
¾ teaspoon nutmeg
1 egg

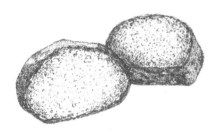

Butter a bowl with about a 3-quart capacity and set it aside to have ready for the dough to rise in.

Place the water in a 1-cup glass measuring cup. Add 1 teaspoon of the sugar (reserve the remaining sugar) and the yeast, stir with a knife, and set aside at room temperature to rise about an inch or two.

Place the milk and butter in a small saucepan over moderate heat to warm to 105 to 115 degrees. It is not necessary for the butter to melt completely.

To make this in a food processor, fit the machine with the metal chopping blade. Place about 3½ cups of the flour in the processor bowl (reserve the remaining ½ cup of flour), add the salt, the nutmeg, and the remaining sugar, and process on/off once or twice to mix; then, through the feed tube, add the warm milk and butter, the egg, and the yeast mixture (which may be stirred down before it is added or not). Process until the mixture forms a ball. If it is sticky add all or part of the remaining ½ cup of flour (as necessary) through the feed tube to make a mixture that can be kneaded. Process for about 45 seconds.

To make this without a processor, in a large bowl beat the egg to mix, mix in the warm milk and butter, the yeast mixture, and then about 3½ cups of the flour, the salt, nutmeg, and the remaining sugar. If the mixture is too sticky to knead add all or part of the remaining flour (as necessary).

Whichever way you have reached this stage, now flour a work surface and turn the dough out onto the floured surface. If the dough was made in a processor, knead it for only about 1 minute. If it was made without a processor, knead it for about 5 minutes, adding additional flour if necessary.

Form the dough into a ball, place it in the buttered bowl, turn it around and around to butter all sides of it, cover with plastic wrap, and set aside to rise (see Rising, page 153) for about 1 hour until doubled in volume.

Then make a fist, punch down the dough, fold in the sides and press down to deflate, turn out onto a lightly floured surface, and form into an even oblong. With a large knife cut the dough into 12 even pieces.

Line two large cookie sheets with baking pan liner paper or with foil shiny side up.

Pick up 1 piece of the dough. Flatten it between your hands. Then, to shape it into a round ball, fold the sides in—tuck them under—toward the bottom and pinch them together (on what will be the bottom of the ball shape).

Shape all of the pieces and place them, pinched sides down, on the two sheets, 6 on each sheet.

Lightly oil or butter two pieces of plastic wrap large enough to cover the balls of dough and place them oiled side down. (Or, if you prefer, sift a little flour over the balls of dough to prevent sticking, and then cover with plastic wrap.)

Set aside to rise in a warm, draft-free spot, for 1 to 1½ hours until double in volume.

Adjust two racks to divide the oven into thirds. (If you are using the oven as a place for the rolls to rise, it is all right to remove the rolls from the oven about 20 minutes before baking and let the sheets stand at room temperature in a draft-free spot.) Preheat the oven to 400 degrees.

Bake the two sheets of rolls at 400 degrees for 10 minutes. (If the rolls on one sheet brown more than the other, reverse the sheets top to bottom during this phase of baking.) Then reduce the temperature to 350 degrees, open the oven door a crack to allow it to cool a bit, and then bake for 15 minutes more (total baking time is 25 minutes).

Remove from the oven and transfer the rolls to racks to cool completely.

The rolls will slice better if they are chilled first either in the refrigerator or freezer.

Meanwhile, heat the oven to 300 degrees.

With a very sharp knife, or a serrated knife, slice the rolls, cutting straight down. Traditionally Zwieback is cut into slices ½ inch wide; I usually cut it a little bit thinner.

Place the slices cut side down (and up) on cookie sheets and bake, reversing the sheets top to bottom and front to back occasionally, and turning the slices over as necessary for the Zwieback to become lightly golden on both sides by the time they feel completely hard to the touch.

Let stand to cool. Store airtight.

Chocolate Bread

I am so in love with making yeast breads and cakes that for about a year when I started this book I thought it was going to be a yeast book. But then one day a new ice cream was born in our kitchen, and several other things came along,

as they do, and I saw that it was not to be a yeast book. But this recipe, which is a bread and not a dessert, refuses to be left out of this book of desserts.

It is a huge loaf that makes giant-size slices,

light and airy in texture, dark as pumpernickel in color. It has a few raisins and nuts. Serve it lightly buttered, or use it for cream cheese or peanut butter and bacon sandwiches, or serve it at the *table with honey butter (mix ½ cup of honey into ¼ pound of unsalted butter).*

¼ cup warm water (105 to 115 degrees)
1 tablespoon plus ½ cup granulated sugar
1 envelope active dry yeast
1 cup milk
2 tablespoons unsalted butter, cut into pieces
About 4 cups unsifted all-purpose flour or
    bread flour
1 teaspoon salt
⅔ cup unsweetened cocoa powder (preferably
    Dutch-process)

2 teaspoons powdered (not granular) instant
    coffee or espresso
2 eggs graded "large," "extra-large," or "jumbo"
1 teaspoon vanilla extract
4 ounces (generous 1 cup) walnuts, cut into ¼- to
    ⅓-inch pieces
2½ ounces (½ cup) dark raisins

Generously butter a large bowl to have ready for the dough to rise in. And butter an 8-cup loaf pan (mine is 9¼ by 5¼ by 2⅞ inches). Set the bowl and the pan aside.

Stir the water and 1 tablespoon of the sugar (reserve the remaining ½ cup of sugar) in a 1-cup glass measuring cup, add the yeast, stir briefly with a knife, and set aside for about 10 minutes until foamy.

Meanwhile, place the milk and butter in a small saucepan over moderate heat until warm (105 to 115 degrees). It is not necessary for the butter to melt.

Place 4 scant cups of the flour, the salt, cocoa, coffee, and the remaining ½ cup of sugar in a large mixing bowl. Stir to mix.

Beat the eggs just to mix, and add them to the flour mixture along with the vanilla, warm milk and butter, and the foamy yeast mixture. Add the walnuts and raisins. Stir as well as you can with a long, heavy wooden spatula. (Or mix these ingredients in a large-size food processor, or in a mixer with a dough hook.)

Turn out onto a lightly floured board and knead for 5 or 6 minutes until smooth and elastic. (If you have used a food processor or an electric mixer, a minute or two of kneading will probably be enough.) Add additional flour (very little at a time) if necessary to make the dough manageable.

Place the dough in the large, well-buttered bowl, turn the dough to butter it on all sides; cover with plastic wrap, and let rise at a temperature of about 80 to 85 degrees (see Rising, page 153) until the dough has doubled in volume—it will take about 1¾ to 2 hours.

Make a fist, punch it into the dough, knead the dough three or four times, and turn the dough out onto a lightly floured board. Cover with plastic wrap and let stand for about 5 minutes.

To shape the dough, form it roughly into an oval and, with a rolling pin, roll it out into a large oval about 8 or 9 inches across the narrow width. Then roll it up the way you would a jelly roll, rolling from one narrow end to the other narrow end, and place the loaf seam side down in the buttered pan.

Loosely cover the pan with a piece of buttered plastic wrap, buttered side down. Let rise again until doubled in size—it will take about 1¼ to 1½ hours.

Before the dough has finished rising, adjust a rack one-third up from the bottom of the oven and preheat the oven to 350 degrees.

Bake the loaf for about 20 to 30 minutes, then cover the top loosely with foil to prevent overbrowning. Continue to bake for 30 to 40 minutes (total baking time is about 60 minutes).

Let the loaf cool in the pan for 5 to 10 minutes and then lift it gently with potholders to remove it from the pan and place it on a rack to cool.

Muffins, Cupcakes, and Tassies

Gingerbread Muffins

It is hard to believe that anything so quick and easy can be so light and delicious; as a matter of fact it is hard to believe that anything can be so light and delicious—quick and easy or not.

Serve as a plain coffee cake or cupcakes or as a dessert with vanilla ice cream and Bittersweet Glaze (see page 181). Or pass them with baked apples.

You need two pans, each for twelve standard-size muffins, although you will use only sixteen of the forms.

16 MUFFINS

1 cup sifted all-purpose flour
1 teaspoon baking soda
¼ teaspoon salt
¼ teaspoon finely ground black pepper, preferably freshly ground
1 teaspoon ground ginger
½ teaspoon ground cloves
½ teaspoon cinnamon
¼ teaspoon dry powdered mustard
1 egg and 1 egg yolk, graded "large"
½ cup granulated sugar
½ cup molasses (preferably dark)
½ cup tasteless salad oil
1 tablespoon granular or powdered instant coffee
½ cup boiling water

Adjust two racks to divide the oven into thirds and preheat the oven to 400 degrees. Butter sixteen standard-size cupcake forms and dust them with fine dry bread crumbs (butter and crumb them even if they are non-stick), tap and turn the pans over a large piece of paper to crumb them thoroughly, and then invert them over the paper to tap out excess crumbs. Set the pans aside.

Sift together the flour, baking soda, salt, pepper, ginger, cloves, cinnamon, and mustard and set aside. In the large bowl of an electric mixer beat the egg and yolk just to mix. Beat in the sugar, molasses, and oil. Then on low speed add the sifted dry ingredients and beat until incorporated.

Dissolve the coffee in the boiling water and on low speed gradually add it to the batter, scraping the bowl with a rubber spatula and beating only until smooth. It will be a thin mixture.

Transfer to a pitcher that is easy to pour from and pour into the sixteen prepared forms, filling them about two-thirds full.

Bake for about 18 to 20 minutes, reversing the pans top to bottom and front to back once during baking to ensure even browning, until the muffins spring back when they are pressed gently with a fingertip. Do not overbake even by a minute.

Remove from the oven, cover each pan with a rack and turn the pan and rack over, remove the pan, and with your fingers turn the muffins right side up.

Serve hot or cooled.

Raisin Date Cupcakes

These are quite sweet and cakelike even though they have very little sugar; the generous amount of dates supply a natural sweetening and a wonderful flavor.

It is more efficient to line the forms for these with paper liners than it is to butter them, because when they are lined the paper makes them *slightly deeper and you need all the room you can get for these.*

12 CUPCAKES

10 ounces (1¼ cups, firmly packed) pitted dates
2½ ounces (½ cup) light raisins
1¾ cups plus 2 tablespoons boiling water
1 teaspoon baking soda
4 ounces (1 stick) unsalted butter
¼ teaspoon salt

1 teaspoon vanilla extract
⅓ cup dark brown sugar, firmly packed
2 eggs graded "large"
1⅓ cups sifted all-purpose flour
Finely grated rind of 1 deep-colored orange (see Note)

Adjust a rack one-third down from the top of the oven and preheat the oven to 350 degrees. Line a standard-size muffin pan (12 2¾-inch muffins) with paper liners and set aside.

Cut each date into 3 or 4 pieces and place them in a small mixing bowl. Add the raisins, the boiling water, and the baking soda and stir to mix. Let stand to cool (either completely or partly).

In the large bowl of an electric mixer beat the butter until soft. Add the salt, vanilla, and sugar and beat to mix. Beat in the eggs one at a time and then on low speed add the flour and beat until incorporated. The mixture will be thick. On low speed, very gradually add the water, raisin, and date mixture, scraping the bowl with a rubber spatula as necessary and beating until smoothly incorporated. (The dates remain in chunks.)

Remove the bowl from the mixer and stir in the grated orange rind. Spoon the mixture into the lined cups (the cups will be three-quarters full). It is not necessary to smooth the tops.

Bake for about 30 minutes until the tops of the cupcakes spring back when pressed gently with a fingertip; check carefully right in the middle of the cupcakes.

Remove from the pan and cool on a rack.

NOTE: *If you wish, you can substitute ¼ teaspoon of almond extract for the grated orange rind. If so, stir it in along with the vanilla.*

Raisin Banana Cupcakes

These are from the Florida Keys, where I think the people know more about banana breads than anyone else. At least they make the best I've had. The most important thing to remember about any banana bread is that the bananas must *be thoroughly ripe with brown/black spots on the skins or the bread will not have any flavor. These are moist, juicy, flavorful—wonderful.*

20 CUPCAKES

3½ ounces (¾ cup) light raisins
1 cup sifted all-purpose flour
¾ teaspoon double-acting baking powder
¾ teaspoon baking soda
¼ teaspoon salt
¼ teaspoon nutmeg

¼ teaspoon cinnamon
3 large (a generous 1¼ pounds) fully ripened bananas (to make 1½ cups, mashed)
1 egg graded "large"
⅓ cup dark brown sugar, firmly packed
¼ cup safflower oil (or other vegetable oil)

Adjust a rack to the middle of the oven and preheat the oven to 375 degrees. Line a standard-size muffin pan (12 2¾-inch muffins) with paper liners, or butter the forms; set aside.

Steam the raisins by placing them in a vegetable steamer or in a strainer over shallow water in a saucepan on high heat, cover the pan, bring the water to a boil, and let it boil for only a minute or two until the raisins are barely moist. Remove the steamer or strainer from the pan and set aside.

Sift together the flour, baking powder, baking soda, salt, nutmeg, and cinnamon and set aside.

To mash the bananas (the way it is done in the Florida Keys) peel them and place them all in the large bowl of an electric mixer. Beat on moderate speed, scraping the sides occasionally with a rubber spatula, until the bananas are mashed coarse. They should not be beaten until they completely liquefy; they should be uneven—some small chunks should remain. Set aside.

Without washing the bowl or beaters, beat the egg, sugar, and oil to mix, add the bananas and beat to mix, then on low speed gradually add the sifted dry ingredients and beat only until incorporated.

Remove the bowl from the mixer and stir in the raisins.

Divide the batter among the prepared forms. (They should be filled two thirds to three quarters of the way.)

Bake for about 25 minutes until the tops spring back when they are pressed gently with a fingertip.

Remove from the pan and cool on a rack.

Apple Cranberry Muffins

These are loaded with goodies; they have the tart flavor of cranberries and apples, the spiciness of nutmeg and ginger, the chewiness of raisins and nuts, and the body of whole wheat flour.

I have made these only with fresh cranberries (as opposed to frozen); remember these when you see fresh cranberries.

12 MUFFINS

1¼ cups fresh cranberries
1 egg graded "large"
Finely grated rind of 1 large deep-colored orange
2½ ounces (½ cup) raisins
⅓ cup orange juice
1 teaspoon vanilla extract
1 or 2 tart apples (to make 1 cup, diced)
½ cup sifted all-purpose whole wheat flour
½ cup sifted all-purpose flour
1 teaspoon double-acting baking powder
¼ teaspoon baking soda

¾ teaspoon cinnamon
¾ teaspoon nutmeg
¼ teaspoon ground ginger
¼ teaspoon allspice
¼ teaspoon salt
½ cup granulated sugar
2 ounces (½ stick) unsalted butter, cold and firm, cut into small pieces
4 ounces (generous 1 cup) walnuts, broken into medium-size pieces
Additional granulated sugar

Adjust a rack to the top position in the oven and preheat the oven to 350 degrees. Line twelve 2¾-inch standard muffin forms with cupcake

paper liners, or butter the forms (even if the pans are nonstick) and set aside.

Wash the berries briefly in a bowl of cold water, drain, and let dry on paper towels.

In a small bowl beat the egg just to mix. Stir in the grated rind, raisins, orange juice, and vanilla and set aside.

Peel, quarter, and core the apples and cut them into ¼-inch dice. Measure 1 cup of the diced apples and set aside.

Sift into a large mixing bowl both the flours, the baking powder, baking soda, cinnamon, nutmeg, ginger, allspice, salt, and sugar. Add the butter and with a pastry blender cut it into the dry ingredients until the mixture resembles coarse crumbs (some particles may be the size of small peas).

Add the egg and orange juice mixture and with a rubber spatula fold together only until the dry ingredients are barely moistened. Then briefly mix in the apples, cranberries, and walnuts; again, do not handle any more than necessary.

Spoon the mixture into the prepared muffin forms. They will be mounded high above the tops; it is all right. Do not smooth the tops.

Sprinkle the tops generously with additional sugar (it gives the tops a light glaze).

Bake for 25 to 28 minutes until the muffins are just barely firm to the touch.

Remove the muffins from the pan and place them on a rack.

Serve warm or at room temperature; the fresher the better.

Vermont Maple Syrup Cupcakes

This wonderful old recipe has lasted through many generations; one taste and you will see why. Quick and easy.

12 CUPCAKES

1¾ cups unsifted all-purpose flour
2½ teaspoons double-acting baking powder
¼ teaspoon salt
1 egg
¼ cup milk
¼ teaspoon almond extract
1 cup maple syrup
2 ounces (½ stick) unsalted butter, melted and
    just barely cooled

2½ ounces (¾ cup) toasted pecans (see To
    Toast Pecans, page 7), broken into large
    pieces
A bit of untoasted wheat germ, a few thinly sliced
    almonds, or a bit of chopped pecans (to be
    used as a topping)

Adjust two racks to divide the oven into thirds (these will bake first on the lower rack and then on the upper) and preheat the oven to 350 degrees. Line standard-size cupcake forms with cupcake paper liners, or butter the forms (even if they are nonstick). Set the pan aside.

Sift together the flour, baking powder, and salt and set aside. In the small bowl of an electric mixer beat the egg just to mix, then beat in the milk and almond extract. On low speed gradually add the sifted dry ingredients in three additions alternately with the maple syrup in two additions, scraping the sides of the bowl as necessary with a rubber spatula. Add the butter and beat briefly only until partly incorporated.

Remove the bowl from the mixer. Stir/fold a bit to finish mixing in the butter, then fold in the nuts only until they are distributed.

The mixture will be rather thin. It is best to ladle it into the prepared pan, distributing the nuts evenly.

Sprinkle lightly with whichever topping you wish.

Bake on the lower rack for about 15 minutes. Then reverse the pan front to back and transfer it to the higher rack and bake for 15 minutes more until the tops spring back when they are pressed gently with a fingertip. (Total baking time is about 30 minutes.)

Remove these from the pan as soon as they are done or they will steam and become soggy. These are especially tender—handle with care as you transfer them to a rack to cool.

Please taste one soon, even before it has cooled.

Pecan Sour Cream Muffins

Mr. Stanley Marcus, chairman emeritus of Neiman-Marcus, is a charming and remarkable gentleman. One of his many talents is his recognition and knowledge of quality in almost every field—and his good taste. When he hired Helen Corbitt to be in charge of all the food served in the Neiman-Marcus stores in Texas, it was because she was "the best." Her reputation as a cook/cateress/

hostess soon became national.

This is a simple little sweet muffin that Helen Corbitt served at breakfast, brunch, or lunch. These muffins and a cup of tea or coffee were a frequent treat during the day for many Texans. Plain, moist, rich, very easy, and beautiful.

12 LARGE MUFFINS

1⅓ cups sifted all-purpose flour
1 teaspoon double-acting baking powder
½ teaspoon baking soda
⅛ teaspoon salt
Generous pinch of nutmeg, preferably freshly grated
2 ounces (½ stick) unsalted butter

⅔ cup granulated sugar
2 eggs graded "large"
¾ cup sour cream
5½ ounces (1⅓ cups) toasted pecans broken into large pieces, plus 12 large toasted pecan halves (see To Toast Pecans, page 7)

Adjust an oven rack to the middle of the oven and preheat the oven to 450 degrees. Either butter twelve 2¾-inch muffin forms or line them with cupcake paper liners. (There will be a difference in the muffins if you butter the forms or line them. The muffins in lined forms come out higher, but they have pale sides and bottoms when the papers are removed. If you butter the forms, the muffins will not rise quite so high but they will have browned sides and bottoms. Frankly, I can't decide which is better; they taste equally good.)

Sift together the flour, baking powder, baking soda, salt, and nutmeg and set aside.

In the small bowl of an electric mixer beat the butter until soft. Beat in the sugar to mix, then add the eggs one at a time, beating until incorporated after each addition. On low speed add half of the sifted dry ingredients, then all of the sour cream, and then the remaining sifted dry ingredients. Beat only until smoothly incorporated. Remove the bowl from the mixer and stir in the 5½ ounces of pecan pieces.

Spoon into the prepared muffin forms. It is not necessary to smooth the tops; the muffins will do it themselves during baking.

Place a pecan half, flat side down, on each muffin; press them only slightly into the muffins.

Bake for 15 to 20 minutes until the muffins spring back when pressed lightly with a fingertip. During baking the muffins will rise with high, nicely rounded, golden-brown tops.

Remove from the pans immediately and place on a rack.

These may be served warm or cooled.

Tassies

These are miniature pastry tarts with a pecan filling. They are buttery, crisp, caramelized, crunchy; they remind me of pecan pie and butter-crunch and caramel and sugar and everything nice all in one. Serve tassies as a dessert or with tea or coffee.

It takes time to prepare these; they are worth it.

Many years ago I attended a drawing class at which the students were mostly chic ladies. It was a quick-sketch class at which we were all told to draw with charcoal. The teacher explained how to hold the piece of charcoal flush with the paper in order to draw with the side of it rather than the point. A lady in the class said she couldn't do it. The teacher said it was because her fingernails were too long. To which the student replied, "Miss So-and-so, if you told me that I could draw like Picasso if I cut my fingernails, I would not do it."

No connection with this recipe except that if you have long fingernails I don't think you will be able to make these.

Tassies are regional food in many different parts of this country. I was told that they originated in Texas. And Georgia. And Virginia. This recipe is based on one that was given to me in San Francisco by Jane Benét and Fran Irwin in the food department of the San Francisco Chronicle.

You need muffin forms with a nonstick finish that measure 1¾ inches in width and ¾ inch in depth. I have four such pans, each with twelve forms. If you have fewer, the tassies do not have to be baked all at once. The remaining dough can be refrigerated and the filling can wait at room temperature, or it can be refrigerated. These pans are generally available in hardware stores. See Miniature Muffin Pans, page 11, for a source.

48 "LITTLE CUPS"

PASTRY

8 ounces cream cheese, preferably at room temperature
8 ounces (2 sticks) unsalted butter

2 cups sifted all-purpose flour
Pinch of salt

In the large bowl of an electric mixer beat the cream cheese and butter until they are soft. On low speed gradually add the flour and the salt and beat until smoothly incorporated.

Turn the mixture out onto a length of wax paper or foil and refrigerate or freeze it briefly until the mixture is not too sticky and can be shaped lightly.

Transfer the dough to a work surface and with your hands form it into an even oblong. Wrap and return to the refrigerator or freezer for about 10 minutes (or much longer, if you wish) until it is firm enough to be cut and handled.

Cut into 4 equal pieces. Cut each piece into 12 equal pieces. Roll each piece between your hands into a ball and place the balls in the (unbuttered) miniature muffin forms.

Keep some flour next to your work space for flouring your fingers. With floured fingertips press each ball of dough into a cup, pressing down in the middle and then working the dough up on the sides. The shaped pastry shells should be flush with the tops of the forms but it does not matter if they are slightly uneven (it will all bake together more or less and the filling will run over the edges in spots anyhow).

FILLING

8 ounces (1 cup, packed) pitted dates
5½ ounces (1½ cups) pecans, toasted (see To
 Toast Pecans, page 7), plus 48 perfect pecan
 halves (untoasted) (to be used on the tops)
4 ounces (1 stick) unsalted butter

1 tablespoon vanilla extract
Pinch of salt
2 cups light brown sugar, firmly packed
1 egg graded "large"

Adjust a rack one-third up from the bottom of the oven (do not bake these any higher or the tops will become too brown). Preheat the oven to 350 degrees. Since these are very rich, some of the butter might bubble and ooze out of the pans; therefore place a cookie sheet or aluminum foil on a rack below. (If your oven does not have a rack below place aluminum foil on the bottom of the oven, if you wish.)

With scissors cut the dates into ¼-inch pieces and set aside. Break up or cut the 5½ ounces of pecans (reserve the remaining 48 halves) into medium-small pieces (it will be difficult to place the filling in the pastry cups if the pieces of nuts are too large) and set aside. In the small bowl of an electric mixer beat the butter until it is soft. Beat in the vanilla, salt, sugar, and the egg. Remove the bowl from the mixer. Stir in the dates and the 5½ ounces of the pecans.

With a small spoon (a demitasse spoon works well) spoon the filling into the unbaked pastry shells. If you have four pans and are making these all at one time, you will see that when you have used up all of the filling the cups will be filled to the tops; that is right.

Then place a pecan half, flat side down, on each tassie, pressing the nut gently into the filling just a bit.

Bake two pans at a time on the same rack for about 35 minutes until the pastry that shows around the edges is lightly browned. During baking, if the tassies are not browning evenly, reverse the pans front to back and left to right.

When the tassies are done, let them stand in the pans until completely cool.

Now, to remove the tassies from the pans. Since some of the filling will have bubbled up and run over the edges of the forms it will tend to stick them to the pans and will not allow them to slip out (nonstick or not); therefore, use the dull side of a table knife and gently and carefully (without cutting into the finish on the pan) cut away any edge that ran over. Then the tassies should lift out easily. If necessary, turn the pan upside down. Or, if necessary, stick the tip of a small, sharp knife into the pastry on an angle and gently pry the tassie up and out of the pan. Whatever, be gentle, because these will break if you are rough with them.

When I make these, if I don't plan to serve them soon, I wrap them individually in plastic wrap and place them in a freezer bag. They can wait at room temperature or in the refrigerator for a day or two or they can be frozen. But when they are very fresh—well, taste one when it is almost but not completely cool.

Miniature Ginger Cakes

Ginger and chocolate are a great combination. These are adorable little honey cakes, as light as a breeze, with an irresistible, spicy, orange and ginger flavor and a thin, dark, bittersweet, mocha chocolate glaze.

Miniature cakes were a popular conceit during the Victorian period, when they were usually very fancy and elaborate. These, which are adapted from an old recipe, are totally simple. If you have tea parties for dolls in your family, they will love these. People love them too, at tea parties, or at a buffet, or along with ice cream or fruit after dinner. Or make them for a cake sale.

By the way, the combination of cream of tartar and baking soda takes the place of baking powder. It was commonly used before baking powders were manufactured.

You will need four pans, each with twelve 1¾ by ¾-inch miniature muffin forms with a non-stick finish. They are generally available at hardware stores and supermarkets. Or see Miniature Muffin Pans, page 11, for a source.

48 1¾-INCH CAKES

3 ounces candied ginger (to make ½ cup, diced)
1½ cups sifted all-purpose flour
3 teaspoons ground ginger
½ teaspoon coriander
½ teaspoon mace
½ teaspoon cinnamon
½ teaspoon cream of tartar
½ teaspoon baking soda

¼ teaspoon salt
Finely grated rind of 1 orange
2 tablespoons orange juice
2 ounces (½ stick) unsalted butter
3 tablespoons granulated sugar
½ cup honey
2 eggs graded "large"
¼ cup milk

Adjust two racks to divide the oven into thirds and preheat the oven to 325 degrees. Butter the miniature muffin forms (above), even though they are nonstick, and set aside.

Cut the ginger into ⅛- to ¼-inch dice and place it in a small bowl. Add about 2 teaspoons of the flour and toss with your fingers to separate and coat the pieces thoroughly. Set aside.

Sift together the remaining flour with the ground ginger, coriander, mace, cinnamon, cream of tartar, baking soda, and salt and set aside.

Combine the rind and juice and set aside.

In the small bowl of an electric mixer beat the butter until soft. Beat in the sugar, then add the honey and beat until smooth. Add the eggs one at a time, beating until incorporated after each addition. On low speed gradually add about half the sifted dry ingredients, then the milk, and then the remaining dry ingredients. Beat until smooth.

Remove the bowl from the mixer and stir in the orange rind and juice mixture and then the diced candied ginger.

Spoon the mixture into the buttered muffin forms; they will be about three-quarters full.

Place two pans side by side on each oven rack and bake for 20 to 23 minutes, reversing the pans top to bottom once during baking (after about 15 minutes) to ensure even browning. Bake only until the tops spring back when they are pressed lightly with a fingertip.

When done, let the cakes stand in the pans for about a minute. Then cover each pan with a rack and turn the pan and the rack upside down. If the cakes do not fall out of the pan easily, tap the pan against the rack to knock them out. Then, with your fingers, turn the cakes right side up to cool.

The glaze can be made while the cakes are baking or after they have baked.

BITTERSWEET GLAZE

This glaze makes a fantastic sauce on vanilla ice cream. If you plan it for ice cream, double the amounts to serve about 6 portions. Serve it slightly warm or at room temperature. If it is made ahead of time, it can be reheated before serving.

¼ cup boiling water
1 teaspoon granular instant coffee
3 ounces semisweet chocolate

1 ounce unsweetened chocolate
1 teaspoon vegetable shortening (e.g., Crisco)

Stir the water and coffee in a very small saucepan over moderate heat, add the chocolates and shortening, and then stir occasionally until the chocolates are melted.

Transfer to the small bowl of an electric mixer and beat briskly until the glaze is as smooth as honey.

The glaze can be warm or cooled when you use it. Transfer it to a small, shallow custard cup.

One at a time, pick up a ginger cake, hold it upside down, and dip the top of the cake into the glaze to coat it. Then turn the cake right side up and place it on the rack again for the glaze to set a bit.

These can be served in about an hour or they can stand for several hours. (The glaze will become dull as it dries. Sorry about that.)

Surprise Cakes

Fancy, dainty, buttery-delicious. These are tiny cupcakes with a crisp butter-cookie base, a jelly and nut surprise filling, and a light, cakelike topping. Make them for a tea party, a shower, a children's party, a cake sale, or just any time you feel like playing in the kitchen.

You will need two miniature muffin pans each with twelve 1¾ by ¾-inch forms and a non-stick finish. These pans are generally available at hardware stores and supermarkets. See page 11 for a source. And you will need a round cookie cutter about 1½ inches in diameter.

The dough for the bottom layer should be refrigerated for an hour or two, or overnight, before it is rolled out and cut.

24 SMALL CUPCAKES

BOTTOM LAYER

1½ cups unsifted all-purpose flour
Pinch of salt
1 teaspoon double-acting baking powder
½ cup granulated sugar
4 ounces (1 stick) unsalted butter, cold and firm,

cut into ½-inch dice (it is best to cut the butter ahead of time and refrigerate it)
1 egg graded "large"
½ teaspoon vanilla extract
¼ cup milk

Sift into a large mixing bowl the flour, salt, baking powder, and sugar. With a pastry blender cut in the butter until the mixture resembles coarse crumbs; there may be some pieces of butter about the size of grains of rice, or even a bit larger—it is all right.

In a small bowl beat the egg, vanilla, and milk to mix. Add it all at once to the flour mixture and stir briskly with a fork until the dry ingredients are all moistened and the mixture just holds together.

Turn the mixture out onto a length of plastic wrap, bring up the sides of the plastic tightly against the dough to form it into a ball, press it together, wrap, and refrigerate for an hour or two or overnight.

When you are ready to bake, adjust a rack to the middle of the oven and preheat the oven to 425 degrees. Butter twenty-four miniature muffin forms (above), even though they are nonstick, and set aside.

Cut the chilled dough in half and work with one piece at a time; refrigerate the other piece. On a lightly floured pastry cloth with a lightly floured rolling pin roll out the dough until it is ⅓ inch thick.

You need a round cookie cutter about 1½ inches in diameter (it should be slightly wider than the base of the muffin forms). Cut out 12 rounds of the dough. Repeat with the remaining half of the dough. Reserve scraps of the dough (see Note).

Place a round of dough into each buttered form, pressing down gently in the middle to make it cup-shaped (it is not necessary to fuss with the shapes—they will take care of themselves during baking).

FILLING

About ⅓ cup red currant jelly, orange marmalade, or any other jam, jelly, or preserves

A few spoons of rather finely chopped walnuts or 24 walnut halves

Place a rounded ½ teaspoon of the jelly in the middle of each muffin form on top of the dough (it does not have to be exactly in the middle), and either sprinkle a bit of the chopped walnuts over the jelly or place 1 walnut half on each.

Set aside while you prepare the top layer.

TOP LAYER

2 ounces (½ stick) unsalted butter, at room
 temperature
¼ cup granulated sugar
1 egg graded "large"

Scant ¼ teaspoon almond extract
2 tablespoons unsifted all-purpose flour
½ teaspoon double-acting baking powder

Adjust a rack to the middle of the oven and preheat the oven to 425 degrees.

In the small bowl of an electric mixer beat the butter until it is soft. Beat in the sugar and then the egg and almond extract. Then add the flour and baking powder and beat until smooth.

Place a teaspoonful of this mixture over the filling in each form; there will be just enough for the 24 cakes.

Bake the two pans side by side on the same rack for 13 to 15 minutes, reversing the pans front to back once after about 10 minutes. When done, the little cakes will be golden with darker rims and the tops will spring back when they are pressed gently with a fingertip.

Let the cakes stand in the pans for about 5 minutes. Then cover each pan with a rack, turn the pan and the rack over, and remove the pans (the cakes will slip out easily). Then, with your fingers, turn the cakes right side up to cool.

NOTE: *You will most probably have some leftover dough from the bottom layer. It makes delicious crisp sugar cookies. Roll it out to a scant ¼-inch thickness, cut with a round cutter or cut into squares with a knife. Place on unbuttered cookie sheets, sprinkle with a bit of sugar or cinnamon-sugar, and bake on a high rack in a 425-degree oven until the cookies are sandy colored with darker rims. Cool on a rack.*

VARIATIONS: *I don't see any reason you could not play with this recipe and substitute other fillings. I think about peanut butter or dates or a piece of chocolate . . .*

Texas Chocolate Muffins

These are not muffins; they are my idea of Brownies baked like cupcakes. But in Texas for some reason they call them muffins. They have two kinds of chocolate and cocoa. They are dense, *rich, and very chocolate. Especially beautiful— totally plain. Quickly and easily mixed in a saucepan.*

12 MUFFINS

1 cup sifted all-purpose flour
Pinch of salt
3 tablespoons unsweetened cocoa powder
    (preferably Dutch-process)
8 ounces (2 sticks) unsalted butter
2 ounces unsweetened chocolate
2 ounces semisweet chocolate

1½ cups granulated sugar
4 eggs graded "large"
1 teaspoon vanilla extract
¼ teaspoon almond extract
7 ounces (2 cups) toasted pecans (see To Toast
    Pecans, page 7), broken into large pieces

Adjust a rack one-third up from the bottom of the oven and preheat the oven to 350 degrees. Line twelve standard-size muffin forms with fluted paper cupcake liners, or butter twelve muffin forms (line them or butter them even if they are nonstick). Set aside.

Sift together the flour, salt, and cocoa and set aside.

Place the butter and both of the chocolates in a heavy 2½- to 3-quart saucepan over moderately low heat and stir frequently with a wooden spatula until melted and smooth. Remove the pan from the heat. Stir in the sugar, the eggs one at a time, the vanilla and almond extracts, and then the sifted dry ingredients. After the dry ingredients are moistened stir briskly until smooth. If necessary, whisk with a firm wire whisk. Then stir in the nuts.

This is a thick and gooey mixture and I find it clumsy to spoon into the prepared muffin forms. Instead, I pour it, part at a time, into a 2-cup plastic measuring cup with a spout (which is wide and easy to pour from). Then, with the help of a teaspoon, I pour it into the forms. This is a large amount of batter for 12 muffins; the forms will be filled to the tops. It is all right. The muffins will mound high during baking but they will not run over. They might run into one another a bit on the sides but they will not stick to each other.

Bake for 33 to 35 minutes, reversing the pan front to back once during baking. To test for doneness, insert a toothpick into the middle of a muffin; it should come out just barely or almost dry and clean. A bit of moist batter may cling to the toothpick. Do not overbake. During baking these will rise with inch-high, perfectly rounded tops with a gorgeous crackly texture.

Remove the muffins from the pan and cool them on a rack. When cool these will develop a hard and crunchy crust that is delicious.

Shortcake, Cobblers, Pandowdy, et Cetera

ABOUT COBBLERS,
PANDOWDIES,
BUCKLES, CRISPS,
GRUNTS, ET CETERA

Cobblers, pandowdies, buckles, crisps, grunts, et cetera, are all combinations of fresh fruit and a quick biscuit or cakelike topping that are baked together. Very very Early American and very very wonderful. As delicious as fruit pies but quick, easy, and foolproof. They are simple and homey and at the same time sophisticated. They are as appropriate, as much at home, and just as appreciated today as they were hundreds of years ago.

You will see that in almost all of these recipes the directions are for serving them hot. Believe me, it really makes a big difference (even if you love them cold also)—please do try them hot.

All of these recipes make fabulous desserts for a luncheon or dinner. They are also divine at breakfast or brunch. Or at a coffee between meals, or late at night. Or at a dessert party.

TO PREPARE
BISCUIT TOPPINGS
AHEAD OF TIME

Some of the desserts in this section are topped with biscuits before they are baked. Some expert biscuit bakers say "don't mix them ahead of time," some say "do mix them ahead of time." I have therefore just completed a series of experiments to find out for myself. Here are the results.

If the biscuits are made with sweet milk and baking powder it is safe to mix them about 1 to 2 hours ahead of time, place them on a tray lined with wax paper or plastic wrap, cover with plastic wrap, and refrigerate. Then, place them on top of the fruit mixture just before baking.

If the biscuits are made with buttermilk and baking soda (plus baking powder) the results are a bit different. Baking soda starts to work as soon as it is mixed with a liquid. Therefore it is best to bake these immediately. I am looking at some that I baked immediately, some that I let stand at room temperature for an hour, some that I let stand at room temperature for several hours, some that I refrigerated for an hour, and some that I refrigerated all day—before baking. There is a difference. Those that I baked immediately rose a tiny bit higher (only a tiny bit) and they rose straight up on the sides with a flat top; those that waited before baking rose with a rounded top (nothing to be ashamed of).

For biscuits to be as good as possible, you can, if you wish, cut the butter into the dry ingredients ahead of time, refrigerate the mixture for hours, and then, as close to baking time as possible, stir in the liquid and shape the biscuits (which you are supposed to do quickly and which should take only a minute or two anyhow).

But if the biscuits are not for a biscuit-baking contest (in which case you would probably use lard instead of butter anyhow), and if it is a big help to you, finish the biscuits (either sweet milk or buttermilk), place them on a covered tray, cover the biscuits and refrigerate (preferably no longer than an hour if the mixture has baking soda and buttermilk—up to a few hours if it has sweet milk and only baking powder), and place the biscuits on top of the fruit just before baking.

NOTE: *At a lovely restaurant in Savannah, Georgia, named Elizabeth's on 37th, we had especially delicious biscuits. Elizabeth told me that she uses margarine instead of butter, she adds a bit of wheat germ to the dough and also a bit of grated cheese (a combination of Cheddar, mozzarella, and*

Swiss, which she always has on hand for topping casseroles), she uses sweet milk and baking powder, and she completes the biscuits up to an hour before baking.

Strawberry Shortcake

If it is made with spongecake it is not shortcake. The dictionary says "a cake made short and crisp with butter—served with fruit usually between the layers." That's shortcake. Consider it if you invite friends for dessert and coffee, or for a Sunday brunch. I grew up with this as a frequent dinner dessert—my mother served it often—sometimes with her own home-grown berries. But home-grown or store-bought, Strawberry Shortcake always made the meal an occasion, a celebration, a festivity.

Strawberry Shortcake is certainly a traditional dessert, but this is an untraditional variation. It is spectacular, and I think easy enough for anyone.

8 PORTIONS

STRAWBERRIES

The berries can be washed, hulled, and drained ahead of time, but wait until the last minute to finish their preparation. (When the berries stand after being mixed with the preserves they give off their juice, which causes them to lose their texture; they are more delicious if they are mixed just before serving.)

3 1-pint boxes (3 pounds, or about 10 to 12 cups) fresh strawberries (or more if you wish)

12 ounces (1 cup) strawberry preserves
2 tablespoons kirsch

Wash, hull, and dry the berries (see To Wash Strawberries, page 14). Refrigerate the berries if they will have to wait more than an hour or so; otherwise they can wait at room temperature.

Place the preserves in a saucepan and let stand until you are ready to put the dessert together. Reserve the kirsch also.

SHORTCAKE

Part of this can be done early in the day or even a day ahead, although it takes only a few minutes from beginning to end. This should be served as soon as it is baked.

2 cups sifted all-purpose flour
1 tablespoon plus 1 teaspoon double-acting baking powder
¼ teaspoon salt
¼ cup granulated sugar
4 ounces (1 stick) unsalted butter, cold and firm, cut into quarters the long way and then cut

into ¼-inch slices (it is best to cut it ahead of time and refrigerate)
1 egg graded "large," cold
⅓ cup milk, cold
If necessary, a bit of ice water
Additional butter, at room temperature, to use after the cake is baked

Before baking, adjust a rack to the middle of the oven and preheat the oven to 450 degrees. Butter two 8-inch layer cake pans and set aside.

Sift together into a wide bowl the flour, baking powder, salt, and sugar. With a pastry blender cut in the butter until the mixture resembles coarse crumbs (some of the pieces may be as large as corn kernels).

In a small bowl beat the egg to mix and beat in the milk.

(If you wish, the two mixtures may be refrigerated, separately, for hours or even overnight.)

To finish the shortcake, slowly drizzle the egg-milk mixture over the flour mixture and, with a table fork, stir vigorously to moisten all of the flour mixture. Stir well. If some dry ingredients remain dry in the bottom of the bowl and you need more liquid, drizzle in a bit of ice water (only about a teaspoonful at a time) where needed and stir to incorporate. When it is just right the ingredients should be only damp enough to hold together when pressed together.

Turn the mixture out onto a lightly floured surface. Handle very little now. Flour your hands and press the ingredients lightly together to form a ball. Flour the ball lightly. With a sharp knife cut the ball of dough in half. Form each half into a ball, flour lightly, flatten slightly, and place the balls in the buttered pans. Flour your fingertips and press out the dough to fill the pans; they will be thin layers.

Bake for about 12 minutes until just done—a medium golden color. Do not overbake.

While the cake is baking, place the preserves over a low-medium heat just to melt. And slice the strawberries into a wide bowl, cutting each berry into three or four slices (or more if the berries are extra large). Drizzle the kirsch over the berries, toss gently with a rubber spatula, and set aside for a few minutes.

(If the cream has not been whipped ahead of time, do it now—see Whipped Cream, below.)

When the cakes are done, cover one with a rack, turn the pan and rack over, remove the pan, cover the cake with a wide platter, and turn the rack and platter over again, leaving the cake right side up. Move the cake to center it if necessary.

Without waiting spread the top of the hot cake with room-temperature butter. It should melt and run into the cake, leaving only a shiny finish.

Pour the melted preserves (which may be warm or at room temperature) over the sliced berries and toss gently with a rubber spatula.

Place about half of the berries over the bottom layer of cake. With your bare hands press down on the berries to form them into a smooth and compact layer. If some of the berries or juices run over the edge of the cake it is all right—it looks nice—but you will have an easier time serving this if the layer of berries is not too thick.

Then cover the second cake with a rack, turn over, remove the pan, cover the cake with a cutting board or a cookie sheet, and turn over again, leaving the cake right side up. Lightly butter the top of this cake (do not use more butter than melts into the cake). And with a long sharp knife cut the cake into eight pie-shaped wedges. With a pie server transfer the wedges to re-form the layer and cover the berries.

Place the remaining berries in a pretty bowl. And place the whipped cream in another bowl. Bring both bowls and the cake plate to the table, with a knife, a pie server, and two large serving spoons. Serve on wide plates, preferably dinner-size plates, a portion of cake in the middle with a mound of berries and their juice on one side of the cake and a mound of the whipped cream on the other side.

WHIPPED CREAM

2 cups whipping cream
¼ cup granulated or confectioners sugar

1 teaspoon vanilla extract

In a chilled bowl, with chilled beaters, whip the ingredients only until they hold a soft shape; this is better if it is not really stiff.

If you whip the cream ahead of time, refrigerate it. Then, just before serving, whisk it a bit with a wire whisk to bring it back to a smooth consistency (it separates a bit while standing).

Washington State Cherry Cobbler

National Sweet Cherry Week is celebrated at the end of June because that is the beginning of the fresh cherry season in the northwest states of Washington, Oregon, Idaho, and Utah. The season is a short one and here in Florida, at the opposite side of the country, it comes and goes before I realize it. (The produce man says, "They're not in yet—come back next week." Then he says, "We had them last week but the season is over now.")

I will continue to wait but, while waiting, I have canned cherries on the shelf always ready to make this wonderful dessert.

It consists of a slightly thickened and mildly spiced cherry mixture in a shallow baking dish, topped with the lightest and tenderest old-fashioned buttermilk biscuits. I like it best very hot—straight from the oven—but it does hold its

heat for about half an hour, and it is still delicious an hour or two later at room temperature.

The cherry mixture can be prepared hours ahead of time; the biscuits can be prepared up to an hour ahead of time, if you wish. If you want to prepare the biscuits ahead, place them on a tray covered with wax paper, loosely cover the biscuits with plastic wrap or wax paper, and refrigerate. Wait until you are ready to bake before placing the biscuits on the cobbler.

This recipe is written for one large baking dish, but it can also be made in individual onion soup bowls or similar ovenproof dishes, with one biscuit on top of each (in which case, cut the biscuits with a slightly wider cutter).

6 PORTIONS

CHERRY MIXTURE

2 cans (16 to 17 ounces each) pitted sweet cherries packed in syrup (gorgeous with black Bing cherries, but light cherries may be used)
¼ cup unsifted all-purpose flour
⅛ teaspoon salt

¼ teaspoon allspice
¼ teaspoon cinnamon
⅓ cup granulated sugar
1 tablespoon unsalted butter
2 tablespoons lemon juice

Place a wide strainer or a colander over a large bowl. Pour the cherries and their syrup into the strainer or colander and let drain. Measure and reserve 2 cups of the syrup.

Sift together into a heavy 1½- to 2-quart saucepan the flour, salt, allspice, cinnamon, and sugar. Gradually add the 2 cups of cherry syrup, stirring with a rubber spatula (or a wire whisk if necessary) until smooth.

Place over moderate heat and cook, stirring and scraping the bottom and sides constantly with a rubber spatula, until the mixture comes to a gentle boil. Then reduce the heat to low and simmer, stirring gently, for 1 minute.

Remove from the heat. Add the butter and continue to stir gently until it is melted. Carefully mix in the lemon juice, then add the drained cherries and stir—always very gently.

Turn the warm mixture into an unbuttered shallow baking dish with at least a 2-quart capacity (11 by 8 by 1¾ or 2 inches). Smooth the top, and set aside.

BUTTERMILK BISCUITS

1 cup minus 2 tablespoons unsifted all-purpose
    flour
1 teaspoon double-acting baking powder
¼ teaspoon salt
¼ teaspoon baking soda

2 teaspoons granulated sugar
2½ tablespoons unsalted butter, cold and firm,
    cut into small pieces (it is best to cut the
    butter ahead of time and refrigerate it)
¼ cup plus 2 tablespoons buttermilk, cold

Adjust a rack one-third up from the bottom of the oven and preheat the oven to 450 degrees.

Sift together into a mixing bowl the flour, baking powder, salt, baking soda, and sugar. Add the butter and with a pastry blender cut it in until the mixture resembles coarse crumbs (small but visible pieces of butter make biscuits flakier than if the butter is cut in too fine). Up to this point the mixture can be made long ahead of time and refrigerated, if you wish.

Make a well in the middle of the ingredients in the bowl. Add the buttermilk all at once to the well and quickly stir with a fork for only 10 to 20 seconds until barely but not completely mixed.

Flour a work surface very lightly (good biscuits do not want any additional flour). Turn the mixture out onto the floured surface. With your hands press the mixture together gently, lightly, and quickly. Then knead it (fold part of the dough over onto itself) very briefly (only three or four times) until the mixture holds together but not until it becomes smooth.

If necessary, reflour the surface lightly, and lightly flour a rolling pin. Roll out the dough into a round shape about 7 inches in diameter and about ¼ to ⅜ inch thick.

Use a round cookie cutter 2 inches in diameter. Dip the cutter into flour before cutting each biscuit. Start cutting at the outside edge of the dough. Cut the biscuits as close to each other as possible. Each time, cut straight down (do not twist the cutter). When they are all cut use a metal spatula to transfer the biscuits to the top of the cherry mixture. Do not press the remaining scraps together (it would make tough biscuits). You can either use the scraps as they are, placing them any which way between the rounds, or place a few scraps next to each other and cut a round out of them, or cut a few half-moon shapes and place them between the rounds.

GLAZE

1 egg yolk   2 to 3 teaspoons granulated sugar
1 tablespoon milk or cream

Mix together the yolk and milk or cream (you will not use it all for this recipe) and brush it lightly over the tops of the biscuits (do not use so much that it runs down the sides). Sprinkle the sugar lightly all over the biscuits and exposed cherry mixture.

Bake for about 15 minutes until the biscuits are well browned and the cherry mixture is bubbling hot.

NOTE: *There are two schools of thought: those who push their biscuit topping down into the soupy part and wait for it to absorb the liquid (they're the Southerners) and those who think the biscuits should be dry and should not become mushy (they're the Northerners). At least that's how it is with my husband and me (he's from Texas, I'm from New York).*

VARIATION: *This is the Cherry Cobbler made with fresh cherries. You need a cherry pitter for this. That is not a silly gadget; it is an essential tool. I don't know any other way to get the pits out. It is surprisingly quick and easy to pit a bowlful of cherries. Most kitchen shops sell cherry pitters.*

2 pounds (generous 6 cups) fresh black Bing   1⅓ cups granulated sugar
     cherries   2 cups cool tap water
¼ cup plus 1 tablespoon unsifted all-purpose flour   1 tablespoon unsalted butter
⅛ teaspoon salt   2 tablespoons lemon juice
¼ teaspoon allspice   Optional: red food coloring
¼ teaspoon cinnamon

Wash, dry, and pit the cherries, then set them aside. Sift together into a heavy 1½- to 2-quart saucepan the flour, salt, allspice, cinnamon, and sugar. Gradually stir in the water, pressing on any lumps of dry ingredients with a rubber spatula or briskly beating with a wire whisk until smooth.

Follow the preceding recipe to bring the mixture to a boil, simmer for 1 minute, stir in the butter and lemon juice, then add the optional food coloring to give the mixture a nice deep rosy hue. Stir in the pitted fresh cherries, turn the mixture into the baking dish, and then continue to follow the above recipe.

New York State Apple Cobbler

This is unusual, and wonderful—you will love it. The secret is grated Cheddar cheese in the topping. It is best when it is hot, although it is also delicious after it has cooled. It can be prepared ahead of time and can stand at room temperature for a few hours, if you wish, before it is baked. It is one of the easiest recipes I know.

6 PORTIONS

TOPPING

6 ounces Cheddar cheese (which may be mild or aged and sharp)
4 ounces (1 stick) unsalted butter

¼ teaspoon salt
1 cup sifted all-purpose flour
½ cup light brown sugar, firmly packed

Grate the cheese either on a standing metal grater or in a food processor. (In a processor, use either the fine or medium grater blade. Or use the metal chopping blade, cutting the cheese into coarse chunks first and then processing it on/off for only a few seconds until coarsely processed.)

Place the cheese and butter in the large bowl of an electric mixer and beat until mixed. Add the salt, flour, and sugar and beat on low speed until mixed. Set aside.

APPLE MIXTURE

2½ to 3 pounds (4 large or 6 medium) tart cooking apples (I use Granny Smith)
½ cup light brown sugar, firmly packed

½ teaspoon cinnamon
¾ teaspoon nutmeg
2 tablespoons bourbon or brandy

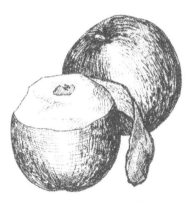

You will need an ovenproof baking dish that measures about 11 by 8 by 2 inches (2-quart capacity); butter the dish and set it aside.

Peel, quarter, and core the apples and cut each quarter into 4 to 6 lengthwise slices, depending on the size of the apples. You should have 8 to 10 cups of sliced apples.

Place the apples in a large mixing bowl with the sugar, cinnamon, nutmeg, and bourbon or brandy. Toss and mix with a rubber spatula until the ingredients are distributed evenly.

Turn the apple mixture into the buttered baking dish; arrange the apples slightly to make a rather smooth layer.

With your fingers crumble the topping over the apples, covering the fruit as completely as possible. Place a piece of wax paper over the surface and, with your hands, press down on the paper rather gently to press the topping into a fairly smooth layer.

Cover airtight with plastic wrap and let stand until you are ready to bake.

Before baking, adjust a rack to the middle of the oven and preheat the oven to 350 degrees.

Uncover the baking dish and bake for about 45 minutes until the apples are tender when tested with a toothpick and the topping is a beautiful golden-brown color.

Serve as is or with ice cream.

Apple and Orange Cobbler

The year was 1937. My family was living on a dairy farm in Connecticut. When we drove into Danbury or New Milford, we passed a little roadside stand where a lady occasionally sold homemade bread. It was fabulous! We always tried to plan our shopping or driving at the time we thought her bread might be ready. Her name was Margaret Rudkin, and her farm was Pepperidge Farm.

She had started to bake bread, which she had never done before, because her son was allergic to certain ingredients in commercial bread. She said it was just as easy to bake several loaves at a time —she loved doing it—and she enjoyed selling the extra loaves. (Her bread sold for twenty-five cents a loaf, which seemed terribly extravagant; other breads cost ten cents.) The first loaves were only whole wheat, and they were sold mainly to doctors, a few specialty stores, and a few lucky neighbors.

Mrs. Rudkin said that her first loaf should have been sent to the Smithsonian Institution as a sample of bread from the Stone Age because it was as hard as a rock and about an inch high.

This wonderful recipe has nothing to do with bread, but it was inspired by a recipe in The Margaret Rudkin Pepperidge Farm Cookbook (Atheneum, 1963), a beautiful book.

The filling for this can be made even a day or two ahead, and the biscuits can be prepared up to a few hours ahead, if you wish. If so, place the biscuits on a tray covered with wax paper, cover them loosely with plastic wrap or wax paper, and refrigerate. Wait until you are ready to bake before placing the biscuits on the cobbler.

If possible, serve this hot, right out of the oven.

9 PORTIONS

APPLE AND ORANGE FILLING

3 pounds (6 to 7 large) cooking apples (preferably Granny Smith)
Finely grated rind of 1 large deep-colored orange
½ cup orange juice
3 ounces (¾ stick) unsalted butter

¾ cup granulated sugar
2 tablespoons flour
¼ teaspoon vanilla extract
3 large seedless navel oranges, sectioned (see page 15)

Peel, quarter, and core the apples. Cut each quarter into 4 or 5 lengthwise strips. You should have 10 to 12 cups of loosely packed sliced apples.

Place the apples, orange rind, orange juice, 2 ounces (½ stick) of the butter (reserve the remaining ¼ stick), and the sugar in a wide, deep, heavy saucepan that has a tight-fitting cover.

Cover and cook over moderate heat, stirring a few times, for about 7 minutes until the apples have given off their juice and are just barely tender.

Pour the mixture into a wide strainer set over a wide bowl. Set aside the apples. Measure the drained syrup; you should have 1½ cups. (If you have less than that, add water or orange juice; if you have more, boil it, uncovered, over high heat to reduce, and set aside.)

In the saucepan that the apples cooked in, melt the remaining ¼ stick of butter over moderate heat, stir in the flour, reduce the heat to low, and simmer, stirring, for about 2 minutes.

Then over moderate heat add the drained 1½ cups of syrup (which should still be warm); pour it in all at once, stir briskly with a wire whisk, and then reduce the heat to low and scrape the pan with a rubber spatula, letting the syrup just simmer gently for about 2 minutes. Stir in the vanilla, let cool for a few minutes, then stir in the cooked apples and the orange sections.

Butter a wide, shallow 2-quart ovenproof baking dish (11 by 8 by about 2 inches). Turn the mixture into the baking dish, smooth the top, and set aside.

Continue with the recipe now or cover and refrigerate the fruit in the baking dish, and continue with the recipe later on.

BISCUIT TOPPING

These are traditional, old-fashioned biscuits made with sweet milk. (If you want to make these separately, to serve as bread, bake them on an unbuttered shiny metal cookie sheet or use any cookie sheet lined with aluminum foil shiny side up. Bake at 450 degrees for about 12 minutes until lightly browned.)

2 cups minus 2 tablespoons sifted all-purpose flour
¼ teaspoon salt
2¾ teaspoons double-acting baking powder
3 ounces (¾ stick) unsalted butter, cold and firm,
cut into ½-inch pieces (it is best to cut the butter ahead of time and refrigerate it)
⅔ cup cold milk
Heavy or light cream
Granulated sugar

Adjust a rack to the middle of the oven and preheat the oven to 450 degrees.

Into a mixing bowl sift together the flour, salt, and baking powder. Add the butter and with a pastry blender cut it in until the mixture resembles coarse meal; there may be a few pieces the size of small dried split peas. The recipe may be prepared ahead of time to this point and refrigerated overnight.)

Make a well in the middle of the ingredients. Pour the milk into the well. With a fork quickly stir around and around to incorporate the dry ingredients. Handle as little as possible. If necessary add a bit more flour or milk but mix or stir only briefly.

Turn the rough mixture out onto a lightly floured board or work the surface and knead it only a few times (only a few seconds—no more) until the mixture is barely smooth.

With a lightly floured rolling pin roll out the dough until it is about 10 inches in diameter and about ½ inch thick.

Use a small, round cookie cutter (the dessert looks fabulous if the cutter is only about 1½ inches wide). Dip the cutter into flour each time before cutting the dough. Start to cut at the outside edge. Cut biscuits as close to one another as possible. Do not twist the cutter. Use a wide metal spatula to transfer the biscuits to the top of the cobbler. Place them only about ½ inch apart (28 to 30 biscuits cut with a 1½-inch cutter will fit the top of an 11 by 8-inch baking dish nicely).

With a pastry brush, brush the tops of the biscuits with heavy or light cream. Then sprinkle granulated sugar generously all over the fruit and the biscuits, using about 2 to 3 tablespoons of sugar. (Do not top the biscuits with cream or sugar if they are to be served as bread.)

Bake for about 15 minutes until the tops of the biscuits are beautifully browned. For the last few minutes, place the baking dish under a broiler to melt the sugar topping; watch it carefully.

Serve plain or with ice cream.

Georgia Peach Cobbler

I have read that possibly the Scottish-Irish brought cobblers with them when they came here in the early 1700s and that possibly the name came from the phrase to "cobble up," which meant to put together in a hurry.

This has a layer of cake batter covered before baking with a juicy peach mixture. During baking most of the peaches sink to the bottom, most of the batter rises to the top, and as they pass each other going up and down the peach

mixture absorbs some of the batter and thickens to a wonderful consistency.

The fruit mixture can be prepared ahead of time and can wait at room temperature. The dry ingredients for the batter can be sifted ahead of time. Then it takes only a few moments to finish the batter and "cobble up" the dessert.

You will need an ovenproof baking dish with at least a 2-quart capacity.

8 PORTIONS

PEACH MIXTURE

About 2 pounds (6 medium-large) just-ripe
    freestone peaches
⅔ cup light brown sugar, firmly packed

1 tablespoon unsalted butter
1¼ cups water

Blanch and peel the peaches (see page 330), cut them in half, remove the pits, and slice them coarse. Place the peaches in a 3-quart heavy saucepan with the sugar, butter, and water. Stir briefly over moderately high heat just until the mixture comes to a boil. Remove from the heat and set aside.

CAKE BATTER

1½ cups sifted all-purpose flour
1 tablespoon double-acting baking powder
Pinch of salt
2 tablespoons unsalted butter

½ teaspoon vanilla extract
¼ teaspoon almond extract
⅔ cup light brown sugar, firmly packed
¾ cup milk

Adjust a rack to the middle of the oven and preheat the oven to 375 degrees. Generously butter a shallow ovenproof baking dish with at least a 2-quart capacity (11 by 8 by 1¾ or 2 inches); it can be larger but not smaller.

Sift together the flour, baking powder, and salt and set aside. In the small bowl of an electric mixer beat the butter with the vanilla and almond extracts. Beat in the sugar to mix. On low speed add in half of the milk, then half of the sifted dry ingredients, the balance of the milk, and the balance of the dry ingredients, scraping the sides of the bowl with a rubber spatula as necessary and beating only until mixed.

Pour the batter into the baking dish and spread it smooth. With a large slotted spoon place the prepared peaches (which may be boiling hot

196

or may be cool) evenly over the batter (reserve the peach syrup for a moment). Place the dish in the oven.

Now, pouring the peach syrup (it will be thin) over the fruit will be easiest if you pour it in two additions into a 2-cup measuring cup, and then reach into the oven and quickly pour it over the top of the fruit in the baking dish. (It is best to do it this way—in the oven—because it will fill the dish almost to the top and might spill if it is moved.)

Place a cookie sheet or a large piece of foil on a rack below the baking dish or on the floor of the oven to catch any juice that might bubble over during baking (it probably will if your dish has a 2-quart capacity).

Bake at 375 degrees for 20 minutes. Then lower the temperature to 325 degrees and bake for 25 more minutes (total baking time is 45 minutes).

Serve immediately or within 20 to 30 minutes on large flat plates or in dessert bowls, spooning some of the thickened syrup from the bottom over or alongside each portion.

Serve plain or with ice cream.

Peach Pandowdy

This is a very old American recipe. Pandowdies were first made in the 1600s in the Middle Colonies—Pennsylvania, New Jersey, and Delaware. Although they were most often made with apples, there were a few with rhubarb, apricots, or peaches. It was customary for the host or hostess to cut into the top of the dessert with a serving spoon and stir the top and bottom together a bit before serving. Hence "Will you please dowdy the pan and serve the dessert."

In a shallow baking dish you will have sweet-ened and flavored uncooked fresh peaches and their delicious juice on the bottom, and a layer of quite plain but wonderful batter similar to a soft biscuit dough over the top.

The peaches should be just ripe, but for the best flavor and texture they should not be overripe.

When I could not stop eating this and my husband tried to reason with me about it, I quoted Mae West's line "Too much of a good thing is wonderful."

6 PORTIONS

PEACH MIXTURE

3 pounds (9 medium-large) fresh just-ripe
    peaches, preferably freestone
⅓ cup dark brown sugar, firmly packed

1 tablespoon lemon juice
1 teaspoon cinnamon
⅓ cup light raisins

Adjust a rack one-third down from the top of the oven and preheat the oven to 400 degrees. Butter a shallow baking dish with a 2-quart capacity (11 by 8 by 2 inches) and set it aside.

Blanch and peel the peaches (see page 330). Cut them in half, remove the pits, and cut each half in 3 or 4 lengthwise slices; you should have 6 generous cups of sliced peaches.

Place the sliced peaches in a bowl, add the sugar and lemon juice, and sprinkle the cinnamon all over. With a rubber spatula toss the fruit gently to mix the ingredients evenly. Let stand for about 10 minutes to draw a bit of the juice.

Then place the mixture in the buttered baking dish, including every bit of the juice that has collected. Smooth the top and sprinkle on the raisins. Let stand while you prepare the topping.

TOPPING

1¼ cups sifted all-purpose flour
1 teaspoon double-acting baking powder
3 tablespoons granulated sugar
¼ teaspoon salt
2 eggs

⅓ cup milk
2 ounces (½ stick) unsalted butter, melted
1 teaspoon vanilla extract
Few drops almond extract

Sift together the flour, baking powder, sugar, and salt and set aside.

In the small bowl of an electric mixer beat the eggs with the milk, butter, and vanilla and almond extracts. On low speed add the dry ingredients and beat briefly only until smooth.

The mixture will be thick but fluid. Either pour it slowly to make a thin layer (it will form a wide ribbon when it is poured) or spoon it by small spoonfuls over the fruit. Do not pour or spoon too much in any one spot or there will not be enough to cover the fruit. Actually, the topping might not cover the fruit completely anyhow, but it should almost cover it. Some of the topping will run down into the spaces between the fruit.

Bake for 28 to 30 minutes. The juices will bubble dark around the rim and through any little spots that the topping did not cover. The topping will darken slightly.

Serve warm as is or with ice cream. However, if it is not possible to serve it warm, then definitely serve the ice cream with it.

Pennsylvania Dutch Peach Cobbler

A thick and juicy peach filling with a cookie-like topping that is both soft and crisp; irresistible.

You will need a shallow ovenproof baking dish about 13 by 8 by 2 inches with about a 3-quart capacity.

If you wish, this can all be prepared a few hours before it is baked and it can wait at room temperature to go into the oven when you sit down to start dinner.

6 TO 8 PORTIONS

TOPPING

1 cup unsifted all-purpose flour
⅔ cup granulated sugar
1 teaspoon double-acting baking powder
¼ teaspoon salt
1 ounce (¼ stick) unsalted butter, at
    room temperature

½ teaspoon vanilla extract
¼ teaspoon almond extract
1 egg graded "large"

Have ready a shallow 3-quart baking dish.

Sift together the flour, sugar, baking powder, and salt and set aside. In the small bowl of an electric mixer beat the butter with the vanilla and almond extracts to mix. Beat in the egg, and then on low speed gradually add the sifted dry ingredients. Beat until the mixture holds together.

Remove the bowl from the mixer and transfer the mixture to a piece of wax paper about 15 inches long. Cover with another 15-inch length of wax paper. Sprinkle a few drops of water on a work surface (to keep the wax paper from slipping) and place the wax papers with the dough between them on the damp surface. With a rolling pin roll over the top paper until the dough measures about 11 inches in length by about 8 inches; it may be an oval shape (or approximately an oval)—it should be about ¼ inch thick. Slide a flat-sided cookie sheet under the bottom piece of paper and transfer to the freezer for 45 to 60 minutes, or for a few hours if you wish.

FILLING

About 4 pounds (12 medium-large) just-ripe
    peaches, preferably freestone
¼ cup unsifted all-purpose flour
¼ cup light brown sugar, firmly packed
¼ cup honey

½ cup water
1 ounce (¼ stick) unsalted butter
1½ tablespoons lemon juice
Nutmeg, preferably freshly grated

Blanch and peel the peaches (see page 330). Cut them in half. Remove the pits. Place them on a towel briefly to drain; then cut each peach into quarters and let the quarters continue to drain on the towel.

Place the flour, sugar, and honey in a 3-quart heavy saucepan. Very gradually add the water, stirring well with a rubber spatula or a wire whisk until the mixture is smooth.

Place over moderate heat and cook for a few minutes, scraping the sides and bottom constantly with a rubber spatula, until the mixture thickens. Reduce the heat and cook, stirring, for 1 minute.

Then add about one third of the peaches (reserve the remaining peaches) and cook, stirring, for another minute.

Remove from the heat; stir in the butter and lemon juice.

Place the reserved two thirds of the peaches in the baking dish and smooth the top. Then pour the cooked mixture over the peaches in the baking dish and smooth the top again. (There must be headroom because the filling will bubble during baking.) Grate about half of a nutmeg over the peaches or sprinkle on about ¼ teaspoon of ground nutmeg.

When you are ready to bake, adjust a rack to the middle of the oven and preheat the oven to 375 degrees.

Remove the firm topping from the freezer. Peel off the top piece of wax paper just to release it, and then replace it. Turn the rolled-out topping (still between both pieces of wax paper) over. Peel off the other piece of paper but do not replace it. With a round cookie cutter (I use a cutter that is 2 inches in diameter—you could use any size) cut as many rounds as possible from the dough, starting at the outside edge and cutting the rounds just touching each other. Don't discard a speck of this dough—it makes great sugar cookies. (The scraps may be pressed together, chilled, rolled, cut, and baked on a foil-lined cookie sheet in a 350-degree oven until lightly colored.)

Place the rounds of dough over the peaches, leaving small spaces between them (they will spread a bit during baking). For my 13 by 8-inch baking dish I use 15 rounds of dough (three rows, 5 in each row).

Bake for 45 minutes, reversing the dish front to back as necessary to ensure even browning. If the top still looks pale after 30 minutes of baking, raise the rack to the highest position for the last 15 minutes.

Serve hot or warm, as is or with ice cream.

Blueberry and Peach Buckle

A delicious and tantalizing flavor and texture—a coffee cake, of sorts—colorful, beautiful, moist, loaded with fruit (with only enough batter to hold the fruit together).

Buckles are in most very old Southern cookbooks. The name, meaning to crumple up, probably came about because of the crumbly topping.

Make this in the summer when fresh blueberries and peaches are in season.

I thought this had to be served hot, right out of the oven. However, I recently made it early in the day to serve at 10:00 A.M. when I had invited friends for coffee, but when my husband and I had it again 12 hours later it was still very good. (But if it stands even longer than that, the moisture in the peaches and berries soaks into the cake and makes it mushy.)

8 PORTIONS

TOPPING

2 ounces (½ stick) unsalted butter
1 teaspoon cinnamon

⅓ cup dark brown sugar, firmly packed
⅓ cup sifted all-purpose flour

In the small bowl of an electric mixer (or in any small bowl) beat the butter until soft, mix in the cinnamon and sugar, and then the flour. Refrigerate.

CAKE

12 ounces (3 cups) fresh blueberries
2 cups sifted all-purpose flour
2 teaspoons double-acting baking powder
½ teaspoon salt
2 ounces (½ stick) unsalted butter
1 teaspoon vanilla extract

¼ teaspoon almond extract
⅔ cup plus 2 tablespoons granulated sugar
1 egg
½ cup milk
3 fresh just-ripe medium-large peaches

Adjust a rack one-third down from the top of the oven and preheat the oven to 375 degrees. Butter a shallow ovenproof baking dish with a 2-quart capacity (11 by 8 by 1½ or 2 inches) and set it aside.

Wash the berries (see To Wash Blueberries, page 14) and let them drain and dry.

Remove and reserve 2 tablespoons of the flour. Sift together the remaining flour, baking powder, and salt and set aside.

In the small bowl of an electric mixer beat the butter until soft. Beat in the vanilla and almond extracts and ⅔ cup of the sugar (reserve the remaining 2 tablespoons of sugar). Beat in the egg. Then, on low speed, add the sifted dry ingredients in three additions alternately with the milk in two additions. The mixture will be thick and stiff. Set it aside.

Place the blueberries in a large mixing bowl. Add the reserved 2 tablespoons of flour. With a rubber spatula toss gently to coat the berries without squashing them. (If some of the flour settles to the bottom of the bowl, spread out a large piece of wax paper, place a wide colander or strainer over the paper, turn the berries and flour into the colander or strainer, and shake gently. Any flour that lands on the wax paper should be folded into the cake batter.)

Then add the floured blueberries and fold gently just barely to mix without squashing the berries.

Turn half of the mixture into the buttered baking dish and spread to level it a bit; it will be a very thin layer.

Blanch and peel the peaches (see page 330), place them on a towel to drain, and then slice them about ½ inch thick on the outside curve. Place the peaches in a layer over the cake batter. (If your dish is the size mentioned above, you will be able to make three lengthwise rows of overlapping slices.) Sprinkle the peaches with 1 tablespoon of the remaining sugar.

Place the remaining batter by very small spoonfuls over the peaches; it will not be enough to cover the peaches completely, but be patient and work slowly to cover as much of the peaches as possible.

With your fingertips sprinkle the refrigerated topping, a bit at a time, over the cake. It will not completely cover the cake, but, again, patience. Sprinkle the remaining 1 tablespoon of sugar over the top.

Bake for 35 minutes until the pale part of the top is medium brown and dry and springs back if pressed lightly with a fingertip.

To serve, cut into squares and remove the squares with a metal spatula. Serve directly from the baking dish either warm or at room temperature.

This is so yummy I do not think it needs anything with it, but Crème Fraîche (see page 361) or whipped cream or ice cream may be passed, or spooned alongside each portion.

Cranberry Grunt

They say that this name came about because when it comes out of the oven it makes a noise similar to a grunt. In my kitchen it does not grunt, it doesn't make a sound—it just smiles.

The first settlers in America found cranberries here just waiting to be picked; different varieties grow from Newfoundland to the Carolinas and west to Arkansas and Minnesota, and in Oregon and the state of Washington. The berries, which are related to blueberries, are in season in the fall

and early winter. But now you can buy them frozen all year, or you can freeze them yourself. (They don't need any preparation; just put them in a freezer bag in the freezer. Do not wash them until you are ready to use them; then rinse quickly in cold water and use them frozen.)

This very old recipe is made in a shallow baking dish. It has a layer of juicy and spicy cranberries and apples which is then covered with light and tender biscuits that resemble slices of jelly roll (they have a filling of strawberry preserves).

It is quick and easy. It is great hot, warm, or at room temperature, but do not bake it more than 2 or 3 hours ahead of time; when it is just baked the biscuits are light and tender and terrific—after a few hours they lose their special tenderness, and the juicy apple and berry mixture becomes less juicy.

Both the fruit and the biscuits can be pre-pared up to a few hours ahead of time, if you wish. If so, cover the fruit mixture and let it wait at room temperature. Place the biscuits on a tray covered with wax paper, cover the biscuits loosely with plastic wrap or wax paper, and refrigerate. Wait until you are ready to bake before placing the biscuits on the fruit layer.

ABOUT 8 PORTIONS

FRUIT LAYER

12 ounces (3 cups) cranberries (fresh or frozen)
2 large apples (see Note), to make a generous
    2 cups, cut up
⅔ cup water
½ cup granulated sugar

1 ounce (¼ stick) unsalted butter
Scant ¼ teaspoon cloves
½ teaspoon nutmeg
Scant ¼ teaspoon allspice

Adjust a rack one-third up from the bottom of the oven and preheat the oven to 425 degrees. Generously butter a shallow ovenproof baking dish with at least an 8-cup capacity (11 by 7 by 1½ or 2 inches).

Quickly wash and pick over the berries, drain, and place them in a heavy 4- to 6-cup saucepan. Peel, quarter, and core the apples; then cut them into small chunky pieces about ½ to ¾ inch. Add the apples and the water to the berries. Bring to a boil over moderate heat, cover, reduce the heat slightly to maintain a simmer, and simmer for about 10 minutes. Remove from the heat, stir in the sugar, butter, cloves, nutmeg, and all-spice, and let the mixture stand, uncovered.

JELLY-ROLL BISCUITS

3 ounces (¾ stick) unsalted butter
1½ cups sifted all-purpose flour
1 tablespoon double-acting baking powder
¼ teaspoon salt

2 tablespoons granulated sugar
⅓ cup milk
¼ cup strawberry preserves (or any other
    red preserves)

Cut ½ stick of the butter into small pieces and refrigerate. Melt the remaining ¼ stick of butter and set aside.

Sift together into a bowl the flour, baking powder, salt, and sugar. Add the cut-up butter and with a pastry blender cut it in until the mixture resembles coarse crumbs. Make a well in the middle, add the milk all at once to the well, and stir with a fork until the flour is just barely moistened.

Turn the mixture out onto a lightly floured board and knead it very briefly (the less the better) only until the flour is incorporated.

Shape the mixture into an oblong. Place it on a lightly floured pastry cloth and with a lightly floured rolling pin roll out the dough until it measures 8 by 12 inches, keeping the shape as even and as neat as you can.

Brush with the melted butter.

Stir the preserves a bit to soften and spread them over the whole surface of the dough, but staying ½ inch away from 1 12-inch side. Then, with your hands, roll up the dough like a jelly roll, starting at the 12-inch side opposite the ½-inch border.

Cut into 12 1-inch pieces.

Transfer the fruit mixture (which may still be warm) to the baking dish, smooth the top, and place the biscuits cut side up (and down) over the fruit layer (I make three rows, 4 biscuits in each row).

Bake for 20 to 25 minutes until the biscuits are well browned and crusty.

Serve hot, warm, or at room temperature. Serve plain or with ice cream, or with ice-cold Ricotta Cream (see page 360); if you are serving 4 or 5 portions, 1 15-ounce container of ricotta cheese will be enough, but for 6 or more portions use 2 15-ounce containers.

NOTE: *I like Golden Delicious apples for this. They are not as sour as Granny Smith apples—the cranberries are sour enough—and they hold their shape and do not fall apart the way some other sweet apples do.*

Rhubarb Crumble

Rhubarb, which is also called pieplant, is, botanically speaking, a vegetable, although we use it as a fruit. Frozen rhubarb is available but use the fresh for this recipe. Generally during April the first young, springtime rhubarb starts to show up in the markets. Watch for it. The season does not last long, and rhubarb is especially delicious when it is young.

This Pennsylvania Dutch recipe is certainly one of the easiest and quickest ever. You can pre-pare it ahead of time (in just a few minutes), you can bake it immediately or bake it later, you can serve it warm or cooled, plain or with ice cream. (The combination of warm tart rhubarb with cold sweet ice cream is great.)

This is a shallow baking dish of the tart rhubarb covered with a buttery brown-sugar, crunchy, crumb topping.

8 PORTIONS

2 pounds fresh rhubarb (to make 8 cups, cut up)
Finely grated rind of 1 large orange
⅓ cup orange juice
3 tablespoons dark rum
⅔ cup granulated sugar

1 cup unsifted all-purpose flour
1 teaspoon cinnamon
1 cup dark brown sugar, firmly packed
4 ounces (1 stick) unsalted butter, cut into
    small pieces

Adjust a rack one-third up from the bottom of the oven and preheat the oven to 350 degrees. You will need a shallow ovenproof baking dish with an 8- to 9-cup capacity (about 11 by 8 by 2 inches); butter it lightly.

Wash the rhubarb with a vegetable brush under cold running water. Cut off any leaves and a thin slice from the top and bottom of each stalk. On a board with a heavy knife cut the rhubarb into 1-inch pieces and place in the baking dish.

Combine the rind, juice, and rum and pour it evenly over the rhubarb. Sprinkle the granulated sugar evenly over the top.

Place the flour, cinnamon, brown sugar, and butter in a wide mixing bowl. With your hands work the ingredients together, rubbing them between your fingertips and then between your palms, to form crumbs. Sprinkle the crumbs evenly over the rhubarb, covering it all.

Bake immediately or set aside and bake later.

Bake for 40 to 45 minutes only until the rhubarb in the middle of the baking dish just tests tender when tested with a toothpick and the juices are bubbly, thick, and shiny and the crumb topping is nicely browned.

Serve hot, warm, or at room temperature, but preferably don't let it wait more than a few hours after baking; the crumb top starts to soften. Serve plain or with ice cream.

Blueberry Crumble

A crisp, nutty, crumbly topping over a thick layer of sweet juicy blueberries. This is easy to make and it is equally good hot or cooled. But if you want it hot (wonderful) it can all be prepared ahead of time, and it can wait in the refrigerator a day, if you wish, before it is baked.

6 TO 8 PORTIONS

BLUEBERRY LAYER

6 cups (2 1-"pint" boxes) fresh blueberries
⅓ cup dark brown sugar, firmly packed
3 tablespoons sifted all-purpose flour

¾ teaspoon cinnamon
2 teaspoons lemon juice

Wash the berries (see To Wash Blueberries, page 14) and let them stand to drain and dry.

Adjust a rack to the middle of the oven and preheat the oven to 375 degrees. Butter a wide, shallow 2-quart ovenproof baking dish (for instance, one 11 by 8 by 2 inches) and set aside.

In a large bowl mix the sugar with the flour and cinnamon. Add the washed and dried berries and turn the ingredients gently a few times with a rubber spatula to mix. Pour the mixture into the dish. Sprinkle any sugar and flour mixture remaining in the bottom of the bowl evenly over the top. Smooth the top. Drizzle the lemon juice all over. Set aside.

CRUMBLE TOPPING

This will stay crisp long after the dessert is baked, even after it has cooled.

½ cup sifted all-purpose flour
¼ teaspoon nutmeg
¼ cup granulated sugar
½ cup dark brown sugar, firmly packed
4 ounces (1 stick) unsalted butter, cold and firm, cut into pieces (it is best to cut the butter ahead of time and refrigerate it)

½ cup "old fashioned" Quaker oats (must be the kind labeled "old fashioned" or the topping will not be as crunchy as it should be)
3½ ounces (1 cup) pecans, toasted (see To Toast Pecans, page 7), cut into medium-size pieces

Sift together into a bowl the flour, nutmeg, and granulated sugar. Add the brown sugar and stir to mix. Add the butter and with a pastry blender cut it in until the mixture resembles coarse crumbs (not too fine). Stir in the oats.

Sprinkle the nuts over the berries, and sprinkle the topping over the nuts.

Bake for 25 to 30 minutes until the berries are bubbly around the edge. Then place the baking dish under the broiler for about a minute or so to darken the top a bit—watch it carefully.

Serve warm or cooled, as is or with Top Secret (see page 359), White Custard Cream (see page 360), or with plain sour cream or unwhipped heavy cream. (But it is delicious alone.)

Peach Crisp

Quick and easy; it is an old Southern recipe from the area of Colonial Williamsburg. A layer of fresh peaches is covered with a crunchy, crumbly, deliciously crisp topping.

6 PORTIONS

3 pounds (about 9 medium-large) just-ripe fresh
   peaches, preferably freestone
1½ tablespoons lemon juice
1 teaspoon vanilla extract
1 cup sifted all-purpose flour

¾ cup granulated sugar
¼ teaspoon salt
¼ teaspoon almond extract
1 egg, beaten
3 ounces (¾ stick) unsalted butter, melted

Adjust a rack one-third down from the top of the oven and preheat the oven to 400 degrees. You will need a shallow ovenproof baking dish with about a 2-quart capacity (it might measure about 11 by 8 by 1½ or 2 inches). Butter the dish and set it aside.

Blanch and peel the peaches (see page 330). Cut them in half, remove the pits, and cut the halves into rather wide slices (if they are thin they will overcook and become mushy). You should have about 6 cups of sliced peaches. Place them in a wide bowl. Combine the lemon juice and vanilla, drizzle it over the peaches, and toss gently with a rubber spatula to mix.

Place the peaches in the buttered baking dish.

Sift together into a mixing bowl the flour, sugar, and salt. Stir the almond extract into the egg. Drizzle it and the melted butter over the dry ingredients and stir very well with a fork until the dry ingredients are barely moistened and the mixture is crumbly.

Sprinkle the crumbs loosely all over the peaches.

Bake for 30 to 35 minutes.

If the topping is still pale place the dish about 12 inches under the broiler to brown a bit; it should not be too close to the broiler or the topping will burn before it browns.

Serve hot, or warm, if possible. Serve alone, or with ice cream.

Peach Kuchen

A quick, easy, and delicious coffee cake, wonderful for breakfast or brunch, or as a dessert (with or without ice cream). This is an unusual recipe that uses yeast (but there is no kneading or rising time) *and also baking powder; they work their magic together in the oven and you will be surprised and delighted.*

TOPPING

½ cup chopped or slivered (julienned) blanched almonds

3 tablespoons unsalted butter

½ cup light or dark brown sugar, firmly packed

1 teaspoon cinnamon

¼ cup unsifted all-purpose flour

Adjust a rack to the middle of the oven and preheat the oven to 350 degrees.

Place the almonds in a shallow pan in the oven to bake for 5 minutes until hot but not colored. Set aside to cool.

In the small bowl of an electric mixer beat the butter until soft. Add the sugar and cinnamon and beat to mix, then add the flour and beat only until the mixture is crumbly. Stir in the cooled almonds.

Set aside the topping to use later.

CAKE MIXTURE

2 tablespoons warm water (105 to 115 degrees)

1 teaspoon plus ½ cup granulated sugar

1½ teaspoons active dry yeast

2 cups unsifted all-purpose flour

1 tablespoon double-acting baking powder

½ teaspoon salt

4 ounces (1 stick) unsalted butter

2 eggs graded "large"

½ teaspoon vanilla extract

¼ teaspoon almond extract

Finely grated rind of 1 large lemon

¼ cup milk

4 to 6 cups blanched, peeled, and sliced fresh peaches (see Note)

Optional: ¼ cup raisins

Butter a 9 by 13 by 2-inch cake pan and place it in the freezer (it is easier to press out a thin layer of dough if the pan is frozen).

Place the warm water in a small bowl, add 1 teaspoon of the sugar (reserve the remaining ½ cup of sugar) and the yeast. Stir briefly with a knife just to mix. Set aside.

Sift together the flour, baking powder, and salt and set aside.

In the large bowl of an electric mixer beat the butter until soft. Add the remaining ½ cup of sugar and beat to mix. Add the yeast mixture, the eggs, the vanilla and almond extracts, and the lemon rind and beat to mix. (It is OK if the mixture looks curdled now.) On low speed mix in half of the sifted dry ingredients, then the milk, and finally the remaining dry ingredients. Beat until well mixed.

Spread half of the mixture (about 1¼ cups) over the bottom of the buttered, frozen pan—it will be a very thin layer.

Place the prepared peaches in rows, each slice just barely touching the one before it, or there may be a little room left between the slices. Or, if you wish, the amount of fruit can be increased slightly and the slices can just barely overlap.

Sprinkle the optional raisins over the fruit.

Next, using two teaspoons—one for picking up with and one for pushing off with—place small spoonfuls of the remaining cake mixture over all the fruit and the bottom layer. There will be places where the fruit shows through; it is OK but you do not want much of it uncovered.

Then, with your fingers, carefully sprinkle the prepared topping to cover as much of the cake as possible.

Bake for 35 to 40 minutes until the top is nicely browned.

ICING

Prepare this 5 minutes before the cake is done.

1 cup sifted confectioners sugar
1½ teaspoons lemon juice

1 tablespoon boiling water

In a small bowl stir the ingredients with a rubber spatula to mix. The icing should be smooth and thick, just barely thin enough to flow when some of it is picked up on the spatula.

As soon as the cake is removed from the oven, drizzle thin lines of the icing every which way over the cake. (I drizzle it off the rubber spatula.)

Serve hot, or let stand in the pan until cool. Cut into large squares and use a wide metal spatula to transfer the portions.

NOTE: *This is equally good with apples, pears, blueberries, or a combination of fruits. If you are using peaches, see the directions on page 330 for blanching and peeling. Then cut them in half, remove the pits, and slice the peaches into wedges about ½ inch thick at the curved edge. If you use apples or pears they should be peeled, quartered, cored, and cut into wedges about ½ inch thick at the curved edge.*

Colonial Blueberries

Especially easy—and especially delicious. It has a thick, juicy, dark purple layer of slightly cooked fresh blueberries covered with a wonderfully light cake (only ¾ inch thick), baked together. It may be served hot or at room temperature but the fresher the better. The blueberry part can be made ahead of time, but it hardly pays, since the whole thing can be made quickly. You need a shallow ovenproof baking dish with a 3-quart capacity (for instance, 9 by 13 by 2 inches).

ABOUT 10 PORTIONS

BLUEBERRY LAYER

1¼ pounds (5 cups) fresh blueberries
1 cup dark brown sugar, firmly packed

3 ounces (¾ stick) unsalted butter
½ teaspoon cinnamon

Wash the blueberries (see To Wash Blueberries, page 14), and let them drain and dry.

Place 3 cups of the berries (reserve the remaining 2 cups) in a heavy 2½- to 3-quart saucepan with the sugar and butter. Stir occasionally with a wooden spatula over low heat until the mixture comes to a low boil. Let simmer gently for 3 minutes. Remove from the heat, cool for about 10 minutes, and then stir in the remaining 2 cups of berries.

Pour the mixture into a 3-quart baking dish, smooth the top, and sprinkle the cinnamon through a fine strainer over the berries.

Set aside. (If this is made hours ahead, it can wait either at room temperature or in the refrigerator.)

CAKE LAYER

1½ cups sifted all-purpose flour
2 teaspoons double-acting baking powder
¼ teaspoon salt
5⅓ ounces (10⅔ tablespoons) unsalted butter
½ teaspoon vanilla extract
¾ cup granulated sugar

2 eggs graded "large"
⅔ cup fresh orange juice (grate the rind of 1 orange before squeezing)
Cognac, bourbon, or more orange juice
Finely grated rind of 1 large deep-colored orange

Adjust a rack to the middle of the oven and preheat the oven to 350 degrees.

Sift together the flour, baking powder, and salt and set aside.

In the small bowl of an electric mixer beat the butter until soft. Beat in the vanilla and sugar. Then add the eggs one at a time, beating until incorporated after each addition.

Place the orange juice in a 1-cup glass measuring cup and add Cognac or bourbon to reach the ¾-cup line (or use ¾ cup of orange juice).

On low speed gradually add the sifted dry ingredients in three additions alternately with the liquids in two additions, beating until smooth after each addition. Remove from the mixer and stir in the grated rind. (The mixture will appear slightly curdled—it is OK.)

Slowly pour the cake mixture over the berries. (The batter will cover all the berries but if there are a few spots uncovered it is OK.)

Bake for 45 minutes. The top of the cake will be richly browned and will spring back when pressed gently with a fingertip.

Serve hot or cooled. To serve, use a wide metal pancake turner and a large serving spoon. Serve on flat dessert plates. Serve as is or with ice cream. Or pass a bowl of Crème Fraîche (see page 361) or whipped cream (whip 2 cups whipping cream with ¼ cup confectioners sugar and ⅓ cup Cognac, bourbon, or Grand Marnier, until thick but not stiff). Or serve with White Custard Cream (see page 360)—divine.

Down Home Apple Casserole

This is a bit like an apple pie without the crust, but this is creamy and has an almond and macaroon topping. It is, as they say, "a cup of tea" to prepare this. It can be prepared ahead of time, it can wait for hours, and then it can be baked (for only 15 minutes) during dinner and served bubbling hot right out of the oven. Or it can be baked ahead of time, refrigerated for several hours, and served very cold. I like it both ways. It is a simple country-style dessert, and at the same time it is elegant enough for almost any occasion.

4 OR 5 PORTIONS

¼ cup crushed dried almond macaroons
⅓ cup thinly sliced unblanched (natural) almonds
2 pounds tart cooking apples (see Note)
½ cup water
About ⅓ cup granulated sugar (see Note)
¼ cup raisins
1 to 2 teaspoons lemon juice (see Note)

½ teaspoon cinnamon
¼ teaspoon nutmeg
Optional: pinch of mace
½ cup whipping cream
1 tablespoon all-purpose flour
1½ tablespoons unsalted butter, cold and firm
1 to 2 tablespoons additional granulated sugar

If you use Italian Amaretti (macaroons—usually available in all better food stores and kitchen shops), they do not have to be dried (they are dry when you get them). Others, which are moist, should be dried ahead of time in a slow oven until they are crisp. Crush them coarse and then grind them in a food processor, or place them between pieces of wax paper and pound with a wide cleaver or any similar tool. Place the ground macaroons in a bowl with the sliced almonds and stir to mix.

Adjust a rack one-third down from the top of the oven and preheat the oven to 400 degrees. You will need a shallow ovenproof baking dish with a 6-cup capacity. Butter it lightly and set aside.

Peel, quarter, and core the apples. Cut them into slices (if the apples are large, cut each quarter into 4 slices; if they are small, cut each quarter into 2 slices).

Place the apples, water, the ⅓ cup sugar, and the raisins in a large, heavy saucepan with a tight lid, but uncovered, over moderate heat. Stir occasionally until the liquid comes to a boil, then reduce the heat slightly, cover, and let cook for about 10 minutes until the apples are barely tender. Uncover again and let boil for a minute or two to reduce the liquid just a bit; do not cook longer than that—there should still be plenty of juice in the pan and the apples should not be overcooked.

Remove from the heat. Add the lemon juice, cinnamon, nutmeg, and optional mace. Stir/fold gently to mix.

In a small bowl whisk the cream and the flour together. Strain through a fine strainer, and then add to the apple mixture. Stir/fold again gently to mix.

Turn into the buttered baking dish. Smooth the top. Sprinkle with the macaroons and almonds, dot with small pieces of the butter, and sprinkle with the additional sugar.

This can be baked right away, or it can be covered and kept at room temperature for hours, or it can be refrigerated. If it is refrigerated, remove it from the refrigerator ahead of time to come to room temperature before baking.

Bake for about 15 minutes until it is bubbling hard around the edges. Then broil for a minute or two (that's all it takes) 7 or 8 inches below the broiler to caramelize the top a bit. Watch it carefully.

Serve this right away or let it cool, refrigerate it, and serve it very cold. Either way, serve it at the table on flat plates. If you serve it hot, the cream will be thin and runny. If you cool and then chill it, the cream will thicken. Either way, spoon some of the cream onto each plate.

Serve just as it is, pass a bowl of cold Crème Fraîche or cold Sweet Sour Cream (see page 361), or serve ice cream with it.

NOTE: *Granny Smith and Jonathan apples are considered best to use for pies or recipes like this one. Granny Smith are more tart. Adjust the amount of sugar and lemon juice depending on the sweetness of the apples. Taste before turning the mixture into the baking dish, and add more sugar if necessary.*

Mousse, Flan, Puddings, et Cetera

Indian Pudding

If you have never had Indian Pudding and you don't know what to expect, you are in for a treat. Soft, creamy, cozy, a delicate flavor, a heavenly texture. It is the oldest New England dessert on record. The original recipe probably came about when all cooking was done on wood-burning stoves. Since this calls for long slow baking it might have been made over the smoldering embers and baked all night or all day. I have raised the temperature a bit and reduced the cooking time a bit but it still has to cook for 3 hours. (If you are baking something else in the oven that takes long slow baking and if you can fit this in at the same time, it would be a shame not to.)

They say that there are as many variations of this recipe as there are days in the year. And in Vermont they say there are as many ways of making this pudding as there are "hairs on a dog." The original and traditional recipe calls for dark molasses, but this recipe calls for maple syrup.

People who were brought up on Indian Pudding can never get enough, and people who eat it for the first time—they can't get enough either.

This is served hot, warm, at room temperature, or chilled.

6 TO 8 PORTIONS

2 tablespoons granulated sugar
1 teaspoon cinnamon
½ teaspoon ground ginger
¼ teaspoon nutmeg
¼ teaspoon salt

5 cups milk
½ cup yellow cornmeal
2 ounces (½ stick) unsalted butter
1 cup maple syrup
½ cup light raisins

Adjust a rack to the middle of the oven (if there is something else in the oven, this may bake higher or lower) and preheat the oven to 350 degrees. Butter a shallow ovenproof baking dish with a 7- to 8-cup capacity. Have ready a shallow baking pan to place the dish in while baking. Set aside.

In a small cup stir the sugar, cinnamon, ginger, nutmeg, and salt and set aside.

Scald 3 cups of the milk (reserve the remaining 2 cups) in a heavy saucepan or in the top of a double boiler over hot water on moderate heat.

Meanwhile, place the cornmeal in an 8- to 10-cup heavy saucepan off the heat. Stir in ¾ cup of the remaining cold milk (reserve the remaining 1¼ cups of cold milk).

When the 3 cups of milk are scalded (when you can see a wrinkled skin on the top or small bubbles around the edge), gradually pour it into the cornmeal, stirring constantly with a wooden spatula. Place over moderate heat and continue to stir constantly for 20 minutes until the mixture thickens a bit. (It may come to a boil and it may simmer but you must not stop stirring. For one thing, this could still become lumpy unless you stir, and for another, it wants to burn on the bottom of the pan, which you might be able to prevent with stirring. Reduce the heat if necessary.)

Then stir in the butter, the sugar and spice mixture, the maple syrup, and the raisins.

Turn the mixture into the buttered baking dish.

You still have 1¼ cups of milk remaining. This is to be poured slowly and gradually over the top of the pudding. (It is a traditional topping.) To prevent the milk from sinking immediately into the pudding hold a large spoon over the pudding—just barely touching—and pour into the spoon; in that way the milk runs off the edges of the spoon (instead of into one spot) and more of it remains on the top of the pudding. While pouring the milk, move the spoon slowly over the surface of the pudding.

Place the baking dish in a large, shallow baking pan and place them both together in the oven. Reach into the oven and pour boiling water about 1 inch deep in the large baking pan.

Bake at 350 degrees for 30 minutes. Then reduce the temperature to 300 degrees and bake for 2½ hours longer (total baking time is 3 hours). The milk that you poured over the top (and did not mix in) will form a skin on top, in some places pale and in other places dark brown—this is the way it should be. The pudding will have the consistency of soft mashed potatoes; it will become firmer as it stands after it is removed from the oven —there will be a noticeable difference after even only 10 or 15 minutes.

Remove the baking dish from the hot water and let stand for 10 to 15 minutes if you can. Serve this hot, warm, at room temperature, or chilled.

Many Yankee cooks say this is best barely warm—with vanilla ice cream—in wide soup plates. Or it may be served with a pitcher of heavy cream, or with whipped cream. Or just plain. With or without the ice cream or other cream, hard sauce is traditionally served with Indian Pudding. Either of the following is especially delicious with hot or warm pudding.

HARD SAUCE (¾ cup)

2 ounces (½ stick) unsalted butter
Pinch of salt
1 cup confectioners sugar

½ teaspoon vanilla extract
1 tablespoon whipping cream
1 to 2 teaspoons rum, whiskey, or brandy

Beat all the ingredients together until smooth, light, and fluffy. Place in a small dish or bowl, cover, and refrigerate. Serve the sauce cold.

RUM BUTTER (1 cup)

⅓ cup superfine granulated sugar
4 ounces (1 stick) unsalted butter

¼ cup dark rum

In the small bowl of an electric mixer beat the butter until soft. Add the sugar and beat well. On low speed gradually add the rum and then continue to beat, increasing the speed when the butter has absorbed the rum (and it doesn't splash). Continue to beat for several minutes longer until the mixture resembles creamy whipped butter. At first it will look as though the butter will not absorb the rum, but it will.

Transfer to a crock or container that will go to the table; cover and refrigerate. Serve cold Rum Butter with hot Indian Pudding. (Or try it on toasted English Muffins.)

American Chocolate Pudding

If you think it doesn't pay to bother making your own when you can buy a box and just add some milk, then you have not tasted the real thing. This has considerably more chocolate (as well as cocoa), and less sugar, and egg yolks that make it custardy and give it body. It is dense, dark, not too sweet, smooth, semifirm, rich; it is marvelous.

This recipe is adapted from two recipes I received recently which were almost identical to each other, and considerably different from the usual. One of the recipes is in Richard Sax's wonderful cookbook, Cooking Great Meals Every Day *(Random House, 1982). And the other recipe is from Larry Forgione, for the dessert he serves at his popular restaurant, An American Place, in New York City. (Where, incidentally, it was served to us after an elegant meal that included three kinds of caviar. It would be just as appropriate after a casual meal.)*

This recipe may be doubled, if you wish.

Using cornstarch correctly is a delicate art. Overcooking or overbeating—even the least little bit—can cause cornstarch to break down and make the mixture too thin. (Although I have written these words dozens of times, it recently happened to me.) Be very careful.

4 PORTIONS—SEE NOTE

1 egg graded "large" or "extra-large" plus
    2 additional egg yolks
2 ounces unsweetened chocolate
3 ounces semisweet chocolate (I used
    Tobler Tradition)
2¼ cups milk
½ cup plus 1 tablespoon granulated sugar
Scant ⅛ teaspoon salt

2 tablespoons unsifted cornstarch
3 tablespoons unsifted, unsweetened cocoa
    powder (preferably Dutch-process)
2 tablespoons unsalted butter, at room
    temperature, cut into small pieces
1 teaspoon vanilla extract
Optional: 1 tablespoon dark rum

Have 10- or 12-ounce stemmed wineglasses or dessert bowls ready. Cut rounds of wax paper to place on top of the puddings, actually touching the puddings) when it is poured into the glasses or bowls. Set aside.

In a bowl beat the egg and yolks to mix and set aside.

On a board, with a long, heavy knife, chop both chocolates (coarse or fine—either is OK).

Remove and reserve ¼ cup of the milk. Place the remaining 2 cups of milk in a heavy saucepan with a 2- to 3-quart capacity. Add ¼ cup of the sugar (reserve the remaining ¼ cup plus 1 tablespoon of the sugar) and the chopped chocolate. Place over moderate heat and whisk frequently with a wire whisk until the milk just comes to a boil (flecks of chocolate will disappear by the time the milk boils).

Meanwhile, sift the reserved sugar, salt, constarch, and cocoa into a mixing bowl. Add the reserved ¼ cup of milk and whisk with a small wire whisk until smooth.

When the milk comes to a boil, pour (or ladle) part of it into the cornstarch mixture, whisking as you pour.

Then add the cornstarch mixture to the remaining hot milk mixture. Stir to mix. Place over moderate heat.

Now, use a rubber spatula and scrape the bottom and sides constantly until the mixture comes to a low boil. Reduce the heat a bit to low-medium and simmer gently, stirring and scraping the pan, for 2 minutes.

Add about 1 cup of the hot chocolate milk mixture to the eggs and whisk or stir to mix. Then add the egg mixture to the remaining hot chocolate milk mixture, stirring constantly.

Cook over low heat, scraping the pan with a rubber spatula, for 2 minutes. Be sure that you do not allow the mixture to come anywhere near the boiling stage after the eggs are added.

Remove from the heat. Add the butter, vanilla, and the optional rum. Stir very gently until the butter is melted.

Without waiting, pour into the wineglasses or dessert bowls. Cover immediately with the rounds of wax paper, placing the paper directly on the puddings (to prevent a skin from forming).

Let stand to cool to room temperature. Then refrigerate for at least a few hours.

WHIPPED CREAM

1 cup whipping cream

½ teaspoon vanilla extract

2 tablespoons confectioners or granulated sugar

In a chilled bowl, with chilled beaters, whip the cream with the sugar and vanilla until it holds a soft shape, not until it is really stiff. Shortly before serving, spoon the cream on top of the puddings. (The cream may be whipped ahead of time and refrigerated; if it separates slightly, whisk it a bit before using.)

At An American Place, the pudding is served in wineglasses, with the pudding filling the glasses only halfway and the whipped cream filling the remaining space to the top.

NOTE: *This recipe is written for good old-fashioned generous portions. But actually they should be smaller if it is to be served after a dinner.*

Apricot Bread Pudding

Serve this as dessert, or serve it as the main course at a breakfast or brunch party. Serve it hot/hot, right from the oven, or only warm, up to an hour after baking. This can be prepared hours ahead of time and can stand in the kitchen until you are ready to bake it. It is a rich, bland, creamy custard combined with the delicious tartness of dried apricots. It tastes wonderful, and looks beautiful; plan to serve it at the table or at a buffet so everyone can see it.

8 GENEROUS PORTIONS

10 slices firm white bread, such as Pepperidge Farm or Arnold

6 ounces (½ to ⅔ cup, packed) dried apricots

⅓ cup dark or light raisins

3 ounces (¾ stick) unsalted butter, at room temperature

2 cups whipping cream

2 cups milk

5 eggs graded "large" plus 4 additional egg yolks

2 teaspoons vanilla extract

Scant ½ teaspoon almond extract

¼ teaspoon salt

½ cup plus 2 tablespoons granulated sugar

The bread should be stale, or as dry as stale bread (not as dry as melba toast). If it is necessary to dry it, place it in a single layer on a cookie sheet in a 250-degree oven for 10 to 15 minutes, or as necessary. Do not remove the crusts.

You will need a large, shallow ovenproof baking dish with a 2½- to 3-quart capacity (13 by 8 by 2 inches). Butter the dish lightly and set aside.

With scissors cut the apricots into slices that measure about ¼ to ½ inch in width. Then steam the apricots as follows. Place the apricots in a vegetable steamer or in a wide strainer over shallow hot water on moderate heat, covered. Bring the water to a boil, then lower the heat to let simmer for about 30 minutes, during which time it will probably be necessary to add additional water. During the last 5 or 10 minutes of steaming add the raisins to the apricots. Then uncover and let stand off the heat.

Meanwhile, butter the bread, stack it in two or three piles, and cut the slices in half into rectangles.

Place about one third of the bread strips, buttered side up, in the dish, leaving spaces between the strips. Sprinkle with one half of the softened apricots and raisins. Place another one third of the bread on top, forming a layer of strips going in the opposite direction from the first layer. Sprinkle with the remaining fruit and top with the remaining strips (in the same direction as the first layer). The design of the strips of bread will show, so plan accordingly.

To scald the cream and milk, place them in the top of a large double boiler over hot water on moderate heat and let cook, uncovered, until a slightly wrinkled skin forms on the surface.

Place the eggs and the yolks in a large bowl. Mix with a wire whisk or a mixer only to mix (the eggs should not become foamy or bubbly). Add the vanilla and almond extracts, the salt, and ½ cup of the sugar (reserve the remaining 2 tablespoons of sugar), then very gradually stir in the hot cream and milk.

Gradually ladle or pour the mixture over the bread. There should not be many of the apricot strips or raisins floating on top; if there are, move them under some of the bread slices.

Place a piece of wax paper or plastic wrap over the top and press down on the paper with both hands to encourage the bread to absorb as much of the liquid as possible. Let stand for 30 minutes, or longer, if you wish.

Before baking, adjust a rack one-third down from the top of the oven (baking this high helps to brown the top) and preheat the oven to 325 degrees.

Remove the wax paper or plastic wrap from the top of the pudding and sprinkle the remaining 2 tablespoons of sugar over the top (this also helps the top brown nicely).

Place the baking dish in a large, shallow pan that must not be deeper than the dish. Put both pans into the oven, then reach in and pour hot water into the large pan about 1 inch deep.

Bake for about 40 minutes or longer (see Note) until a small, sharp knife inserted gently into the middle comes out just barely dry. During baking carefully reverse the pans front to back to ensure even browning.

If the top is still too pale when the pudding tests down, place it under the broiler for a few moments to help it brown; it should be a rich golden color.

I think this is most delicious served right away. Or any time during the next hour. After that it is still wonderful, but it would be a second choice.

This does not actually need a sauce, but here's a quick and easy one that is very good. Simply mix some apricot preserves with a tiny bit of rum, bourbon, or water, and heat just before serving. It is not necessary to strain the preserves.

NOTE: *If the pudding waits a long time before it is baked the ingredients will cool off and might therefore need a little longer baking time.*

Fried Bread Pudding

This is sensational! We had some leftover Apricot Bread Pudding in the refrigerator, and I used it for lunch for unexpected guests. If I had thought about and planned the meal weeks ahead it could not have been more of a hit. We had just this,

with maple syrup, and bowls of fresh strawberries.

This will remind you somewhat of French toast, but better. The inside of the fried slices is unbelievably light/moist/custardy; the outside is divinely crisp/crunchy.

This is made with Apricot Bread Pudding (preceding recipe) that has cooled and been refrigerated overnight. The remaining preparation can be done hours before serving or immediately before serving.

For each two or three people you plan to serve, beat 1 egg with ¼ cup milk lightly just to mix. Place the egg and milk mixture in a wide, shallow soup plate or serving dish. Place a generous amount of dry bread crumbs on a large piece of wax paper or foil.

In the baking dish cut the cold pudding into slices 1 inch thick. Cut each slice into pieces 3 or 4 inches long. Carefully cut around the sides of the dish to loosen the slices. Then, with a wide metal spatula, transfer the slices one at a time to the egg and milk mixture.

Handle the slices of pudding very carefully—they are delicate. It is safer to handle the slices while they are very cold than if they have been standing at room temperature for a while. Turn each slice over gently in the egg mixture and then in the bread crumbs to coat it thoroughly.

Place the prepared slices on wax paper. They can now stand for a short time at room temperature or they can be refrigerated for a few hours.

To sauté the slices it is best to use clarified butter (see below). Regular butter burns and the slices will not be the gorgeous color they become with clarified butter.

Use a larger frying pan than you think you will need (preferably nonstick) so that you will have room for turning the slices easily. Place the pan over moderate heat. Add a generous spoonful of clarified butter. When the butter is melted and hot, carefully place the slices in the pan. Fry on each side until golden brown and crisp. Turn the slices gently and carefully with two wide metal spatulas, one in each hand.

Drain the fried slices briefly on a brown paper bag.

Serve quickly on warmed plates. You may sprinkle a bit of confectioners sugar through a fine strainer over the slices, if you wish, or serve with maple syrup or preserves or marmalade.

If you are making this for more than three people I suggest that you use two large frying pans at the same time.

I served 3 generous slices as an entrée portion; 1 or 2 would be enough for a dessert portion.

CLARIFIED BUTTER Since this keeps indefinitely and since I use it whenever I fry eggs or potatoes, calves liver, or blintzes, et cetera, I make several pounds of it at a time. (I often give a jar of it as a gift.)

Use unsalted butter. Place it in a saucepan, uncovered, over moderate heat. When the butter has melted and starts to bubble, use a large serving spoon to skim off every bit of foam from the top—and discard it. Boil gently for a few minutes, skimming the top as the foam rises.

Then pour the clear, hot butter slowly and carefully into a container; do not include the milky sediment that remains in the bottom of the pan—discard it.

This may be stored in the freezer or refrigerator.

Bread Pudding with Peaches

This is a real peachy, peaches-and-cream, country-style pudding that is superdelicious and "as pretty as a picture." It can be prepared hours before baking and the baking can be timed so the pudding is served HOT—when it is at its best. Serve this as a dinner dessert or as a main course for a breakfast or brunch party. Or serve it at a coffee party. But get it while it's hot!

10 PORTIONS

9 to 10 slices firm white bread, preferably a
    square-sliced sandwich loaf such as
    Pepperidge Farm or Arnold
Unsalted butter, at room temperature
⅓ cup light raisins
2 pounds (6 or 7 medium-size) just-ripe
    freestone peaches
½ cup apricot preserves
4 eggs graded "large"
½ cup light brown sugar, firmly packed

¼ teaspoon salt
1 cup milk
1 cup whipping cream
3 tablespoons dark or light rum
1 teaspoon vanilla extract
¼ teaspoon almond extract
Additional ⅓ cup whipping cream } to be used just
⅓ cup granulated sugar } before baking

You will need a shallow ovenproof baking dish with at least a 2-quart capacity (about 11 by 8 by 1¾ or 2 inches). Butter the dish and set it aside.

The bread should be stale, or you can dry it a bit. If necessary, place the slices in a single layer on a cookie sheet in a 250-degree oven for about 15 minutes. Do not remove the crusts from the bread. Butter one side of each slice of bread. Stack 3 or 4 slices of bread at a time and cut through the pile, cutting the slices into three fingers. Place the fingers, buttered side up, touching one another, to cover the bottom of the baking dish, fitting the bread slices tightly together. If necessary, trim the slices to fit the dish. This first layer of bread should use about half of the total amount of bread.

Sprinkle the raisins over the bread.

Blanch and peel the peaches (see page 330). Cut the peaches in half, remove the pits, cut each half into about 4 lengthwise slices. Place the slices neatly overlapping in rows to cover the bread and raisins, fitting the slices close together.

Stir the apricot preserves in a small bowl with a small wire whisk just to soften, and then drizzle over the peaches.

Cover with the remaining bread fingers buttered side up, fitting them close together. If necessary, trim the slices.

In a bowl beat the eggs just to mix. Add the brown sugar, salt, milk, cream, rum, and the vanilla and almond extracts, beating after each addition just to mix.

With a ladle, gradually ladle the egg-milk mixture over the bread.

Cover the bread with a long piece of wax paper or plastic wrap. With your hands gently press down on the paper to encourage the bread to absorb the egg-milk mixture, but watch the edges of the dish and do not allow the liquids to run over. Then, to encourage the top layer to absorb still more of the liquids, place small items as weights on the paper or plastic wrap. (I use boxes and bars of chocolate; they are the right size and shape and weight and they are always at hand. One-pound boxes of brown sugar are good too.) Gradually, as the bread absorbs the liquids, you will be able to apply more pressure without having it run over.

The pudding can wait this way at room temperature for an hour or two or in the refrigerator for several hours.

Before baking, adjust a rack to the middle of the oven and preheat the oven to 325 degrees. Remove the wax paper or plastic wrap.

Drizzle the ⅓ cup whipping cream over the bread (it will not become absorbed and it will not be an even or smooth layer—OK—leave it as it is) and sprinkle the granulated sugar over the top. (The cream and sugar on top make a crisp, crunchy, candylike topping that is wonderful.)

Wipe the rim of the baking dish and place it in a wide, shallow baking pan. Put the pans in the oven, then reach in and pour hot water about 1 inch deep in the large pan.

Bake for about 1 hour and 10 or 15 minutes until a small, sharp knife inserted gently between bread fingers in the middle of the baking dish comes out clean. (If the pudding was refrigerated before baking it will probably need more baking time; test it carefully to be sure it is done.)

Then, if the top is pale (and it probably will be) place the baking dish under the broiler briefly, watching it closely, until the top is a lovely golden brown all over.

Remove the baking dish from the hot water and let stand for about 10 minutes before serving.

Mother's Spanish Cream

It is not Spanish and it does not have cream (although whipped cream is usually served alongside). When my mother and father were married, Spanish Cream was a popular dessert of the time. It was in all the American cookbooks and it appeared often in newspapers and magazines (so my mother told me). She served it regularly for many, many years; we never got tired of it, we could never get enough of it.

One hundred years ago they called this Quaking Custard—it has custard ingredients plus gelatin. But in this recipe the yolks and the whites are beaten separately and folded together. It is then poured into a mold and refrigerated. When it is turned out of the mold there will be a layer of a smooth and shiny mixture on top with a light, airy, spongy layer on the bottom—and a thin brown line of macaroon crumbs between the two layers.

This may be served with or without whipped cream and with or without fresh berries, fresh peaches, or any stewed fruit. Mother always surrounded it with a generous amount of strawberries and passed a bowl of softly whipped cream. For a party she doubled the recipe, poured it into two melon molds, unmolded them end-to-end on a huge platter, formed mounds of whipped cream at both ends, and piled strawberries along the long sides. Spectacular!

You will need a mold with a 7-cup capacity; it should preferably be thin metal (the dessert comes out more easily than if it is heavy pottery), and it should be a simple shape: a round bowl will do, a ring mold is nice (put the berries around the outside and the cream in the middle). Years ago everyone who cooked had a melon mold. Then, for years, manufacturers stopped making them. Now, happily, they seem to be available again. You can buy a heavy tinned steel French melon mold with an 8-cup capacity from The Chef's Catalog, 3915 Commercial Avenue, Northbrook, Illinois 60062. I have also used an 8 by 3-inch one-piece cheesecake pan (see page 241) and it looked wonderful.

6 TO 8 PORTIONS

Dry almond macaroons (see Note), to make ½
    cup crumbs
3 cups milk
2 envelopes unflavored gelatin
½ cup cold water
3 eggs graded "large" or "extra-large," separated

½ cup granulated sugar
½ teaspoon vanilla extract
¼ teaspoon almond extract
Generous pinch of salt
Optional: fresh or stewed fruit

Coarsely break up the macaroons and crumb them in a food processor or a blender, or put them in a plastic bag, wrap them in a towel and pound with a hammer. It is best if they are not all powdery; there should be some slightly coarser pieces. Set aside.

Place the milk in a heavy saucepan over moderate heat and let cook, uncovered, until you see heavy steam coming off the top and a few tiny bubbles on the surface.

Meanwhile, sprinkle the gelatin over the water and let stand.

In a medium-size bowl beat the yolks a bit with a wire whisk. Remove and reserve 2 tablespoons of the sugar; gradually add the remaining sugar to the yolks and whisk briskly for a minute or two until it is slightly pale in color.

(It helps with this next step if you place the bowl of yolks on a folded towel to prevent slipping.) Very gradually at first add the hot milk to the yolks, whisking constantly. Then return the yolk mixture to the saucepan and cook over low-medium heat, scraping the bottom and the sides constantly with a rubber spatula, until the mixture thickens enough to coat a spoon (in this case that will be 180 degrees on a candy thermometer).

Remove from the heat. Add the softened gelatin and whisk or stir gently until the gelatin is completely melted and incorporated. Stir in the macaroon crumbs and the vanilla and almond extracts. Set aside briefly.

In the small bowl of an electric mixer add the salt to the egg whites and beat until the whites barely hold a firm shape. Reduce the speed to moderate, gradually add the reserved 2 tablespoons of sugar, increase the speed to high again, and beat briefly only until the whites hold a straight peak when the beaters are raised. Remove from the mixer.

The yolk-milk mixture should still be very hot. It is going to be folded gradually into the whites; it is most convenient to use a ladle to add the hot yolk-milk mixture, about ½ cup at a time, and fold it in with a rubber spatula. After adding about half of the hot mixture the remainder will not want to blend well. Don't fight it—it is all right. When necessary transfer to a larger bowl and add the final third or quarter of the hot mixture all at once. Fold briefly.

Pour ice water into a mold with at least a 7-cup capacity, shake it out (leaving the mold cold and wet), pour the dessert into the mold, and refrigerate for at least 3 hours, or all day if you wish.

To unmold: Before unmolding onto a large platter, rub the platter lightly with a bit of oil (to make it easy to move the dessert a bit if necessary—and it usually is).

Fill a large bowl or dishpan with hot tap water; with a small, sharp knife cut around the top of the mold to release the edge, and place the mold in the hot water to the depth of the dessert—hold it there for about 15 seconds. Remove the mold, quickly dry it, cover with the oiled platter, and, holding the mold and platter together, turn them over. This dessert always comes out easily for me but if you have any trouble, dip it in the hot water again for a few seconds.

Refrigerate.

Before serving, surround the mold any way you wish with optional fresh or stewed fruit.

Cut with a sharp knife and serve with a pie server.

WHIPPED CREAM

If you are going to serve 4 to 6 portions, 1 cup of cream is enough; for 8 portions use 2 cups of cream. For each cup of cream add 2 tablespoons of confectioners or granulated sugar and ½ teaspoon vanilla extract. In a chilled bowl, with chilled beaters, whip the ingredients until the cream holds a soft shape.

If you prepare this ahead of time, refrigerate it. Then whisk it a bit before serving.

NOTE: *I use Amaretti di Saronno crisp Italian almond macaroons. They are available at most fine food stores around the country. They may be bought at, or ordered by mail from, Manganaro Foods, 488 Ninth Avenue, New York, New York 10018. Or Williams-Sonoma, P.O. Box 7456, San Francisco, California 94120-7456.*

Wild Rice Pudding

This was created at the Soho Charcuterie restaurant in New York City; this recipe is adapted from the cookbook The Soho Charcuterie Cookbook (William Morrow & Company, 1983).

Wild rice, which was originally called Indian rice, is a rare luxury. When the first white men who came to America traveled west, they found wild rice growing in the lakes and rivers of what later became Minnesota, Michigan, and Wisconsin. It is the only truly native grain in North America. Actually, wild rice is not rice; it is a grain —a form of grass or wheat.

This is a luxuriously and unbelievably smooth, rich, velvety, and seductive custard, with firm, chewy, nutty wild rice; the combination of textures is sensational. It is baked in individual soufflé dishes or custard cups.

The wild rice is cooked ahead of time. Cooked wild rice may be refrigerated for a few days or it may be frozen, if you wish. Since it takes about an hour to cook, you might like to keep some already cooked in the freezer.

6 PORTIONS

WILD RICE

You can divide this and cook as little as you want; here are the directions for 1 cup of wild rice, which will make 4 cups when cooked.

1 cup wild rice
½ teaspoon salt

3 cups cold tap water

Place the rice in a strainer in a large bowl of cold water; swoosh it around to wash it, raise the strainer to drain, and transfer the wild rice to a heavy saucepan with a tight lid. Add the salt and water. Place over high heat, stir once or twice, and bring to a boil. Then reduce the heat to allow the water to boil gently, cover the saucepan, and cook the rice for about 1 hour. But there are many different varieties of wild rice and they do not all take the same time to cook. So taste it frequently. It is important not to overcook it; it should be al dente. When it is just done, there might not be any water remaining in the saucepan; if there is some left, drain it. Set the cooked wild rice aside and let stand. (To freeze it, just place it in a freezer container or a freezer bag, airtight, and freeze. Thaw completely before using.)

WILD RICE CUSTARD

2 cups whipping cream
4 egg yolks from eggs graded "large" or "jumbo"
¼ cup granulated sugar
Pinch of nutmeg
Pinch of salt

½ teaspoon vanilla extract
¼ teaspoon almond extract
¼ cup light raisins
Scant ¾ cup cooked wild rice

Adjust a rack one-third up from the bottom of the oven and preheat the oven to 325 degrees.

Scald the cream by placing it in the top of a large double boiler, uncovered, over hot water on moderate heat until you see a slightly wrinkled skin on the top or tiny bubbles around the edge.

Meanwhile, place the yolks in a medium-size mixing bowl. Beat them with a wire whisk just to mix. Gradually whisk in the sugar, nutmeg, and salt. Add the vanilla and almond extracts. Very gradually stir in the hot cream. Taste the mixture carefully. Often it needs an additional pinch of salt (which seems to bring out the vanilla and almond flavors, or a bit more vanilla or almond, although the vanilla should be a mild flavor and the almond should be only barely discernible).

Stir in the raisins and ½ cup of the cooked wild rice.

Return to the top of the double boiler over hot water on moderate heat. Stir and scrape the bottom and sides with a rubber spatula for 10 minutes (reduce the heat a bit for the last few minutes), during which time the mixture will thicken only very slightly. (It is not necessary to take the custard's temperature, but when it is ready it will register 174 degrees on a candy thermometer.)

Arrange six 5-ounce individual soufflé dishes or custard cups in a shallow pan that is no deeper or only slightly deeper than the dishes or cups. With a ladle, ladling from the bottom (in order to get an equal amount of wild rice and raisins in each portion), divide the mixture among the dishes.

Then, spoon the remaining cooked wild rice onto the custards (using a scant teaspoonful on each)—it will partly sink into the custards but with luck a few pieces will remain on the surface (for looks).

Pour boiling water into the larger pan at least 1 inch deep.

Bake for 25 to 30 minutes. To test for doneness, wiggle one of the dishes a bit and when the mixture no longer appears liquid, it is done. Do not overbake.

Remove the pan from the oven. To remove the dishes from the hot water it might be helpful to use a wide metal spatula, but be careful. Let cool to room temperature. Then refrigerate for at least a few hours.

Serve the pudding in the individual dishes.

Banana Pudding

Banana Pudding is an old Southern recipe; my husband was brought up on it as a child in Texas, and it seems that many of his happiest memories involve this Banana Pudding. It is a luscious combination of cold, smooth, and creamy vanilla custard pudding (made with cornstarch), sliced bananas, and bought Vanilla Wafers, all layered in a serving bowl. The wafers absorb some of the moisture from the pudding and they become deliciously soft and chewy instead of crisp. (I had to try it to believe it. Soggy, I thought. Well, soggy it is—delightfully and deliciously soggy, you will agree.)

This is best 4 to 8 hours after it is made.

6 TO 8 PORTIONS

⅓ cup unsifted cornstarch
½ cup granulated sugar
¼ teaspoon salt
4 cups milk
2 eggs graded "large" or "extra-large"
2 tablespoons butter, cold and firm, cut into small pieces (it is best to cut the butter ahead of time and refrigerate it)
1 teaspoon vanilla extract
About 8 ounces bought Vanilla Wafers
4 large just-ripe bananas (not the least overripe)

You will need a wide serving bowl similar to a spaghetti bowl, or a shallow baking dish (for instance 8 by 11 by 1¾ or 2 inches) with an 8- to 10-cup capacity.

In the top of a large double boiler off the heat stir the cornstarch, sugar, and salt to mix thoroughly (it is important that these ingredients be completely mixed). Then, very gradually at first, add the milk, stirring well to make sure there are no lumps; use a wire whisk if necessary.

Place over shallow hot water on moderate heat; stir gently and scrape the pan slowly and constantly with a rubber spatula for 12 to 15 minutes until the mixture thickens and reaches 185 degrees on a candy thermometer.

Remove the top of the double boiler and set aside temporarily.

In the small bowl of an electric mixer (or in any other bowl and using a wire whisk) beat the eggs to mix. Very gradually at first, on low speed, beat about half of the thickened milk mixture into the eggs. Then stir the eggs into the remaining milk mixture.

Replace over the hot water on moderate heat and stir slowly and extremely gently for only 2 minutes.

Remove the top of the double boiler. Add the cold butter and stir gently until melted.

Stir in the vanilla.

Do not let the pudding stand now; without waiting complete the dessert. Place about one third of the vanilla wafers over the bottom of the baking dish, placing them about 1 inch apart.

Peel the bananas and cut them into round slices ¼ to ⅓ inch thick. Place half of the slices over and between the wafers.

Pour half of the custard pudding over the banana layer.

Then make a second layer of cookies, place the remaining banana slices over the wafers, and the remaining pudding over the bananas. Be sure the banana slices are all covered. Place the remaining one third of the cookies over the top.

Cover with wax paper or plastic wrap, letting it touch the top (to prevent a skin from forming on the exposed pudding).

Refrigerate.

Serve this at the table; it should be very cold and is best on chilled plates or in chilled dessert bowls.

Cream Cheese Flan (Flan de Queso Crema)

This is a Miami-Cuban custard, but that simple statement doesn't begin to tell it. This deserves a special name, and a special award; it is thick and dense, smooth as honey, creamy, a taste thrill. (The Cubans have brought some wonderful cooking to this country.) It is an exciting and extraordinary dessert. It is both simple and elegant, appropriate for a casual meal or for a fancy party.

Make it a day before serving or early in the day for that night.

You will need a 2-quart straight-sided oven-proof soufflé dish (7 inches wide and 3 inches deep) and a large baking pan that is wider but not deeper than the soufflé dish (for hot water).

10 TO 12 PORTIONS

¾ cup granulated sugar
8 ounces cream cheese, at room temperature
3 eggs graded "large" plus 6 additional egg yolks
1 14-ounce can sweetened condensed milk
1 13-ounce can evaporated milk
Generous pinch of salt
1 teaspoon vanilla extract

3 tablespoons lime juice (before squeezing the
    juice, grate the rind of 1 lime to use below)
Finely grated rind of 1 large lime
Optional (but highly recommended): several
    packages Birds Eye Quick Thaw Raspberries
    frozen in syrup (see Note)

Adjust a rack one-third up from the bottom of the oven and preheat the oven to 350 degrees. Place a large kettle of water on to boil and then just keep it hot until you are ready for it.

First, caramelize the sugar, as follows, to coat the soufflé dish. Place the sugar in a wide frying pan (an 11-inch nonstick pan is best). Place over high heat and stir constantly with a woden spatula. When the sugar begins to melt, gradually reduce the heat. The sugar will form lumps before it all melts; just continue to cook and stir. When the lumps begin to melt and the sugar begins to caramelize, reduce the heat even more (it should be about low-medium by now) and cook until it is all smoothly melted and is a rich butterscotch color. If it is too pale it will not have any flavor; if it is too dark it will taste burnt.

Pour the caramelized sugar into the soufflé dish. Immediately, holding the dish on both sides with potholders, tilt the pan from side to side to coat the bottom of the dish and about an inch (more or less) up the sides. Continue to tilt the pan until the caramel stops running. Set the dish aside. (The caramel might crack while it stands—don't worry.)

When the dish has cooled, spread butter on the sides above the caramelized part. You can use a brush and melted butter, or spread soft butter with your fingertips.

In the small bowl of an electric mixer beat the cheese until soft. Beat in the eggs one at a time and then the yolks in several additions, scraping the bowl with a rubber spatula and beating until smooth after each addition. Gradually beat in the condensed milk. Transfer the mixture to the large bowl of the electric mixer. Beat on rather low speed while you add the evaporated milk, salt, vanilla, and lime juice. When the ingredients are mixed and smooth remove the bowl from the mixer and stir in the grated lime rind.

Pour the mixture into the caramelized dish.

Place in the wider but not deeper pan. Place in the oven and then reach in and pour hot water from the kettle 1 to 1½ inches deep in the larger pan. Cover the soufflé dish with a cookie sheet.

Bake, covered, for 1½ hours until a small, sharp knife inserted gently in the middle just comes out clean. (If you tap the dish to wiggle it, the flan will shake and look as though it is not set enough, but if the knife comes out clean it is done.)

Uncover, remove from the water, and let stand until completely cool. Refrigerate for 6 to 8 hours or overnight.

DO NOT unmold until only moments before serving; this is glorious looking—smooth liquid gold and shiny the moment it is unmolded. It loses the shine and becomes dull as it stands. To unmold, you will need a dish at least as wide as but preferably wider than the soufflé dish, with a slight rim to catch the caramel, which will run like a sauce. With a small, sharp knife cut around the rim of the flan to loosen it, and then cut all the way down around the sides. Cover with the serving dish, hold them together firmly and carefully, turn them both over, wait a few seconds for the flan to slip out of the dish, remove the soufflé dish, and serve immediately.

Cut the portions with a knife and serve as though it were cheesecake, on flat dessert plates (preferably chilled).

NOTE: *Serve with a generous spoonful of the optional frozen raspberries. Plan on 1 package of the berries for each 2 or 3 portions. The berries should not be thawed ahead of time; they should be barely thawed when served. About 5 minutes before you unmold the flan, place the bag of berries in a bowl of warm water. Separate the berries with your fingers. When they are just barely thawed, pour the berries and a bit of their syrup (not all of it) into a serving bowl.*

Now, unmold the flan.

California Lemon Pudding

A light, delicate, smooth pudding that separates while baking into a soft cake layer on top and a softer sauce on the bottom. All lemony and creamy.

This is a very old recipe that has been popular all around the country for a long long time. It has stood the test of time not only because it is quick and easy but because it is so good. It is baked in individual pottery custard cups and is inverted onto flat plates (see Note).

This is best about 3 hours after it is baked. The longer it stands the more dense it becomes. But if necessary it can wait all day.

5 OR 6 PORTIONS

1 tablespoon unsalted butter
¾ cup granulated sugar
2 eggs graded "large," separated
¼ cup lemon juice (before squeezing the juice, grate the rind of 1 lemon to use below)

2 tablespoons sifted all-purpose flour
1 cup milk
Finely grated rind of 1 large lemon

Adjust a rack to the middle of the oven and preheat the oven to 350 degrees. Butter five 6-ounce or six 5-ounce pottery custard cups (with additional butter to that called for). Place the buttered cups in a shallow baking pan that must not be deeper than the cups. Set aside.

In the small bowl of an electric mixer beat the butter with ½ cup of the sugar (reserve the remaining ¼ cup of sugar) to mix.

Beat in the egg yolks (reserve the whites). Then beat in the lemon juice, the flour (scraping the sides of the bowl as necessary with a rubber spatula), and add the milk gradually at first. When the mixture is smooth remove the bowl from the mixer. Stir in the grated rind.

If you do not have an additional small bowl for the mixture transfer the mixture to any other bowl and wash the bowl.

In the small bowl, with clean beaters, beat the whites until they hold a soft shape. On moderate speed gradually add the remaining ¼ cup of sugar. Then increase the speed again and beat briefly until the whites hold a straight shape when the beaters are slowly raised. The beaten whites will resemble a thick marshmallow fluff; do not beat until they are stiff or dry.

Very gradually at first, in many small additions, fold about half of the lemon mixture into the whites, and then fold the whites into the remaining lemon mixture.

Transfer to a pitcher or use a ladle and pour or ladle the mixture into the buttered cups, dividing the mixture evenly and filling the cups almost to the top.

Pour hot water about 1 inch deep into the larger pan.

Bake for 35 minutes until the tops are puffed up (they will have deep cracks) and are golden. During baking reverse the pan front to back once to ensure even browning.

Remove the cups from the water and let cool. While cooling, the puddings will sink down to their original level and they will look wrinkled and cracked. They are supposed to look that way. Refrigerate. These should be served very cold.

Immediately before serving cut around the pudding with a table knife or a small metal spatula, cover with a plate, turn the plate and the cup over, if necessary tap the cup and plate together against the work surface to release the pudding, remove the cup, and use a spoon or a rubber spatula to scrape out every bit of the sauce that remains in the cup.

This is wonderful just as it is, or with a few fresh strawberries or raspberries.

NOTE: *It is more casual, not as fancy, to serve these directly from the cups they were baked in. If you do serve these in the custard cups you might want to top each portion with a bit of whipped cream and/or a few berries.*

Hot Chocolate Mousse

It sounds like a mousse, looks like a cake, tastes like a soufflé; is served piping hot but without the hectic timing involved with a soufflé—it will not fall even if it waits until it cools. Delicious, exciting, very chocolate—semisweet. Make it for a dinner party.

Most of this can be prepared during the day and can wait until just before baking for the beaten whites. It takes 45 minutes to bake and about 15 minutes to cool a bit before serving; so it can be comfortably placed in the oven to bake just before you sit down to dinner.

You will need a nonstick 10-inch Bundt pan with a 14-cup capacity.

8 PORTIONS

5 ounces unsweetened chocolate
4 ounces (1 stick) unsalted butter, at room temperature
1 cup boiling water

8 eggs graded "large," separated
¾ cup granulated sugar
Pinch of salt

Adjust a rack one-third up from the bottom of the oven and preheat the oven to 350 degrees. Prepare a nonstick 10-inch, 14-cup Bundt pan as follows. With a pastry brush, brush soft but not melted butter (not melted because that would run down to the bottom of the pan) all over the pan (using additional butter to that called for). Sprinkle sugar (additional) all over the pan—to get the sugar on the tube sprinkle it with your fingertips, then turn the pan over paper and tap out excess. When you are ready to bake, you will also need a pan wider but not deeper than the Bundt pan.

Place the chocolate, butter, and boiling water in a 2- to 3-quart heavy saucepan over low heat and stir with a wooden spatula until the chocolate and butter are melted. Remove from the heat and let cool completely. Then place in the freezer to chill for about 15 minutes and stir with a wire whisk until perfectly smooth and slightly thickened. Set aside.

Start to beat the egg yolks in the small bowl of the electric mixer. Gradually add ½ cup of the sugar (reserve the remaining ¼ cup of sugar) to the yolks. Beat at high speed for about 10 minutes until very pale and very thick.

Remove the bowl from the mixer. Gradually fold in the chocolate mixture. Then transfer to a very large mixing bowl and set aside. (You can let everything wait now for a few hours, if you wish. If you are going to wait don't preheat the oven until 20 minutes before baking.)

Add the salt to the egg whites in the large bowl of the electric mixer and with clean beaters beat at high speed until the whites have increased in volume and hold a soft shape. Reduce the speed to moderate and gradually add the remaining ¼ cup of sugar; then again on high speed continue to beat briefly until the whites hold a definite shape when the beaters are raised, but not until they become stiff or dry.

Stir a large spoonful of the beaten whites into the chocolate mixture. Then fold in about half of the whites without being too thorough, and then fold in the remaining whites only until the mixtures are barely blended.

Pour the mousse into the prepared pan, pouring first into one side of the pan and then into the opposite side. If the top of the mousse mixture is not level, smooth it a bit.

Place the Bundt pan into a larger pan (not deeper) and fill the larger pan to about half the depth of the Bundt pan with hot water.

Place in the oven and bake for 45 minutes, covering the top loosely with foil for about the last 15 minutes if it is getting too dark.

When the mousse is done, remove the foil, remove the pan from the hot water, and let it stand for 5 minutes. Then cover the pan with a wide, flat platter and, holding the pan and the platter together, carefully turn them over. Do not remove the pan immediately; let stand for 15 minutes, then remove the pan.

Serve with whipped cream.

WHIPPED CREAM

The cream can be whipped ahead of time, if you wish. Refrigerate it and then, just before serving, whip it a bit with a wire whisk to reincorporate it.

2 cups whipping cream
¼ cup confectioners sugar
2 tablespoons Cognac ⎫
2 tablespoons Grand ⎬ or 1 teaspoon vanilla
    Marnier or rum ⎭ extract

In a chilled bowl, with chilled beaters, whip the ingredients only until the cream barely holds a soft shape. Do not whip until the cream is stiff.

Do not serve the cream on top of the mousse; the heat from the mousse would melt it. Instead, place it alongside the mousse on the individual plates.

East Hampton Chocolate Icebox Cake

It had been a perfect summer day. There was a riot of hot colors in the sky and water, and every-where we looked there were graceful sea gulls and sleek sailboats. We were on the terrace of the Clubhouse Restaurant at Wings Point Yacht Club overlooking 3-Mile Harbor in East Hampton, New York.

Everything was magical, but even so, I could not believe the dessert. They called it a Chocolate Mousse Cake; it is a traditional icebox cake. I thought I had made or at least tasted every varia-tion of chocolate mousse as well as chocolate ice-box cake, but this one was different and wonderful. (The difference is a larger proportion of chocolate, and the chocolate is a combination of both semi-

sweet and milk chocolate, which makes a rich, creamy, dense but not heavy, extraordinarily deli-cious mousse.)

I was invited into the kitchen, where I met the pastry chef, Linda Nessel, a darling young lady who had just graduated from a cooking school in Rhode Island. In her baker's whites she looked like a kid in her father's pajamas. But when I asked her about the recipe she spoke with detailed precision and an air of experience and authority.

You will need a 9 by 3-inch springform pan. This dessert can be made a day ahead or it can be served about 6 hours after it is made.

8 TO 10 PORTIONS

2 3-ounce packages ladyfingers
7 ounces semisweet ⎫
    chocolate   ⎬ (I used Hershey's
9 ounces milk   ⎬ semisweet and milk
    chocolate   ⎭ chocolates)
6 eggs graded "large," separated

½ teaspoon vanilla extract
¼ cup Grand Marnier
½ teaspoon unflavored gelatin
1 teaspoon cold tap water
Pinch of salt
¼ cup granulated sugar

Separate the strips of ladyfingers but do not separate each individual lady-finger. Place strips of them, top sides against the pan, around the sides of an unbuttered 9 by 3-inch springform pan. Then cover the bottom of the pan with ladyfingers, placing them any which way and cutting them as you please (the pattern on the bottom will not show). You will prob-ably use about 40 ladyfingers; there will be some left over that you will not need.

Break up both chocolates and place them in the top of a large double boiler over warm water on low heat. Cover the top with a folded paper towel (to absorb steam) and with the pot cover. Stir occasionally. When the chocolates are almost melted, remove the top of the double boiler and stir until completely melted and smooth. Set aside.

While the chocolates are melting, beat the egg yolks in the small bowl of an electric mixer at high speed for about 5 minutes until pale and thick. Stir in the vanilla and about one third of the Grand Marnier (reserve the remaining Grand Marnier). Let stand.

Sprinkle the gelatin over the water in a small glass custard cup and let stand for 3 to 5 minutes to soften. Then add the remaining Grand Marnier; place the custard cup in shallow hot water in a small pan over low heat; stir occasionally with a table knife until the gelatin is dissolved.

Quickly beat the warm gelatin mixture into the egg yolks, adding it all at once and beating at high speed. Then reduce the speed to moderate and beat in the melted chocolate, beating until the two mixtures are smoothly blended. Remove the bowl from the mixer.

In the large bowl of an electric mixer, with clean beaters, beat the whites with the salt until they hold a soft shape. Reduce the speed to moderate and gradually add the sugar. Increase the speed to high again and beat until the whites hold a definite shape but not until they are stiff or dry.

In about three additions, with a rubber spatula fold about a third of the whites into the chocolate, folding gently and not thoroughly. Then add the chocolate to the remaining whites and again fold gently—this time fold until thoroughly incorporated, but do not handle any more than necessary.

Gently pour the chocolate mixture into the ladyfinger-lined pan. The chocolate mixture will not fill the pan to the top of the ladyfingers.

If you cover the pan (even loosely) with plastic wrap, moisture will form on the bottom of the plastic, it will drip onto the mousse, and although there will not be much of it you don't need any. Therefore, unfold a lightweight paper napkin, place it loosely over the pan, and cover the napkin loosely with plastic wrap. The paper will absorb moisture and the plastic will prevent the mousse from drying out.

Refrigerate for about 6 hours or overnight.

WHIPPED CREAM

1 cup whipping cream   2 tablespoons confectioners sugar
½ teaspoon vanilla extract

In a chilled bowl, with chilled beaters, whip the ingredients until they hold a definite shape. (If you whip the cream ahead of time, refrigerate it until shortly before serving. Then, if it has separated a bit, beat it briefly with a wire whisk or a beater to incorporate.)

Place the cream by spoonfuls around the outer edge of the mousse, up against the ladyfingers—or transfer it to a pastry bag fitted with a rather large star-shaped tube and form rosettes of the cream in a circle around the outer edge. If you wish, sprinkle the whipped cream with coarsely grated semisweet chocolate. And cut 2 slices of navel orange about ⅓ inch thick. Remove the seeds but do not remove the rind. Cut each slice into

6 pie-shaped wedges. Place the wedges, point down, into the whipped cream.

Before serving, release the catch on the side of the pan and gently and slowly remove the sides of the pan.

Serve directly on the bottom of the springform on a folded napkin on a serving plate. It is possible to transfer this if you prefer and if you are very careful. First release the bottom with a long, sharp knife. Then, raise one edge a bit with a wide metal spatula, and slip a flat-sided cookie sheet slowly and gently under the cake. Using the cookie sheet as a spatula, carefully transfer the cake to a large flat platter.

Raspberry Pâté

It's in the pink—it's the berries—it's gorgeous, creamy, a dessert pâté. It may be prepared a day ahead. It has a brilliant shocking-pink sauce and also white whipped cream; when it is served the sauce will go on one side of a portion, the cream on the other. It is appropriate for a fancy party or a simple meal.

You need a loaf pan with a 6-cup capacity.

ABOUT 8 PORTIONS

3 10-ounce packages frozen red raspberries in
    syrup, thawed (see Notes)
1 envelope unflavored gelatin
¼ cup cold tap water
1 cup whipping cream

8 ounces cream cheese, at room temperature
½ cup granulated sugar
Pinch of salt
3 tablespoons lemon juice

Prepare a loaf pan with a 6-cup capacity as follows. Turn the pan over. Fold one long piece of aluminum foil the long way shiny side out to fit the length of the pan including the two small sides of the pan (it may extend a bit above the sides). Also, fold a length of aluminum foil the long way to fit the width including the two large sides (this may extend a bit above the sides also). The pieces of foil should not be the least bit too wide or they will wrinkle and the pâté will not be smooth. Carefully place one piece over the pan and fold down the two sides to fit. Remove and set aside. Then place the other piece over the pan and fold down the two sides to fit. Remove. Turn the pan right side up. Carefully place one piece of foil in place in the pan, and then do likewise with the second piece of foil (there will be a double thickness on the bottom). If the foil is longer than necessary, fold the ends out over the rim of the pan. Set the pan aside. (Do not butter or oil the foil.)

Place the thawed berries in a wide strainer over a wide bowl to drain. Reserve ¼ cup of the drained syrup; you will not need the remaining syrup for this recipe.

Place the drained berries in the bowl of a food processor fitted with the metal chopping blade and process for about 20 seconds until puréed. (Or, in a blender, purée a small amount at a time. Or work the berries through a food mill.)

Now, to strain the seeds out of the berries, place a wide but fine strainer (if it is not fine enough the seeds will go through—and you really do not want them) over a wide bowl and push the berries through the strainer. (I use a rather firm rubber spatula or a wooden spoon for pushing the berries through, but many professionals use the back of the bowl of a ladle.) You should have 1¼ cups of strained purée. Let stand.

Sprinkle the gelatin over the water in a 1-cup glass measuring cup or in a Pyrex custard cup. Let stand for about 5 minutes.

Meanwhile, in the small bowl of an electric mixer, whip the cream only until it is softly whipped; it should just hold a shape but it should not be firm. Refrigerate.

In the large bowl of the mixer beat the cheese until it is soft and smooth. Beat in the sugar, salt, and the lemon juice. Then beat in the puréed raspberries. Let stand.

To melt the gelatin place the cup in a pan of warm water only as deep as the gelatin mixture over low heat. Let stand for a few minutes until the granules are dissolved. Remove from the water. Quickly and briefly stir in the reserved ¼ cup of drained raspberry syrup and, with the mixer at medium speed, beat the gelatin, which may be warm, into the raspberry and cheese mixture. Beat for a few moments, scraping the bowl with a rubber spatula. Be sure it is all thoroughly mixed.

The raspberry and cheese mixture should thicken slightly before the whipped cream is folded in. Place the bowl into a larger bowl of ice and water and stir frequently until the mixture thickens slightly. (Actually, this mixture should become almost as thick as the softly whipped cream.)

In three additions fold about three quarters of the berry mixture into the cream, and then fold the cream into the remaining raspberry mixture. If the mixtures resist blending into each other, pour back and forth gently from one bowl to another once or twice until smooth.

Pour into the lined pan (it will not fill the pan to the top). Cover the pan with plastic wrap or aluminum foil.

Refrigerate for 6 hours or overnight.

RASPBERRY SAUCE

This can be prepared ahead of time.

The amount of sauce to prepare depends on how many people you plan to serve. (With enough sauce, the pâté will serve ten people.) For each three or four people, use one 10-ounce package of red raspberries frozen in syrup (see Notes). Thaw the berries. Drain in a strainer over a bowl; reserve the drained syrup. Purée the berries in a food processor or a blender or a food mill. Force through a fine strainer to remove the seeds. Add 1 teaspoon of kirsch, framboise, cassis, or lemon juice for each package of berries. And then stir in enough of the drained syrup to make a sauce that is not too thick. I use about three quarters of the syrup. Refrigerate.

WHIPPED CREAM

For each three or four people use 1 cup of whipping cream, 1 tablespoon of granulated or confectioners sugar, and ½ teaspoon of vanilla extract.

In a chilled bowl, with chilled beaters, whip the ingredients until the cream is softly whipped; it should hold a soft shape, not firm. Think "sauce." Refrigerate.

If the cream is whipped ahead of time, it will separate slightly and should be whisked a bit with a wire whisk just before serving.

To serve: Remove the covering from the pan. Fill a dishpan with hot tap water. Place the pan of pâté in the hot water for only 3 or 4 seconds (see Notes). Dry the pan quickly. The pâté will slip out of the pan quickly when it is turned over; you'd better be ready. First, wet the serving platter with cold water (which will make it possible for you to move the pâté if necessary). And second, be sure to center the serving platter over the pâté. Hold the pan and platter together firmly and turn them over. Remove the pan. Peel off the foil. If the surface of the pâté needs to be smoothed (which I doubt), dip a small metal spatula into very hot water, shake it off lightly, and with the hot and wet spatula smooth the surface.

If you serve this at the table, the sauce and whipped cream should be in pitchers, or in bowls with ladles.

Serve on wide (luncheon-size) flat plates (chilled). The pâté slices perfectly. Use a sharp knife and cut slices about 1 inch wide. With a pie or cake server place a slice of the pâté on a plate. Pour or ladle Raspberry Sauce generously on the plate next to one long side of the pâté, and Whipped Cream next to the other long side. (The Raspberry Sauce and the Whipped Cream should just run into each other at the top and bottom sides of the slice.)

NOTES: 1. *The new Birds Eye red raspberries frozen in light syrup (less sugar) make a dessert that might not be quite sweet enough for many people; the original frozen berries in regular syrup are probably better here.*

2. *The only reason for dipping the pan into the hot water is to help to loosen the pâté in the corners of the pan, because the pan is probably flared and, if so, the foil does not fill in the corners.*

Strawberry Yogurt Cream

This is typical of new American desserts; it is made with fresh fruit and yogurt, it is made quickly, it can be made weeks ahead and frozen (although it is served at refrigerator temperature), and it is pink and pretty. Delicious.

This is prepared in individual dishes, glasses, or molds and is served either in the dishes or glasses or unmolded onto individual flat plates.

6 PORTIONS

1 1-pound box washed fresh strawberries (see To Wash Strawberries, page 14)
1 envelope unflavored gelatin
2 tablespoons plus 2 teaspoons cold tap water
¼ cup granulated sugar
Optional: red food coloring

¾ cup unflavored yogurt
1 tablespoon lemon juice
2 tablespoons dark rum or brandy
Pinch of salt
1 teaspoon vanilla extract
½ cup whipping cream

234

Wash and hull the berries. Remove 6 large berries for decoration and refrigerate them. Drain the remaining berries.

Sprinkle the gelatin over the water in a small cup and let stand.

Place the drained berries in a food processor fitted with the metal chopping blade and process until smoothly puréed/liquefied. Or purée them in batches in a blender. Or mash them on a plate with a fork. You should have 1 cup of purée.

Stir the purée and sugar in a small saucepan over moderate heat until the mixture comes to a boil. Add the gelatin, stir to dissolve, remove from the heat, stir in a bit of the optional red food coloring to give the dessert a nice rich color, and set aside briefly.

In a bowl, with a wire whisk, beat the yogurt until it is soft and smooth. Gradually whisk in the warm strawberry mixture.

To remove the tiny strawberry seeds, press the mixture through a wide but fine strainer set over a bowl.

Stir in the lemon juice, rum or brandy, salt, and vanilla.

Place the bowl into a larger bowl of ice and water and stir and scrape the bowl frequently with a rubber spatula until the mixture just begins to thicken slightly.

Meanwhile, in a small chilled bowl, with chilled beaters, whip the cream until it just holds a shape.

Gradually, a little bit at a time, fold the berry mixture into the cream.

If you would like to prepare this in portions to be unmolded, use small cups (preferably metal or Pyrex—oval tin *oeuf en gelée* molds are wonderful) with a 5- to 6-ounce capacity. Rinse the containers with ice water just before filling them; they should be cold and wet when they are filled. Or prepare this in individual soufflé dishes or stemmed wineglasses to serve without unmolding.

Cover individually with foil and refrigerate from 4 hours to overnight. Or freeze them (see Note).

To unmold, cut around the tops of the desserts with a small, sharp knife to release, hold the container in a bowl of hot tap water as deep as the dessert itself for 10 to 20 seconds (the time depends on the material of the container), dry quickly, then, holding the container at about a 45-degree angle, bang it sharply against the side of your left hand a few times. It will force the dessert away from the container and will make it easy to unmold (wiggle the container a bit and you will see that the dessert is no longer clinging to the container—if it is, bang it again). Cover with a flat plate—center the plate carefully—and turn the plate and container over. (The dessert will probably slip out when you least expect it to. It cannot be moved once it is out, so always be sure to hold the container in the middle of the plate.)

Use the reserved 6 strawberries to decorate the desserts either in cups or glasses or on plates. The berries may be left whole or sliced. And if the desserts have been unmolded onto plates and if you have plenty of room and if you have more berries, use them, if you wish.

NOTE: *To freeze, just place the dishes, glasses, or molds in the freezer for up to 2 weeks. Thaw several hours or overnight in the refrigerator. Do not serve frozen.*

Grand Marnier Strawberry Soufflé

You need six 5-ounce individual soufflé dishes, fresh strawberries, egg whites, and someone special to share this happiness with. It is fluffy, gorgeous —it must be served immediately.

6 PORTIONS

2 1-pound boxes fresh strawberries
½ cup plus 1 tablespoon granulated sugar
Grand Marnier
1½ teaspoons lemon juice
A few ladyfingers or a small piece of any sponge
   cake, pound cake, or a sweet bun (you can
   even use white bread)

7 egg whites from eggs graded "large" (they may
   be whites that were frozen and then thawed;
   they should measure 7 liquid ounces)
⅛ teaspoon salt

Butter six 5-ounce soufflé dishes. To make collars for them tear off six 6-inch lengths of aluminum foil (keep the foil smooth and neat). Fold each piece in half the long way, shiny side out. Butter about half of the length of one long side of the pieces of foil (buttered part should be 12 by 1½ or 2 inches). Carefully wrap the pieces of foil, buttered side up and in, around the dishes; wrap a piece of string around each dish and tie it carefully and tightly to make the foil secure. Sprinkle about a teaspoonful or more of sugar (additional to that called for) in each dish. Working over wax paper or foil, turn and tap each dish to coat the dish and its collar with the sugar. Then turn the dishes over and tap to shake out excess sugar. Place the prepared dishes on a jelly-roll pan and set aside.

Adjust a rack to the bottom position in the oven and preheat the oven to 400 degrees.

Wash, hull, and drain the berries (see page 14); you will not use them all.

Coarsely slice or cut up 6 to 8 large berries. Place them in a small bowl. Add 1 tablespoon of the sugar (reserve the remaining ½ cup of sugar) and 2 tablespoons of Grand Marnier. Let stand at room temperature, stirring occasionally.

Measure about 1½ cups of the remaining berries. Purée/liquefy them in a food processor fitted with the metal chopping blade or mash them fine on a plate with a fork.

Place a wide but fine strainer over a wide bowl. Press the puréed berries through the strainer to remove the seeds.

Measure the strained berries. You need 1 cup; if necessary purée or mash more. Stir in the lemon juice and set aside.

You need 6 small pieces, 1 for each dish, of the ladyfingers, pound cake, or whatever (to absorb the Grand Marnier, which will perfume the whole soufflé). The pieces should be about the size of lump sugar, or almost as large as a domino. Place 1 piece in each prepared dish. Then divide the sliced berries and all their juice among the dishes. If you wish, drizzle an additional ½ teaspoonful of Grand Marnier into each dish.

All of the above (except lighting the oven) can be done early in the day, if you wish; if so, let the dishes stand at room temperature.

Place the egg whites in the large bowl of an electric mixer, add the salt, and beat until the whites hold a soft shape. Reduce the speed to moderate, gradually add the remaining ½ cup of sugar, then increase the speed to high again and continue to beat until the whites hold a peak when they are lifted with a rubber spatula but not until they are stiff or dry. Remove from the mixer.

Gradually, in small additions at first, with a rubber spatula fold the strained berries into the beaten whites. Do not fold or handle any more than necessary; if the mixtures are just barely blended that is fine.

With a large spoon divide the mixture among the dishes. Then, with a teaspoon, smooth the tops just a bit and immediately place the soufflés in the oven.

Bake for 18 to 20 minutes. Remove from the oven and quickly cut the strings with scissors (if you have someone to help right now, you will be glad), remove the foil collars, and with a wide metal spatula or pancake turner quickly place each soufflé on a plate and serve IMMEDIATELY. A bit of the soufflé might have run down the sides of the dishes and might have caramelized on the jelly-roll pan. Do not pay any attention to it; do not take one second longer than necessary. These will be gloriously high.

If you wish, place one or more of the remaining strawberries on each flat plate.

Apple Cranberry Pudding

This is so easy there is nothing to it. The buttery part on the top is sweet and chewy and pudding-like. The cranberry part on the bottom is deliciously tart. If you like a tart flavor you will be wild about this—I do and I am. It is scrumptious served warm with vanilla ice cream.

6 TO 8 PORTIONS

BOTTOM LAYER

2 cups fresh cranberries
2 large, firm cooking apples (preferably Granny Smith or Jonathan)

½ cup pecans, toasted (see To Toast Pecans, page 7), broken into medium-size pieces
½ cup granulated sugar

Adjust a rack to the middle of the oven and preheat the oven to 325 degrees. Butter a shallow ovenproof baking dish with about a 2-quart capacity (11 by 8 by 1¾ or 2 inches). Set aside.

Place the berries in a bowl of cold water to wash, pick over them, and then drain on a towel. Let stand.

Peel, quarter, and core the apples. Cut each piece into ½-inch chunks.

In a bowl mix the cranberries with the apples, pecans, and sugar. Turn into the baking dish and smooth the top.

TOP LAYER

2 eggs graded "large"
1 cup granulated sugar

1 cup unsifted all-purpose flour
6 ounces (1½ sticks) unsalted butter, melted

In the small bowl of an electric mixer beat the eggs to mix. Beat in the sugar, then add the flour and the melted butter at the same time and beat until smooth.

Pour the batter evenly over the bottom layer.

Bake for about 50 minutes until the top is golden and a toothpick inserted into the center comes out clean.

Serve hot, warm, or at room temperature, preferably with vanilla ice cream.

Cheesecakes

A CHEESECAKE PAN   A professional cheesecake pan, the kind that is generally used by bakers and pastry chefs, is a one-piece pan, because cheesecakes are frequently baked in a pan of water. And they are deeper than layer cake pans. They come in a variety of widths. Many of these recipes call for an 8 by 3-inch cheesecake pan. They are available at almost all well-equipped kitchen shops. They can be bought at, or ordered by mail from, Bridge Kitchenware, 214 East 52nd Street, New York, New York 10022.

Bull's Eye Cheesecake

"How did you do it?"—"I can't believe it"—"I never saw anything like it."

You will have two mixtures, one dark and one light. When you work your magic with them they will form a series of concentric circles (a bull's eye) of dark and light cheesecake to produce this photogenic and delicious creation. When you cut into the cake you will see gracefully curved, vertical stripes that are incredibly precise; they

practically happen by themselves.

The recipe is foolproof and not difficult.

Although this tastes perfectly delicious any time at all, the design will be more clearly defined after the cake has been refrigerated for at least 8 hours or overnight.

You need a one-piece 8 by 3-inch cheesecake pan (see above).

10 PORTIONS

32 ounces cream cheese (preferably at
    room temperature)
¼ cup sour cream
1 teaspoon vanilla extract
¼ teaspoon almond extract
¼ teaspoon salt
4 eggs graded "large"

⅔ cup granulated sugar
⅔ cup dark brown sugar, firmly packed
1 teaspoon powdered (not granular) instant coffee
2 teaspoons unsweetened cocoa powder
About ¼ cup graham cracker crumbs or crumbs
    made from Amaretti or any other crisp
    cookies (to be used after the cake is baked)

Adjust a rack one-third up from the bottom of the oven and preheat the oven to 350 degrees. Carefully butter an 8 by 3-inch one-piece cheesecake pan all the way up to the rim and including the inside of the rim itself (or the cake will stick to the rim as it rises and will therefore not rise evenly). You will also need a larger pan (for hot water) to place the cake pan in while baking; the larger pan must not be as deep as the cheesecake pan, and it must be wide enough so it will not touch the sides of the cake pan. Set aside.

In the large bowl of an electric mixer beat the cheese until it is soft and smooth, frequently scraping the sides of the bowl (with a rubber spatula) and the beaters themselves (with your finger) to be sure the cheese is uniformly smooth. Beat in the sour cream, then the vanilla and almond extracts, and the salt, and then the eggs one at a time, scraping the bowl occasionally and beating after each addition until it is incorporated.

Remove the bowl from the mixer. You will have about 6 cups of the mixture. Place half of it (3 cups) in another bowl that is large enough to allow you to stir in it.

Add the granulated sugar to one bowl and the brown sugar to the

other bowl. With a rubber spatula for each bowl stir the ingredients for about a minute until the sugar has dissolved and the mixtures have thinned out.

To the dark mixture, add the instant coffee and, through a fine strainer, the cocoa. Stir. Stir some more until the coffee and cocoa have dissolved and there are no visible specks of either. If there are specks, strain the mixture through a fine strainer.

Now, to form the design. You have a scant 4 cups of each mixture. The two mixtures will be placed alternately in the pan. Each segment will be one quarter or a scant 1 cup of the mixture. I use two 1-cup glass measuring cups, one for the dark mixture and one for the light. (But you can do this any way you wish, even without measuring if that suits you better.)

If you are using the two 1-cup measuring cups, pour a scant cupful of one mixture into one cup and a scant cupful of the other into the other (use separate rubber spatulas to assist for each color).

It does not matter which color you use first. Pour the scant cupful of either directly into the middle of the prepared cake pan. (It will spread out by itself to cover the bottom of the pan.) Then pour the same amount of the other mixture directly into the middle of the first mixture. (That will spread out by itself also.) Then use the first color again, right in the middle. Do you see the bull's eye design forming?

Continue until you have used all of both mixtures (or four additions of each mixture).

Now, handle the pan very carefully in order not to disturb the design. Place the cake pan in the larger pan and pour hot water into the larger pan about 1½ inches deep. (If the larger pan is aluminum add about 1 teaspoon of cream of tartar to the hot water to keep the pan from discoloring.)

Carefully transfer to the oven and bake for 1½ hours.

Then remove the cake pan from the hot water and set aside to cool. (During baking the top of the cake will darken to a rich honey color and will rise up to and sometimes above the top of the pan; during cooling it will sink down to its original level.)

When the bottom of the cake pan has reached room temperature the cake is ready to be unmolded.

There are several versions of this cake in my other books. Occasionally, people have complained that a bit of the cake stuck in the pan when it was unmolded. Somehow a solution never occurred to me. One day, my friend Ellen Safian, of Great Neck, New York, told me that she never has any trouble because she dips the bottom of the cake pan in a wide frying pan of boiling water for 10 to 15 seconds before unmolding. Such a simple solution, and it works so well. Thanks, Ellen.

After dipping the bottom of the pan in boiling water, dry the pan, cover it with a flat plate or board (clear, lightweight plastic cutting boards from the hardware store are wonderful for this), carefully hold the cake pan and the board firmly together, and turn them over.

If the cake doesn't slip out of the pan easily, bang the pan and the plate or board against the work surface. Remove the pan. Sprinkle the crumbs over the cake (this will become the bottom and the crumbs will keep it from sticking to the plate), cover with a serving plate, a board, or another plastic cutting board, and very carefully (the cake is still soft and tender—do not press down on it) turn it all over again, leaving the cake right side up.

Refrigerate.

This will slice best if you dip the knife into a deep pitcher of very hot water before making each cut. Or, if you are serving from the kitchen, hold the knife under very hot running water—the hotter the better.

8-Hour Cheesecake

The fun and excitement, the challenge, the satisfaction, the hoopla of cooking will never fade. On the contrary, for me it gets more so.

Surely I have had enough cheesecake to be satiated and to feel that I have had it—with cheesecakes. But recently a friend sent me a page from a New Jersey newspaper, and on the back was a story about cheesecakes written by Andrew Schloss, who writes regularly about food for the Philadelphia Inquirer. Mr. Schloss had a whole new theory about cheesecake. I did not need another cheesecake recipe or another theory, but when I read his story I couldn't wait to make the cake. And then with each bite I swooned.

Mr. Schloss points out that cheesecake is really just a custard: eggs, sugar, and cream cheese instead of milk or cream. He says that after years

of trial and error he concluded that with a lower temperature "the ingredients simply melted together yielding a mousselike texture." When he says low he means low. The cake is baked at only 200 degrees for 8 hours.

You will have a pure creamy-white cake that is stark in its simplicity, it will have an extremely creamy texture, the top will not crack or color or rise or fall, and when you serve the cake it will not cling to the knife. The "flayvah" (as Lauren Bacall says) is sensational.

I have adapted this recipe from the original. I make it in an 8 by 3-inch one-piece cheesecake pan (see page 241); Schloss uses a 2-quart soufflé dish.

10 TO 12 PORTIONS

2 pounds cream cheese, preferably at
 room temperature
1 cup granulated sugar
2 tablespoons (repeat, 2 tablespoons)
 vanilla extract

2 tablespoons Cognac
2 tablespoons Myers's Dark Rum (see Note)
5 eggs graded "large"

Adjust a rack one-third up from the bottom of the oven and preheat the oven to 200 degrees. Correct oven temperature is vital for this recipe (and most others) since you will not "bake until done," but you will bake for the specified time based on correct oven temperature (see Oven Temperature, page 9). Butter an 8 by 3-inch one-piece cheesecake pan or a 2-quart soufflé dish and set aside.

Have ready a large pan in which to place the cake pan or soufflé dish. It must not be deeper than the cake pan but it must be wider.

In the large bowl of an electric mixer beat the cheese until soft and perfectly smooth. To ensure the smoothness, scrape the bowl and the beaters a few times during mixing.

When the cheese is as smooth as possible, gradually beat in the sugar, vanilla, Cognac, and rum. Then add the eggs one at a time, beating well after each addition.

Pour the mixture into the buttered pan or dish. Place the pan or dish into the larger pan. Pour hot water about 2 inches deep into the larger pan and place in the oven.

Bake for 8 hours. Then remove from the hot water and let stand for several hours or overnight. Or if you bake the cake during the night let it cool for most of the day; it should stand for at least a few hours after it has reached room temperature.

To unmold, let a few inches of very hot tap water run into a dishpan. Hold the cheesecake pan or soufflé dish in the hot water for about 10 seconds, dry the pan or dish, cover it with a flat cake plate or serving board, and turn the pan or dish and plate over. If the cake does not slip out, gently bang the pan or dish and plate on the work surface once or twice. Serve the cake upside down.

If you serve this before refrigerating or freezing (it freezes well), it will be especially delicate, creamy, tender, and custardy. If you do freeze or refrigerate the cake, bring it to room temperature before serving. (However, if it is cold when you serve it, it is still wonderful, only different—that's all.)

Serve this as it is, perfectly plain, or serve any fresh berries alongside.

NOTE: *I am not suggesting that you buy a bottle of Myers's rum for the 2 tablespoons you need. I mention the brand because it is the kind I use and because I have been told that no other dark rum tastes the same. But for such a small amount I think you can use any.*

Emilio's Cheesecake

The New Yorker *magazine, in their issue of March 27, 1971, published a recipe for a cheesecake made by Emilio Braseco which they said was the best cheesecake in New York.*

I tore the page out of the magazine and put it on my desk in the kitchen, planning to make it soon, but I didn't. Eventually I said to myself, "You haven't made it yet; what makes you think you ever will?" (I don't keep files of recipes.)

A few days after I threw it away I received a letter from a friend in Mobile, Alabama, asking if I would like the world's best cheesecake recipe, and he mentioned, casually, that it was originally from an old issue of The New Yorker.

I wrote back immediately and said, "Yes, please." This time I did not wait; I made it minutes after the recipe arrived.

The story is that the cake was from a cafeteria for graduate students at the City University of New York. At the time the story was written The New Yorker *said the cake was so popular that the cafeteria never had enough—and it soon became the talk of the town.*

Incidentally, this cake is not like Lindy's, or the so-called New York–style cheesecake. It is not as heavy or dense or cheesy; it is more creamy. It has no crust. It is quick and easy to make. It is wonderful for a large party. You will ♥ it.

The following recipe has been adapted from the recipe for Emilio's; the adapting was done partly in Mobile, Alabama, and partly in my kitchen in Florida.

16 TO 24 PORTIONS

2 pounds cream cheese, at room temperature
4 ounces (1 stick) unsalted butter, at
    room temperature
1 tablespoon vanilla extract
1½ cups granulated sugar
½ cup less 1 tablespoon cornstarch
7 eggs graded "large"
2 cups whipping cream
¼ cup lemon juice

Adjust a rack one-third down from the top of the oven and preheat the oven to 350 degrees. Butter a 13 by 9 by 2-inch pan and set aside.

In the large bowl of an electric mixer beat the cheese and butter until soft and smooth. Add the vanilla, sugar, and cornstarch, and beat, scraping the bowl with a rubber spatula as necessary, until smooth. Beat in the eggs one at a time and then on low speed gradually add the cream. Continue to scrape the bowl as necessary; the mixture will be thin, and it should be as smooth as honey. Add the lemon juice last and beat only to mix.

Pour the mixture into the prepared pan. Place the pan in a larger pan that must not be deeper than the cake pan. (I use a large roasting pan that came with my oven; it is 1¼ inches deep.)

Place the pan on the rack in the oven and pour hot water almost 1 inch deep in the large pan.

Bake at 350 degrees for 30 minutes; then, to ensure even browning, carefully turn both pans together front to back; raise the oven temperature to 375 degrees and bake for 10 to 15 more minutes (total baking time is 40 to 45 minutes). Bake only until the top is a pale golden brown.

Carefully remove from the oven and remove the cake pan from the hot water. Let stand until the bottom of the pan is completely cool. (Do not refrigerate the cake until it has been removed from the pan.)

Cover the cake with a large serving board or tray. (I use a lightweight clear plastic board from a hardware store, or a wooden cutting board.) Center the board or tray very carefully over the cake. Hold the board or tray and the cake pan firmly together and turn them over. Remove the cake pan.

Refrigerate the cake (as it is—upside down).

My friend in Alabama likes this best after it has been refrigerated for 3 days. I have served it after a few hours in the refrigerator, as well as the following day. We loved it both ways.

In Mobile they serve this with strawberries and a mountain of whipped cream. I served it recently with the blueberries from the Blueberries and Cream recipe (see page 334). After the prepared berries have been refrigerated they might thicken a bit too much to be used as a sauce (as in this case, with the cheesecake). If so, thin them slightly with a bit of water, orange juice, kirsch, or Grand Marnier.

Triple-Threat Cheesecake

This is a variation of the cheesecake that I made every day for years for my husband's restaurants. There are three variations of it in my first book and one in my chocolate book. Now this. In this recipe the cake is baked in a springform pan—it has a crumb crust on the bottom—and the cheese mixture is put into the pan alternately with ribbons and globs and lumps, large and small areas, of very thick, almost black, chewy, not-too-sweet chocolate sauce made with unsweetened chocolate, semisweet chocolate, and cocoa. Sensational!

The cake should be refrigerated for 5 to 6 hours or overnight before serving. (Nevertheless, I had this once at room temperature before it had been refrigerated. It was as custardy as crème brûlée and wonderful, the chocolate sauce was still a bit saucy, which made it run a little when served. It was so good my conscience tells me that I must let you know about it. But I think you should become familiar with it chilled first.)

10 TO 12 PORTIONS

CRUST

1 cup graham cracker crumbs
1 tablespoon granulated sugar
1 tablespoon unsweetened cocoa powder
    (preferably Dutch-process)

1 teaspoon cinnamon
½ teaspoon powdered (not granular) instant
    coffee or espresso
2 ounces (½ stick) unsalted butter, melted

You will need an 8 by 3-inch springform pan. With the sides and bottom in place carefully butter only the sides up to and including the inside of the rim.

Place the crumbs in a mixing bowl and add the sugar, cocoa, cinnamon, and coffee. Stir with a rubber spatula to mix. Add the butter, stir, and press down with the spatula to mix thoroughly (the mixture will not hold together).

Turn the mixture into the pan. With your fingertips distribute the crumbs loosely but evenly over the bottom of the pan. Then, with your fingertips and/or bent finger joints, press on the crumbs firmly to make a compact layer.

This will be baked in a larger pan of shallow hot water. To make the springform pan watertight tear off a large square of wide heavy-duty aluminum foil. Place the pan in the center of the foil and, with your hands, bring up the sides of the foil and press them firmly against the sides of the pan. Then, with scissors, cut the foil even with the top of the pan or just below the top; or instead of cutting it you can fold it down to just below the top. Set aside.

CHEESECAKE MIXTURE

2 pounds cream cheese, at room temperature
Pinch of salt
1 teaspoon vanilla extract

1¾ cups granulated sugar
4 eggs graded "large"

Adjust a rack one-third up from the bottom of the oven and preheat the oven to 350 degrees.

In the large bowl of an electric mixer beat the cheese until it is soft and perfectly smooth, scraping the bowl frequently with a rubber spatula. Do not underbeat at this stage. Beat in the salt, vanilla, and the sugar.

Beat well again, scraping the bowl, for several minutes until thoroughly mixed. Then, on moderate speed, add the eggs one at a time, beating until thoroughly incorporated after each addition. (But do not overbeat after adding the eggs; the mixture should not become airy.) Set aside.

TRIPLE-THREAT CHOCOLATE SAUCE

½ cup whipping cream
2 ounces (½ stick) unsalted butter
2 ounces unsweetened chocolate
3 ounces semisweet chocolate
⅓ cup granulated sugar

⅓ cup dark brown sugar, firmly packed
2 teaspoons powdered (not granular) instant coffee
Pinch of salt
½ cup unsweetened cocoa powder (preferably Dutch-process)

In a 1½-quart heavy saucepan place the cream, butter, unsweetened chocolate, and semisweet chocolate. Whisk occasionally over rather low heat until the chocolate and butter are melted and the mixture is smooth. Add both sugars and stir over moderate heat until the granules are dissolved. Add the powdered coffee, salt, and cocoa. Stir with a wire whisk. Remove from the heat. Whisk or, if necessary, beat with a mixer until perfectly smooth.

This must be used right away while it is warm; as it cools it becomes too thick to pour. Here's how.

First, the cheese mixture should be divided into three parts, one part equal to half of the mixture and the other two parts each equal to one quarter of the mixture. (You can just guess, or measure. To measure: There is a total of about 7 cups. Therefore, place half of it—or 3½ cups— in a bowl or a 1-quart measuring cup. And place the two smaller parts— 1¾ cups each—in small bowls or 2-cup measuring cups.)

The chocolate sauce should be divided in half. (You can just guess, or measure. To measure: There is a total of about 1½ cups; therefore, divide it into two ¾-cup parts.)

Pour the larger amount of the cheese mixture into the cake pan. Then, with a fork, slowly drizzle one of the parts of the chocolate sauce in a thin stream all over the cheese mixture, in a crisscross design or in circles or whatever pleases you; the only thing to concentrate on is that the mixture should not flop out in large globs. Cover the chocolate with one of the smaller parts of the cheese mixture, again pouring slowly, all over—not in large globs. Repeat drizzling the second half of the chocolate. And then repeat with the third and last part of the cheese mixture. When you pour this final layer of cheese mixture, remember that it will be the top of the cake, and it will look best if you do not allow any of the chocolate to show through. It is a help to pour very slowly (however, if a little bit of chocolate does show through it is OK).

Place the cake pan in a larger pan that must not be deeper than the cake pan (1½ inches is deep enough). Pour hot water about 1 inch deep into the larger pan. Carefully transfer to the oven.

Bake for 1½ hours. If, after about 1 hour of baking, the top seems to be browning too much, carefully lower the rack to the lowest position and continue baking. When done, the top of the cake will be a beautiful, smooth medium-brown color.

Remove the pan from the oven. Carefully remove the cake pan from the water and transfer it to a rack. After about 20 minutes remove the foil. Let the pan stand on the rack until it is completely cool; or for at least 4 or 5 hours.

Carefully release and remove the sides of the pan.

Refrigerate for 5 to 6 hours or overnight.

The cake can be served from the bottom of the cake pan (which should be put on a folded napkin on a cake platter) or it can be transferred to a cake platter. To transfer it, first release the bottom of the cake as follows. Insert a heavy knife with about a 6½-inch blade and carefully work it around the cake to be sure the cake is not sticking. Then, with an extra-large wide metal spatula, or with two wide metal spatulas (one under each side), carefully lift and transfer the cake.

Chocolate-Brownie Cheesecake

This is a white cheesecake with chunks of extra-chocolate Brownies throughout. First you bake the Brownies. Then, mix the cheesecake and fold in small chunky pieces of the Brownies. When the cake is baked the Brownies do not fall apart or sink to the bottom or lose their identity—they remain like black nuggets in the creamy cheesecake. It is fascinating to eat both cheesecake and Brownies in the same bite. And it is gorgeous.

People ask me, "Where do you get your ideas?" Usually I don't know where; they just happen. But this one came from my husband. When I told him I was making Chocolate Cheesecake Brownies (see page 266), he came back with, "Why not Chocolate-Brownie Cheesecake?" I think he was joking. But it is no joke; it is wonderful.

You will need a one-piece 8 by 3-inch cheesecake pan (see page 241).

10 PORTIONS

BROWNIES FOR CHEESECAKE

1 cup sifted all-purpose flour
3 tablespoons unsweetened cocoa powder
    (preferably Dutch-process)
4 ounces (1 stick) unsalted butter
2 ounces unsweetened chocolate
1 teaspoon powdered or granular instant coffee
½ teaspoon vanilla extract

¼ teaspoon almond extract
Pinch of salt
1 cup granulated sugar
2 eggs graded "large"
3½ ounces (1 cup) walnuts, broken into rather
    large pieces

Adjust a rack one-third up from the bottom of the oven and preheat the oven to 350 degrees. Prepare an 8-inch square cake pan as follows: Invert the pan on the work surface, center a 12-inch square of foil shiny side down over the pan. With your hands press down on the sides and corners to shape the foil to the pan. Remove the foil, turn the pan over, place the foil in the pan, and with a potholder or a towel press against the foil to fit it smoothly into the pan. Place a piece of butter in the pan (additional to that called for) and place the pan in the oven to melt the butter. Then, with a brush or with crumpled wax paper, spread the butter all over the foil. Set the pan aside.

Sift together the flour and cocoa and set aside.

Place the butter and the chocolate in a 2½- to 3-quart heavy saucepan. Stir occasionally over rather low heat until melted. Remove from the heat.

Stir in the coffee, vanilla, almond extract, and the salt. Then add the sugar, mix well, and add the eggs one at a time, mixing well after each addition. Then add the sifted ingredients and stir to mix. Finally stir in the nuts.

Turn the mixture into the prepared pan, smooth the top, and bake for 23 to 25 minutes until a toothpick inserted gently in the middle comes out clean and dry.

Remove from the oven and let stand until cool. Then place the pan in the freezer until the cake is very firm. Cover with a rack, turn the pan and rack over, remove the pan, peel off the foil, cover with another rack or a cookie sheet, and turn over again, leaving the cake right side up.

The cake of Brownies should be frozen or at least very cold when you cut it. Cut the cake into quarters. One quarter will be left over for you to do something else with. The remaining three quarters should be cut into ½-inch dice (they will be barely 1 inch deep). Return them to the freezer until you are ready for them. (If they are not very cold when they are folded into the cheesecake, they might crumble.)

CHEESECAKE

2 pounds cream cheese, at room temperature
1 teaspoon vanilla extract
Pinch of salt
1½ cups granulated sugar

4 eggs graded "large"
⅓ cup graham cracker crumbs (to be used after the cake is baked)

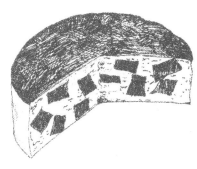

Adjust a rack one-third up from the bottom of the oven and preheat the oven to 350 degrees. Generously butter an 8 by 3-inch one-piece round cake pan (see page 241) up to and including the rim. The cake pan will be placed in a larger pan of water during baking—the larger pan should not be deeper than the cake pan; 1½ to 2 inches is deep enough. (I use a 13 by 9 by 2-inch pan.)

In the large bowl of an electric mixer beat the cheese until it is soft and smooth. Scrape the sides and the bottom of the bowl frequently with a rubber spatula during the mixing. Add the vanilla, salt, and sugar. Beat well until you are sure that it is thoroughly mixed, with no lumps of cheese remaining. Then, on moderately low speed, add the eggs one at a time, beating only until incorporated after each addition. (Do not beat any more than necessary after adding the eggs; this should not be an airy mixture.)

Remove the bowl from the mixer. Pour enough of the mixture into the prepared pan to make a layer about ½ inch thick.

Add the cold diced Brownies to the remaining batter. Very gently, fold together, being careful not to break up or crumble the Brownies, and turn into the pan. With the bottom of a spoon, smooth the top.

Place the cake pan in the larger pan and add hot water about 1½ inches deep to the larger pan.

Bake for 1½ hours. The top of the cake will rise about ¼ inch above the rim of the pan during baking, and it will become a lovely shade of brown. When the cake is done, remove the cake pan from the hot water and place it on a rack to cool. While cooling, the cake will sink back to its original level.

Let stand for 2 or 3 hours until the bottom of the pan is cool. (See Notes.)

Place a flat cake plate or lightweight board over the cake pan. Hold the plate or board and cake pan together and turn them over. (The cake will fall out of the pan. Do not leave the cake upside down any longer than necessary or the crust might stick.) Quickly remove the cake pan, sprinkle the graham cracker crumbs over the bottom of the cake, cover with a cake plate or a serving board (I use my second lightweight plastic board), and quickly turn the cake and the plate or board over again, leaving the cake right side up. Do this without pressing on the cake or you will squash it. (In order to avoid the tricky business of inverting the cake the second time, some people serve it upside down without the graham cracker crumbs.)

This cake may be served at room temperature or refrigerated. Frankly, it is more deliciously creamy/custardy at room temperature. But it is firmer and therefore slices a little better when cold. My choice now is room temperature (although either way—it's great).

NOTES: *1. For unmolding this cake, and other similar cheesecakes, I have the best results when I use two 8½-inch square lightweight clear plastic cutting boards (they have handles) that are available at most good hardware stores.*

2. Here's a trick to make the unmolding of this and Bull's Eye Cheesecake (see page 241) less precarious. After the cake has cooled, place it (still in the cake pan) in the refrigerator to become firm. Then, before you turn it out, dip it briefly in a large container of very hot water as though you were unmolding a gelatin dessert.

Blackberry with Scotch Cheesecake

This was created by a friend of mine, Marcia Hamann, who owns the Springhill Bakery in Portland, Oregon. It is a small bakery that supplies delicious desserts for some of the best restaurants in the Portland area. She says, "This is a Northwesterly cake with a shortbread crust; the cheese mixture is flavored with cinnamon, Drambuie, and blackberries, and it is topped with sour cream."

Blackberries grow in the Portland area but Marcia uses the frozen ones because "they hold their shape better and do not discolor the whole of the cake the way fresh berries do." Since fresh blackberries are available in Florida for about forty-five minutes every year, I am delighted (and

I am sure you will be) to use the frozen ones.

The blackberries that are embedded in the pale and creamy cheese mixture become an incredibly gorgeous shade of shocking pink. It slices like a dream; you will be thrilled to cut into it. And when you taste it you will probably just go limp as I did; the buttery and crunchy crust along with the smooth and mellow, sweet and tart cheesecake is pure cheesecake heaven.

You will need a springform pan 9 or 9½ inches in diameter, 2½ or 3 inches deep. (The completed cake is 2 inches high when it is made in a 9-inch pan.)

12 PORTIONS

CRUST

1 cup sifted all-purpose flour
¼ cup granulated sugar

4 ounces (1 stick) unsalted butter, cold and firm

Adjust a rack one-third up from the bottom of the oven and preheat the oven to 375 degrees.

Place the flour and sugar in a large bowl, or place them in the bowl of a food processor fitted with the metal chopping blade. Cut the butter into about ½-inch squares. Either cut the butter into the dry ingredients with a pastry blender until the mixture resembles coarse crumbs or add it to the processor bowl and process with quick on/off pulses for 15 seconds until the mixture resembles coarse crumbs. If you have used a processor, now transfer the mixture to a wide bowl.

Gently rub the crumb mixture between your hands to form smaller crumbs. It should become almost a powdery mixture that does not hold together.

Turn the mixture into an unbuttered 9- or 9½-inch springform pan and distribute it evenly over the bottom of the pan. Then press down on the mixture firmly with your fingers to make a compact crust on the bottom only.

To prevent butter in the crust from leaking out of the pan during baking, place the pan on a 12-inch square of aluminum foil and fold the foil firmly up around the sides of the pan.

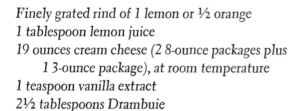

Bake for about 25 minutes until the edges of the crust begin to brown and it is sandy or golden in the center. (The crust will not darken any more even though it will bake more after the filling is added.) Don't worry if the crust puffs up a bit during baking; it will settle down again.

CHEESECAKE MIXTURE

This can be prepared while the crust is baking, or the baked crust can wait.

Finely grated rind of 1 lemon or ½ orange
1 tablespoon lemon juice
19 ounces cream cheese (2 8-ounce packages plus
   1 3-ounce package), at room temperature
1 teaspoon vanilla extract
2½ tablespoons Drambuie

½ teaspoon cinnamon
¾ cup granulated sugar
3 eggs graded "large"
8 ounces (2 cups) dry-packed frozen blackberries,
   not thawed

Place rind and juice in a small cup and let stand.

In the large bowl of an electric mixer beat the cheese until soft and smooth. Beat in the vanilla, Drambuie, cinnamon, and then the sugar. Add the eggs one at a time, beating until smooth after each addition. Remove from the mixture and stir in the rind and juice mixture. Set aside for a moment.

To butter the sides of the pan, melt a bit of butter and, with a pastry brush, brush it around the sides of the pan (which may be warm), carefully buttering all the way to, and touching, the crust.

Pour the cheese mixture over the crust. Now, carefully place the frozen blackberries one at a time evenly all over the cheese mixture with small spaces between them. Then, with your finger, press each berry down into the cheese; the berries should be just barely covered with the cheese mixture.

Bake at 375 degrees for 35 to 40 minutes until the sides are slightly risen and lightly browned, and the center—when pressed gently with a fingertip—feels as though it may be barely set (dry to the touch but soft inside).

The top of the cake might crack a bit; don't even look at it, it won't show.

Remove the cake from the oven and let stand for 20 minutes. Do not turn off the oven.

SOUR CREAM TOPPING

2 cups sour cream   1 teaspoon vanilla extract
1 tablespoon granulated sugar

In a bowl stir the sour cream with the sugar and vanilla. Pour over the cheesecake. With the bottom of a spoon spread and smooth the mixture.

Bake for 5 minutes. Remove from the oven. Remove the foil. Let stand until cool.

When the cake is thoroughly cool, cut around the sides gently with a small, sharp knife to release the cake. Remove the sides of the pan. Place the cake, still on the bottom of the pan, in the refrigerator for several hours or overnight.

The cake may be served from the bottom of the pan. It should be placed on a folded napkin (to prevent slipping) on a cake plate or serving board. But I remove it from the bottom of the pan; it is not difficult to do and I think it is nicer. Use a heavy chef's knife with a blade about 6 inches long, ease the blade gently and carefully under the crust at one spot, and then gently and carefully work the blade all around under the crust. (The crust will not be stuck to the pan; it will be crisp and it will separate from the pan quite easily.) Then, without removing the knife completely (hold the tip of it under the crust) ease a wide metal pancake turner under one half of the crust and then ease another wide metal pancake turner under the other half of the crust.

Holding one handle in each hand, raise the cake and transfer it to a flat plate or serving board.

Apple Cream Cheese Pie

Cheesecake is so popular in America that some people believe we should change "as American as apple pie" to "as American as cheesecake." How about a combination of the two?

This is a cream cheese pie in a graham cracker crust. But under the cheese is a surprise: a gen-

erous layer of apples, walnuts, raisins, ginger, cinnamon, brown sugar, and butter. The combination is delirious, delicious, delovely. The whole experience—that's American.

6 GENEROUS PORTIONS

1 9-inch baked graham cracker crust (see page 256)
2 large or 3 medium tart cooking apples
      (preferably Granny Smith)
1 tablespoon butter
3 tablespoons dark or light brown sugar,
      firmly packed
1 to 2 teaspoons lemon juice (depending on the
      tartness of the apples)

1 teaspoon cinnamon
¼ teaspoon nutmeg
¼ cup raisins
½ cup walnuts, broken into medium-size pieces
3 to 4 tablespoons candied or preserved ginger,
      cut into ¼-inch pieces

Prepare the baked graham cracker crust.

Peel, quarter, and core the apples. Cut them into about ¾-inch chunks.

Melt the butter in a large frying pan. Add the apples, sugar, and lemon juice. Stir to mix. Cover and let steam for a few minutes, stirring occasionally until the apples are barely tender. Then uncover and cook, stirring until the liquid is almost all evaporated. Stir in the cinnamon, nutmeg, raisins, walnuts, and the ginger, and continue to cook, stirring, for a few minutes until the liquid has evaporated and the apples are just tender. Set aside to cool.

Prepare the cheese mixture.

CHEESE MIXTURE

12 ounces cream cheese, preferably at room
      temperature
1 teaspoon vanilla extract
½ cup granulated sugar

⅓ cup whipping cream, sour cream, or Crème
      Fraîche (see page 361)
2 eggs graded "large"

Adjust a rack one-third up from the bottom of the oven and preheat the oven to 350 degrees.

In the small bowl of an electric mixer beat the cheese until it is soft and smooth. Beat in the vanilla and sugar until mixed, then beat in the cream and finally the eggs one at a time, scraping the bowl with a rubber spatula and beating until smooth. (Do not beat any more than necessary after adding the eggs; this should not become airy.)

Turn the apple mixture into the crust and smooth the top.

Pour the cheese mixture very slowly over the center of the apples. Do not add it quickly or all at once. Depending on the size of the apples and on the depth of the crust, you might or might not have room for all of the cheese mixture. Don't take a chance. If it looks as though the cheese mixture might run over the edge, do not use it all.

Bake for 25 minutes.

Cool to room temperature, and then refrigerate for several hours or overnight.

Blueberry Cream Cheese Pie

When blueberries are at the height of their season and you can find big beautiful ones, this is the dessert to make. It is scrumptious and easy, and it can be made hours or a day ahead, if you wish.

You must make the crust ahead of time. (If you have a graham cracker crust all baked and ready to go in your freezer, then making this pie is a snap.)

1 9-inch baked graham cracker crust (see page 256)
12 ounces cream cheese, preferably at
    room temperature
1 teaspoon vanilla extract

½ cup granulated sugar
⅓ cup whipping cream, sour cream, or Crème
    Fraîche (see page 361)
2 eggs graded "large"

Prepare the baked graham cracker crust.

Adjust a rack one-third up from the bottom of the oven and preheat the oven to 350 degrees.

In the small bowl of an electric mixer beat the cheese until it is soft and smooth. Add the vanilla and sugar and beat until mixed. Beat in the cream and then the eggs one at a time, scraping the bowl with a rubber spatula and beating until smooth. (Do not beat any more than necessary after adding the eggs; this should not become airy.)

Pour the filling into the crust and bake for 25 minutes.

Remove from the oven and let stand until cool. Refrigerate for about an hour, or overnight, if you wish.

TOPPING

3 cups fresh blueberries

About ½ cup red currant jelly

Wash the berries (see To Wash Blueberries, page 14) and drain to dry.

In a small, shallow pan, melt ½ cup of the jelly over moderate heat, stirring occasionally. Bring the jelly to a boil and simmer gently for a minute or two.

With a pastry brush, brush a thin layer of the jelly over the top of the pie (directly onto the cream cheese filling). Set the remaining jelly aside to cool a bit and thicken slightly.

When the jelly has just barely begun to thicken and the berries are thoroughly dry (and the cream cheese filling is cold), place the berries and the jelly in a bowl and very gently, with a rubber spatula, fold the berries and the jelly together until the berries are thoroughly coated.

Turn the mixture out over the top of the pie. With your fingers, carefully move the berries around as necessary so that they touch the crust on the sides and they cover the top nicely.

A bit of the jelly should run out between the berries to fill in the spaces between the berries and the rim. If it does not, melt a few more tablespoons of the jelly and, with a small spoon, gradually drizzle on a bit more jelly so there is just enough to cover the cheese where it shows next to the rim, but be careful not to use so much that it runs out over the crust.

Refrigerate for a few hours, or all day, or overnight.

Peach Cream Cheese Pie

Peaches and blueberries are in season at the same time. That poses a serious problem: which cheesecake to make? Should it be the preceding blueberry one, or this? They are equally fabulous. It probably depends on which fruit is nicer. But there is one other consideration. This peach recipe does not hold up overnight. However, you can have the crust all made and in the freezer, you can make the cream cheese filling the day before serving, and then finish the peach part just an hour or two before serving (it only takes a few minutes). For a party make both and let your guests have their choice.

6 GENEROUS PORTIONS

1 9-inch baked graham cracker crust (see page 256)
12 ounces cream cheese, preferably at
    room temperature
1 teaspoon vanilla extract

½ cup granulated sugar
⅓ cup whipping cream, sour cream, or Crème
    Fraîche (see page 361)
2 eggs graded "large"

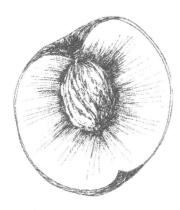

Prepare the baked graham cracker crust.

Adjust a rack one-third up from the bottom of the oven and preheat the oven to 350 degrees.

In the small bowl of an electric mixer beat the cheese until it is soft and smooth. Add the vanilla and sugar and beat until mixed. Beat in the cream and then the eggs one at a time, scraping the bowl with a rubber spatula and beating until smooth. (Do not beat any more than necessary after adding the eggs; this should not become airy.)

Pour the filling into the crust and bake for 25 minutes.

Remove from the oven and let stand until cool. Refrigerate for an hour, or overnight if you wish.

PEACH TOPPING

About 3 large, just-ripe fresh freestone peaches
About ½ cup apricot preserves

¼ teaspoon almond extract

Peel the peaches (see page 330) and place them in a bowl of acidulated water (water mixed with the juice of a lemon to keep the peaches from discoloring).

Place the preserves in a small, shallow pan over moderate heat. Stir occasionally until the preserves come to a boil, simmer for a minute or two, and then force the preserves through a strainer. Stir in the almond extract.

Brush a thin layer of the preserves over the top of the pie (directly onto the cream cheese filling).

Then drain the peaches on a large, heavy towel. Cut each peach in half, remove the pit, and then cut each half into about 6 lengthwise slices. Drain the slices briefly on the towel. Then arrange the slices so that they overlap slightly and make a nice, even ring at right angles to, and touching, the crust. Cut the remaining peaches into ⅓- to ½-inch chunks. Place the chunks in the middle of the pie.

With a pastry brush, gently and generously brush the remaining preserves all over the peaches and over any spaces between the peaches. If you do not have enough, melt and strain a bit more.

Refrigerate.

If the pie stands for more than an hour or two, the glaze will dry and the peaches will become dull. If this happens, just before serving, melt and strain still more preserves and brush over the peaches again.

Lemon Cream Cheese Pie

The smooth and creamy filling is a combination of cream cheese and cottage cheese or ricotta, which makes a slightly lighter mixture than many others. And the smooth and creamy topping is a mixture of half sour cream and half sweet cream.

A sensational dessert. It is easy and you will love it.

6 TO 8 PORTIONS

CRUMB CRUST

1¼ cups graham cracker crumbs
1 tablespoon granulated sugar
1 teaspoon cinnamon
½ teaspoon nutmeg

½ teaspoon ground ginger
Pinch of allspice
3 ounces (¾ stick) unsalted butter, melted

Combine the above ingredients. Use a 9-inch pie plate and follow the directions for Crumb Crusts (see page 25) to line the pan with foil, then with the crumb mixture, to bake, cool, freeze, and then to remove the foil. Set aside.

FILLING

Finely grated rind of 1 lemon
3 tablespoons lemon juice
¾ cup creamed cottage cheese or ricotta cheese
    (may be large or small curd, regular or low fat)

8 ounces cream cheese, at room temperature
¾ cup granulated sugar
½ teaspoon vanilla extract
2 eggs graded "large"

Adjust a rack to the middle of the oven and preheat the oven to 350 degrees.

Mix the rind and juice and set aside. In a processor fitted with the metal chopping blade, or in a few additions in a blender, process or blend the cottage cheese or ricotta cheese until it is as smooth as honey (it takes a full minute in a processor).

In the small bowl of an electric mixer beat the cream cheese until it is perfectly smooth. Add the smooth cottage cheese or ricotta cheese and beat to mix. Then add the sugar, vanilla, and the eggs one at a time, scraping the bowl with a rubber spatula and beating until smooth after each addition.

When the filling is perfectly smooth, remove the bowl from the mixer, stir in the lemon rind and juice, and pour into the prepared crust.

Bake for 30 minutes.

Remove from the oven and cool completely. Then prepare the topping.

TOPPING

1 cup whipping cream
1 cup sour cream
2 tablespoons granulated sugar

Optional: a few green pistachio nuts, chopped
(to sprinkle on top)

In a chilled bowl, with chilled beaters, whip the whipping cream until it holds a firm shape when the beaters are raised (but be careful not to overbeat).

In a bowl stir the sour cream until it is soft and smooth. Stir in the sugar. Then gently fold the sour cream and the whipped cream together.

Just pile the topping loosely on top of the pie, letting some of the filling show around the edges. Or, if you prefer, smooth it all over the filling.

Refrigerate for at least a few hours.

I like this plain, but I have sprinkled a few chopped green pistachio nuts (see Pistachio Nuts, page 7) right on the center before serving, and I liked that too.

Cottage Cheese and Jelly Tart

This is a shallow cheese tart with a thin layer of jelly under the cheese. Cottage cheese makes a lighter cake than cream cheese, but with the same slightly tart flavor. This recipe was originally made in Virginia hundreds of years ago; versions of it have been popular since then. Traditionally it is made in a pie plate, but since the filling is so shallow (¾ inch deep) I suggest a shallow tart or quiche pan instead of a pie plate. It is quite easy and makes a delicious dessert.

It is best to serve this tart the same day it is made. You will need a food processor (a great time-saver over the original procedure of forcing the cheese through a linen towel) and a loose-bottomed tart or quiche pan 10 inches across the top and a scant 1 inch deep, preferably made of black or blue-black metal instead of a shiny silver-colored metal—the dark color encourages the pastry to brown.

8 PORTIONS

Prepare Pie Pastry for a 10-inch crust (see page 21) and refrigerate it overnight, if possible, or for at least a few hours.

On a floured pastry cloth with a floured rolling pin roll out the dough until it is 13 to 13½ inches in diameter (keep the thickness as even as possible). Drape the pastry over a rolling pin and unroll it over the tart or quiche pan, centering it carefully. Ease the sides down into the pan; do not stretch the pastry. If the pastry is too narrow in spots and too wide in other spots, cut away the part that is too wide, wet the edges of the piece you have cut away with water, and place it where needed. Flour your fingertips and press the pieces together.

With scissors trim the edge, leaving a ½- to ¾-inch overhang. Fold the overhang over onto itself, folding in toward the center of the pan, to form a narrow hem at the top of the pastry, which should extend about ¼ inch above the sides of the pan.

If you have pastry pincers, use them to decorate the hem of the pastry; if not, use the dull edge of a knife and score little lines on an angle about ¼ inch apart around the hem. Then pierce the bottom at ½-inch intervals with a fork.

Place the pastry shell in the freezer for about 20 minutes (or for days or weeks, if you wish, in which case wrap it when it is firm).

To bake, adjust a rack one-third up from the bottom of the oven and preheat the oven to 450 degrees. Place a 12-inch square of foil shiny side down in the frozen pastry shell; press it into place (let the edges and corners stand up straight), and fill the foil at least ½ inch deep with dried peas or beans (which should be saved to be reused for the same purpose) or with aluminum pellets called pie weights.

Bake for 13 minutes. Then carefully remove the foil and beans or weights by lifting the four corners of the foil. (You may prepare the following cheese filling while the crust is baking, if you wish.)

Return the tart shell to the oven for only 2 or 3 minutes more until the bottom looks dry. Watch the pastry; if it starts to puff up, pierce it carefully with a cake tester.

You will need an egg white now (to keep the crust crisp). If you have prepared the cheese filling while the crust was baking, you will have 2 leftover egg whites.

Beat the white until it is just barely foamy and, with a pastry brush, brush the white over the bottom of the hot baked shell. The heat will set the white quickly. After a few moments brush on another layer of egg white. This time place the pastry shell in the oven for a moment or two to set the second layer of egg white. Remove the shell from the oven but do not turn the oven off.

If the filling is ready, it may be poured into the hot shell and baked immediately. If not, set the shell aside while you prepare the filling.

COTTAGE CHEESE FILLING

12 ounces large-curd cottage cheese (preferably regular or 4 percent butterfat)
⅛ teaspoon salt
½ cup granulated sugar
1 teaspoon vanilla extract
Finely grated rind of 1 large lemon
1 teaspoon lemon juice
2 eggs graded "large" or "extra-large" plus 2 additional egg yolks

1½ tablespoons unsalted butter, melted
½ cup sour cream
½ cup black raspberry jelly (or any other smooth jelly; currant is good too)
1 teaspoon cinnamon
1 teaspoon granulated sugar } mixed together

Place the cottage cheese in a food processor bowl fitted with the metal chopping blade and process for a full minute until the cheese is as smooth and as thick as sour cream. Stop the machine once or twice and scrape down the sides. Then stop the machine, remove the top, add the salt, the ½ cup sugar, the vanilla, lemon rind, lemon juice, eggs and egg yolks, melted butter, and sour cream. Process again briefly until everything is smoothly blended.

Stir the jelly in a bowl until it is soft and spread it over the bottom of the pastry.

Very slowly pour the filling into the prepared shell without disturbing the jelly any more than necessary. The filling will almost fill the shell to the top; it is all right—it will not run over (unless you have some low spots on the shell, in which case do not use all of the filling).

Sprinkle the cinnamon-sugar over the top through a fine strainer.

Bake at 450 degrees for 10 minutes; then reduce the temperature to 375 degrees and bake for 20 minutes longer (total baking time 30 minutes). During baking the filling will rise very high and it will form cracks, but it will all settle down to its original height when it cools.

Let cool. Refrigerate for at least a few hours, and serve cold.

When the tart is cold, remove the sides of the pan and with a wide metal spatula ease the tart onto a flat cake plate.

Serve this plain or with any fresh or stewed fruit. It is delicious with a Raspberry Pear (see page 331) or a Stewed Peach (page 330)—drained of its juice.

Brownies

When I was about 10 years old, I had a hugely successful Brownie business. My father saved his empty cigar boxes for me, I painted them inside and out, and made elaborate sealing wax designs on them. Then I baked the Brownies, wrapped them individually, and packed them in the boxes. All our relatives were my customers. I think I charged a dollar a box. Everything I took in was profit (I didn't have any expenses), so I made a lot of money.

Since I have grown up it has been a dream of mine to sell my Brownies in New York City on the corner of 57th Street and Fifth Avenue in front of Tiffany's, from a pushcart.

Within the last year or so I have heard from many people around the country who are going into the Brownie business. I wish them all great success, but I am sorry it is them and not me. I am jealous.

**DON'T LEAVE HOME
WITHOUT THEM**

To most people that means American Express; to me it means Brownies. When I was quite young I learned the best way to win friends and influence people. Dale Carnegie had his system; mine, in a word, is Brownies. A few Brownies in my pocket or pocketbook have charmed, bribed, influenced—worked magic.

I am telling you all this to explain why each of these Brownie recipes says "wrap individually." There is no way I could carry Brownies otherwise. They can be wrapped in foil or wax paper or gold leaf or gift wrapping paper or anything but plastic wrap (I don't use that only because it is infuriating and not fun), but the best wrapping is clear cellophane. It is not easy to find a place to buy it. See page 16 for a source for cellophane and directions for wrapping.

"Brownie" Schrumpf's Brownies

Brownies are totally American. I don't know of any other country where they are made. Their history and origin are unknown and only guessed at. One theory is that someone once forgot to use the leavening and the chocolate cake did not rise. There is a rumor that this historical event occurred in Bangor, Maine, in the early 1900s.

At the Maine Historical Society in Bangor, Mrs. "Brownie" Schrumpf, a local food authority and an octogenarian, remembers a cookbook published by the local YWCA in 1914. It had a recipe for Brownies. That might have been the first Brownie recipe in print.

Here is "Brownie" Schrumpf's recipe. The ingredients are the usual but the proportions are slightly different (less butter).

These are old-fashioned, traditionally huge, plain, down-home Brownies—crusty on top, moist and chewy inside, and delicious.

You will need a 13 by 9 by 2-inch pan.

16 MONSTER OR 32 NORMAL BROWNIES

4 ounces unsweetened chocolate
4 ounces (1 stick) unsalted butter
2 teaspoons vanilla extract
½ teaspoon salt
2 cups granulated sugar

4 eggs graded "large"
1 cup sifted all-purpose flour
8 ounces (generous 2 cups) walnuts, broken into
    large pieces

Adjust a rack one-third up from the bottom of the oven and preheat the oven to 350 degrees. Line a 13 by 9 by 2-inch pan as follows. Turn the pan over, center a 17- or 18-inch length of aluminum foil over the pan shiny side down, fold down the sides and the corners to shape the foil, then remove the foil and turn the pan over again. Place the foil in the pan and press it gently into place. To butter the foil place a piece of butter in the pan, heat it in the oven to melt, and brush it all over with a pastry brush or with crumpled wax paper. Set aside.

Place the chocolate in the top of a small double boiler over shallow hot water on moderate heat. Cover with a folded paper towel (to absorb steam) and the pot cover. Let cook until almost completely melted, then remove the cover and stir with a rubber spatula until smooth. Remove the top of the double boiler and set aside.

In the large bowl of an electric mixer beat the butter until it is soft. Add the vanilla, salt, and sugar and beat well. Then add the eggs one at a time, scraping the bowl with a rubber spatula and beating until incorporated after each addition. Add the melted chocolate (it can be warm or cool) and beat until incorporated. On low speed add the flour and beat only until smooth. Remove the bowl from the mixer and stir in the nuts.

Turn into the prepared pan and smooth the top.

Bake for 30 to 33 minutes until a toothpick inserted gently in the middle comes out almost but not completely clean; there should be a few specks of moist Brownie clinging to the toothpick. Do not overbake.

Cool to room temperature in the pan. Then cover with a cookie sheet, turn the pan and cookie sheet over, remove the pan, peel off the foil, cover with a clean piece of foil and then with another cookie sheet, and turn over again, leaving the cake right side up.

It is best to chill the cake before cutting it (however, I think that is not what they did in Bangor in 1914). Place it in the freezer for about an hour or in the refrigerator for a bit longer. Then, with a long, thin, sharp knife, cut into 16 huge or 32 regular Brownies.

Barron's Brownies

September 4, 1982, was the big day. It was the party of all time. Craig Claiborne gave the party at his home in East Hampton on Long Island. It was a triple celebration: publication of A Feast Made for Laughter, *Craig's autobiography, his birthday, and twenty-five years as food editor of* The New York Times. *It was referred to as an international covered-dish party, with chefs from around the world bringing food or preparing it in Craig's sumptuous kitchen. There were about sixty chefs and about four hundred celebrity guests.*

My husband and I drove up from Florida with a carful of desserts; among them were 350 Brownies. The Brownies were a new recipe that I had made up in honor of the occasion. They had more chocolate and less flour than any others I had made and were therefore more chocolaty and more moist.

The occasion was covered by all the news services and publications, including Barron's, *the prestigious financial newspaper.*

A few days after the party, I received a phone

call from Barron's, saying that they would like to print the recipe for the Brownies. It would be the first time they had ever printed a recipe, and they would like to call it Barron's Brownies.

When it appeared (September 27, 1982) it was as part of a large story on gourmet foods. They asked Craig, "WHAT'S GOURMET?" He answered, "It's any food that is cooked conscientiously, with intelligence, with great care, with enthusiasm. If it's done with your heart and soul, it's bound to be gourmet."

Barron's then printed this recipe as a working model of "gourmet."

Incidentally, it was the greatest party ever!

16 BROWNIES

2 ounces unsweetened chocolate
4 ounces semisweet chocolate (see Note)
4 ounces (1 stick) unsalted butter
¼ teaspoon salt
½ teaspoon vanilla extract

1 cup granulated sugar
2 eggs graded "large"
¼ cup sifted all-purpose flour
4 ounces (generous 1 cup) walnut halves or large pieces

Adjust a rack one-third up from the bottom of the oven and preheat the oven to 325 degrees. Prepare an 8-inch square cake pan as follows. Turn the pan over, center a 12-inch square of foil shiny side down over the pan, fold down the sides and corners to shape the foil, then remove the foil and turn the pan over again. Place the foil in the pan and press it gently into place. To butter the foil, spread it all over using a brush or crumpled wax paper with melted butter (additional to that called for), and set aside.

Place both of the chocolates and the butter in a 2½- to 3-quart heavy saucepan over moderately low heat. Stir occasionally until melted, whisk if necessary until smooth. Remove from the heat, stir in the salt, vanilla, sugar, and then the eggs one at a time, stirring after each addition until incorporated. Add the flour and stir briskly for about a minute until the mixture is smooth and shiny and comes away from the sides of the pan. Then stir in the nuts.

Turn the mixture into the pan and smooth the top.

Bake for 40 minutes or until a toothpick inserted gently into the middle comes out clean and dry.

Remove from the oven. Cool completely in the pan. Then place the pan in the freezer for about an hour until the cake is firm.

Cover with a cutting board or a cookie sheet and turn the pan and the board or sheet over. Remove the pan. Slowly and carefully peel off the foil. Then turn the firm cake over again.

Mark the Brownies with a ruler and toothpicks (marking the cake into quarters is enough—you can cut the rest freehand). Use a long, thin, sharp knife or a long, finely serrated knife. Cut the cake into quarters and then cut each quarter into 4 Brownies.

Wrap individually, if you wish.

If these are served cold (refrigerated) they have a chocolate caramel candy quality.

NOTE: When I made these for the party I used Maillard's Eagle Sweet chocolate for the semisweet chocolate.

Chocolate Cheesecake Brownies

This is a dense, dark, chewy Brownie with pecans and coconut topped with a dense, dark, creamy chocolate cheesecake—all baked together.

I made these for the state dinner at the 1983 World Economic Summit Meeting in Williamsburg. The heads of state and other guests sent back to the kitchen for seconds.

16 SQUARES OR 32 BARS OR TRIANGLES

BROWNIE LAYER

2 ounces unsweetened chocolate
4 ounces (1 stick) unsalted butter
Pinch of salt
1 cup granulated sugar
½ teaspoon vanilla extract

2 eggs graded "large"
⅓ cup unsifted all-purpose flour
4 ounces (generous 1 cup) pecan halves, toasted
    (see To Toast Pecans, page 7)
2 ounces (½ cup) shredded coconut, firmly packed

Adjust a rack one-third up from the bottom of the oven and preheat the oven to 350 degrees. Prepare a 9 by 9 by 1¾-inch square cake pan as follows. Turn the pan over, center a 12-inch square of aluminum foil shiny side down over the pan, fold down the sides and corners of the foil, then remove the foil and turn the pan over again. Place the shaped foil in the pan and press it gently into place. To butter the foil, place a piece of butter (additional to that called for) in the pan, heat it in the oven to melt, and then brush it all over with a pastry brush or with a piece of crumpled wax paper. Set aside.

Place the chocolate and butter in a 2- to 3-quart heavy saucepan over low heat and stir occasionally until melted. Stir in the salt, sugar, and vanilla. Remove the pan from the heat and stir in the eggs one at a time. Add the flour and stir well to mix. Stir in the pecans and coconut.

Turn into the prepared pan and smooth the top. Set aside.

CHOCOLATE CHEESE CAKE LAYER

8 ounces cream cheese, at room temperature
½ cup granulated sugar
3 tablespoons unsweetened cocoa powder
    (preferably Dutch-process)
½ teaspoon vanilla extract
Optional: a few drops almond extract

2 eggs graded "large"
1 tablespoon flour
Cocoa powder, either sweetened or
    unsweetened (to be used after the cake
    is baked)

In the small bowl of an electric mixer beat the cheese until it is soft and smooth. Add the remaining ingredients one at a time, beating until incorporated after each addition.

Pour the mixture over the top of the Brownie layer and smooth the top.

Bake for about 40 minutes until a toothpick inserted gently in the middle comes out clean.

Cool until tepid.

Sprinkle the top with cocoa through a strainer. Cover with a piece of wax paper and a cookie sheet. Turn the pan and cookie sheet over, remove the pan, peel off the foil, cover with a cutting board or another cookie sheet, and then turn over again, leaving the cake right side up. Then chill in the freezer or refrigerator until firm.

Cut into 16 large squares or 32 bars or triangles, wiping the blade with a damp cloth as necessary between cuts.

These may be wrapped individually, if you wish. But if you do so, strain additional cocoa over the tops before wrapping to prevent sticking.

Store these in the refrigerator. Serve them chilled or at room temperature.

Cristina's Brownies

An executive at the Hershey company told me that the taste and flavor of a chocolate candy bar seem to change depending on its thickness or thinness. (He said that the Hershey Golden Almond Bar is the same chocolate as that used in the regular Hershey bar; it only tastes different because it is thicker.) Could be. And the same could be true of Brownies. These are almost 1¾ inches thick (3 ounces each), which is extra thick indeed, and they are extra good; extra large, extra dark/ dense/chewy chocolate, with extra nuts.

The recipe (made with cocoa instead of the usual chocolate) is from Cristina Giovanoli of Queens Village in New York. Cristina is a student at The Culinary Institute of America, and a weekend pastry chef and dessert maker at a local Italian restaurant. Squisito; molte grazie, Cristina.

24 EXTRA-LARGE BROWNIES; 4½ POUNDS

1 pound (4½ cups) walnut halves or large pieces
1¼ cups unsifted unsweetened cocoa powder (see Notes)
1¼ cups unsifted all-purpose flour
½ teaspoon salt

12 ounces (3 sticks) unsalted butter
3 cups granulated sugar
7 eggs graded "large"
2 teaspoons vanilla extract

Adjust a rack one-third up from the bottom of the oven and preheat the oven to 350 degrees. Line a 13 by 9 by 2-inch pan as follows: Turn the pan upside down, center an 18-inch length of aluminum foil shiny side down over the pan, press down the sides and corners of the foil to shape it to the pan, remove the foil, turn the pan right side up, place the shaped foil in the pan and gently press it into place (it might be easiest to press against the foil with a potholder or folded towel). To butter the foil, place a piece of butter in the pan and place the pan in the oven only until the butter is melted. Then, with crumpled wax paper, spread the butter all over the foil, and set the pan aside.

Look over the nuts carefully; walnuts frequently include a piece of shell. Set the nuts aside.

Sift together into the large bowl of an electric mixer the cocoa, flour, and salt, and set aside.

In a 3-quart heavy saucepan over low heat melt the butter. Remove the pan from the heat and with a heavy wooden spatula stir in the sugar, then the eggs two or three at a time, and then the vanilla. Add the butter mixture to the sifted dry ingredients, pouring it in all at once. Beat on low speed, scraping the bowl as necessary with a rubber spatula, until the ingredients are completely mixed. Remove the bowl from the mixer and stir in the nuts.

Turn the mixture into the prepared pan and bake for 50 to 60 minutes until a toothpick gently inserted in the middle comes out not quite clean. Actually, these are best if a bit of chocolate is clinging to the toothpick. Do not overbake.

Cool in the pan at room temperature. When the bottom of the pan is just tepid (not completely cool), cover the pan with a length of wax paper and then with a flat cookie sheet or a board. Turn the pan and the sheet or board over, then remove the pan and slowly peel off the foil.

Leave the cake upside down and transfer to the refrigerator overnight or to the freezer for a few hours.

Cover the chilled cake with a cookie sheet or a board and turn it over again, leaving the cake right side up now. Remove the sheet or board and wax paper from the top of the cake.

Use a ruler and toothpicks to mark the cake into quarters, and with a long, strong, sharp knife or a long and finely serrated knife cut the cake into quarters (cutting once in one direction and then once in the opposite direction). Next, cut each quarter in half, cutting from one long side to the opposite long side, making 8 pieces. (If the cake is not cold enough to be cut perfectly, please stop cutting, chill the cake longer, and then continue to cut.) Finally, cut each piece into 3 bars.

Wrap the Brownies individually in clear cellophane (preferably) or wax paper or aluminum foil, or package them in an airtight box. Or do as Cristina does and place them in Ziploc bags.

NOTES: 1. *Cristina uses Hershey's cocoa; I use any Dutch-process cocoa— usually Droste, or Guittard from Williams-Sonoma, P.O. Box 7456, San Francisco, California 94120–7456.*

2. I served these recently at a tea party. They had been frozen; I let them thaw about 10 minutes, then cut each one the long way into 2 thin bars, and served them very cold—almost frozen. They helped to make it a wonderful party. Incidentally, do you know about Hédiard's fabulous French food store? They make my favorite tea; it is called Four-Red-Fruit Tea (a combination of black tea with raspberries, cherries, straw-berries, and red currants). It has a wonderful flavor and a fantastic perfume —the whole room will smell like fresh raspberries. You can buy it at many good specialty food stores.

"Rich and Beautiful" Brownies

Extremely dark, extravagant, sumptuous. You will make a classic Brownie mixture and spread it in a 13 by 9-inch pan to make a thin layer. Then you will make a chocolate, cream, and egg yolk mix-ture similar to a rich custard or a pot de crème and pour it over the Brownie layer. When it is baked it will only barely show that there are two layers, although the top will remain softer and rather like some magical fudgy icing. But these are still Brownies and can be served as finger food, or they can be served on a plate with ice cream and chocolate sauce.

This is all mixed in a saucepan.

BOTTOM LAYER

2½ ounces unsweetened chocolate
4 ounces (1 stick) unsalted butter
Pinch of salt
1 teaspoon powdered or granular instant coffee
½ teaspoon vanilla extract

1 cup granulated sugar
2 eggs graded "large"
½ cup unsifted all-purpose flour
6 ounces (1½ cups) walnuts, broken into
    medium-size pieces

Adjust a rack one-third up from the bottom of the oven and preheat the oven to 350 degrees. Line a 13 by 9 by 2-inch pan as follows. Turn the pan over, cover it with a 17-inch length of aluminum foil shiny side down, fold down the sides and corners of the foil, remove the foil, turn the pan over again, place the foil in the pan, and press it gently into place all over. Place a piece of butter (additional to that called for) in the pan, place the pan in the oven to melt the butter, spread the butter all over with a pastry brush or a piece of crumpled wax paper, and set the pan aside.

Place the chocolate and butter in a 2- to 3-quart heavy saucepan over low heat and stir occasionally until melted. Stir in the salt and coffee. Remove from the heat. Stir in the vanilla and sugar, and then the eggs one at a time. Add the flour, stir until smooth, and then stir in the nuts.

Turn the mixture into the prepared pan and spread it smooth.

(The bottom layer can wait in the pan while you make the top layer, or you can start the top layer in another 2- to 3-quart heavy saucepan while you are making the bottom layer.)

TOP LAYER

4 ounces (1 stick) unsalted butter
8 ounces semisweet chocolate (I use Maillard's
    Eagle Sweet for this)
2 tablespoons granulated sugar
½ cup whipping cream

Pinch of salt
1 teaspoon powdered or granular instant coffee
1 teaspoon vanilla extract
1 egg graded "large" plus 4 additional egg yolks

Place the butter and chocolate in a 2- to 3-quart heavy saucepan over low heat and stir occasionally until melted. Add the sugar, cream, salt, coffee, and vanilla and stir to mix. Remove the pan from the heat and gradually, one at a time, whisk in the egg and the yolks. Stir or whisk briskly until as smooth as honey.

Pour this mixture over the bottom layer and smooth the top.

Bake for 28 to 30 minutes until a toothpick inserted in the middle comes out clean.

Cool in the pan. Then chill in the freezer or refrigerator for an hour or more.

Cover the cake pan with a cookie sheet. Turn the pan and the sheet over, remove the pan, peel off the foil, cover with another cookie sheet, and turn over again, leaving the cake right side up.

This cuts best when it is thoroughly chilled. Cut into 32 Brownies or 64 bite-size, candylike petits fours.

Wrap individually, if you wish. Serve these at room temperature, cold, or very cold (almost frozen).

Hershey's Brownies

In February 1983, at the Hershey company's First Great Chocolate Festival at Hershey, Pennsylvania, everything was chocolate: soup, cereal, salad dressing, cocktail dip, cheese spread, poached fish, either the hot dogs or the mustard (by then I couldn't tell them apart), et cetera. And that is aside from all the usual. A lady visitor there begged me to taste a certain Brownie they served, adding that if I knew how to make them

she would give anything for the recipe.

It is a delicious, moist Brownie with a great icing. I got the recipe from the pastry chef at the Hershey Hotel, but by then the lady was gone.

The Brownies are made with cocoa, and the candylike icing has unsweetened chocolate, semisweet chocolate, and milk chocolate.

16 BROWNIES

½ cup unsifted all-purpose flour
⅓ cup unsweetened cocoa powder (preferably Dutch-process)
¼ teaspoon double-acting baking powder
¼ teaspoon salt
4 ounces (1 stick) unsalted butter

1 cup granulated sugar
1 teaspoon vanilla extract
2 eggs graded "large"
4 ounces (generous 1 cup) walnuts, broken into large pieces

Adjust a rack to the middle of the oven and preheat the oven to 350 degrees. Line a 9-inch square cake pan as follows. Turn the pan over, center a 12-inch square of foil over the pan shiny side down, fold down the sides and corners to shape the foil, remove the foil, turn the pan over again, and place the shaped foil gently in the pan, pressing it smooth against the bottom and sides. To butter the foil place a piece of butter (additional to that called for) in the pan and place the pan in the oven to melt the butter. With a pastry brush or with crumpled wax paper spread the butter all over the foil and set the pan aside.

Sift together the flour, cocoa, baking powder, and salt and set aside.

Melt the butter in a 10- to 12-cup heavy saucepan over moderate heat. Remove from the heat, stir in the sugar and vanilla, and then the eggs one at a time. Now stir in the sifted dry ingredients and then the nuts.

Spread smoothly in the prepared pan. Bake for 20 to 25 minutes until a toothpick inserted in the middle just barely comes out clean.

Cool in the pan for about 15 minutes. Then cover with a rack and turn the pan and the rack over. Remove the pan and the foil lining. Cover with a cookie sheet or a cutting board or anything flat and turn over again, leaving the cake right side up.

Let stand until cool.

2 ounces (½ stick) unsalted butter

1 ounce unsweetened chocolate

3 ounces semisweet chocolate

4½ ounces milk chocolate

½ teaspoon vanilla extract

In a medium or small heavy saucepan over low heat melt the butter, unsweetened chocolate, and semisweet chocolate, stirring frequently.

Break up the milk chocolate and when the other chocolates are melted add the milk chocolate, remove from the heat, and stir until the milk chocolate is melted. Stir in the vanilla.

Transfer to the small bowl of an electric mixer and beat at moderate or high speed for about a minute until very smooth. (Beating now not only smooths the mixture but keeps the icing from becoming streaked or discolored after standing.)

Pour the icing (which can be warm or cool) over the cake. With a long, narrow metal spatula spread it to cover the top. Let stand until set enough to cut.

Cut into 16 squares.

Raspberry Brownies

This is one of the best Brownies ever. It is Katharine Hepburn's marvelous recipe (it has less flour than most and the Brownies are therefore more moist) to which I have added a thin layer of raspberry preserves in the middle before baking. If they gave Oscars for Brownies, this would win.

A few years ago someone complimented Katharine Hepburn about her figure and asked how she managed to maintain it all her life. She answered, "You see before you the results of a lifetime of eating chocolate." We should all be so lucky.

These are easy but they do take longer to make than the usual because of the procedure used to layer the preserves; half of the Brownie mixture is spread in the pan, then it is frozen (that takes time), then the preserves are spread over the firm frozen layer, and then the remaining Brownie mixture is poured over the preserves. And before baking the pan must stand at room temperature for half an hour or more for the frozen layer to thaw.

16 OR MORE BROWNIES

2 ounces unsweetened chocolate

4 ounces (1 stick) unsalted butter

¼ teaspoon salt

½ teaspoon vanilla extract

1 cup granulated sugar

2 eggs graded "large"

¼ cup unsifted all-purpose flour

4 ounces (generous 1 cup) walnuts, broken into
    medium-size pieces

⅓ cup seedless red raspberry preserves

(Do not preheat the oven now.) Prepare an 8 by 8 by 2-inch square cake pan as follows. Turn the pan over, center a 12-inch square of aluminum foil over the pan, fold down the sides and corners to shape the foil, then remove it, turn the pan over again, place the foil in the pan, and press it gently into place. Brush the foil all over with melted butter (additional to that called for) or spread the butter with crumpled wax paper, and set the pan aside.

Place the chocolate and butter in a large, heavy saucepan over low heat. Stir frequently until melted. Remove the pan from the heat, stir in the salt, vanilla, sugar, and then the eggs one at a time, stirring until incorporated after each addition. Add the flour and stir briskly with a rubber or wooden spatula until smooth. Then stir in the nuts.

You will have about 2½ cups of batter. Pour half of it (about 1¼ cups) into the prepared pan. Tilt the pan to level the mixture or spread it with the bottom of a spoon.

Place the pan in the freezer for about 30 minutes or longer until the mixture is just firm enough for you to spread a thin layer of preserves on top.

Spread the preserves all over the top; it will be a very thin layer— barely enough to cover the Brownie mixture.

Now, pour or spoon small amounts at a time of the remaining Brownie mixture over the preserves, and smooth with the back of a spoon.

Let stand at room temperature for at least 30 minutes (or longer) until the frozen layer has thawed.

Meanwhile, adjust a rack one-third up from the bottom of the oven and preheat the oven to 325 degrees.

Bake for 40 minutes until a toothpick inserted gently in the middle comes out barely clean.

Let stand in the pan until the cake reaches room temperature. Then place the pan in the freezer until the cake is firm. Cover with a small cutting board or a cookie sheet, turn the pan and board or sheet over, remove the pan, peel off the foil, and with your hands turn the cake right side up.

With a long, thin, sharp knife cut the Brownies into 16 squares or 32 small finger-shaped pieces.

Wrap these individually, if you wish. Serve at room temperature, cold, or very cold (almost frozen).

VARIATION: *Peanut Butter and Jelly Brownies. Any experienced Brownie baker will immediately see that the recipe for Raspberry Brownies opens up a whole new world of Brownies: cherry preserves, ginger marmalade, apricot preserves, et cetera. I have tried many. Here's a word of caution. Keep the new ingredients to a small amount; if you overdo it, it will not be a Brownie any more.*

This is one of the best variations I have made: chewy, gooey, yummy— I love them frozen. Follow the preceding recipe but in place of the raspberry preserves use ¼ cup of smooth peanut butter mixed with 2 tablespoons of grape jelly. (Mix the peanut butter and jelly in a small bowl with a rubber spatula.)

If you use plain peanut butter without the jelly it will taste wonderful, but the top and bottom of the Brownies will come apart when they are handled.

Brownies with Milk Chocolate Icing

Recipes similar to this have been winning blue ribbons at county fairs all across the country. As soon as the Brownie part is baked it is covered with bars of milk chocolate and put back in the oven for 30 seconds (that's all it takes to soften *the chocolate), then the chocolate is spread and covered with chopped walnuts. Fun to make and no one will believe how easy. These are very much like candy.*

16 BROWNIES

1 ounce unsweetened chocolate
4 ounces (1 stick) unsalted butter
1 teaspoon vanilla extract
1 cup granulated sugar
2 eggs graded "large"

3 tablespoons unsweetened cocoa powder
    (preferably Dutch-process)
½ cup sifted all-purpose flour
2 ounces (generous ½ cup) walnuts, broken into
    medium-size pieces

Adjust a rack one-third up from the bottom of the oven and preheat the oven to 325 degrees. Prepare an 8 by 8 by 2-inch square cake pan as follows. Turn the pan over, center a 12-inch piece of aluminum foil shiny side down over the pan, fold down the sides and corners of the foil to shape it, remove the foil, turn the pan over again, place the foil in the pan, and smooth it carefully into place. To butter the foil place a piece of butter (additional to that called for) in the pan and put the pan in the oven to melt the butter, then spread with a pastry brush or with crumpled wax paper. Set the pan aside.

Place the chocolate in the top of a small double boiler over warm water on moderate heat and stir occasionally until melted. Remove the top of the double boiler and set aside.

In the large bowl of an electric mixer beat the butter until it is soft. Add the vanilla and sugar and beat to mix. Beat in the eggs one at a time, and then beat in the cocoa powder and the melted chocolate (which may be warm or cool). On low speed add the sifted flour and beat only until incorporated. Remove the bowl from the mixer and stir in the walnuts.

Turn the mixture into the prepared pan and smooth the top. Bake for about 35 minutes until a toothpick inserted into the middle comes out clean and dry.

TOPPING

4 to 5 1.45-ounce bars of milk chocolate
    (I use Hershey's; use any kind but they must
    be thin)

2 ounces (generous ½ cup) walnuts, chopped into
    fine pieces

While the cake is baking, prepare the milk chocolate. Simply lay out as much as you will need to cover an 8-inch square.

As soon as the cake tests done, place the chocolate bars on the cake to cover the top completely and put the pan back in the oven for 30 seconds (no more) and then with the bottom of a spoon spread the chocolate, which will be soft, then quickly, before it starts to set, sprinkle the chopped nuts all over the top. With a wide spatula or the bottom of a large spoon, press down on the nuts to embed them in the chocolate.

Let stand until cool and then place the pan in the freezer for about

30 minutes (or the refrigerator for a bit longer) until cold and firm. Then cover the pan with a piece of foil, fold down the sides and corners (to prevent any loose nuts from flying around), cover the foil with a small cutting board and turn the pan and the board over, remove the pan, peel off the foil, turn the cake over again, and remove the remaining foil.

Now, about cutting this into squares. If the cake is cold and firm it will cut beautifully, but at the same time, when it is cold and firm the icing will crack when you cut it. Here's how to solve the problem: use a serrated knife to cut through the milk chocolate and then use a plain knife to cut through the cake. Or cut through the whole thing with a serrated knife. Whichever works best.

These may be wrapped individually, if you wish.

It is best to bring these to room temperature before serving.

Caramel Fudge Pecan Brownies

This is a "cotton country" Brownie from Alabama, where one family that grows pecans has been making it as far back as they can remember. These are thick (1¼ inches thick), moist, chewy, *like caramel candy and like chocolate fudge, sweet, very dark—delicious Southern hospitality.*

24 HUGE OR 48 MODERATE BROWNIES

2 cups sifted all-purpose flour
¼ teaspoon salt
½ teaspoon double-acting baking powder
8 ounces (2 sticks) unsalted butter
4 ounces unsweetened chocolate
1 ounce semisweet chocolate

½ cup granulated sugar
1 1-pound box dark brown sugar
4 eggs graded "large" or "extra-large"
2 teaspoons vanilla extract
8 ounces (2¼ cups) pecan halves, toasted (see
    To Toast Pecans, page 7)

Adjust a rack one-third up from the bottom of the oven and preheat the oven to 350 degrees. Line a 13 by 9 by 2-inch pan as follows. Turn the pan over, cover it with a piece of aluminum foil long enough to cover the bottom and sides and to extend above the sides about ½ inch, placing the foil shiny side down. Fold down the sides and corners of the foil to shape it. Remove the foil and turn the pan over again. Put the shaped foil in the pan and press it gently into place (pressing with a potholder or a folded towel does a nice neat job). Place a piece of butter (additional to that called for) in the pan, place the pan in the oven to melt the butter, then spread the butter all over the foil with a pastry brush or a piece of crumpled wax paper. Set the pan aside.

Sift together the flour, salt, and baking powder and set aside.

Place the butter and both of the chocolates in a heavy saucepan that has at least a 10-cup capacity and place it, uncovered, over low heat. Stir occasionally with a long wooden spatula until melted. Remove from the heat.

Stir in both of the sugars. Add the eggs one at a time, stirring until incorporated after each addition.

Stir in the vanilla and then the sifted dry ingredients, stirring only until incorporated. Mix in the pecans.

Turn the mixture into the prepared pan and smooth the top.

Bake for 40 to 45 minutes until a toothpick inserted gently all the way to the bottom in the middle comes out just barely clean and dry.

Let stand in the pan (on a rack or not) until cool.

Then place the pan in the freezer for about an hour, or a bit longer in the refrigerator, until the cake is rather firm.

Cover with a cutting board or a cookie sheet and turn the pan and the board or sheet over. Remove the pan and peel off the foil. Carefully turn the cake right side up.

Using a ruler and toothpicks as a guide, cut the cake into quarters. (If the edges of the cake are a bit too dark, and if you would like to cut them away, it is easiest to cut one quarter of the cake at a time. Turn the quarter upside down and use a long, finely serrated knife to trim the edges.)

Place each quarter right side up and use a smooth-bladed knife to cut each piece into 6 or 12 Brownies.

Wrap individually, if you wish.

Lattice-Topped Brownies

Incredible—artistic—creative—gorgeous. These are very fancy; they are not quick and easy. First there is a buttery cookie dough similar to a shortbread; half of it is layered in the pan and baked. The baked layer is then brushed with melted chocolate, which is covered with a moist and fudgelike Brownie mixture, and that is topped with a lattice design of strips of the cookie dough. When it is *baked the lattice will become a beautiful amber color and will sink slightly into the Brownie part, which will be dark and shiny and will show through the openings in the lattice.*

They're Brownies all right, but at their dressed-up and fanciest best.

16 TO 32 BROWNIES

COOKIE DOUGH

1½ cups plus 2 tablespoons sifted all-purpose
    flour
⅔ cup granulated sugar

5 ounces (1¼ sticks) unsalted butter
1 egg yolk

Adjust two racks in the oven; one should be one-third up from the bottom and the other should be at the highest position in the oven. Preheat the oven to 400 degrees. Prepare an 8-inch square cake pan as follows. Turn the pan over, center a 12-inch square of foil shiny side down over the pan, fold down the sides and corners of the foil to shape it, remove the foil, turn the pan over again, place the foil in the pan, and smooth it gently into place. To butter the foil, place a piece of butter (additional to that called for) in the pan and place it in the oven to melt. Then brush it all over with a pastry brush or with crumpled wax paper. Set aside.

The cookie dough can be mixed in a processor or a mixer. If using a processor, place 1½ cups of the flour (reserve the remaining 2 tablespoons of flour) and the sugar in the processor bowl fitted with the metal chopping blade. Cut the butter into ½-inch slices and add it to the bowl. Process until the mixture holds together. If using a mixer, beat the butter until it is soft, beat in the sugar and then 1½ cups of the flour, and beat until the mixture holds together.

Whichever way you have mixed the ingredients, now place the dough on a large work surface, knead it slightly to be sure it is smooth, form it into a ball, and cut it in half. One piece will be the bottom crust; set it aside. Place the other piece, which will be the top lattice strips, either in the bowl of the processor or in the mixer bowl. Add the egg and the remaining 2 tablespoons of flour and process or mix until smooth. Set aside.

Form the bottom crust into a square, place it between two sheets of wax paper, and with a rolling pin roll over the paper until the dough is a square shape that will just fit into the bottom of the lined pan. If the shape is not perfect, cut away excess dough and place it where you need it to make a perfect square that just fits. Trim the sides. Slide a flat-sided cookie sheet under the rolled-out dough and both pieces of wax paper and place it in the freezer until it is firm, then remove the top piece of paper. Turn the firm square of dough over into the pan and remove the remaining piece of wax paper.

Bake on the lower rack for 13 minutes until lightly browned on the edges and barely sandy colored in the middle. Remove from the oven and set aside.

Reduce the oven temperature to 350 degrees.

Form the remaining cookie dough into a square, place it between two pieces of wax paper, and with a rolling pin roll over the top paper to form the dough into a square that is the same size as the inside measurement of the top of the pan. Again, cut away excess dough and place it where you need it. Trim the edges neatly. (Leftover dough makes delicious cookies.) Slide a flat-sided cookie sheet under the bottom piece of wax paper and transfer the dough—and the papers—to the freezer.

BROWNIE LAYER

3 ounces semisweet or bittersweet chocolate (Tobler Tradition or Lindt Excellence or Tobler or Lindt Extra-Bittersweet or any other that you like)
4 ounces (1 stick) unsalted butter
2 ounces unsweetened chocolate
2 teaspoons powdered (not granular) instant coffee or espresso

¼ teaspoon salt
½ teaspoon vanilla extract
1 cup granulated sugar
2 eggs graded "large"
⅓ cup sifted all-purpose flour
4 ounces (generous 1 cup) walnuts, cut into small pieces (about the size of dried split peas)

Break up or chop coarse the semisweet or bittersweet chocolate, place it in the top of a small double boiler over hot water on low heat. Stir occasionally until melted. Pour the melted chocolate over the baked bottom layer (which may still be slightly warm) and spread with a rubber spatula or with the bottom of a spoon up to ¼ inch from the edges. Place this in the freezer or in the refrigerator just until the chocolate is set and then let stand at room temperature.

Meanwhile, make the Brownie layer. Place the butter and the unsweetened chocolate in a 2- to 3-quart heavy saucepan over low heat. Stir occasionally until melted. Remove from the heat. Stir in the powdered instant coffee, salt, vanilla, and sugar. Then stir in the eggs one at a time, and then the flour. When the mixture is smooth, stir in the nuts, and set aside to cool to room temperature.

Meanwhile, remove the firm layer of dough from the freezer. Remove the top piece of wax paper. With a ruler and the tip of a small, sharp knife mark the dough into ½-inch widths. Then, using the ruler as a guide, cut the dough into strips ½ inch wide.

Pour the cooled Brownie mixture over the layer of melted chocolate.

Then place half of the strips of dough in one direction, leaving about ½ inch of space between each 2 strips, and place the other half of the strips at right angles to the first strips. (The strips should be just the right length to fit into the pan perfectly.)

Bake on the high rack at 350 degrees for 35 to 40 minutes until the lattice strips are pale golden and the Brownie mixture just tests done (test by inserting a toothpick into the middle of the cake, but not all the way to the bottom because the chocolate that was spread on the bottom layer will be soft and will stick to the toothpick; the toothpick should come out barely dry).

If the lattice is colored before the cake tests done, transfer the pan to the lower oven rack to finish baking.

Remove from the oven. Let stand until completely cool. Then cover with a small board or cookie sheet, turn the pan and the board or sheet over, remove the pan, peel off the foil, cover with another board or sheet, and very carefully turn the cake over again, leaving it right side up.

This cuts best at room temperature, or only slightly chilled (that is, about 15 minutes in the refrigerator). The bottom layer is extremely crisp, and if you are not very careful in cutting, the bottom might crumble. And the Brownie layer is extra moist. Work slowly. And carefully. Use a long, thin, sharp knife (like a ham slicer). Or, if necessary, try different knives. Cut into 16 outrageous monsters or 32 more respectable bars.

These may be wrapped individually, if you wish.

Chocolate Cookies

Savannah Chocolate Chewies

In Savannah, Georgia, we went to one of America's great bookstores, E. Shaver. As soon as I introduced myself, the lovely ladies who run the store and love to cook screamed and giggled and swooned (just thinking about chocolate). They asked me if I knew how to make Chocolate Chewies, a Savannah specialty, and a deep dark secret. I was told they are made at Gottlieb's, a 100-year-old local bakery. When they phoned Isser

Gottlieb at the bakery he rushed right over, picked us up, drove us to the bakery, showed us the kitchen, fed us tastes of everything, and gave me this recipe. Talk about Southern hospitality!

The cookies are large, very dark, very chewy, and since they have egg whites and no yolks (and no butter) they are a sort of meringue; a decidedly chocolate meringue.

12 LARGE COOKIES

8 ounces (generous 2 cups) pecans
3 cups confectioners sugar
⅔ cup unsifted, unsweetened cocoa powder
  (preferably Dutch-process)
1 teaspoon powdered (not granular) instant
  coffee or espresso

2 tablespoons unsifted all-purpose flour
Pinch of salt
3 egg whites from eggs graded "large" (they may
  be whites that were frozen and thawed)
½ teaspoon vanilla extract

Adjust a rack to the middle of the oven and preheat the oven to 350 degrees. Line cookie sheets with baking pan liner paper or with aluminum foil shiny side up.

The pecans should be chopped rather fine. If you do it in a food processor fitted with the metal chopping blade, process on/off 10 quick times (10 seconds), or chop the nuts on a board using a long French chef's knife. Some pieces will be larger than others, but none should be larger than a green pea, and some will be smaller. Set aside.

Place the sugar, cocoa, coffee or espresso, flour, salt, egg whites, and vanilla in the small bowl of an electric mixer. Beat slowly at first until the dry ingredients are moistened, and then beat at high speed for 1 minute. Remove the bowl from the mixer and stir in the nuts.

It is important now to spoon out the cookies as soon as possible. Once they are spooned out they can wait before baking, but if they remain in the mixing bowl for any length of time, they will not be beautifully shiny when baked. Use a tablespoon for spooning out the cookies (not a measuring spoon)—make each cookie one rounded tablespoonful of the dough—and use another spoon for pushing off the mounds of dough. Place the cookies at least 1 inch apart on the prepared sheets.

I think these bake best if you bake only one sheet at a time. Bake for 15 minutes, reversing the sheet front to back once during baking to ensure even baking. When done, the cookies should be dry and crisp on the outside, wet and chewy inside.

If you have used baking pan liner paper the cookies may be removed from the paper with a wide metal spatula as soon as they are done and transferred to a rack to cool. If you have used foil, the cookies will have to stand on the foil until they can then be lifted easily with your fingers (or, if you have trouble, peel the foil away from the backs of the cookies).

Store these airtight.

At Gottlieb's they told me that if these are not served the day they are made, they should be frozen or they will dry out. I packed them in a freezer bag and let them stand on the counter overnight (just to test) and they were still moist and delicious. I also let some stand uncovered overnight (just to test) and they were still just as wonderful. (Maybe there's something in the air.)

Incidentally, this is Gottlieb's number one best-selling cookie.

Chocolate Gingersnaps

Crisp, dark and gingery, made with three kinds of ginger—ground, fresh, and candied. Gingerful!

ABOUT 50 COOKIES

1 ounce (a piece about 2 inches long and 1 inch thick) fresh ginger (see Fresh Ginger, page 8)
2 cups sifted all-purpose flour
¼ cup unsweetened cocoa powder (preferably Dutch-process)
½ teaspoon cinnamon
½ teaspoon salt

½ teaspoon ground ginger
1½ teaspoons baking soda
6 ounces (1½ sticks) unsalted butter
1 cup dark brown sugar, firmly packed
1 egg graded "large"
¼ cup dark molasses
¼ cup candied ginger, finely diced

Adjust two racks to divide the oven into thirds and preheat the oven to 350 degrees. Line cookie sheets with aluminum foil shiny side up, and set aside.

Grate the fresh ginger and set it aside.

Sift together the flour, cocoa, cinnamon, salt, ground ginger, and the baking soda, and set aside.

In the large bowl of an electric mixer beat the butter until soft. Add the grated fresh ginger and the sugar and beat to mix. Then beat in the egg and molasses. When mixed gradually add the sifted dry ingredients on low speed, scraping the sides of the bowl as necessary with a rubber spatula, and beating only until incorporated. Remove the bowl from the mixer and stir in the diced candied ginger.

Cover an additional cookie sheet or a jelly-roll pan with aluminum foil shiny side up. Using a barely rounded teaspoonful of the dough for each cookie, form mounds close together on the foil. Transfer to the freezer for about 10 minutes or longer in the refrigerator until the mounds are not sticky.

Roll the mounds between your hands into marble-size balls. Place them about 1½ inches apart on the prepared cookie sheets.

Bake two sheets at a time for about 15 minutes, reversing the sheets top to bottom and front to back once during baking. Bake until the cookies just barely feel springy if they are gently pressed with a fingertip. If you bake one sheet at a time, bake it on the lower of the two racks; one sheet will bake in about 13 minutes.

Immediately transfer the cookies with a wide metal spatula to racks to cool.

Store airtight.

David's Cookies

These are the famous chocolate chunk cookies that took New York City and suburbs by storm a few years ago; David now has shops all over the country—and in Japan, where they are wild about homemade cookies, especially chocolate. David's trademark is that his cookies are made with coarsely chopped semisweet chocolate bars instead of with morsels. As far as I know this recipe has been and still is a closely guarded secret—but here it is.

It is best to bake these on baking pan liner paper. If you line the sheets with foil, or if you butter them, the cookies spread out too much and the edges become too thin and brittle. If you butter and flour the sheets the cookies tend to burn. But if there is no baking pan liner paper available, butter and flour the sheets, bake the cookies on double cookie sheets to protect the bottoms from burning, and watch them carefully.

40 TO 50 SMALL COOKIES

8 ounces semisweet or bittersweet chocolate
    (David uses Lindt. Tobler is equally good.
    Poulain and Callebaut are wonderful. Use the
    best you can get.)
8 ounces (2 sticks) unsalted butter
½ teaspoon salt

½ teaspoon vanilla extract
1 cup light or dark brown sugar, firmly packed
1 egg graded "large" or "extra-large"
2 cups sifted all-purpose flour
Optional: 4 ounces (generous 1 cup) pecans or
    walnuts, broken into large pieces

Adjust two racks to divide the oven into thirds and preheat the oven to 400 degrees. Cut baking pan liner paper to fit cookie sheets. Or butter and flour the sheets and have enough other sheets ready so you can place each one on another to bake on double sheets.

Place the chocolate on a cutting board and with a long, heavy, sharp knife cut the chocolate first in one direction and then in the opposite direction, making uneven ¼- to ½-inch (or larger) pieces. Set aside.

In the large bowl of an electric mixer beat the butter until soft. Beat in the salt and vanilla, then the sugar, until well mixed. Add the egg and beat, scraping the bowl with a rubber spatula, until mixed. Then, on low speed, add the flour and beat until incorporated. Remove from the mixer.

With a heavy wooden spatula stir in the chopped chocolate and the optional nuts. The mixture will be thick and sticky.

Use two teaspoons to shape the cookies, one for picking up the dough and one for pushing it off. Use a rounded teaspoonful of dough for each cookie. Do not make these too large. Place the cookies 2 inches apart.

If you are using the baking pan liner paper, now slide a cookie sheet (easiest if the sheet has three flat sides) under the paper. Or place the buttered and floured sheet on another sheet.

Bake two sheets at a time for 8 to 10 minutes, reversing the sheets top to bottom and front to back as necessary to ensure even browning. Bake only until the edges of the cookies start to brown (see Note). If some are done before others, remove them as they become ready, and bake the rest as necessary. If they are too soft to handle, let them wait on the sheet for a few seconds and they will become firmer. With a wide metal spatula transfer the cookies to racks to cool.

NOTE: *To make these like David's, do not overbake. Actually, David underbakes them (6 to 8 minutes baking time), but I like 8 to 10 minutes or* even a little longer if necessary. David's are very soft; mine are slightly crisper.

VARIATION: *I have often made these huge, and they are wonderful. I make only 9 or 10 cookies with the full amount of dough. Here's how:*

Preheat the oven to only 350 degrees (instead of the 400 degrees used for the smaller-size cookies).

Place a large piece of aluminum foil on the counter next to the sink. Use ¼ cup of the dough for each cookie (measure with a ¼-cup metal measuring cup) and place the mounds any which way on the foil. Wet your hands with cold water, shake the water off but do not dry your hands, roll a mound of the dough between your cold, wet hands to form a ball, and then flatten the ball to about ½-inch thickness. Place only 3 cookies on each lined cookie sheet.

Bake the cookies for 20 to 22 minutes, reversing the sheets top to bottom and front to back as necessary to ensure even browning, until the cookies are lightly colored and just barely spring back when pressed lightly with a fingertip.

Let the cookies cool briefly on the paper until they are firm enough to be moved, and then use a wide metal spatula to transfer them to racks to cool.

Extra-Bittersweet Chocolate Chunk Monster Cookies

These are huge shortbreads with an inconceivable amount of unusually large chunks of extra-bittersweet chocolate and large pieces of walnuts and barely enough dough to hold them together. Rich, buttery, and crisp/crunchy. A far cry from chocolate chip cookies, yet related—distantly.

The recipe can be multiplied by any number, and any semisweet chocolate can be used in place of the extra-bittersweet.

8 LARGE COOKIES

9 ounces extra-bittersweet chocolate (I use
    3-ounce bars of Tobler Extra-Bittersweet)
4 ounces (generous 1 cup) walnuts
4 ounces (1 stick) unsalted butter
¾ teaspoon vanilla extract

¼ teaspoon almond extract
⅓ cup granulated sugar
½ teaspoon salt
1 cup sifted all-purpose flour

Adjust two racks to divide the oven into thirds and preheat the oven to 350 degrees. Line three cookie sheets with aluminum foil shiny side up and set aside.

With a large, heavy knife or with a Chinese cleaver cut the chocolate into chunks approximately ½ inch square; they may be even a bit larger but preferably not smaller. Set aside.

Break the walnuts into large pieces; each half may be broken in half, but they shouldn't be smaller. Set aside.

In the large bowl of an electric mixer beat the butter until just barely soft. Beat in the vanilla and almond extracts, then the sugar and salt, and finally the flour.

Remove from the mixer and with a heavy wooden spatula stir in the nuts and chocolate.

Place a large piece of foil or wax paper next to the sink. Use a ⅓-cup metal measuring cup to measure the amount for each cookie. Place 8 ⅓-cup mounds of the dough any which way on the foil or wax paper next to the sink.

Wet your hands with cold water, shake off the water but do not dry your hands (they should be cold and damp); pick up a mound of the dough, roll it between your hands into a ball, and then flatten it a bit between your hands. Place 3 cookies on each of two sheets, and 2 cookies on one sheet. Then, with your fingertips, press the cookies a bit to flatten them to about ½-inch thickness and 3½ inches in width. Keep the shape round.

Bake two sheets at a time, reversing the sheets top to bottom and front to back as necessary to ensure even browning. Bake for 16 to 18 minutes until the cookies are a pale golden color, darker on the rims. When these are done the tops will feel too soft (they will become crisp as they cool); time them by their looks (color) rather than by their feel.

Remove from the oven and let stand for about a minute.

Meanwhile, bake the one remaining sheet on the higher of the two racks. One sheet will bake in a minute or two less time than it takes for two sheets.

With a wide metal spatula, transfer the cookies very carefully and gently to racks to cool.

Store airtight.

Brownie Cookies

These delicious drop cookies (actually they are dropped, but then rolled into balls between your hands) are made with Brownie ingredients. They are semisoft and chewy, very dark, dense, fudge-like, not-too-sweet chocolate. Quick and easy, they are mixed in a saucepan.

ABOUT 28 COOKIES

2 ounces unsweetened chocolate
4 ounces semisweet chocolate
4 ounces (1 stick) unsalted butter
½ teaspoon salt
½ teaspoon vanilla extract

1 cup granulated sugar
2 eggs graded "large"
1½ cups sifted all-purpose flour
6 ounces (generous 1½ cups) walnuts, cut or
    broken into medium-size pieces

Adjust two racks to divide the oven into thirds and preheat the oven to 375 degrees. Line two cookie sheets with baking pan liner paper or with aluminum foil shiny side up and set aside.

In a 3-quart heavy saucepan over low heat melt both of the chocolates and the butter, stirring frequently with a heavy wooden spatula. Remove

from the heat. Add the remaining ingredients, in order, stirring briskly after each addition.

Place a long piece of aluminum foil next to the sink. Use two teaspoons, one for picking up the dough and one for pushing it off. Use a heaping teaspoonful of dough for each cookie. Place the mounds any which way on the foil.

Then wet your hands with cold water, shake off the water but do not dry your hands. Pick up a mound of the dough, roll it between your hands into a ball, and place it on one of the lined cookie sheets. Continue to roll the balls of dough and place them about 1 inch apart. Wet your hands again if dough begins to stick.

With the bottom of a fork, press each ball of dough lightly to flatten it to about ½- or ⅝-inch thickness (no thinner).

Bake for 10 to 12 minutes, reversing the sheets front to back and top to bottom once during baking. Bake only until the tops of the cookies lose their shine and become dull and feel dry but soft when pressed gently with a fingertip. The cookies become firmer as they cool.

With a wide metal spatula transfer the cookies to racks to cool. Store airtight.

Chocolate Whoppers

We were at the Soho Charcuterie, one of my favorite restaurants in New York City. They brought us a dish of huge, gorgeous, dark chocolate cookies that we had not ordered. They smiled secretively and knowingly, and watched me. I tasted one; it was wonderful. I was just about to ask for the recipe when they said, "These are yours." I soon learned that they meant it both ways; the cookies were mine to eat or take with me, and also, the recipe was from my first book (page 163).

They had increased the size of the cookies and made a few other little changes and they called them Chocolate Gobs. They told me that they could not make them fast enough.

This recipe is based on their adaptation.

At Sonrisa bakery in beautiful Rancho Santa Fe in southern California these are called Charlie's Cookies, in memory of a friend of ours who was a great World War II naval pilot and a top ace. His name was Charles Stimpson, and he shot down seventeen Japanese planes. These were Charlie's favorites.

2 ounces unsweetened chocolate
6 ounces semisweet chocolate
3 ounces (¾ stick) unsalted butter
¼ cup sifted all-purpose flour
¼ teaspoon double-acting baking powder
½ teaspoon salt
2 eggs graded "large"
¾ cup granulated sugar
2 teaspoons powdered (not granular) instant coffee or espresso

2 teaspoons vanilla extract
6 ounces (1 cup) semisweet chocolate morsels (see Note)
4 ounces (generous 1 cup) walnuts, broken into large pieces
4 ounces (generous 1 cup) toasted pecans (see To Toast Pecans, page 7), broken into large pieces

Adjust two racks to divide the oven into thirds and preheat the oven to 350 degrees. If you are baking only one sheet, adjust a rack to the middle of the oven. Line cookie sheets with baking pan liner paper (first choice) or aluminum foil shiny side up (second choice); you will need three pieces of paper or foil for three cookie sheets. If you don't have enough sheets, one or two pieces of paper or foil can wait their turn.

Place the unsweetened chocolate, semisweet chocolate, and the butter in the top of a small double boiler over hot water on moderate heat. Cook, covered, for a few minutes. Then stir occasionally until melted and smooth. Remove the top of the double boiler and set aside, uncovered, to cool slightly.

Sift together the flour, baking powder, and salt and set aside.

In the small bowl of an electric mixer beat the eggs, sugar, coffee or espresso, and vanilla at high speed for a minute or two.

Beat in the melted chocolates and butter (which may still be quite warm) on low speed just to mix. Add the sifted dry ingredients and again beat on low speed just to mix, scraping the sides of the bowl as necessary with a rubber spatula to incorporate the ingredients. Remove from the mixer and transfer to a larger bowl.

Stir in the chocolate morsels, the walnuts, and the pecans.

Use a ⅓-cup metal measuring cup to measure the amount of batter for each cookie. Put 5 cookies on each cookie sheet, 1 in the middle and 1 toward each corner. Use a rubber spatula to push the mixture into the measuring cup and then to scoop it out onto the lined sheet (the dough is gooey). Do not flatten the tops.

Bake two sheets at a time, reversing the sheets top to bottom and front to back once during baking to ensure even baking. Bake for 16 to 17 minutes—no longer. The surface of the cookies will be dry but the insides will still be soft. There is really no way to test these; just use a portable oven thermometer before baking to be sure your oven is right, and then watch the clock.

If the sheets have four rims the cookies and papers or foil will have to wait on the sheets until cool. If you have used cookie sheets with only one or two raised rims, you can slide the papers or foil off the sheets and let stand until the cookies are cool. (It is not necessary to let the sheet cool before sliding it under another paper or foil with unbaked cookies on it.)

When the cookies have cooled, use a wide metal spatula to release them and turn them over to air the bottoms a bit.

I wrap these individually in clear cellophane, and I know of a few bakeries that do the same and charge up to $2.00 for each cookie.

NOTE: *If you wish, in place of semisweet morsels, use 6 ounces of Tobler Tradition or Lindt Excellence or any similar chocolate, cut into ½-inch chunks.*

Cookie Kisses

Hershey's Milk Chocolate Kisses are about as American as can be. Everybody knows them. These are delicious peanut butter cookies shaped by being rolled between your hands. The kisses are put on top as soon as the baked cookies are taken out of the oven. Fun to make and fun to serve.

This is a variation of an old American recipe that is sometimes called Sombreros (they do look like them), Blossoms, or Silver Tipped Blossoms. (Does that mean that they did not remove the foil from the kisses?)

48 COOKIES

48 Hershey's Milk Chocolate Kisses
1¾ cups sifted all-purpose flour
1 teaspoon baking soda
¼ teaspoon salt
½ cup granulated sugar
½ cup light brown sugar, packed

1 egg graded "large"
1 teaspoon vanilla extract
2 tablespoons milk
4 ounces (1 stick) unsalted butter
½ cup smooth peanut butter
Additional granulated sugar

Adjust two racks to divide the oven into thirds and preheat the oven to 375 degrees. These should be baked only 12 cookies at a time on a foil-lined 15½ by 12-inch cookie sheet. Therefore, line four sheets with foil shiny side up or simply tear off four 15½-inch pieces of foil and place them on the counter shiny side up.

Remove the wrapping from the kisses and set them aside.

This dough can be prepared in a food processor or in the large bowl of an electric mixer.

In a processor: Place the flour, baking soda, salt, granulated sugar, and brown sugar in the processor bowl fitted with the metal chopping blade and process on/off quickly 2 or 3 times to mix. Place the egg, vanilla, and milk in a 1-cup glass measuring cup and set aside. Cut up the butter and add it and the peanut butter to the bowl of the processor. Turn the machine on and pour the egg mixture through the feed tube. Process until the mixture forms a ball and is thoroughly mixed.

Or in a mixer: Sift together the flour, baking soda, and salt and set aside. Reserve both sugars. Place the egg, vanilla, and milk in a small cup and reserve. Place the butter and peanut butter in the large bowl of the mixer and beat until soft. Add both sugars and beat to mix. Then add half of the sifted dry ingredients, the egg mixture, and the remaining dry ingredients. Beat until thoroughly mixed.

Place a long piece of wax paper or foil on the work surface. Divide the dough into 48 mounds, each one a rounded teaspoonful. (You can either just pick up the cookie-size mounds and place them on the paper or foil, or roll the dough into a long sausage shape and cut it into 48 even pieces.)

Place additional granulated sugar (about 1 cup) on a wide plate and have it handy. One at a time, roll the mounds of dough between your hands to make balls, roll them around in the granulated sugar to coat the cookies, and then place them on the foil, placing only 12 cookies on each length of foil. Then if the foil is not on cookie sheets, slide two sheets under two pieces of foil.

Place one sheet in the oven; wait a few minutes before placing the second sheet in the oven so that they do not come out of the oven at the same time. (If you might forget which sheet went into the oven first, roll up a little bean-size piece of foil and place it in a corner on the first sheet.) Reverse the sheets top to bottom once during baking to ensure even browning. Bake for 12 to 13 minutes. The cookies will be only lightly colored and will still feel soft to the touch.

Immediately as you remove a sheet from the oven place a chocolate kiss, point up, in the middle of each cookie, pressing it down firmly. Then, with a wide metal spatula, transfer the cookies to racks to cool.

The chocolate kisses will soften from the heat of the cookies and they will remain soft for quite a while. Therefore, if you are packing these, or stacking them, be sure that the kisses have become firm; if necessary, chill the cookies.

Chocolate Peanut Butter Cookies

This is a chocolate version of plain old-fashioned peanut butter cookies; easy to make; they keep well, mail well, and they are deeelicious.

48 COOKIES

2 ounces unsweetened chocolate
1 ounce semisweet chocolate
1½ cups sifted all-purpose flour
¾ teaspoon baking soda
½ teaspoon salt
4 ounces (1 stick) unsalted butter

½ teaspoon vanilla extract
½ cup granulated sugar
½ cup dark or light brown sugar, firmly packed
½ cup smooth peanut butter
1 egg graded "large"

It is best to bake these one sheet at a time (or some might burn before others are done); adjust a rack to the middle of the oven and preheat the oven to 375 degrees. Cut baking pan liner paper or aluminum foil to fit cookie sheets (see Note). Set aside.

Place both kinds of chocolate in the top of a small double boiler over warm water on moderately low heat. Cover with a folded paper towel (to absorb steam) and with the pot cover. Let stand until the chocolate is almost all melted. Then uncover and stir until completely melted and smooth. Remove the top of the double boiler and set aside to cool.

Sift together the flour, baking soda, and salt and set aside.

Place the butter in the small bowl of an electric mixer and beat until soft. Add the vanilla and both sugars and beat until well mixed. Then add the peanut butter, beat to mix, add the melted chocolate and beat to mix, beat in the egg, and finally add the sifted dry ingredients and beat on low speed until incorporated.

Turn the mixture out onto a piece of wax paper or foil and shape it into an even oblong. Cut it into 48 equal pieces. Roll the pieces one at a time between your hands into balls about 1 inch in diameter and place them 2 inches apart on the prepared baking pan liner paper or aluminum foil (12 cookies fit on a 15½ by 12-inch piece of paper or foil).

Press the tops of the cookies gently with the bottom of the tines of a fork, pressing in one direction only, forming a ridged pattern and flattening the cookies to about ½-inch thickness.

Slide a cookie sheet under the foil or paper and bake one sheet at a time for about 15 minutes, reversing the sheet front to back once during baking to ensure even browning. Watch the cookies carefully to see that none of them becomes too dark. When they are done they will feel dry and semifirm when pressed lightly with a fingertip, but they should not darken much or they will taste burnt. These will harden and become crisp as they cool.

NOTE: *These directions are for a cookie sheet that has only one raised rim and is flat on the other three sides. If you do not have that type, it will probably be best to line the sheets with the paper or foil before putting the cookies in place.*

Candy Cookies

The narrow dividing line between candy and cookies becomes even narrower with this dessert. This recipe is a combination of two American favorites, chocolate chip cookies and candy bars. The candy bars (crisp toffee covered with milk chocolate) are coarsely cut up and are used in place of chocolate chips (the candy does not melt during baking). Fabulous!

24 LARGE COOKIES

9 ounces Heath Bars
4 ounces (1 stick) unsalted butter
½ teaspoon salt
½ teaspoon vanilla extract
⅓ cup granulated sugar
⅓ cup dark brown sugar, firmly packed

1 egg graded "large"
1¼ cups unsifted all-purpose flour
½ teaspoon baking soda
½ teaspoon hot water
4 ounces (generous 1 cup) walnuts, broken into
    large pieces

Adjust two racks to divide the oven into thirds and preheat the oven to 375 degrees. Line cookie sheets with aluminum foil shiny side up.

Cut the Health Bars into four ½-inch pieces and set aside.

In the large bowl of an electric mixer beat the butter until soft. Add the salt, vanilla, and both sugars and beat to mix. Then beat in the egg. On low speed add the flour, scraping the bowl as necessary with a rubber spatula and beating only until incorporated.

In a small cup combine the baking soda and water and beat it into the dough. Remove the bowl from the mixer, then add the walnuts and the cut-up Heath Bars and stir with a heavy wooden spatula until evenly mixed.

Use a rounded tablespoon of the dough for each cookie. Place them 2 inches apart on the lined sheets.

Bake two sheets at a time for 13 to 15 minutes, reversing the sheets top to bottom and front to back as necessary to ensure even browning. Bake until the cookies are lightly browned all over.

Slide the foil off the sheets (unless your sheets have raised sides, in which case just let the foil stand on the sheets). Let the cookies stand on the foil for about 5 minutes. Then use a wide metal spatula to transfer the cookies to racks to cool.

Store airtight.

Chocolate Chip-Chocolate Oatmeal Cookies

These are drop cookies that combine several qualities of America's favorite cookies: 1) chocolate, 2) chocolate chips, 3) oatmeal. Plus quick and easy. The original recipe was worked out by the Gold Medal flour people at General Mills to help introduce unbleached flour, which by now needs no introduction, but a few years ago the average homemaker had never even seen it.

Incidentally, General Mills celebrated its 100th birthday a few years ago. Congratulations.

46 COOKIES

1¼ cups sifted unbleached all-purpose flour
½ teaspoon baking soda
½ teaspoon salt
⅓ cup unsweetened cocoa powder (preferably Dutch-process)
8 ounces (2 sticks) unsalted butter
1 teaspoon vanilla extract
¼ teaspoon almond extract

1½ cups granulated sugar
1 egg graded "large," "extra-large," or "jumbo"
2 teaspoons instant coffee
¼ cup hot water
6 ounces (1 cup) semisweet chocolate morsels
3 cups quick-cooking (not "instant") rolled oats
10 ounces (2½ cups) walnuts, broken into medium-size pieces

Adjust two racks to divide the oven into thirds and preheat the oven to 350 degrees. Line cookie sheets with aluminum foil shiny side up and set aside.

Sift together the flour, baking soda, salt, and cocoa and set aside.

In the large bowl of an electric mixer beat the butter until it is soft. Add the vanilla and almond extracts and then the sugar, beating until well mixed. Beat in the egg. Mix the coffee and water and add. Now, on low speed, add the sifted dry ingredients, beating only until incorporated.

Remove from the mixer. With a heavy wooden spatula stir in the chocolate morsels, the oats, and the nuts.

Spread out a long piece of foil next to the sink.

Use a rounded tablespoon of the mixture for each cookie; place any which way on the foil.

Wet your hands with cold water and pick up a mound, roll it into a ball, flatten between your hands to ½-inch thickness, and place 2 inches apart on the foil-lined sheets, six to eight on a sheet.

Bake for 14 to 16 minutes, reversing the sheets top to bottom and front to back once during baking to ensure even baking. Bake until the cookies just barely spring back when they are pressed lightly in the center. They will feel soft when they are removed from the oven but they will become dry and crisp when they cool.

Let the cookies cool briefly on the foil; then use a wide metal spatula to transfer them to racks to cool.

Store airtight.

Chocolate Miracles
(a.k.a. Chocolate Fudge Cookies)

This is from Barbara (Mrs. Paul) Leand of Brooklandville, Maryland. The recipe has been in her family for many many years. Dense/dark/candy-like—as black and shiny as wet tar—like a combination of chewy macaroons, Tootsie Rolls, and caramel. The miracle is how easy they are to make. You need baking pan liner paper (see Note).

25 COOKIES

2 ounces unsweetened chocolate
1 14-ounce can sweetened condensed milk
4 ounces (generous 1 cup) pecans, toasted (see To Toast Pecans, page 7), cut into medium-small pieces

Place the chocolate in the top of a large double boiler over warm water on moderate heat. Cover for a few minutes, with a folded paper towel (to absorb steam) and pot cover, then uncover and cook until the chocolate is melted. Raise the heat to high (the water in the bottom of the double boiler should boil after the chocolate has melted). Add the condensed milk. With a rubber spatula, stir and scrape the bottom and sides of the pan, cooking (over boiling water) for 5 minutes, during which time the mixture will thicken very slightly.

Remove the top of the double boiler; stir the mixture briskly a bit with a wire whisk until very smooth. Let stand, stirring occasionally with the spatula, for 10 to 15 minutes, during which time the mixture will thicken considerably more.

Meanwhile, adjust two racks to the two top positions in the oven and preheat the oven to 350 degrees. Line two cookie sheets with baking pan liner paper.

By now the chocolate mixture will have thickened still more. Stir in the nuts. Transfer to a small bowl for easier handling.

Use two teaspoons to shape the cookies, one for picking up with and one for pushing off with. Use a rounded teaspoon of dough for each cookie. Place them 1½ to 2 inches apart on the baking pan liner paper.

Bake for 15 minutes, reversing sheets top to bottom and front to back once during baking to ensure even baking. (During baking the cookies will flatten and spread out only slightly.) They will feel very soft when done but will become more firm as they cool.

With a wide metal spatula transfer the cookies to racks to cool. (If the cookies stick to the spatula turn the spatula over into the palm of your left hand—onto a folded napkin to protect your hand from the heat—lift away the spatula, and then place the cookie right side up on the rack.)

It would be great if you could serve these immediately, because as soon as they cool, and for about 12 hours after that, they are crisp on the outside and soft inside: a divine condition. But after they've been standing for a long time the moisture from inside the cookies works its way out and the crispness disappears. If they are wrapped or stored airtight, the moisture is contained and the crispness disappears even sooner. (However, the flavor remains and they are still outstanding.) Therefore, if you plan to serve these either the same day or a day later, do not store them airtight; they may be covered loosely with wax paper. Or, if you must make these way ahead of time, package them airtight and freeze them until a few hours before serving time. Then, thaw before unwrapping.

NOTE: *These work like magic on baking pan liner paper. If you use foil instead, they stick. If you butter the sheets, the cookies want to burn.*

VARIATION: *If you wish, each cookie may be topped with a pecan half. It should be done immediately after shaping each cookie, before the surface of the cookie has time to dry out. Press each pecan half into the cookie dough so that it will not fall off after baking. (These halves may be toasted or not before they are used.)*

Down East Chocolate Cookies

Thin and crisp, intensely chocolate and almond. No flour. They are brittle and hard until they go into your mouth; then they become chewy and caramel-like. The perfect cookie to nibble on with ice cream or custard, or any other time.

This recipe calls for bought almond paste. It is available at specialty food stores; the brand I use is Odense, which comes in a 7-ounce package. It is stored on the grocer's shelf and lasts indefinitely.

28 TO 30 THIN COOKIES

1½ ounces unsweetened chocolate
3 ounces (¾ stick) unsalted butter
¾ cup granulated sugar
⅛ teaspoon salt

3½ ounces (⅓ cup, tightly packed) almond paste (see Note)
1 egg graded "large"
½ teaspoon almond extract

Place the chocolate and butter in the top of a large double boiler, uncovered, over warm water on moderate heat. Stir frequently until melted. Add the sugar and salt and stir to mix. Then add the almond paste. Stir with a wooden or rubber spatula, pressing down on the almond paste until it is completely blended; if necessary, stir with a wire whisk. (If the butter separates it is all right.)

Remove the top of the double boiler from the heat. Add the egg and almond extract. Beat with an electric mixer, an eggbeater, or a wire whisk until smooth.

Cool and then place in the freezer for about 30 minutes, stirring a few times, until quite thick.

Before baking, adjust two racks to divide the oven into thirds and preheat the oven to 300 degrees. Preferably, use cookie sheets that have only one raised rim (flat on three sides). Or, if you must use the ones with raised rims (or jelly-roll pans), turn the sheets (or pans) over and use the bottoms. Cover the sheets (or pans) with aluminum foil shiny side up. Set aside.

Use two teaspoons, one for picking up with and one for pushing off with, to make drop cookies. Use a slightly rounded teaspoonful of the dough for each cookie; these will spread. Do not make them too large, do not flatten them, and do not place more than 6 cookies on a sheet. Do take your time and shape them carefully in order to have nice round cookies when baked.

Bake for 21 or 22 minutes, no less, reversing the sheets top to bottom and front to back once during baking to ensure even baking. If you bake only one sheet at a time, bake it on the lower of the two racks. The cookies will rise a little and then settle down very flat during baking.

These must cool completely on the foil. I like to let them cool on the foil still on the cookie sheets. However, if you need the sheets now for baking more cookies, you can slide the foil off the sheets.

When completely cool, peel the foil away from the beautifully smooth and shiny backs of the cookies. (If the cookies were not baked enough they will stick to the foil. If that should happen, place the foil and cookies in the freezer for a few minutes; then peel the foil away.)

I store these in an airtight jar on the coffee table. They last wonderfully; they seem to get even better after a few days.

NOTE: *Leftover almond paste should quickly be wrapped airtight in plastic wrap and then aluminum foil (see Patching the Pastry, page 24).*

Chocolate Fudge Candy-Cookies

The MOST chocolate! Like dark chocolate fudge candy; softer and smoother. Chewy. Heavenly. And about the easiest cookies I have ever made.

55 RATHER SMALL COOKIES

12 ounces (2 cups) semisweet chocolate morsels
2 ounces (½ stick) unsalted butter
1 14-ounce can sweetened condensed milk
1 teaspoon vanilla extract

1 cup sifted all-purpose flour
8 ounces (2¼ cups) pecans, toasted (see To Toast Pecans, page 7), broken into large pieces

Adjust two racks to divide the oven into thirds and preheat the oven to 350 degrees. Line cookie sheets with aluminum foil shiny side up, being careful not to crease the foil.

Place the chocolate morsels and the butter in the top of a large double boiler over warm water on moderate heat. Stir occasionally until melted and smooth.

Remove the top of the double boiler. Stir in the condensed milk and vanilla, then the flour, and then the pecans.

Use a rounded teaspoonful of the mixture for each cookie; pick it up with one teaspoon and push it off with another. Place the cookies 1 to 2 inches apart on the foil.

Bake two sheets at a time, reversing the sheets top to bottom and front to back once during baking. Bake for exactly 7 minutes. The cookies will still feel soft; they will become firmer as they cool.

If you bake only one sheet at a time, bake it in the middle of the oven and reverse it front to back once during baking.

(Before baking, the dough will be as shiny as varnish; after baking it will have changed to the dull look of fudge candy.)

If you have used a cookie sheet with only one raised rim, as you remove it from the oven slide the foil off and let stand until the cookies are completely cool. (You can slide the hot cookie sheet under another piece of foil with unbaked cookies on it.) If the cookie sheet has raised rims all around, the foil must stand on the sheet until the cookies are completely cool. When they have cooled, use a wide metal spatula to transfer the cookies to racks and let stand until the bottoms become dry.

Store with wax paper or plastic wrap between the layers.

Pennsylvania Squares

I met a lady who works in the test kitchen at the Hershey company. She spends all her time testing chocolate recipes. I asked if she had a favorite. She didn't hesitate and gave me this recipe. They are very thin brown sugar cookie squares covered with milk chocolate and chopped walnuts. The result is like a combination of chewy butterscotch and English toffee. Quick, easy, foolproof, won-

derfully delicious candylike cookies.

You need rather small (1.45 ounces each) thin bars of Hershey's milk chocolate, although I don't see any reason you couldn't use any other brand of milk chocolate, and if the bars are not the same size, approximately the same size will do.

32 COOKIES

8 ounces (2 sticks) unsalted butter
1 teaspoon vanilla extract
¼ teaspoon salt
1 cup dark brown sugar, firmly packed

1 egg yolk
2 cups sifted all-purpose flour
8 1.45-ounce bars of Hershey's milk chocolate
5 ounces (1¼ cups) walnuts

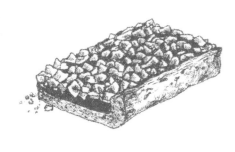

Adjust a rack one-third up from the bottom of the oven and preheat the oven to 350 degrees. Butter a 9 by 13-inch baking pan with additional butter to that called for and set aside.

In the large bowl of an electric mixer beat the butter until soft. Beat in the vanilla, salt, and sugar. Then add the egg yolk and beat well. On low speed gradually add the flour, scraping the bowl as necessary with a rubber spatula and beating until incorporated. (It might be necessary to finish the beating by hand.)

To make a thin layer of the dough in the buttered pan it will be best if you first place the dough by rounded teaspoonfuls over the bottom of the pan. Cover with a length of wax paper and, with the palm of your hand and your fingertips, press down on the paper to press the mounds of dough together into a rather smooth layer. Remove the wax paper.

Bake for 23 minutes. (During baking the dough will rise and then settle down.)

Meanwhile, as the cake is baking, unwrap the chocolate bars and set them aside. And, on a large chopping board, with a long, heavy French chef's knife, chop the nuts into rather small pieces. Small is better than large for these cookies. Set the nuts aside.

Remove the baked layer from the oven and immediately, without waiting, place the chocolate bars on the hot cake. Keep them about ¼ inch away from the sides of the pan. Break the bars into pieces wherever necessary and fit them together to cover the cake; a few empty areas—uncovered—will be all right.

In about a minute or two the chocolate will have softened from the heat of the cake. With the bottom of a teaspoon smooth over the chocolate. Then, with your fingertips, sprinkle the nuts all over the chocolate. Cover with a length of plastic wrap or wax paper and, with the palms of your hands and your fingertips, press down gently on the nuts to make sure that they are all embedded in the chocolate. Remove the plastic wrap or wax paper.

With a small, sharp knife cut around the sides of the cake to release. Let stand until cool. Then refrigerate only until the chocolate is set.

With a small, sharp knife cut the cake into 32 rectangles. (Or cut it into 16 rectangles and, after removing them from the pan, cut each one in half.)

To remove the first 1 or 2 cookies from the pan it might be helpful to use a fork to pry the cookie up; then use a metal spatula to remove the remaining cookies.

Wrap the cookies individually in clear cellophane or wax paper or aluminum foil, if you wish, or place them on a tray and cover with plastic wrap until serving time.

Other Cookies

COOKIE CLUBS

When my cookie book was printed, I heard from many people about their favorite occupation—I was going to say "hobby," but many of them have made it a "business." But "hobby" or "business" or both, baking cookies is their favorite occupation. And they let me know about their cookie clubs, which were news to me.

This is how it works. They get together a group of about ten or twelve people who all love to bake cookies. They meet about once a month. Each person bakes one batch of cookies and makes enough copies of the recipe for all the club members. He or she brings the cookies, packed so that each member can take some of them home and can also eat some of them at the meeting. The host or hostess for each meeting supplies beverages as well as cookies.

These cookie clubs are all around the country, in big cities and small towns. They have men, women, and children as members. That's fun!

Tea Cakes

Scotty was about 16 years old, although she looked more like 12, when she knocked on our door looking for domestic work. She was scared stiff. She had absolutely no experience. She told me, in a whisper, that her parents worked as a live-in domestic couple for friends of ours. When Scotty lived with them she was never allowed into the kitchen or the main part of the house. When her grandmother was still alive, she occasionally visited her in Georgia. Scotty looked so sad and pleading that I had to say, "OK, let's try it." She was bright and learned quickly. But she did not get over being afraid. I thought if I could teach her to cook something, she might relax and gain a little confidence; she had never cooked a thing. I asked her what she would like to make and she answered Tea Cakes, like her grandma used to.

I had no idea what Tea Cakes were. We played Twenty Questions until I found out that they were very old-fashioned, extremely plain Southern cookies. I looked through old Southern

recipes and picked one that sounded close to what Scotty had described. I made them, and they were wonderful. Scotty could not believe it—she said they were her grandma's Tea Cakes. Then I taught her to make them, and she was thrilled beyond words.

Incidentally, they became our favorite plain cookies and we were seldom without them.

Once Scotty started cooking she couldn't stop. She was a wonderful cook, and I had as much fun teaching her as she did learning. She stayed with us for several years.

When I wrote my first book I used this recipe (page 153); here it is again because it is so American and so wonderful. (These have no salt or flavoring—typical of many very old recipes—but they are neither tasteless nor too bland.)

The dough must be refrigerated overnight before it is rolled out with a rolling pin, cut with a round cutter, and baked.

36 VERY LARGE COOKIES

½ teaspoon baking soda
5¼ cups sifted all-purpose flour
8 ounces (2 sticks) unsalted butter

3 cups granulated sugar
3 eggs graded "large" or "extra-large"
1 cup whipping cream

Sift the baking soda with 1 cup of the flour (reserve the remaining 4¼ cups of flour) and set aside.

In the large bowl of an electric mixer beat the butter until soft. Gradually add the sugar and beat for about a minute. Scrape the bowl as necessary with a rubber spatula all during the mixing. Add the eggs one at a time, beating until incorporated after each addition.

On low speed beat in the 1 cup of flour that has been sifted with the baking soda. Then add the remaining 4¼ cups of flour in five additions, alternating with the cream in four additions. Beat only until smooth after each addition.

Divide the dough roughly in quarters and wrap them individually in aluminum foil. Refrigerate overnight or longer.

Before baking, adjust two racks to divide the oven into thirds, preheat the oven to 400 degrees, and cut aluminum foil to fit cookie sheets.

Work with one quarter of the dough at a time, keeping the rest refrigerated. On a floured pastry cloth with a floured rolling pin roll out the dough until it is ¼ to ⅓ inch thick. Work quickly before the dough softens.

Cut out the cookies with a 3½-inch (or larger or smaller) round cutter, dipping the cutter into flour as necessary to prevent sticking.

With a wide metal spatula transfer the cookies to the foil shiny side up, placing them about 2 inches apart. Slide a cookie sheet (the kind with only one raised rim) under the foil.

Bake for 13 to 15 minutes, reversing the sheets top to bottom and front to back once during baking to ensure even browning; bake until the cookies are lightly colored.

With a wide metal spatula transfer the cookies to racks to cool.

If you bake only one sheet at a time, bake it on the upper rack.

Leftover pieces of the dough should be pressed together, wrapped, and rechilled before rolling.

My Mother's Gingersnaps

These are the cookies that my mother and I made together probably more often than any other. Although they seem like a Christmas cookie we had jars and boxes of them around the house all year. For 30-odd years my father did his radio news broadcasts from home; that meant that people were coming and going all day and often late into the night. With plenty of these gingersnaps we were always prepared, and many famous people left the house carrying a box or a bag.

Crisp, chewy, large and thin, spicy and peppery but mellow. The dough should be refrigerated overnight before rolling, cutting, and baking.

35 COOKIES

3½ ounces (½ cup) candied ginger, loosely packed
2 cups unsifted all-purpose flour
1½ teaspoons baking soda
¾ teaspoon salt
¾ teaspoon finely ground black pepper
    (preferably freshly ground)
1½ teaspoons ground ginger

8 ounces (2 sticks) unsalted butter
1 cup granulated sugar
¾ cup dark molasses
1 egg graded "large"
1¼ teaspoons cider vinegar (see Note)
1 cup unsifted all-purpose whole wheat flour

Cut the ginger into pieces ¼ inch or less and set aside.

Sift together the all-purpose flour, baking soda, salt, pepper, and ground ginger and set aside.

In the large bowl of an electric mixer beat the butter until it is soft. Add the sugar and beat to mix. Beat in the molasses, egg, and vinegar (it might look curdled; it is OK). Then beat in the cut candied ginger. Add the sifted dry ingredients and the whole wheat flour and beat on low speed until incorporated.

Spread out three lengths of wax paper or foil. Place one third of the dough on each paper. Wrap and refrigerate overnight. (If you can't wait, freeze the packages for about an hour.)

Before baking, adjust two racks to divide the oven into thirds. Preheat the oven to 350 degrees. Line cookie sheets (preferably the kind with only one raised rim) with aluminum foil shiny side up.

To roll the dough, generously flour a pastry cloth and rolling pin. Place one piece of the chilled dough on the cloth, press down on it a few times with the rolling pin, turn the dough over to flour both sides, roll out the dough until it is ¼ inch thin. Work quickly. Do not leave the dough unattended; it becomes sticky and gooey if it is allowed to reach room temperature (which seems to happen quickly). Reflour the cloth and the pin as necessary.

With a round cookie cutter measuring 3⅛ inches in diameter (or any other size) cut out the cookies; start cutting at the outside edge of the dough and cut the cookies just barely touching each other. Reserve the scraps and press them together (the dough will be too sticky for you to press the scraps together with your hands—it is best to put the scraps in a bowl and mix them together with a spatula), wrap, and rechill.

With a wide metal spatula quickly transfer the cookies to the foil-lined sheets, placing them 2 inches apart (if the cookies are 3⅛ inches wide I place only 5 cookies on a 15½ by 12-inch sheet—they spread).

Bake two sheets at a time, reversing the sheets top to bottom and front to back once during baking to ensure even baking. As they bake, the cookies will rise and then settle down into thin waferlike cookies. They will take about 15 minutes to bake; if you bake only one sheet, use a rack in the middle of the oven—one sheet might bake in slightly less time.

When the cookies are done, remove the sheets from the oven and let stand until they are just barely cool. (If you have used the sheets with only one raised rim, slide the foil off the sheet and slide the sheet—which may be hot—under another piece of foil already prepared with cookies on it, and continue baking.)

Then lift the cookies away from the foil, or transfer the cookies with a wide metal spatula (if the backs of the cookies stick to the foil the cookies were not baked long enough—return them to the oven).

Place the cookies on racks to finish cooling or just turn them over to allow the bottoms to dry.

Store airtight.

NOTE: *It is best to pour some vinegar into a cup and spoon out the amount you need. If you pour it into a spoon held over the mixing bowl there is a very good chance you might pour more than you need.*

100 Percent Whole Wheat Ginger Cookies

Thick, semisoft, wholesome/wheaty and spicy. Made with a huge amount of fresh ginger; they are irresistible. Don't even THINK about these without a cup of hot coffee or a glass of cold milk.

The dough must be well chilled before baking. This recipe is written for a food processor.

24 COOKIES

2½ ounces (a piece about 2½ inches long and about 1½ inches thick—to make ½ cup grated) fresh ginger (see Fresh Ginger, page 8)
4 ounces (1 stick) unsalted butter, cold
½ teaspoon vanilla extract
¼ teaspoon salt

½ teaspoon ground cloves
1 teaspoon cinnamon
2 egg yolks graded "large"
1 cup dark brown sugar, firmly packed
2 cups sifted all-purpose whole wheat flour (preferably stone ground from a health food store); see Notes

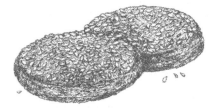

Grate the fresh ginger—do not remove it from the processor bowl.

Cut the cold butter in half lengthwise and then cut it crosswise into ½-inch pieces. With the motor going add the pieces one at a time, pausing briefly between additions. Process until the butter is soft and thoroughly mixed with the ginger. Adding and processing the butter should take about 30 seconds.

Remove the cover of the machine, add the vanilla, salt, cloves, cinnamon, and egg yolks, and process on/off just to mix. Remove the cover again, add the sugar and about half of the flour, and process to mix. Then add the remaining flour and process until the mixture is smooth; it might be necessary to stop the machine and stir the ingredients once or twice with a rubber spatula to help the mixing.

Remove the mixture from the processor to a piece of wax paper, wrap in the paper, and refrigerate for several hours (or overnight if you wish), or freeze for about 1 hour until firm enough to be rolled out.

Before baking, adjust two racks to divide the oven into thirds and preheat the oven to 350 degrees. Line two cookie sheets with aluminum foil shiny side up.

Lightly flour a pastry cloth and rolling pin. Place the chilled dough on the floured cloth, roll it a bit, then turn the dough over to flour the other side. Roll out the dough until it is ⅜ inch thick (it will be an oval or oblong about 12 by 9 inches).

With a 2-inch round cookie cutter, cut out cookies starting at the outside edge of the rolled-out dough and cutting the cookies so they just touch each other.

Place the cookies about 1 inch apart on the foil-lined sheets. (I do not flour the cutter when cutting these cookies because it does not seem to make any difference with this dough, but you might like to try it.)

Chill, reroll, and cut the scraps in the same manner.

Bake these plain—as they are—or with the following optional topping. (The cookies are equally good with or without the topping, but sesame seeds, known as benne seeds in the South, are supposed to bring good luck.)

About 2 tablespoons sesame seeds (bleached or natural)   Milk

To bring out the flavor of the seeds they must be toasted before they are used. (I don't understand why they don't become toasted on top of the cookies in the oven while the cookies are baking, but they don't.) Place them in a small, heavy frying pan over moderate heat. Shake the pan frequently for the first few minutes and then constantly as the seeds start to color. It should take about 5 to 7 minutes for the seeds to toast to a nice golden color (some will be darker than others).

Brush the cookies with milk and, while they are still wet, sprinkle them generously with the toasted seeds.

Bake for about 25 to 28 minutes, reversing the sheets top to bottom and front to back once during baking to ensure even browning. The cookies should become only slightly darker and almost but not completely firm to the touch.

With a wide metal spatula transfer the cookies to racks to cool. Store airtight.

NOTES: 1. *Any flour that is too coarse to go through the sifter should be stirred into the part that did go through.*

2. You will probably see fibers of ginger on the edges of the cookies, both before and after baking. Think of it as seeds of a vanilla bean in ice cream; you know it's the real thing.

Granny's Old-Fashioned Sugar Cookies

These are crisp/crisp, large, thin plain cookies with a divine lemon and cinnamon flavor. Everyone raves about them and asks for the recipe.

It is best to refrigerate this dough overnight before rolling it out and cutting it with a cookie cutter.

18 TO 24 LARGE COOKIES

1¾ cups unsifted all-purpose flour
2 teaspoons double-acting baking powder
¼ teaspoon salt
4 ounces (1 stick) unsalted butter
Finely grated rind of 2 lemons

1 tablespoon lemon juice
1 cup granulated sugar
1 egg graded "large"
2 tablespoons whipping cream

Sift together the flour, baking powder, and salt and set aside. In the large bowl of an electric mixer beat the butter until it is soft. Beat in the lemon rind and juice and then add the sugar. Beat in the egg and the whipping cream. Then, on low speed, gradually add the sifted dry ingredients and beat until smoothly mixed. Remove from the mixer.

Turn the dough out onto a length of wax paper or plastic wrap, wrap it, and refrigerate overnight. (In a hurry, I have used the freezer instead of the refrigerator—only until the dough was cold and firm but not frozen.)

When you are ready to bake, adjust two racks to divide the oven into thirds and preheat the oven to 375 degrees. Line cookie sheets with baking pan liner paper or with foil shiny side up. Set aside.

Spread out a pastry cloth, flour it well, and flour a rolling pin. Unwrap the dough, cut it into thirds, and place one piece on the floured cloth. If it was refrigerated overnight, it will be too stiff to roll out; pound it firmly with the floured rolling pin, turning the dough over occasionally until it is soft enough to be rolled. Roll it out until it is quite thin, about ⅛ to 3/16 inch thick.

Use a large round cookie cutter about 3½ inches in diameter (more or less). Start to cut the cookies at the outside edge of the dough and cut them so close to each other that they are touching. With a wide metal spatula transfer the cookies to the lined sheets, placing them ½ inch apart.

It is best not to reroll the scraps if possible because they would absorb additional flour and would become a bit tougher than otherwise. Here's a hint: Do not press the scraps together but, with smaller cutters, cut out as many smaller cookies as you can. Or use a knife and cut squares or triangles. There will still be some leftover scraps, but much less than otherwise. Reserve the scraps. Roll and cut the remaining dough. Then press all the scraps together, refrigerate if necessary (it probably will not be), roll it out, and cut with a knife or with cutters.

CINNAMON-SUGAR

1 tablespoon granulated sugar	Pinch of nutmeg
⅓ teaspoon cinnamon	

Mix the above ingredients and, with your fingertips, sprinkle over the cookies.

Bake for 10 to 13 minutes, reversing the sheets top to bottom and front to back as necessary to ensure even browning. When done, the cookies will be only sandy colored, slightly darker on the rims.

With a wide metal spatula transfer the cookies to racks to cool.

Store airtight. These last well if you stay away from them.

HALF MOON–SHAPED COOKIES

Here is an easy way to cut cookies into an attractive shape and have only a minimum of leftover scraps. (This procedure may be used for any recipe that calls for a cookie cutter. I am placing it here because I have often made the preceding Granny's Old-Fashioned Sugar Cookies this way.)

After rolling out the dough, use a large—or not large—round cookie cutter and, with the cutter, cut away a small (about 1 inch) section at the edge of the dough; that piece will be a scrap. Now move the cutter away from you and place it on the dough, forming a wide—or narrow—half moon. Cut the cookie and move the cutter again to cut the next cookie. In this way the outside curve of each cookie becomes the inside curve of the next cookie, and there are no scraps except along the edge of the rolled-out dough.

Savannah Crisps

On a recent trip to Savannah I heard raves about a cookie—a sweet cracker—called Brittlebread®; paper thin . . . golden brown . . . crisp and crunchy . . . mildly sweetened . . . its thinness is unusual and hard to believe, its flavor is buttery and delicious. Do you know lavosh? This is somewhat like a sweet lavosh, but more tender.

It saves time when making these if you have many cookie sheets. The dough is quickly and easily mixed in a food processor, or it can be made without a processor.

These keep well, they stay dry and crisp for weeks in our house, but handle with care; they are fragile.

20 6- TO 7-INCH WAFERS

4 ounces (1 stick) unsalted butter, cold
2¾ cups unsifted all-purpose flour
¼ cup granulated sugar
½ teaspoon salt

½ teaspoon baking soda
8 ounces unflavored yogurt (I use Dannon low fat)
Crystal sugar (see page 4) or additional
    granulated sugar

It is best to bake these on large cookie sheets, doubled (one placed on top of another); have the cookie sheets ready, unbuttered. Adjust as many racks to the middle area of the oven as you have double cookie sheets. Preheat the oven to 350 degrees.

Cut the butter into quarters lengthwise, and then across into ½-inch widths, and refrigerate.

To make this in a processor: Place the flour, sugar, salt, and baking soda in the processor bowl fitted with the metal chopping blade. Process on/off a few times to mix. Add the butter and process for about 5 seconds until the mixture resembles coarse crumbs. Then uncover, add the yogurt, and process for 10 to 15 seconds until the mixture holds together and clears the sides of the bowl.

To make this without a processor: Sift the dry ingredients into a mixing bowl. Add the butter and with a pastry blender cut it in until the mixture resembles coarse crumbs. Add the yogurt and stir well until thoroughly mixed.

Turn the mixture out onto a lightly floured surface and knead briefly for a few seconds. With your hands form the mixture into an even sausage-like roll 10 inches long. With a long-bladed knife cut the roll in half the long way. Then cut each half into 10 1-inch pieces. Cover the pieces with plastic wrap to prevent drying out.

One at a time, with your hands, roll each piece into a ball and then, on a lightly floured board with a lightly floured rolling pin, roll out the ball until it is paper thin, turning it over as necessary to keep both sides floured enough not to stick. Reflour the board and rolling pin as necessary. The rolled-out circle of dough should be about 7 inches in diameter. Do not worry about making the circle perfect.

Place the rounds of dough close to each other on an unbuttered cookie sheet. Two or three crackers will fit on each sheet, depending on its size.

Sprinkle the tops of the crackers with the crystal sugar or granulated sugar, using about a teaspoonful for each cracker.

To press the sugar into the crackers it is best to press down on it firmly with the heel of your hand and/or your fingertips until you are sure that the sugar is there to stay.

Bake the crackers until they are honey-colored, reversing the sheets front to back (and also top to bottom if you are baking on more than one rack) as necessary to ensure even browning. Do not underbake; adequate baking not only assures crisp cookies but it also improves the flavor. If you bake on only one rack at a time, the crackers might be done in about 10 to 12 minutes; if you bake on two or three racks at the same time, the crackers might take 14 to 16 minutes or longer.

Cool completely on the cookie sheets. Then store airtight in plastic freezer boxes or plastic bags.

VARIATION: *There is a less sweet variation of this that is made with a bit of coarse salt sprinkled on top instead of sugar. Make 1 or 2 as samples, using very little salt until you are sure of how much (or how little) to use. Serve this salted cracker plain or with soft cheese.*

Charleston Cheesecake Bars

When we recently visited Charleston, South Carolina, I found a wonderful cookie recipe in the News and Courier, *a Charleston newspaper that is the South's oldest daily paper. When we returned home I made the cookies before unpacking the suitcases. They have a crunchy, nutty oatmeal base, a lemon–cream cheese filling, and a layer of the crunchy oatmeal sprinkled over the top. They are unusual and wonderful, fancy enough for a party, but easy to make. These should be stored in the refrigerator.*

16 SMALL SQUARES

OATMEAL LAYER

1 cup sifted all-purpose flour
¼ teaspoon salt
½ teaspoon cinnamon
4 ounces (1 stick) unsalted butter

½ cup dark brown sugar, firmly packed
2 ounces (½ cup) pecans, toasted (see To Toast Pecans, page 7), chopped fine
1 cup quick-cooking (not "instant") rolled oats

Adjust a rack one-third up from the bottom of the oven and preheat the oven to 350 degrees. Line an 8-inch square cake pan with foil as follows. Turn the pan over, place a 12-inch square of foil shiny side down over the pan, press down on the sides and corners to shape the foil, remove the foil, turn the pan over again, place the foil in the pan, and press it gently into place. To butter the foil, place a piece of butter in the pan and place it in the oven to melt; then spread it with a pastry brush or with crumpled wax paper. Set the pan aside.

Sift together the flour, salt, and cinnamon and set aside. In the small bowl of an electric mixer beat the butter until soft, beat in the sugar, then on low speed add the sifted dry ingredients, the nuts, and the rolled oats. When well mixed remove and reserve 1 cup of the mixture.

Turn the remaining mixture into the prepared pan. With your fingertips spread it evenly over the bottom of the pan and then press firmly to make a compact layer.

Bake for 15 minutes.

CREAM CHEESE LAYER

Finely grated rind of 1 lemon
1 tablespoon lemon juice
8 ounces cream cheese

½ cup granulated sugar
1 egg
2 tablespoons sour cream

Combine the rind and juice and set aside.

In the small bowl of an electric mixer beat the cheese until it is soft. Beat in the sugar and then the egg and sour cream. When smooth, remove from the mixer and stir in the rind and juice.

Pour the mixture over the baked bottom crust (which may still be hot). Smooth the top.

Now, with your fingertips, sprinkle the reserved oatmeal mixture as evenly as you can to cover the cheese mixture completely (or almost completely). Then, with your fingertips, press the oatmeal mixture slightly into the cheese mixture so that none of it will remain loose, and also to smooth the top.

Bake for 25 minutes.

Set aside to cool completely.

Place the cooled cake in the freezer for about an hour. Then cover the top of the pan with a piece of foil, and fold down the sides. Cover the foil with a board or a cookie sheet, turn the pan and the board or cookie sheet over, remove the pan, peel off the foil lining, cover the cake with a board or cookie sheet, turn over again, and remove the remaining foil (it was put there only to catch any loose bits of topping that might fly around when the pan is turned over).

Now, to cut the cake. Use a strong, sharp knife. If the cheese mixture sticks to the blade, hold the blade under very hot running water before making each cut (cut with the hot, wet blade). If the cheese mixture squashes out even a bit, place the cake in the freezer again for 10 to 20 minutes (or as necessary) until it is firm enough.

Cut into quarters and then cut each quarter into 4 pieces. Cover and refrigerate until serving time. These may be frozen; if so, thaw in the refrigerator for an hour or two, or longer.

California Fruit Bars

We were living in La Jolla in a house right on the beach. It was a spectacular location with a picture-postcard view. But the thing I looked forward to the most each day was food shopping; the fruits

and vegetables bowled me over. Even when we didn't need anything I went just to look. In my favorite market, located in what had been a private home, and staffed by a crew of friendly young people, they sold these fruit bars to customers who arrived early enough; the bars sold out quickly. When I brought them some Chocolate Cheesecake Brownies they offered me this recipe.

These are butterless, wonderfully chewy, full of nuts and dried fruits, brown-sugar caramel-like, and delicious. They keep well, they travel well, they are good for mailing. As a matter of fact, they are good for everything.

ABOUT 32 BARS

1 cup assorted dried fruits, firmly packed (in La Jolla they use dates, figs, apricots, and raisins —see Variation)
4 eggs graded "large"
1 1-pound box (2¼ cups, packed) light brown sugar

¼ teaspoon salt
1 teaspoon vanilla extract
2 cups sifted all-purpose flour
7 ounces (2 cups) walnut halves or large pieces

Adjust a rack one-third up from the bottom of the oven and preheat the oven to 400 degrees. Line a 10½ by 15½ by 1-inch jelly-roll pan with foil as follows: Turn the pan over. Center a length of foil about 18 inches long shiny side down over the pan. With your hands fold down the sides and corners to shape the foil, remove it, turn the pan over again, put the foil in the pan, and press it firmly into place. To butter the foil, place a piece of butter in the pan and put it in the oven to melt. Then, with a pastry brush or crumpled wax paper, spread the melted butter over the foil and set aside.

With scissors cut the dried fruit (except the raisins) into small pieces. Then steam all the fruit by placing it in a vegetable steamer over shallow water (not touching the fruit) in a saucepan, covered, on high heat. When the water comes to a boil reduce the heat and let simmer for 15 minutes. Uncover and set aside. The fruit should be very soft and moist.

In a 2½- to 3-quart saucepan, beat the eggs with a beater or a whisk to mix well. Add the sugar and stir with a rubber spatula to mix.

Place over low-medium heat, stir and scrape the bottom and sides with the rubber spatula for 10 to 15 minutes until the sugar is dissolved; taste to test. Remove from the heat.

Add the salt, vanilla, and the flour 1 cup at a time. Beat briskly with a heavy whisk to incorporate the flour smoothly. Then stir in the fruit and mix well to be sure that the fruit is not lumped together. Now stir in the nuts.

Turn into the prepared pan and spread to distribute the fruit and nuts all over. Smooth the top. It will be a thin layer; be sure it is the same thickness all over (watch the corners).

Bake for 15 or 16 minutes until the top is a rich golden color and shiny. As it bakes, if the cake is not browning evenly reverse the pan front to back after 10 to 12 minutes.

Let stand until cool. Cover with a cookie sheet, turn the pan and the sheet over, remove the pan, and very gradually peel off the foil. Cover with wax paper and another cookie sheet and turn over again.

Slide the cake and the wax paper off onto a cutting board. With a ruler and toothpicks mark the cake into even sections. Use a long, sharp knife. These are chewy and they might want to stick to the knife (they will stick if you cut them too soon, but not if you wait awhile); if you have any trouble spray Pam on the blade.

I recommend that you wrap these individually in clear cellophane (see page 16) or wax paper or foil; plastic wrap is too hard to handle.

VARIATION: *The "1 cup assorted dried fruits" called for is a variable ingredient. I recently made these with 1 cup (8 ounces) dried apricots and 1 cup (8 ounces) dried figs. I cut both the apricots and the figs, with scissors, into slices—some rather coarse. The cookies were yummy. (Because of this larger amount of fruit the cake is thicker and takes a little longer to bake.)*

And I made California Pecan Bars: Omit the dried fruits and use 3 cups pecans, toasted (see To Toast Pecans, page 7) in place of the 2 cups of walnuts.

World War II Raisin Squares

This old recipe was called Depression Cake when we first used it because it was made during the Great Depression, when people could not afford expensive ingredients. And we made it during the war, when butter and eggs were rationed. We mailed it to men in the service, we ate it at home, we brought it to the local U.S.O., and it was always delicious. It is still delicious, even if you are rich or even if you have a dairy farm or are in the butter and egg business.

It is soft, spicy, moist, cakelike, and easy to make.

Incidentally, in Colorado they call this River Rafting Cake because it travels so well on rafting and camping trips (see Notes).

16 SQUARES

8 ounces (generous 1½ cups) dark raisins
2½ cups water
⅓ cup plus 1 tablespoon tasteless salad oil
¾ cup granulated sugar
1 teaspoon baking soda
1 cup sifted all-purpose flour
1 cup sifted all-purpose whole wheat flour
1 teaspoon cinnamon
1 teaspoon allspice

1 teaspoon cloves
½ teaspoon nutmeg
¼ teaspoon ground ginger
½ teaspoon salt
1 tablespoon unsweetened cocoa powder
    (preferably Dutch-process)
1 tablespoon powdered (not granular) instant
    coffee or espresso (see Notes)
Finely grated rind of 1 large lemon

Adjust a rack one-third up from the bottom of the oven and preheat the oven to 375 degrees. Line a 9 by 9 by 1¾-inch pan as follows: Turn the pan over, cover it with a 12-inch square of aluminum foil, press down the sides and corners of the foil to shape it, then remove the foil, turn the pan over again, place the foil in the pan, and press it into place. To butter the foil place a piece of butter in the pan and place it in the oven to melt, then spread it over the bottom and sides with a pastry brush or crumpled wax paper and set aside.

Put the raisins and the water in a 3- to 4-quart heavy saucepan. Bring to a boil, then reduce the heat, allowing the water to boil gently or simmer, and continue to cook, partly covered, for 15 to 20 minutes.

Pour the raisins and their water into a strainer set over a bowl.

Measure the water; you will want 1 cup of it. If you have less, add warm water; if you have more, discard excess. Pour the water into a large bowl. Stir in the oil, sugar, and baking soda (it will fizz). Set aside briefly.

Sift together both the flours, the cinnamon, allspice, cloves, nutmeg, ginger, salt, cocoa, and coffee.

Add the sifted ingredients to the water (which may still be warm), stir or whisk until smooth, then stir in the lemon rind and the drained raisins.

Turn into the prepared pan and smooth the top.

Bake for 30 to 35 minutes until the top springs back when it is pressed gently with a fingertip.

Cool in the pan for 10 to 15 minutes. Then cover with a rack, turn the pan and rack over, remove the pan, peel off the foil, cover with another rack, and turn over again, leaving the cake to cool right side up.

When cool, slide the cake onto a cutting board and cut it into portions.

If you wish, these may be wrapped individually in clear cellophane, wax paper, or aluminum foil. Or arrange them on a serving dish and cover the whole thing with plastic wrap until serving time.

NOTES: 1. *My friends in Colorado who make this like to take it right in the pan when they go camping. They do not line the pan with foil, they butter it and leave the cake in it until ready to serve.*

2. *If you do not have powdered instant coffee or espresso you can omit it from the recipe or you can use granular (or freeze-dried) coffee; stir it into the measured 1 cup of warm water after the raisins are drained.*

Johnny Appleseed Squares

Recently, during a beautiful drive through the Appalachian Mountains and along the spectacular Skyline Drive in Virginia, we picked up some local literature and learned about Jonathan Chapman, better known as Johnny Appleseed. During the 1800s Chapman personally planted a veritable forest of apple trees throughout Pennsylvania, Indiana, and Ohio. He later sold the grown trees to early settlers for a penny each—ah, those were the good old days.

At a local gift shop we bought some wonder-

ful apple cookies. I had only to ask for the recipe; they had had it typed and printed and were so happy I asked.

The recipe consists of a chewy and chunky oatmeal mixture that is spread thinly in a pan, covered with sliced apples, and topped with another layer of the oatmeal mixture. It is unusual for bar cookies to have a layer of juicy apples in the middle. They are extremely deliciously chewy, and easy and fun to make. They may be frozen.

16 TO 24 COOKIES

1 cup sifted all-purpose flour
½ teaspoon baking soda
Scant ½ teaspoon salt
1 teaspoon cinnamon
¼ teaspoon nutmeg or mace
1½ cups quick-cooking (not "instant") rolled oats
⅔ cup dark or light brown sugar, firmly packed

4 ounces (1 stick) unsalted butter, melted
1 egg graded "large" or "extra-large"
1 teaspoon vanilla extract
2 to 3 firm cooking apples (preferably Granny Smith or Jonathan)
½ cup pecans, toasted (see To Toast Pecans, page 7), cut or broken into medium-size pieces

Adjust a rack to the middle of the oven and preheat the oven to 350 degrees. Line a 9 by 1¾-inch square pan as follows: Turn the pan over, center a 12-inch square of foil shiny side down over the pan, fold down the sides and corners to shape the foil, remove the foil, turn the pan over again, place the foil in the pan, and, with a potholder, firmly press the foil into place. Butter the pan by placing a piece of butter in the pan and then placing it in the oven to melt. Spread the butter with a brush or a piece of crumpled wax paper. Place the prepared pan in the freezer (it is easier to spread a thin layer of dough in a frozen pan).

Sift together into a mixing bowl the flour, baking soda, salt, cinnamon, and nutmeg or mace. Stir in the oats and sugar. In a small bowl stir the butter, egg, and vanilla and mix into the oat mixture.

With your fingertips press half (1 cup) of the dough into the prepared pan; it will be a very thin layer. Set aside.

Place the remaining dough between two 12-inch lengths of wax paper and with a rolling pin roll over the top piece of paper to roll out the dough into a 9-inch square; it will be very thin. You may remove the top piece of paper, cut off pieces of the rolled-out dough, and place them where you need them, to make the square even. Slide a flat-sided cookie sheet under the dough and the wax paper and transfer it to the freezer for a few minutes.

Meanwhile, peel, quarter, and core the apples and cut each quarter lengthwise into 5 or 6 slices.

Place the apples in rows, each slice slightly overlapping another, to cover the bottom layer of dough. Sprinkle with the nuts.

Remove the rolled-out square of dough from the freezer, peel off the top piece of paper, turn the dough over the apples, remove the remaining paper, and press down on the edges of the dough.

Bake for 25 to 30 minutes, reversing the pan front to back once during baking to ensure even browning. About 10 minutes before the cake is done, if the top has not started to brown, raise the rack to a higher position to encourage browning.

Cool in the pan. Then cover with a rack or a cookie sheet, turn the pan and rack or sheet over, remove the pan, peel off the foil, cover the cake with a cookie sheet or a cutting board, and turn it over again, leaving the cake right side up.

It is best to chill the cake a bit before cutting it into squares, but this has a good texture and will cut well even if it is not chilled.

Cut into squares or bars.

Sycamore Cookies

This is an old recipe from deep in the heart of peanut country, Sycamore, Georgia, from a friend of my husband's who is a peanut farmer and a marvelous cook.

The cookies are quick and easy to make. They are thin, crisp, buttery, irresistible brown-sugar peanut cookies. Serve them with tea or coffee, or alongside vanilla ice cream.

16 LARGE OR 32 SMALL COOKIES

1 cup salted peanuts
1 cup sifted all-purpose flour
¼ teaspoon baking soda
½ teaspoon cinnamon

4 ounces (1 stick) unsalted butter
1 teaspoon vanilla extract
½ cup dark brown sugar, firmly packed
1 egg, beaten

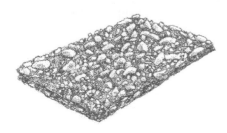

Adjust a rack to the middle of the oven and preheat the oven to 325 degrees. Butter a 10½ by 15½-inch jelly-roll pan and place it in the freezer. (It will be easier to spread the very thin layer of dough in a frozen pan.)

Chop the peanuts fine (do not grind them or powder them); to do this in a food processor place them in the processor bowl fitted with the metal chopping blade and process on/off as briefly as possible 10 times (it should take less than 10 seconds); set aside.

Sift together the flour, baking soda, and cinnamon and set aside. In the small bowl of an electric mixer beat the butter until soft. Add the vanilla and sugar and beat to mix. Then mix in 2 tablespoons of the egg (save the remaining beaten egg to use below), the sifted dry ingredients, and half of the chopped peanuts (reserve the remaining chopped peanuts).

Place the batter by large spoonfuls all over the frozen pan and with the bottom of a spoon spread it to cover the pan as well as you can. It will be a very thin layer and it might have a few bare spots.

Drizzle the remaining beaten egg over the top and with a brush spread it all over. Sprinkle the remaining peanuts over the top.

Bake for 25 minutes, reversing the pan once front to back after about 15 minutes. The top will be nicely but lightly browned and will feel soft to the touch; it will become crisp when cool.

Let stand for about 5 minutes only until just firm enough to cut. With a small, sharp knife cut into 16 large oblongs and immediately, while they are warm, remove the cookies from the pan with a wide metal spatula. Either place them on a rack to cool or, if you want smaller cookies, place them on a board and cut the oblongs in half; then place on a rack to cool.

Store airtight.

Raisin Pillows

This is an old-fashioned Early American cookie that I have updated and simplified a bit by using a food processor. You will make a thick and chewy raisin filling (see Notes) and a deliciously buttery, crisp but tender dough somewhat like sugar cookies. After the filling and the dough are both chilled for an hour or so, the dough is rolled out, cut into rounds, sandwiched together with the raisin filling, and baked. Making these will keep you busy for a few hours; it is fun, gratifying, and the cookies are something special.

24 TO 36 COOKIES

RAISIN FILLING

1 large deep-colored orange
½ cup granulated sugar
10 ounces (2 cups) dark raisins
⅔ cup orange juice (or partly juice and partly water)

1 tablespoon plus 1 teaspoon lemon juice
Optional: 2 tablespoons dark rum
1 tablespoon butter

312

With a vegetable parer remove the thin orange-colored rind from the orange. Place the sugar and the pared rind in the bowl of a food processor fitted with the metal chopping blade. Process for a few minutes until the rind is cut into small pieces. Add the raisins and without waiting, with the machine running, add the juice (or juice and water) through the feed tube and—now be very careful—process for only 5 to 10 seconds, just until the raisins are chopped coarse; they should not be in too-small pieces and should definitely not be processed until ground. If the mixture looks like large-egg caviar it is just right.

In a 2½- to 3-quart saucepan stir the raisin mixture frequently over high heat until the sugar melts and the mixture comes to a boil. Then adjust the heat to allow the mixture to boil slowly and stir occasionally for about 15 minutes until the mixture thickens, but do not overcook; the mixture will thicken more as it cools. Add the lemon juice and the optional rum, boil for about 3 more minutes, remove from the heat, add the butter, stir to melt, cool to room temperature, and then chill in the refrigerator or freezer.

COOKIE DOUGH

3 cups sifted all-purpose flour
1 tablespoon double-acting baking powder
¼ teaspoon salt
8 ounces (2 sticks) unsalted butter

2 teaspoons vanilla extract
1 cup granulated sugar
1 egg graded "large"
⅓ cup milk

Sift together the flour, baking powder, and salt and set aside. In the large bowl of an electric mixer beat the butter until soft. Beat in the vanilla and the sugar. Add the egg and then, on low speed, gradually add the milk and the sifted dry ingredients, scraping the bowl as necessary with a rubber spatula until thoroughly mixed.

The dough will be soft and sticky. Transfer it to a large piece of wax paper or foil. Fold over the ends of the paper or foil to enclose the dough, or cover it with another long piece of wax paper or foil. Press down on the dough to flatten until it is about 1 inch thick. Slide a cookie sheet under the package of dough and transfer it to the freezer for 30 to 60 minutes, or to the refrigerator for a longer time; it must be chilled enough so you can peel away the wax paper or foil without it sticking to the dough.

Before baking, adjust two racks to divide the oven into thirds and pre-heat the oven to 350 degrees. Line cookie sheets with aluminum foil shiny side up.

Generously flour a pastry cloth and a rolling pin.

Cut off about one third of the dough and replace the remainder in the freezer or refrigerator. On the floured cloth, turn the piece of dough over to flour both sides, pound it lightly with the rolling pin to soften it a bit, and then roll it out to ⅛-inch thickness. It must not be any thinner; a little thicker will not hurt, but if it is thinner the cookies will not hold together.

With a round cookie cutter measuring about 2⅜ inches in diameter cut out cookies; start cutting at the outside edge of the dough, flour the cutter as necessary, and cut the cookies as close to one another as possible.

Arrange half of the cookies 2 inches apart (these spread) on the foil-lined sheets. (Leftover scraps may be pressed together and rechilled before rolling—be sure to chill this thoroughly or the dough will absorb too much flour and will not be as tender.)

Place a scant teaspoonful (more or less depending on the diameter of the cookies) of the raisin filling in the center of each cookie; keep the filling away from the edges. Then top each cookie with another round of the dough (it is best to use a small metal spatula to transfer the dough). With your fingertips gently press the edges of the cookies together; the top cookie will not reach out to the rim of the bottom cookie—it is OK, they will blend together when baked and the filling will not run out of the sides.

Now, dip the prongs of a fork in flour and with the back of the prongs press down gently (not too hard) all around the rims, to seal the tops and bottoms together and to make a slightly ridged design around the rim.

Repeat directions to shape all the cookies.

Bake two sheets at a time for about 20 minutes, reversing the sheets top to bottom and front to back as necessary to ensure even browning. Bake until the cookies are an attractive golden color. Do not underbake; these should not be too pale. (If they bake until golden brown the flavor of the browned butter is delicious.)

With a wide metal spatula transfer to a rack to cool.

NOTES: 1. *To make these without a processor, grate the orange rind on a grater, chop the raisins on a board with a long, heavy, sharp knife, and then just mix the rind, sugar, raisins, and orange juice.*

2. Leftover Raisin Filling makes a delicious spread with toast and butter.

Mrs. L.B.F.'s Moonrocks

These are large and thick spice cookies with crisp, chewy edges and semisoft centers. Real old-fashioned "down home" cookies for filling cookie jars. Lady Bird says that "children love them." In our home, and surrounding territory, everyone loves them. While they are baking they perfume the house with an irresistible sweet and spicy aroma.

48 LARGE COOKIES

4 cups sifted all-purpose flour
1 teaspoon baking soda
⅛ teaspoon salt
1 teaspoon cloves
1 teaspoon cinnamon
1 teaspoon allspice
1 teaspoon nutmeg
8 ounces (2 sticks) unsalted butter
1½ cups granulated sugar

3 eggs graded "large"
½ cup dark corn syrup
3½ ounces (1 cup, packed) shredded coconut
    (sweetened or unsweetened)
5 ounces (1 cup) raisins (dark, light, or half of each)
8 ounces (1 cup, packed) dates (each date cut into
    about 4 pieces)
7 ounces (2 cups) walnuts, broken into large pieces

Adjust two racks to divide the oven into thirds and preheat the oven to 350 degrees. Cut aluminum foil to fit cookie sheets.

Sift together the flour, baking soda, salt, cloves, cinnamon, allspice, and nutmeg and set aside.

In the large bowl of an electric mixer beat the butter until it is soft. Beat in the sugar. Then add the eggs one at a time, beating until incorporated after each addition. Beat in the corn syrup. On low speed add the sifted dry ingredients and beat until incorporated.

Remove from the mixer and with a large, heavy wooden spoon or spatula stir in the coconut, raisins, dates, and nuts.

Use a well-rounded tablespoon of the dough for each cookie. Place the mounds of dough 2 inches apart on the foil shiny side up.

Slide a cookie sheet (with only one raised rim) under the foil. Bake two sheets at a time, reversing the sheets top to bottom and front to back as necessary to ensure even browning. Bake for 18 to 20 minutes until the cookies are golden all over.

With a wide metal spatula transfer the cookies to racks to cool.

Store airtight.

Old-Fashioned Spiced Pecan Cookies

These are dark, thick, and semisoft, sharply spiced, gingery/peppery/wheaty. They are wonderful for a cookie jar, lunch box, or a satisfying snack at any time, although somehow I think of these as winter rather than summer cookies.

The dough must be well chilled before it is shaped (rolled into balls between your hands) and baked.

32 TO 36 RATHER LARGE COOKIES

Optional: 2 teaspoons instant coffee
¼ cup boiling water
1 cup sifted all-purpose flour
1 teaspoon baking soda
1 teaspoon cinnamon
1½ teaspoons ground ginger
¾ teaspoon cloves
½ teaspoon salt
1 teaspoon finely ground white pepper
½ teaspoon nutmeg

4 ounces (1 stick) unsalted butter
1 cup dark brown sugar, firmly packed
2 eggs graded "large," "extra-large," or "jumbo"
¼ cup dark molasses
1½ cups sifted all-purpose whole wheat flour
6 ounces (1½ cups) pecans, toasted (see To Toast Pecans, page 7), cut or broken into medium-size pieces
32 to 36 additional pecan halves, toasted (as above)

Stir the optional coffee into the boiling water and set aside to cool; if you do not use the coffee, simply measure ¼ cup of room-temperature water and set aside. Sift together the all-purpose flour, baking soda, cinnamon, ginger, cloves, salt, pepper, and nutmeg and set aside.

In the large bowl of an electric mixer beat the butter until soft. Beat in the sugar. Add the eggs one at a time and beat to mix after each addition. Beat in the molasses and coffee or water (the mixture will appear curdled—it is OK). On low speed beat in the sifted flour mixture and then the whole wheat flour, and beat until incorporated.

Remove from the mixer and stir in the 1½ cups of pecans.

Transfer to a smaller bowl (or leave it in the mixer bowl, if you wish), cover airtight, and refrigerate until firm enough to handle, preferably overnight.

Before baking, adjust two racks to divide the oven into thirds and preheat the oven to 350 degrees. Line cookie sheets with aluminum foil shiny side up.

Place a long piece of foil on the counter next to the sink. With a tablespoon, spoon out about 10 or 12 mounds of the dough, each one a well-rounded tablespoonful (they may be placed right next to one another). Return the remaining dough to the refrigerator.

Wet your hands with cold water; shake them off but do not dry them (they should be damp and cold). Pick up a mound of dough, roll it between your hands into a ball, and place it on a foil-lined sheet. Continue to shape the balls and place them 2½ to 3 inches apart (7 balls on a 15½ by 12-inch cookie sheet).

Place a pecan half on top of each cookie and press it down slightly to flatten the cookie only a little bit (the cookies should remain rather thick).

Bake two sheets at a time for about 15 minutes, reversing the sheets front to back and top to bottom once during baking to ensure even browning. To test for doneness, press the top of a cookie gently with your fingertip; when the cookies just barely spring back, they are done.

With a wide metal spatula transfer the cookies to racks to cool.

Peanut Butter Icebox Cookies

Crisp, plain, crunchy, sandy; like a peanut butter shortbread. Divine to serve with ice cream or tea or coffee. A jar of these makes a wonderful gift.

The dough must be well chilled before the cookies are sliced and baked.

40 TO 48 COOKIES

2 cups unsifted all-purpose flour
¼ teaspoon baking soda
¼ teaspoon cinnamon
4 ounces (1 stick) unsalted butter
⅓ cup smooth peanut butter

1 teaspoon vanilla extract
⅛ teaspoon almond extract
⅓ cup granulated sugar
⅓ cup dark brown sugar, firmly packed
1 egg graded "large"

Sift together the flour, baking soda, and cinnamon and set aside.

In the large bowl of an electric mixer beat the butter and peanut butter until soft and smooth. Add the vanilla and almond extracts and both sugars and beat until incorporated. Beat in the egg. Then, on low speed, add the dry ingredients and beat until thoroughly mixed.

Turn the mixture out onto a work surface, knead it a bit, and then "push off" the dough as follows. Form the dough into a ball. Start at the farther end of the dough and, using the heel of your hand, push off small pieces (about 2 tablespoons), pushing against the work surface and away from you. Continue until all the dough has been pushed off. Re-form the dough and push it off (or "break" it) again. Re-form the dough. (It will feel like clay.)

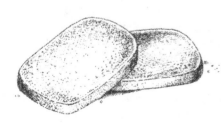

316

Form the dough into a long round shape or a long oblong. Either way, the shape should be 10 to 12 inches long and 1¾ to 2 inches in diameter.

Wrap in plastic wrap and refrigerate for several hours until firm (or longer if you wish—even when it is frozen it will not be too firm to slice), or place the wrapped dough in the freezer for 45 to 60 minutes until firm.

When you are ready to bake, adjust two racks to divide the oven into thirds and preheat the oven to 350 degrees. Line cookie sheets with aluminum foil or baking pan liner paper. Slice the firm dough into ¼-inch slices. Place them ½ to 1 inch apart on the lined sheets.

Bake for 18 to 20 minutes until lightly colored (darker on the rims), reversing the sheets top to bottom and front to back once during baking to ensure even browning.

With a wide metal spatula transfer the cookies to racks to cool.

8-Layer Cookies

Icebox cookies, thin and crisp, made up of contrasting layers of dark and light doughs. Too pretty to eat. Force yourself—they're delicious. These are the ones to make for a fancy party.

40 COOKIES

2¼ cups sifted all-purpose flour
¾ cup cornstarch, unsifted
½ teaspoon double-acting baking powder
½ teaspoon salt
9 ounces (2¼ sticks) unsalted butter
1 teaspoon vanilla extract

1 cup minus 2 tablespoons granulated sugar
4 yolks from eggs graded "large"
½ teaspoon almond extract
¼ cup unsweetened cocoa powder (preferably Dutch-process)
½ teaspoon powdered (not granular) instant coffee

Sift together the flour, cornstarch, baking powder, and salt and set aside.

In the large bowl of an electric mixer beat the butter until soft. Beat in the vanilla and then the sugar, beating until completely mixed. Add the yolks one at a time, beating until incorporated after each addition. On low speed gradually add the sifted dry ingredients and beat until incorporated (it will be a thick mixture).

Remove and set aside half (1½ cups plus 2 tablespoons) of the dough.

Beat the almond extract into the remaining dough until incorporated. Remove the almond-flavored dough from the mixing bowl, and return the other half of the dough to the bowl. On low speed gradually add the cocoa and the powdered coffee and beat until incorporated. Remove this chocolate dough from the mixing bowl; if it is not a perfectly even color, knead it with your hands.

With your hands, form each piece of the dough into a 5-inch square, 1 inch thick. Wrap the squares in wax paper or plastic wrap and refrigerate for about 1 hour, or freeze for less time until barely firm.

Cut each square into quarters, making 2½-inch squares.

Then, on a lightly floured pastry cloth with a lightly floured rolling pin, roll each square of dough out slowly and carefully until it measures 10 by 4 inches. Make the edges as even as possible; you will not be able to make them perfectly even—it is OK, they will be trimmed later. As each piece is rolled, transfer it to a piece of wax paper (as large as the rolled-out dough or slightly larger); the easiest way is to roll them the long way over the rolling pin, and then unroll them onto the wax paper. The pieces of rolled-out dough (each on a piece of wax paper) can be stacked on top of each other. Slide a flat-sided cookie sheet (or anything else flat) under the pile and transfer them all to the freezer for 15 to 20 minutes, until the dough is firm enough to handle but is not brittle. Remove them from the freezer.

Place 1 piece of the dough in front of you on a work surface. Brush the top lightly with cold tap water. Place a piece of the other color dough on top of the wet one. Press down gently all over the surface of the top dough to seal the pieces together. Brush the top with water again and cover with a contrasting piece, press down, wet, et cetera. Continue to stack the pieces as evenly as possible, alternating the colors.

Wrap the whole pile of 8 layers in plastic wrap and refrigerate for a few hours or overnight. Or freeze briefly until firm enough to slice very neatly; the dough should be refrigerated but not frozen when it is sliced.

Before baking, adjust two racks to divide the oven into thirds, and preheat the oven to 375 degrees. Line cookie sheets with aluminum foil, shiny side up.

Unwrap the dough. With a very sharp knife carefully trim one narrow end. (At this stage it seems as though the thing to do is to trim the two long sides also, but actually I have much better results and make neater cookies if I slice them and then trim the uneven ends.) With a ruler and the tip of a small sharp knife mark the dough every ¼ inch. Then, carefully, slice a few cookies, trim the ends individually, and transfer the cookies to the lined sheets, placing them about ½ inch apart. (Reserve all the scraps of dough.)

Bake two sheets at a time for 15 to 20 minutes, reversing the sheets top to bottom and front to back as necessary to ensure even browning. Bake until the cookies are lightly colored on the edges, paler in the centers. Watch them carefully; these are too beautiful to chance over-baking.

With a wide metal spatula, transfer the cookies to racks to cool.

The trimmed edges that you reserved may be pressed together to make attractive marbleized cookies. On a lightly floured pastry cloth with a lightly floured rolling pin, roll out the marbleized dough to ¼-inch thickness, cut out cookies with a knife or with a cookie cutter, and bake as above.

Kansas Cookies

Margie McGlachlin of Sedgwick, Kansas, won first place in a Kansas State Fair with these very unusual and wonderfully delicious cookies. They are soft, moist, and chewy, and they stay that way.

(In a recent poll the results showed that most Americans' favorite cookies are soft and moist.)

There is a lemon filling similar to lemon cheese, an English spread, mixed with a generous amount of shredded coconut. The cookie dough has molasses and cinnamon; it is all a luscious combination. You will find making these is a bit of a challenge and a lot of fun. The dough and the filling can both be made a day ahead if you wish. This recipe is an adaptation of the original.

40 COOKIES

COOKIE DOUGH

2¼ cups sifted all-purpose flour
½ teaspoon baking soda
¼ teaspoon salt
1 teaspoon cinnamon

4 ounces (1 stick) unsalted butter
1 cup granulated sugar
1 egg graded "large"
¼ cup light molasses

Sift together the flour, baking soda, salt, and cinnamon and set aside.

In the large bowl of an electric mixer beat the butter until it is soft. Add the sugar and beat until mixed. Beat in the egg and then the molasses. (The mixture will appear curdled—it is OK.) On low speed gradually add the sifted dry ingredients and beat, scraping the bowl with a rubber spatula, until the mixture holds together and is smooth. Remove the bowl from the mixer.

Turn the dough out onto a piece of wax paper about 15 inches long. Fold up the long sides of the paper and with your hands form the dough into a fat sausage shape about 12 inches long, the same thickness all over.

Bring up the long sides of the paper to wrap the dough and carefully transfer it to the refrigerator to chill for at least 2 hours or longer. (To save time, it may be placed in the freezer for about 15 minutes and then transferred to the refrigerator for an hour.) This will be much easier to work with if it is thoroughly chilled (but not frozen); at room temperature it is too soft.

Meanwhile, make the filling.

LEMON COCONUT FILLING

2 eggs graded "large"
½ cup granulated sugar
¼ teaspoon salt
Finely grated rind of 2 lemons

¼ cup lemon juice
3½ ounces (1 cup, packed) shredded coconut (may be sweetened or unsweetened)

Place the eggs in the top of a small double boiler off the heat and beat them with a small wire whisk until thoroughly mixed. Gradually beat in the sugar and then the salt, the lemon rind, and lemon juice.

Place over shallow hot water on moderate heat and stir and scrape the sides constantly with a rubber spatula for 7 to 8 minutes until the mixture thickens to the consistency of a soft mayonnaise.

Remove the top of the double boiler and mix in the coconut. Set aside to cool. (The dough must be cold when you use it, but the filling can be cold or at room temperature.)

To shape and bake the cookies: Adjust a rack to the middle of the oven and preheat the oven to 350 degrees. Have ready several unbuttered cookie sheets.

Cut the dough crossways into equal quarters.

Lightly flour a large work surface and transfer one piece of the cold dough to the floured surface. Return the remaining pieces of dough to the refrigerator. With your hands elongate the cold dough's sausage shape. Then, roll it back and forth under your fingers on the floured surface into a very thin sausage shape 15 inches long. Roll it toward you a few inches in order to reflour the surface under the dough. Then roll it back onto the floured surface. With your fingers carefully press down on the dough to flatten it a bit. Or roll over it with a rolling pin until it is 3 inches wide, still 15 inches long. The edges should not be thicker than the rest, they do not have to be perfectly straight.

You have a generous cupful of the filling. Therefore, you will use a slightly generous ¼ cupful of the filling for each piece of dough. Measure it in a graded ¼-cup measuring cup.

To make a narrow strip of the filling down the length of the rolled-out dough, use a small spoon and spoon out scant ½ teaspoonfuls just barely touching each other down the middle of the dough. If you use too much filling in any one spot you will not be able to close the sides of the dough over the filling, and you will not have enough to go around. It is not necessary to stay away from the narrow ends; the filling does not run.

Now, to raise the long sides of the dough and have them meet over the top of the filling, here are a few hints. First, work quickly before the dough becomes too soft to handle. Second, use either a long, narrow spatula or a wide metal pancake turner to help lift the dough. The aim is to get the two sides to meet on the top and overlap about ½ inch. It is not necessary to wet the dough to make it stick to itself. And it is a waste of time to fuss too much to try to make this very neat, because it runs a bit (just enough to camouflage any irregularities) during baking. Don't worry about little cracks in the dough.

With a ruler score the strip into 1½-inch lengths. With a sharp knife cut the strip at the scored lines and, using a metal pancake turner, transfer the cookies to an unbuttered cookie sheet, placing them topside up or down about 1½ inches apart.

Bake one sheet at a time for 15 minutes, reversing the sheet front to back once during baking to ensure even browning. When they are done they will just barely begin to darken and the tops will crack a bit. (Everything's under control.)

Use a wide metal spatula to transfer the cookies to a rack to cool.

Shape and bake the remaining dough and filling.

Store airtight.

Bow Ties

These were made in Poland, Rumania, Hungary, Germany, and other Middle-European countries. When so many people from those countries emigrated to America and brought their recipes for Bow Ties, they became a standard item at almost all Jewish-American bakeries. They are very popular, but somehow I think that very few people, if any, make them at home. Why? They are as simple as can be, fun to make, quick and easy. They are plain, airy, crisp, wonderful with tea, coffee or wine.

This recipe calls for powdered ammonium carbonate, a leavening agent that gives the cookies an especially light texture. For the last few years it has become more and more difficult to buy ammonium carbonate. However, I found it at H. Roth & Son, 1577 First Avenue, New York, New York 10028. They will fill mail orders. It comes in a 2-ounce jar labeled "ammonia crystals," and it is powdered. It lasts well, tightly closed, away from the heat and light. I have had a jar for 6 months and it is still alive and well. Don't be concerned by the ammonia odor, especially during baking; it will not affect the cookies.
You will need baking pan liner paper.

34 LARGE COOKIES

1 teaspoon whole anise seeds
2½ cups sifted all-purpose flour
½ teaspoon salt
1 teaspoon powdered ammonium carbonate
2 tablespoons granulated sugar
5 eggs graded "large"
½ cup tasteless salad oil
½ teaspoon vanilla extract
¼ teaspoon almond extract
Additional flour
Additional granulated sugar

Coarsely crush the anise seeds with a mortar and pestle, or whirl them for just a few seconds in a blender (a processor does not do anything to them). Set aside.

Sift together the flour, salt, ammonium carbonate, and the 2 tablespoons of sugar and set aside.

Open 4 of the eggs into a 1-cup glass measuring cup. Separate the remaining egg, add the yolk to the measuring cup, and add a bit of the white if necessary for the eggs to reach the 1-cup line. (You will not need the remaining egg white for this recipe.)

Place the eggs in the small bowl of an electric mixer, beat to mix, add the oil and vanilla and almond extracts, and beat again to mix.

Gradually, on low speed, mix in about half of the sifted dry ingredients. Beat at high speed for about 5 minutes; the mixture will crawl up on the beaters—adjust the speed as necessary. Then stir in the remaining dry ingredients—the mixture will be thick, sticky, and gooey.

Spread a generous layer of additional flour on a rather large piece of aluminum foil, turn the dough out onto the flour, sift a bit of flour lightly over the top, and let stand, uncovered, for 30 minutes.

Meanwhile, adjust two racks to divide the oven into thirds and preheat the oven to 350 degrees. Line two large cookie sheets with baking pan liner paper and set aside.

Now spread a thick layer of the additional granulated sugar on a large board or on a pastry cloth.

The dough will still be sticky; pick it up with your fingers (with only the flour that clings to it—no more) and transfer it to the sugared surface. Sprinkle sugar over the top of the dough too.

With a rolling pin roll out the dough, sugaring it more as necessary, into an oblong about 12 by 6 inches, ½ inch thick.

With a long, sharp knife cut the dough into strips 6 inches long and

¾ inch wide. If the knife sticks to the dough, turn the blade in the sugar to coat it. Next, cut the strips into 3-inch lengths, cutting them a few at a time with one cut.

Pick up a strip by its ends and twist the ends once in opposite directions, then place the cookies about 1 inch apart on the prepared cookie sheets. Continue to cut and shape all of the cookies.

Bake for 25 to 30 minutes, reversing the sheets top to bottom and front to back as necessary to ensure even browning. Bake only until the cookies are pale golden.

With a wide metal spatula transfer the cookies to a rack to cool. Store airtight.

Cinnamon Crisps

Would you believe this? The pastry is made with ice cream—ice cream, melted butter, and flour— just mixed together. It is a real "Believe It or Not." My guess is that someone was out of milk, sugar, and vanilla (maybe even eggs), but he or she had vanilla ice cream, leftover and melted. And whoever-it-was was a creative and inventive cook. And that is how a new recipe was born. A recipe that tastes different from any other. Amazing.

48 SMALL COOKIES

4 ounces (1 stick) unsalted butter
½ cup vanilla ice cream

Pinch of salt
1 cup unsifted all-purpose flour

Place the butter in a heavy 6- to 8-cup saucepan over moderate heat to melt. Remove the pan from the heat, add the ice cream, stir with a wooden spatula until melted, add the salt and flour, and stir briskly with the wooden spatula until the mixture forms a ball and comes away from the sides of the saucepan.

Either in the saucepan or in a bowl, chill the mixture briefly in the freezer or refrigerator for 10 to 20 minutes. Then stir again to incorporate any butter that has separated. Divide the mixture in half (each half will be ½ cup plus a slightly rounded tablespoon of the pastry). Wrap each half in plastic wrap, form each piece into a flattened square, and refrigerate for a few hours or overnight. Or to save time, freeze the wrapped pastry until it is firm enough to be rolled out. (However, you might find it slightly easier to roll and handle this dough if it is refrigerated overnight or at least for several hours.)

FILLING

About 2 tablespoons unsalted butter, melted
¼ cup granulated sugar ⎱
2 teaspoons cinnamon ⎰ mixed together

Scant ½ cup currants
1 cup walnuts, chopped fine

Roll one half of the dough at a time, leaving the other half in the refrigerator until you are ready to use it.

On a lightly floured pastry cloth with a lightly floured rolling pin, roll out the dough until it is paper thin. During rolling, turn the dough over a few times to keep both sides lightly floured. Keep the shape as square as you can. Roll the dough into a 12-inch square.

Brush the rolled-out dough with half of the melted butter, stopping about ½ inch from the farther side. Sprinkle with half (2 tablespoons and 1 teaspoon) of the cinnamon-sugar, keeping it ½ inch away from the farther side too. Sprinkle with half of the currants and half of the nuts, all on top of the butter and cinnamon-sugar, leaving the ½-inch strip.

With your fingertip pat a bit of cold water on the uncovered ½-inch end. Then, using the pastry cloth to help roll up the dough, start the roll at the edge closest to you and roll toward the wet, uncovered end. Roll it tight. After the first few turns it will not be necessary to use the pastry cloth, just roll the dough with your fingers. When it is all rolled up (you will have a roll 12 inches long and about 1 inch in diameter), place a piece of plastic wrap alongside the length of the roll. Roll the pastry over onto the plastic, wrap it, and place it on a tray or cookie sheet.

Repeat with the remaining ingredients. Refrigerate the rolls for 5 or 6 hours or overnight before slicing the cookies and baking them (when I am impatient or in a hurry I have placed the rolls in the freezer for about 30 minutes and then sliced them).

If you are planning ahead, you may freeze the rolls for weeks and then refrigerate overnight before slicing.

To bake: Adjust an oven rack to the middle of the oven and preheat the oven to 350 degrees. (Oven temperature is extremely important for these; if the oven is any hotter the cookies will burn before they dry out enough.)

Unwrap a roll of the pastry. With a very sharp knife trim the ends and carefully cut the roll into ½-inch slices. Place them on an unbuttered cookie sheet about ½ inch apart.

Bake for about 25 minutes, reversing the sheet front to back once during baking until the cookies are lightly colored all over (possibly a bit paler right in the center)—these must be crisp all the way through when cool. If the cookies are a bit thicker or thinner it will affect the baking time.

With a wide metal spatula transfer the cookies to a rack to cool.

Store airtight.

Fresh Fruit

Vermont Baked Apples

I had heard about the Phoenix in Sugarbush Village, Warren, Vermont. A friend had told me, "Next time you leave Florida, if you go north, don't miss their chocolate desserts. They have dozens of them—all wonderful."

So when we next went north, I remembered the Phoenix. We drove to a perfectly gorgeous area in the mountains of Vermont, to a ski village. The chocolate desserts were everything I had heard. We had some of each—literally dozens. All carefully and beautifully made by Peter Sussman,

the owner. We had a wonderful and deliciously good time.

When we left we took away gallons of maple syrup and a small, prized collection of local maple syrup recipes. This is one.

The apples will be mildly spiced, shiny, dark, crunchy, and chewy; made with both honey and maple syrup. Serve these with Honey Ricotta Cream (see page 360). Divine! Wonderful for a brunch or for any casual meal.

6 PORTIONS

⅓ cup pitted dates, firmly packed
¼ cup light honey
¼ cup pecans, cut into small pieces
Finely grated rind of 1 large lemon
¼ cup graham cracker crumbs
1 teaspoon cinnamon

¼ teaspoon nutmeg
¼ teaspoon ground ginger
6 large baking apples (preferably Rome Beauty)
2 ounces (½ stick) unsalted butter, melted
⅔ cup maple syrup
⅓ cup boiling water

Adjust a rack one-third up from the bottom of the oven and preheat the oven to 400 degrees. Have ready a shallow baking dish that measures about 11 by 8 inches.

With scissors cut the dates into small pieces (¼ to ½ inch). In a small bowl combine the dates with the honey, pecans, and grated lemon rind. Set aside.

In a small bowl combine the crumbs with the cinnamon, nutmeg, and ginger and set aside.

Wash the apples. With a vegetable parer peel the top third of each apple. With an apple corer remove the cores from the stem end to about three quarters of the way down; do not cut through the bottoms.

With a pastry brush, brush the peeled part of the apples with the melted butter and, after you brush each one, roll it in the crumbs to coat the buttered part. You will have some leftover butter and leftover crumbs; reserve them.

Place the apples in the baking dish. Then, with a small spoon, fill the apples with the date mixture. Using your fingertips, press it firmly down into the holes in the apples; then mound some of the mixture on top of the apples. All the remaining crumb mixture should be sprinkled over the apples and/or placed in the baking dish. Pour the reserved butter into the dish over the crumbs.

Pour the maple syrup and boiling water in the baking dish around the apples over the crumbs and butter.

Bake for about 30 minutes. Baste several times with the maple syrup mixture, or spoon it over the apples. Whichever, basting or spooning, it should be done slowly and gently with a light touch in order not to dislodge the crumb mixture from the apples.

Test the apples with a cake tester and bake only until they are just barely tender. By the time the apples are done, the sauce should be thick and darkly caramelized.

Set aside and serve warm (warm, these are luscious) or at room temperature or refrigerated (refrigerated, the filling and sauce will thicken and become caramel-candylike and fabulous).

Serve with ice-cold Honey Ricotta Cream (see page 360).

It is best to serve the apples and any of the date and nut mixture on flat dessert plates (preferably rather wide plates) with a small, sharp knife and a fork and spoon for each serving. And pass the Honey Ricotta Cream with a large spoon or a ladle; you will be surprised at how fast this cream disappears.

American Beauty Apples

These apples are basted while they bake, with puréed frozen raspberries flavored with honey and cassis. The apples become the color of American Beauty roses.

The apples will be slightly tart; if you do not enjoy slightly tart desserts, add another 1 to 2 spoons of honey or add 1 to 2 spoons of sugar.

This is best during the winter, when Rome Beauty apples are available.

6 PORTIONS

2 10-ounce packages frozen red raspberries in syrup, thawed
3 tablespoons honey

2 tablespoons crème de cassis
6 large baking apples (preferably Rome Beauty)

Adjust a rack to the middle of the oven and preheat the oven to 350 degrees. You will need a baking dish about 8 by 11 by 2 inches, or any shallow baking dish that will hold the apples comfortably, with a bit of room around each one. Do not butter the dish.

In a food processor, a blender, or a food mill purée the raspberries with their syrup and work the mixture through a fine strainer resting over a bowl (do not use a narrow fine strainer—it will take too long). Stir the honey and cassis into the purée and set aside.

Wash the apples and remove the cores with an apple corer, but do not cut all the way down; leave the bottoms of the apples intact. Then, with a vegetable parer, remove the peel from the top halves of the apples. Place the apples in the baking dish.

Pour the raspberry mixture into and over and around the apples. Bake uncovered. With a bulb baster, or with a spoon, baste or spoon the raspberry mixture over the apples about every 10 minutes. Bake until a toothpick inserted into the apples lets you know they are just barely tender; it should take about 1 hour.

Remove from the oven and set aside to cool, still basting or spooning the raspberry mixture frequently over the apples while they cool. By the time they are cool there will be only a few spoonfuls of the raspberry mixture (it thickens and it evaporates).

Refrigerate.

Serve the apples on chilled flat dessert plates with a knife and fork, pouring whatever bit of raspberry syrup remains over the apples.

These are perfect just as they are, but they are even more so with a bit of Crème Fraîche (see page 361) or Honey Ricotta Cream (see page 360) alongside or over each apple.

Brandied Apples

This must be served immediately, but it takes five minutes to make, is very pretty—and delicious. Serve this after a luncheon or a dinner.

You need a large nonstick frying pan (preferably about 12 inches in diameter), and a plain or scalloped 2½-inch round cookie cutter, as well as

a plain or scalloped ¾-inch round cutter or an apple corer.

Two apples make 2 to 4 portions depending on whether you serve them plain or with ice cream or sour cream. To double the recipe, see Notes.

2 TO 4 PORTIONS

2 large tart apples (preferably Granny Smith)
1 tablespoon unsalted butter
¼ cup granulated sugar

2 ounces Calvados (apple brandy—see Notes)
⅓ cup whipping cream
Optional: ice cream or sour cream

Place an unpeeled apple on its side. Cut it into slices about ⅜ inch wide, discarding the two ends. You should get five or six slices from an average large apple. Slice the other apple.

With a plain or scalloped round cookie cutter about 2½ inches wide cut the apple slices, cutting away the peel. Then, with a plain or scalloped round cutter about ¾ inch wide, cut out the cores. If you do not have a small enough round cutter you can core the apples with an apple corer before slicing them.

Melt the butter over high heat in a 12-inch nonstick frying pan, add the apple slices in a single layer, sprinkle on the sugar, and sauté, turning the slices frequently (with two wide metal spatulas) for about 2 minutes. The apples should be just barely tender when tested with a toothpick.

Add the Calvados and, holding a match at arm's length, light the brandy (it will make a high flame). Twirl the pan briefly until the flame subsides. Add the cream, and twirl the pan a bit more, then shake it back and forth for about a minute to allow the sauce to thicken slightly.

Transfer the apples to individual flat plates, placing the slices in an overlapping row. Raise the heat and boil the sauce for a few seconds longer until it turns a light caramel color, then divide the sauce over the apples.

Serve as is or with a scoop of ice cream or a large spoonful of sour cream alongside the apple slices. Serve quickly while the apples are hot.

NOTES: 1. *Applejack or any other brandy or Cognac or dark or light rum can be used in place of the Calvados, but Calvados is wonderful.*

2. *To double the recipe use two large frying pans. If you double the amount of Calvados in one pan the flame will be dangerously high.*

Sugarbush Mountain Peaches

Pure, sweet, and simple. Peaches baked in maple syrup—that's it. Make this when peaches are at the height of their season and when you can get large ones that are just ripe but not overripe. Or buy them underripe and let them stand in a single layer at room temperature for a day or two until they just barely give when pressed lightly in your hand. Then, if you wish, they can be refrigerated for a few days before you use them.

Use 1 large freestone peach for each portion. Add 2 tablespoons of maple syrup for each peach (that's ¾ cup for 6 peaches). Blanch and peel the peaches (see below), then cut them in half. Place them cut side down in a lightly buttered shallow baking dish. Pour the maple syrup over the peaches.

Bake in the middle of a preheated 350-degree oven for about 20 to 22 minutes, basting the syrup with a bulb baster frequently over the peaches. Fresh peaches are best if they are baked only until they are not quite done. Test them with a toothpick. When they are ready, remove them from the oven and use the bulb baster to transfer all of the syrup to a small saucepan.

Place the saucepan over high heat and let the syrup boil hard, uncovered, for about 3 minutes or until it registers 230 degrees on a candy thermometer.

Pour the boiled syrup over the peaches. Let stand, basting occasionally, until cool. Then refrigerate and serve cold.

Serve the chilled peaches on chilled flat dessert plates with a bit of the thick syrup spooned over them. It is easier to eat these with a knife and fork than with a spoon.

Or cut the baked peaches into bite-size pieces and serve them over vanilla ice cream, in dessert bowls.

Or, my favorite: a cold peach and a mound of cold Top Secret (see page 359) on a flat plate. I could swim in it.

Stewed Peaches

During peach season, when they are large and juicy and full of flavor, plain, whole (pit-in) stewed peaches are as delicious as any dessert I know. (This recipe is from my first book.)

6 large ripe but firm freestone peaches
1½ cups water

1 cup granulated sugar
1 6- to 8-inch vanilla bean

To peel the peaches: Have ready a large bowl of ice-cold water, a slotted spoon, and a saucepan of boiling water deep enough to cover the peaches.

With the slotted spoon, place the peaches in the boiling water, 2 or 3 at a time. If the peaches are fully ripe they will need only about 15 seconds in the boiling water; if not quite ripe they will need more. With the slotted spoon raise a peach from the water and move your thumb firmly over the skin. If the skin has loosened enough it will wrinkle and feel loose. At that point transfer it to the ice water.

Peel with your fingers, starting at the stem end, and return the peeled fruit to the ice water. Partially peeled peaches may be returned to the boiling water for additional blanching if necessary. Continue to blanch and peel all of the peaches.

In a saucepan large enough to hold the peaches in a single layer, place the water and sugar. Slit the vanilla bean and scrape the seeds into the water; add the pod also. Bring to a boil, stirring, and let boil for about 5 minutes to make a syrup. With the slotted spoon add the peaches and adjust the heat so that the syrup simmers gently. Cook, partially covered, turning the peaches a few times with two rubber spatulas in order not to mar them. Baste occasionally with the syrup.

Test for doneness with a cake tester or a toothpick. Do not overcook. When they are just barely tender, transfer the peaches with the slotted spoon to a wide bowl.

Raise the heat and boil the syrup, uncovered, for a few minutes to reduce slightly. Taste the syrup and continue to boil until it tastes right— sweet enough and not watery. Pour the hot syrup over the stewed peaches. Do not remove the vanilla bean. Set aside to cool, basting occasionally with the syrup.

Cover and refrigerate. Serve cold.

Serve in shallow dessert bowls with a spoon and a fork (sometimes you need the fork to hold the fruit in place while you cut it with the spoon). Serve with a generous amount of the syrup, or with a scoop of ice cream.

VARIATION: *Stewed Pears—follow the above recipe, substituting firm but ripe pears for the peaches; pears to be stewed should be a little more firm than those for serving raw. Instead of blanching the pears to peel them, peel with a swivel-bladed vegetable parer, leaving the stems on. As you peel the pears, place them in a bowl of cold water that contains the juice of a lemon, to keep them from discoloring. If necessary, cut the bottoms a bit to allow the pears to stand upright.*

Raspberry Pears

Brilliant, shiny, deep-raspberry-colored pears; poached in a purée of frozen raspberries. Sensational looks and a fantastic flavor. A spectacular dessert—along with a variety of cookies—for a Christmas dinner. Or for any night of the week.

4 PORTIONS

1 10-ounce package frozen red raspberries in syrup, thawed
2 tablespoons honey

2 tablespoons plus 1 teaspoon framboise or kirsch
Juice of ½ lemon
4 large ripe but firm pears (see Note)

Place the berries and their liquid in a food processor or a blender and process or blend until puréed. Force through a rather fine but wide strainer set over a bowl, to remove the seeds. Or just mash the berries and strain them. Stir in the honey and 2 tablespoons of the framboise or kirsch (reserve the remaining 1 teaspoon) and set aside.

Stir the lemon juice into a bowl of cold water that is large enough to hold the pears (to prevent discoloring). Peel the pears with a vegetable parer; do not remove the stems or the cores. Place the pears in the lemon water until they are all ready.

Use a deep, heavy saucepan with a tight cover, one that the pears will just fit in, either standing up or lying on their sides. Remove the pears from the water, place them in the saucepan, pour the raspberry mixture over the top, cover, and place on moderate heat until the mixture comes to a boil. Then reduce the heat so the syrup just simmers, and cook, basting a few times with a bulb baster.

(If the pears are lying down, turn them around very gently occasionally; use two rubber spatulas or, if the pears have stems, you can lift the stems with your fingers or with tongs to turn the pears over gently.)

To test for doneness, pierce the pears carefully with a toothpick at the widest part. When they begin to feel tender, but before they are done (probably after about 20 to 30 minutes or less), let them continue to cook, only partially covered now (for the sauce to thicken a bit), and cook only until tender (probably 35 to 45 minutes or less in all, depending on the pears' ripeness—do not overcook).

Remove from the heat, transfer the pears gently to a wide bowl, stir the remaining 1 teaspoon of framboise or kirsch into the syrup, and pour it over the pears.

Let stand to reach room temperature. Then refrigerate, uncovered (if they are covered they sweat and the wonderfully thick syrup becomes thin).

Serve the pears cold on chilled flat dessert plates with a knife and fork. There will not be much syrup, but pour or spoon whatever there is over and around the pears—even just a bit of the syrup is a real treat.

Serve plain or with White Custard Cream (see page 360) or Crème Fraîche (see page 361) or Top Secret (see page 359).

NOTE: *Winter pears, grown in Oregon, Washington, and northern California, are available from September into the spring. The best varieties for cooking are Anjou, light green or yellow green, almost egg shaped; Bosc, golden brown, with a long tapering neck; and Comice, green to greenish yellow, with a chubby shape and a short neck. Bosc is most frequently recommended for poaching, but I have used others with equally good results. The pears must not be overripe, but if they are underripe they will not have any flavor. The flesh should barely give when pressed firmly with a fingertip.*

Broiled Peppered Pears

Quick, easy, light, peppery, sweet, and hot; served right from the broiler. This is unusual and wonderful. The pears should be almost but not completely ripe when you use them. Pears are one of the few fruits that do not ripen well on the tree; they are picked when fully grown but still firm. The Bosc variety is excellent for cooking, but there are others equally good. Generally, I buy pears about a week ahead and let them stand at room temperature. If they begin to ripen before you are ready to use them, refrigerate to slow down the ripening process.

For each portion serve 1 large half or 2 smaller halves. This recipe can easily be divided for just 2 people.

6 PORTIONS

Juice of 1 lemon
Cold tap water
3 large or 6 medium pears
3 tablespoons mild honey

Scant 1 tablespoon unsalted butter
⅜ teaspoon pepper (see Note)
6 tablespoons Cognac or dark rum
Granulated sugar

Bosc Pear

Anjou Pears

First prepare a bowl of acidulated water to keep the pears from darkening: stir the juice of 1 lemon into a bowl of 1 to 2 quarts cold tap water.

With a vegetable parer peel the pears. Halve them lengthwise. With the tip of a small, sharp knife cut a shallow groove to remove the stem from each pear. Remove the core and seeds with a melon ball scoop or with a serrated grapefruit spoon. Place the prepared pears in the acidulated water (this can be done hours ahead, if you wish, in which case, refrigerate).

Before broiling, adjust a rack 3 to 4 inches below the broiler and preheat the broiler. Lightly butter a shallow baking dish that the pear halves will fit in. Drain the pears and place them curved side up close together in the dish. Drizzle the honey over the tops. Cut the butter into tiny pieces and distribute over the pears. Grind on the pepper (or sprinkle if you ground in a mortar and pestle). Pour the Cognac or rum into the bottom of the baking dish.

Place under the broiler and baste a few times with a bulb baster. Test the pears for doneness with a cake tester or a toothpick. When they are just barely tender and slightly golden on the tops, sprinkle sugar generously over them. Replace under the broiler. Now, do not baste any more, but just broil to caramelize the sugar. Watch carefully.

The total broiling takes from 10 to 15 minutes, depending on the ripeness of the pears. The sugar on top should melt and caramelize to a golden color.

Serve on warm, flat dessert plates. Each person should have a fork and a spoon.

If you wish, pass sour cream with this, and/or any dessert cheese.

NOTE: *The pepper should be ground fine and preferably freshly ground. It may be black, white, or dried green peppercorns (the green ones should be ground with a mortar and pestle).*

Blueberries and Cream

Quick, easy, classy, extra-delicious; made with fresh or frozen berries.

4 TO 6 PORTIONS

2 tablespoons water
3 tablespoons lemon juice
½ cup granulated sugar
Pinch of salt
4 cups fresh blueberries (washed and dried) or 1
    1-pound package frozen dry-packed blue-
    berries (not thawed)

¼ cup cold tap water
2 tablespoons cornstarch
Sweet Sour Cream (see page 361) or The
    Governor's Crème Fraîche (see page 362),
    very cold

Place the 2 tablespoons of water, lemon juice, sugar, and salt in a 2-quart heavy saucepan. Stir over moderate heat until the mixture boils and the sugar dissolves.

Add the berries, reduce the heat a bit (if the berries are frozen wait until the liquid comes to a boil again before reducing the heat), and simmer for 5 minutes.

Place the ¼ cup of cold tap water in a small cup, add the cornstarch, stir to dissolve, stir into the berry mixture, and reduce the heat still a bit more. This should cook slowly, uncovered, without coming to a boil for 4 to 5 minutes, during which time the mixture should be stirred gently and occasionally with a rubber spatula. The mixture will thicken soon after the cornstarch is added, but do not remove it from the heat too soon; it needs these few extra minutes of gentle cooking to remove the raw taste of cornstarch. (Cooking over too-high heat, cooking too long, or stirring too hard would prevent the cornstarch from thickening the mixture properly.)

Remove from the heat. Stir/fold gently with a rubber spatula occasionally until cool. Transfer to a covered container and refrigerate until very cold, or overnight.

To serve, spoon the berry mixture into 4 to 6 wineglasses or dessert bowls and spoon the sauce gently over the tops.

Raspberry Oranges

This is unusual, exotic, fresh, easy, and light. Use wonderful oranges, or the dessert will not be all that wonderful.

This should be prepared at least a few hours ahead or a day ahead.

4 PORTIONS

4 seedless sweet oranges
2 10-ounce packages frozen raspberries in syrup,
    thawed
⅓ cup mild honey
¼ cup framboise or kirsch

1 cup The Governor's Crème Fraîche (see page
    362), which may be prepared several days
    ahead (the Crème Fraîche itself, see page 361,
    may be prepared as much as 3 or 4 weeks
    ahead)

Peel the oranges (see page 15) and cut them crossways into rounds ⅓ inch thick. Set aside.

In a food processor or a food mill purée the berries and, to remove the seeds, strain them through a wide but fine strainer set over a bowl.

Stir in the honey and framboise or kirsch. Add the orange slices, thoroughly moistening each slice on both sides with the raspberry syrup.

Cover and refrigerate for several hours or overnight.

A few hours before serving, remove the orange slices from the raspberry syrup. Transfer the syrup to a saucepan over moderate heat and let boil for a few minutes, stirring occasionally, until the mixture is well thickened; you should have ⅓ to ½ cup of the reduced syrup.

Let cool, and then pour the syrup over, under, and around the slices again. Refrigerate.

To serve, place the slices overlapping one another on chilled flat dessert plates. Divide the sauce over or around the oranges.

Pass The Governor's Crème Fraîche at the table and let the guests spoon it onto their plates.

When I serve this, I serve a knife, fork, and spoon with it, and I find that most guests use them all.

Connecticut Strawberries

Easy and beautiful. A simple strawberry mixture served with a sensational sauce; the sauce has to be made ahead of time.

6 PORTIONS

White Custard Cream (see page 360)
6 to 8 cups fresh strawberries
1 10-ounce jar strawberry or raspberry preserves
　　　or jelly
¼ cup kirsch

Prepare the White Custard Cream and refrigerate.

Wash and hull the berries (see To Wash Strawberries, page 14), dry thoroughly, and refrigerate.

In a small saucepan over low heat stir the preserves or jelly and kirsch until melted smooth. Set aside.

(The above can all be done hours before serving.)

Place the berries in a large dessert bowl—clear glass, if possible.

Just before serving, pour the melted and cooled preserves or jelly over the berries.

Serve at the table, either on chilled flat dessert plates or in chilled bowls.

Pass the White Custard Cream with a ladle or a large spoon.

Ice Cream

These ice creams are all made in a churn. Mine is a 4-quart electric churn, and I love it. I love ice cream anyhow, but making it is such a wonderful experience that every time I do I want to shout about it from the housetop.

In one of my other books I wrote important directions about softening the ice cream before serving; some of them freeze too hard to serve. But not these. These will be just right to serve directly from a zero-degree deep freezer with no special attention and no advance notice.

Ice cream is one of the most popular desserts in America. I think I have eaten every commercial brand sold; good, not-so-good, and this-must-be-heaven. The best of them are not as good as these homemade ones.

Spago's Sensational Caramel Ice Cream

This is one of the famous ice creams made by Nancy Silverton, the pastry chef at Spago, Wolfgang Puck's sensational restaurant in Beverly Hills.

Spago is my favorite restaurant. They serve this heavenly stuff with apple pie. Well, with or without, this is an experience.

1½ QUARTS

CUSTARD

2 cups milk
2 cups whipping cream
8 egg yolks from eggs graded "large"

⅔ cup granulated sugar
1 teaspoon vanilla extract (see Note)

Place the milk and cream in a saucepan over medium heat, uncovered, until scalded (or until you see small bubbles on the surface).

Meanwhile, beat the egg yolks and the sugar in the large bowl of an electric mixer at high speed for 2 minutes.

Then, on low speed, gradually add the hot milk and cream to the egg yolk mixture, scraping the sides of the bowl with a rubber spatula as necessary.

Transfer the mixture to the top of a large double boiler over hot water on moderate heat and cook, stirring, until the mixture thickens enough to coat a spoon or registers 168 to 170 degrees on a sugar or candy thermometer.

Remove from the heat and strain into a large bowl.

The custard should still be hot when the following caramel is added to it. Therefore, without waiting, prepare the caramel.

CARAMEL

⅔ cup whipping cream

1 cup granulated sugar

You will now heat the ⅔ cup cream and caramelize the sugar at the same time.

Place the cream in a small saucepan over low heat; by the time the sugar is caramelized the cream should be almost boiling.

To caramelize the sugar: Place the sugar in a 10- to 12-inch frying pan (use a nonstick pan if possible) over moderate heat and stir occasionally with a wooden spatula until the sugar starts to melt. Then stir constantly as the sugar continues to melt and to caramelize. (If a large chunk of the melted sugar becomes stuck to the spatula use a table knife or a metal spatula to scrape it off.) When the sugar is pretty well melted but not completely smooth, lower the heat a bit and continue to stir until it becomes smooth and a rich caramel color.

Then, off the heat, with a long-handled wooden spatula, gradually stir the almost boiling cream into the hot, caramelized sugar. If adding the cream causes a few lumps of caramelized sugar to form, just place the pan over low heat and stir again until smooth.

Slowly and gradually stir the hot caramel mixture into the still warm (or hot) custard. Then, if the mixture is not perfectly smooth (that is, if there are any lumps of caramel), place it in a saucepan and stir over low heat until smooth. Although the chances are that any lumps of caramel would melt by themselves just from the heat of the custard.

Pour the mixture into a bowl, cool, and stir in the vanilla. Then cover and refrigerate for at least a few hours—or overnight. Or, to save time, chill the mixture by placing the bowl into a larger bowl of ice.

Freeze the chilled mixture in an ice cream churn following the manufacturer's directions.

NOTE: *At Spago they use a vanilla bean instead of the extract. To use a vanilla bean, slit it the long way, scrape out most of the seeds, and add the seeds and the bean to the milk and cream while they are heating for the custard. Remove the bean when the mixture is added to the beaten egg yolks and sugar.*

Little-Havana Coconut Ice Cream

Many Cuban-Americans speak lovingly of a coconut ice cream they remember having eaten in Havana, where it was often served in half a coconut shell by street vendors. After much experimenting, some of my Cuban-American friends arrived at this fabulous recipe, which is adapted from one created by Roland Mesnier, President and Mrs. Reagan's White House pastry chef. As smooth as honey, as rich as Rockefeller, with an evasive but posi-
tively tantalizing coconut flavor.

I have served this weeks after making it, and it was just as good.

It is best to prepare the mixture the day before freezing it.

Serve this remarkable concoction in small portions either by itself, with any chocolate sauce, or with fresh strawberries.

GENEROUS 2 QUARTS

2½ cups whipping cream
4 cups light cream (a.k.a. coffee cream—it is heavier than half-and-half)
12 ounces canned or packaged sweetened shredded coconut

16 egg yolks from eggs graded "large"
1 cup granulated sugar
2 tablespoons canned Cream of Coconut (see Note)

Place 1½ cups of the whipping cream (reserve the remaining 1 cup) in a very large, heavy saucepan. Add the light cream and shredded coconut. Stir frequently with a long-handled wooden spatula over moderate heat until the mixture comes to a low boil. Reduce the heat and let the mixture barely simmer, stirring, for about 5 minutes. Remove from the heat and let stand for 30 minutes.

Place a very large strainer over a very large bowl. Place a thin linen or cotton towel in a single layer over the strainer, letting the ends drape over the outside of the bowl.

Slowly and carefully pour the scalded coconut mixture onto the towel in the strainer (if the saucepan is too heavy to pour from, ladle the mixture). Let drain. (If the drained cream reaches the bottom of the strainer, pour it into another bowl and reserve it; you will use the cream but not the coconut.)

Twist the corners of the towel together and squeeze to remove every bit of the coconut-flavored cream. (If it is too hot to handle, wait until you can.)

Discard the coconut.

In the small bowl of an electric mixer beat the yolks for a minute or so, add the sugar and the Cream of Coconut, and beat for a few minutes. With a ladle gradually add a cup or two of the warm drained cream mixture to the egg yolk mixture and mix together.

Then, very gradually, add the egg yolk mixture to the remaining warm drained cream mixture, stirring constantly with a large wire whisk or a long-handled wooden spatula.

Transfer the mixture to a large, heavy saucepan over moderate heat and cook, stirring constantly and scraping the bottom of the pan with a large rubber spatula until the mixture thickens enough to coat a spoon, or until it registers 178 degrees on a candy or sugar thermometer. (Do not let the mixture come to a boil or the egg yolks will scramble and the mixture will not be smooth.)

Immediately, in order to stop the cooking, pour through a wide but fine strainer set over a bowl. Then stir in the remaining 1 cup of whipping cream.

Stir occasionally until cool. Then cover and refrigerate overnight. Or, if you are in a hurry, place the mixture in the freezer for about 1 hour, stirring a few times.

Freeze the ice cream in a 3- to 4-quart churn, following the manufacturer's directions.

NOTE: *Cream of Coconut is canned by a company named Lopez in Puerto Rico. It is generally available in liquor stores (because it is most frequently used in mixed drinks) and in some large food stores.*

Sugarbush Maple Ice Cream

This is smooth, creamy, mellow—sensational. Incidentally, grade B maple syrup is generally recom- *mended for cooking—it is more flavorful and darker than grade A.*

4 QUARTS

6 egg yolks
2 cups maple syrup
5 cups whipping cream

1 teaspoon vanilla extract
½ teaspoon almond extract

In the small bowl of an electric mixer beat the yolks for 5 to 7 minutes until very pale and thick. Meanwhile, heat the maple syrup in a saucepan, uncovered, over moderately high heat until it almost comes to a boil; you will know it is ready when it forms a pale (almost white) layer on top.

To make it easier to handle, I suggest that you transfer the hot syrup to a pitcher with a spout that is easy to pour from and, without waiting (while the syrup is almost boiling hot), gradually add it to the yolks, while beating on medium speed. Scrape the sides occasionally to be sure the ingredients are well mixed.

Transfer the mixture to the top of a large double boiler over hot water on moderate heat and cook, scraping the bottom and sides almost constantly with a rubber spatula, for about 5 minutes until a candy or sugar thermometer registers 178 to 180 degrees.

Now transfer the mixture to a rather wide, large bowl. Stir frequently until completely cool and then chill the mixture in the refrigerator or freezer. Or cool it in the wide bowl by placing the bowl into a larger bowl of ice and water and stirring until chilled.

Meanwhile, chill the large bowl of the electric mixer and the beaters. In the chilled bowl, with the chilled beaters, whip the cream only until it holds a soft shape, not until it is stiff.

Stir the vanilla and almond extracts into the chilled maple syrup mixture.

Gradually, in several additions, fold about one third of the maple syrup mixture into the whipped cream and then fold the whipped cream into the remaining maple syrup mixture.

Freeze in a 4-quart ice cream freezer according to the manufacturer's directions.

After the ice cream has been churned, it will still be a little softer than most ice creams that have just been churned. And then it will take a little longer than usual to become as firm as most ice creams. Actually, it takes overnight. If it is served before then, it will have an incredible texture—you will love it—like an airy mousse–ice cream; wonderful. If you freeze it longer until it becomes firmer, it will still be wonderful. Whichever.

Devil's Food Chocolate Ice Cream

Dense, rich, ravishing, never too firm, always smooth and voluptuous—with a mild honey flavor.

Churn this at least 8 hours before serving; it takes longer to freeze solid than most others.

You need a heavy 2- to 3-quart saucepan, a heavy 5-quart saucepan, and a sugar or candy thermometer.

3 QUARTS

21 ounces semisweet chocolate (see Note)
2 cups milk
¾ cup honey

14 egg yolks from eggs graded "large"
1⅓ cups granulated sugar
4 cups whipping cream

Break up the chocolate and place it, with the milk and honey, in a 2- to 3-quart heavy saucepan over moderate heat. Scrape the bottom and sides constantly with a rubber spatula until the chocolate is melted and then whisk the mixture until smooth.

Meanwhile, place the yolks in the large bowl of an electric mixer and beat to mix. Gradually add the sugar and beat until the mixture becomes slightly pale in color. Then, very slowly and on low speed, add the warm chocolate mixture and beat until smooth. It will be a thick mixture.

Transfer the mixture to a 5-quart heavy saucepan. Cook over rather low heat; you must scrape the bottom and sides constantly with a large and wide rubber spatula, until the mixture registers 140 degrees on a sugar or candy thermometer.

Pour the mixture through a wide but fine strainer set over a 4- to 5-quart bowl.

Gradually whisk in the cream.

Stir occasionally until cool.

Chill in the freezer or refrigerator until very cold and then freeze in an ice cream churn according to the manufacturer's directions.

This is fabulous with Devil's Food Chocolate Sauce (see page 368) at room temperature or slightly warmed.

NOTE: *Use any good semisweet chocolate. I made this first with Poulain and then with Tobler Tradition and then others; always sensational.*

Candy

Judy's and Joan's Chocolate Truffles

Wonderfulwonderfulwonderful.
These must be served frozen.

14 ounces semisweet chocolate (see Notes)
1 cup plus 3 tablespoons whipping cream
5½ tablespoons unsalted butter, cut into small
  pieces at room temperature

¼ cup dark rum (see Notes)
Unsweetened cocoa powder (preferably Dutch-
  process) to be used as a coating (see Notes)

Chop the chocolate rather fine on a large board with a long, heavy knife. Place the chopped chocolate and the cream in a 2-quart saucepan over low or medium-low heat. Cover and stir occasionally with a wooden spatula until the chocolate is almost melted. Then stir with a wire whisk until the mixture is perfectly smooth.

Remove from the heat, add the butter gradually, and continue to whisk until the butter is all melted and the mixture is perfectly smooth again. Stir in the rum and let stand until cool.

Then either transfer the mixture to a bowl or leave it in the saucepan and place it in the freezer for at least a few hours or longer until firm.

Line a large cookie sheet with aluminum foil.

Use two teaspoons to form mounds of the frozen mixture, one spoon for picking up with and one for pushing off with; use a rounded teaspoonful of the mixture for each truffle (of course you can make them smaller, if you wish) and place the mounds on the foil-lined sheet.

Place the cookie sheet in the freezer to refreeze the mounds.

Meanwhile, spread out a length of wax paper or foil and strain or sift a generous amount of cocoa powder onto the paper.

Have a large tray ready, lined with foil or wax paper, to receive the shaped and coated truffles. The mounds will now be shaped and rolled in cocoa. If the mixture is not frozen enough, it will be sticky to handle. Therefore it is best to remove only a few of the mounds at a time from the freezer.

One at a time, roll the mounds between your hands to shape them into balls, which can be even or uneven like real truffles. If the mixture is too sticky and too difficult to roll, simply use your fingertips and press or push the mixture into even or irregular shapes.

Then roll the truffles in the cocoa to coat them generously. Or, if you have trouble rolling the balls, you might find it helpful to drop the mounds into the cocoa, roll them around until they are coated, and then roll them into balls.

Place the coated truffles on the lined tray or in fluted paper candy cups.

Cover airtight and store in the freezer.

Serve frozen. These do not melt the way ice cream does but after standing at room temperature for 15 minutes they become soft.

I can't say for how much or how little time these can remain frozen. They won't actually spoil even after an indefinite period, but the flavor seems to diminish after weeks in the freezer. I think they are best within a week or so.

NOTES: 1. *I have used different chocolates at different times for these—Maillard's Eagle Sweet, Poulain, Tobler Tradition, Lindt Excellence, and also Tobler Extra-Bittersweet. They were all delicious. Use the best you can get.*

2. The original recipe called for the "liquor of your choice." I chose Myers's dark rum and loved it so much I have not used any other.

3. The original recipe said that the coating could be either cocoa powder; toasted, peeled, and ground hazelnuts; or melted white or dark chocolate. I have tried all three coatings and although the melted dark chocolate makes a heavenly candy, I recommend the cocoa powder until you have had a great deal of experience coating candies, in which case you are on your own. (Incidentally, when I did coat the truffles with melted chocolate I used the same chocolate that I had used in the candy itself. You do not have to temper the chocolate for these because, since they stay frozen, the chocolate does not discolor.)

SERVING SUGGESTION: *I was recently introduced to a new way of serving truffles as a dessert. We were at The Pink Elephant, an extraordinary and beautiful restaurant in a charming little hide-away town, Boca Grande, which is nestled on a narrow finger of land that reaches out into the Gulf of Mexico in southwest Florida. They served three truffles (somewhat similar to these) in a small, glass dessert bowl with about 2 tablespoons of Cognac under the truffles and a generous mound of soft whipped cream on top. The name, Boca Grande, which is Spanish for big mouth, probably came about because of the wide mouth of a river there. Or were they talking about truffles?*

Texas Truffles

These are huge—for truffles; they would even be large for golf balls. There is a creamy milk chocolate fudge wrapped around a large marshmallow center, then all of this rolled in chopped nuts. Even for Texas they are spectacular. And much fun to make. What's more, they keep indefinitely. They are wonderful to have on hand for the Christmas holidays, not only to serve but to wrap and give as gifts. They mail well and they travel well.

When I made these for a large party where there was a lot of food I cut them in half before serving. Gorgeous.

Allow plenty of time to make these (2 hours maybe).

36 TO 40 LARGE CANDIES

About 2 pounds (9 cups) pecans or walnuts (see Note)
18 ounces milk chocolate

1 14-ounce can sweetened condensed milk
1 7-ounce jar marshmallow creme
36 to 40 regular-size (large) marshmallows

The nuts must be chopped fine, but they should not be ground. It is best to place them, part at a time, on a large cutting board. Use a long, heavy

French chef's knife and chop them into fine pieces (there will be some larger pieces and some smaller—it is OK as long as there are not many pieces that are too large—the largest pieces should not be quite as large as corn kernels). Set the chopped nuts aside on a tray or just leave them on the board, if you wish. (You will be able to work with them from either place.)

Break up the chocolate and place it in the top of a large double boiler. Add the condensed milk and the marshmallow creme. Place over warm water on moderately low heat. Stir frequently with a large wooden spatula until melted and smooth. If necessary, while melting, scrape the sides with a rubber spatula. When the mixture is smooth, remove the top of the double boiler. Stir frequently to cool slightly for about 5 or 10 minutes. (The mixture might appear too thick, but it is not; it should form a very thick coating on the marshmallows.)

Cover a large tray or cookie sheet with aluminum foil.

Drop a marshmallow into the fudge. Use two long-pronged forks (preferably two-pronged, if you have them) to roll it around, lift it, brush the bottom against the rim of the pan to remove excess (but leave a coating at least ¼ inch thick), and then place it on the chopped nuts. With your hands roll the truffle around to coat it thoroughly with the nuts.

Set it aside (on a counter top or a tray or wax paper). After a few minutes, look at the candy. The chances are that some of the fudge will have run down the sides, making a thicker bottom. Use your fingers and palms to reshape the truffle, reroll it in nuts if necessary, turn the truffle upside down if you wish, and set aside again. Check on it several times and reshape it as necessary until the fudge stops running.

Place the truffle on the foil-covered tray. Continue shaping and coating the remaining truffles. Then place the tray in the freezer or refrigerator until the chocolate mixture is firm.

These can be placed in fluted paper cupcake liners (small cupcake size is the right size for these) or they can be placed directly on a tray. Cover airtight. Or they can be wrapped individually (in a square of plastic wrap twisted at the top).

Serve refrigerated or at room temperature.

NOTE: *You will not use all of the chopped nuts for this recipe, but it is easiest to coat the truffles if you work with more nuts than you need, and you can freeze and save the rest for another use.*

Brownie Truffles

These are large, chunky, nutty truffles—chocolate on chocolate. There is a small square of moist and chewy apricot Brownie flavored with Grand Marnier or Cointreau, coated with milk chocolate, and rolled around in chopped walnuts. They keep well, they may be frozen or not, they make a luxurious gift, and nobody but nobody will guess that the fudgy and caramel-like center is a quick and easy Brownie.

The apricots should be prepared the night before baking.

64 LARGE CANDIES

4 ounces (½ cup, tightly packed) dried apricots
3 tablespoons Grand Marnier or Cointreau
2 ounces unsweetened chocolate
4 ounces (1 stick) unsalted butter
Pinch of salt

1 cup granulated sugar
2 eggs graded "large"
½ teaspoon vanilla extract
¼ cup unsifted all-purpose flour

With scissors cut the apricots into strips about ¼ inch wide. Steam them as follows. Place them in a vegetable steamer or a strainer over shallow hot water in a covered saucepan on high heat. Bring the water to a boil and let it boil for 2 or 3 minutes until the apricots are well moistened. Remove the apricots and spread them out on paper towels to drain. Pat the tops with paper towels to dry. Then place the apricots in a small jar with a leakproof top. Add the Grand Marnier or Cointreau. Let stand overnight, turning the jar occasionally from top to bottom and from side to side. (It is best to place the jar in a small bowl in case it leaks.)

When you are ready to bake, adjust a rack one-third up from the bottom of the oven and preheat the oven to 325 degrees. Prepare an 8 by 8 by 2-inch square cake pan as follows. Turn the pan over, center a 12-inch square of aluminum foil shiny side down over the pan, fold down the sides and corners of the foil to shape it, remove the foil, turn the pan over again, place the foil in the pan, and press it gently into place. To butter the foil, place a piece of butter (additional to that called for) in the pan and put it in the oven to melt, then spread it all over with a pastry brush or with crumpled wax paper. Set the pan aside.

Place the chocolate and butter in a 2- to 3-quart heavy saucepan over low heat. Stir occasionally until melted. Remove from the heat. Stir in the salt, sugar, and then the eggs one at a time, stirring briskly after each addition. Stir in the vanilla and then the flour. Now add the apricots, including any liquid that has not been absorbed.

Turn into the pan and smooth the top. Bake for 40 to 45 minutes until a toothpick inserted gently all the way to the bottom in the middle comes out clean.

Cool, then chill in the freezer or refrigerator until firm. Cover the pan with a small cutting board or cookie sheet, turn the pan and board or sheet over, remove the pan and the foil lining, and then turn the cold and firm cake right side up.

With a sharp knife cut the cake into quarters and then cut each quarter into 16 small squares. The little squares should be cold when they are coated with the chocolate mixture; place them in the refrigerator or the freezer now.

CHOCOLATE COATING

1½ pounds milk chocolate
6 tablespoons solid vegetable shortening (e.g., Crisco)

1 pound (4½ cups) walnuts

Break up the chocolate and place it in the top of a large double boiler over warm water on low heat. Add the shortening. Cover the pot with a folded paper towel (to absorb steam) and with the pot cover and cook, stirring occasionally, until melted and smooth. Then set aside to cool completely.

Meanwhile, chop the nuts into very small pieces, but do not grind them. It is best to chop them on a large board with a long, heavy French chef's knife; the pieces will be uneven, but there should not be any pieces larger than small kernels of corn. The nuts can be left on the board or they can be transferred to a tray or to wax paper.

Cover a large tray or cookie sheet with aluminum foil to hold the chocolate-coated truffles.

When the chocolate mixture is ready, remove the top of the double boiler from the hot water.

Use two long-pronged forks (preferably two-pronged, if you have them) to coat each little Brownie. Drop the Brownie into the chocolate, use the forks to turn it and coat it on all sides, then to lift it (hold it over the pan for a moment for excess chocolate to run off, or wipe it a bit on the edge of the pan—but the chocolate should be a thick coating), and then drop the chocolate-coated Brownie into the chopped nuts. With your fingers turn it to coat all sides, and then place it on the foil-lined tray or sheet. Repeat the directions to coat all of the Brownies. As you use up some of the chocolate coating mixture, transfer the remainder to a smaller container to make the dipping process easy. And, if the chocolate coating becomes too stiff while you are working with it, replace it briefly over hot water as necessary.

If necessary, chill the truffles in the freezer or refrigerator until the chocolate is set and not runny. Then remove them to room temperature. They may be placed in fluted paper candy cups, if you wish.

Serve these at room temperature.

Apricot and Date Rocky Road

Rocky Road is made in small towns and big cities from coast to coast. It is almost an American staple. People outdo each other making it more thick, exotic, lavish, creative, and original. Marshmallows and milk chocolate are in all the variations I have ever seen; this one also has pecans, dried apricots, and dates. Quick, easy, foolproof, fun.

24 LARGE CANDIES—2 POUNDS

1 pound milk chocolate
About 14 large marshmallows
10 pitted dates
10 to 12 dried apricots (my favorite brand is Bee Ritchie's, available in better food stores)

6 ounces (1½ cups) pecan halves, toasted (see To Toast Pecans, page 7)

You will need an 8 by 8 by 2-inch square cake pan. To line the pan, turn it over, center a 12-inch square of aluminum foil over it, fold down the sides and corners to shape the foil, remove the foil, turn the pan over again, place the foil in the pan, and press it carefully into place. Do not butter the foil. Set aside.

It is important to melt the chocolate very very slowly to prevent it from discoloring after it becomes firm again. Break it into pieces and place it in the top of a large double boiler over warm water on very low heat. Cover with a folded paper towel (to absorb steam) and with the pot cover. Let heat for about 10 minutes until the chocolate only begins to melt. Then remove the cover and the paper and stir frequently with a rubber or wooden spatula until completely melted and smooth (it should take about 20 to 30 minutes altogether to melt).

Remove the top of the double boiler, dry the underside of the top, set aside, and stir occasionally until cool.

Meanwhile, cut the marshmallows into quarters. (It is easy to cut them with scissors; dip the blades occasionally into cold water and shake off the water but do not dry the blades.) Cut the dates into quarters. Cut the apricots into strips about ¼ inch wide (scissors are a help with the dates and apricots also). Set aside the marshmallows and the prepared fruit.

Pour about one third of the cooled melted chocolate into the pan to make a very thin layer; spread it smooth. Place a layer of the cut marshmallows over all of the chocolate (do not place the cut sides of the marshmallows against the foil on the sides—they might stick); the pieces of marshmallow should be very close together, even touching in places.

Sprinkle the dates over and among the marshmallows. Place the apricot strips over everything. Then place about one third of the pecans on top.

Now, hold the pot with the remaining melted chocolate over the pan and tilt the pot to allow the chocolate to run out in a thin ribbon all over the ingredients in the pan. There may be a few spots where the ingredients show through—that's OK as long as everything is at least partly covered so nothing will fall off.

Place the remaining pecans, one by one, flat side down on the chocolate. The nuts should be pressed into the chocolate a bit to be sure that they will not fall off later when the candy is cut into pieces.

Cover the pan with foil or plastic wrap and refrigerate until firm.

Remove from the refrigerator, cover with a cutting board, turn the pan and the board over, remove the pan and peel off the foil. Carefully turn the block of candy right side up.

It is not a good idea to cut the candy into pieces while it is very cold. It will crack. Cover it with plastic wrap and let it stand at room temperature until you can cut it neatly. That will depend on how long it was refrigerated and the temperature of your kitchen.

Use a long, thin, sharp knife or a serrated knife (try both to see which works better) and cut the block of candy into quarters. Then cut each piece in half, making two strips. Finally cut each strip into three bars.

These are gorgeous when they are wrapped individually in clear cellophane. Or arrange them on a tray and cover with plastic wrap.

Serve at room temperature.

Everybody's Favorite Fudge

My chocolate book has a fudge recipe; it is the classic, traditional fudge which, frankly, is temperamental and tricky to make. Since the publication of that book I continue to receive other fudge recipes from readers, recipes that are foolproof. They are all variations on a theme that includes evaporated milk, marshmallow, and chocolate morsels. This is the one that seems to be everybody's favorite. This is never too soft to eat or too hard to handle or too sugary; always smooth and creamy.

A BIT MORE THAN 2½ POUNDS—24 LARGE PIECES

Optional: 7 ounces (2 cups) pecans, toasted (see
    To Toast Pecans, page 7), or walnuts,
    halves or pieces
5 or 5⅓ ounces (about ⅔ cup) evaporated milk
1 7-ounce jar marshmallow creme

2 ounces (½ stick) unsalted butter
1½ cups granulated sugar
¼ teaspoon salt
12 ounces (2 cups) semisweet chocolate morsels
1 teaspoon vanilla extract

Line an 8-inch square pan with aluminum foil as follows: turn the pan upside down, center a 12-inch square of foil shiny side down over the pan, press down the sides and corners of the foil to shape it to the pan, remove the foil, turn the pan right side up, place the shaped foil in the pan and gently press the foil (with a potholder if you wish) into place in the pan. Set aside the lined pan.

Pick over the optional nuts carefully (sometimes they include a piece of shell), and remove and reserve about ½ cup of the best-looking halves or pieces to decorate the fudge. Set the nuts aside.

Pour the evaporated milk into a heavy 2½- to 3-quart saucepan. Add the marshmallow creme, butter, sugar, and salt. Place over low to low-medium heat and stir constantly with a wooden spatula until the mixture comes to a boil. This mixture wants to burn; adjust the heat as necessary, and scrape the bottom of the pan occasionally with a rubber spatula to be sure it is not burning.

As soon as the mixture comes to a full boil start timing it; let it boil, and continue to stir, for 5 minutes. (After the 5 minutes are up, the mixture will have caramelized slightly. It is not necessary to test the mixture with a thermometer—just time it—the temperature will be 226 to 228 degrees when the boiling time is up).

Remove the saucepan from the heat and add the morsels, stir until melted and smooth—a strong wire whisk is a big help—stir in the vanilla, and then the 1½ cups of nuts. Quickly pour into the lined pan, smooth the top, and place the reserved ½ cup of nuts onto the top of the fudge, spacing them evenly and pressing down on them enough so they will not fall off.

Let stand until cool. Then chill until firm. Remove the fudge and foil from the pan by lifting the corners of the foil. Or, cover the pan with wax paper and a cookie sheet, turn the pan and sheet over, remove the pan and foil, cover the fudge with a cookie sheet or a cutting board, and turn it over again, leaving the fudge right side up.

With a long, sharp knife carefully cut the fudge into pieces. Wrap them individually in clear cellophane, wax paper, or aluminum foil. Or place the fudge in an airtight freezer box. If you want to store for more than a few days, freeze it.

Spiced Pecans

Deeelicious, and so quick and easy there's nothing to it. These make a wonderful gift. Or place a bowl of them on the table after dinner with coffee (the guests will go nuts). Spiced pecans are an old Southern custom.

You will need two saucepans, one narrow enough for a candy thermometer to reach the shallow syrup and another wide enough to stir 2 cups of pecans with the syrup. (My small one is 6 inches across the top and 4 inches deep; the large one is a standard 2½- to 3-quart saucepan, 8 by 3½ inches.) You also need a candy thermometer.

1 POUND—SEE NOTE

7 ounces (2 cups) large pecan halves, toasted (see
    To Toast Pecans, page 7)
1 cup granulated sugar
Optional: pinch of salt
1 teaspoon cinnamon
1 teaspoon ground ginger
¼ teaspoon nutmeg
¼ teaspoon cream of tartar
¼ cup water
½ teaspoon vanilla extract

Set the oven temperature to 150 to 200 degrees. Place the toasted nuts in a 2½- to 3-quart saucepan in the oven to stay warm (because this works best if the nuts and the saucepan are warm).

In a narrow saucepan (see Introduction to this recipe) mix the sugar with the optional salt, the cinnamon, ginger, nutmeg, cream of tartar, and water. Stir over high heat and bring the mixture to a boil. Reduce the heat to moderate, insert a candy thermometer, and let boil for a few minutes until the syrup reaches 238 degrees (the soft-ball stage).

Remove from the heat, quickly stir in the vanilla, pour over the warm pecans in the warm saucepan, and, without waiting, stir gently but quickly and constantly with a large wooden spatula for a very few minutes until the syrup turns to sugar (it will take only 2 to 3 minutes). Let stand to cool, or turn the nuts out onto a length of aluminum foil and let cool.

Store airtight.

NOTE: *Although you use only 7 ounces of nuts, when they are sugared they will weigh about a pound.*

Hot Peppered Pecans

The first time I made the above Spiced Pecans my husband said, as he usually does, "It needs some pepper." Some time later, when I planned to make pounds and pounds of these for a friend, I decided this was the time for pepper.

I used the above recipe with the addition of 1 teaspoon of freshly ground black pepper. Ralph said it needed more, so I made it again with

1¼ teaspoons of black pepper, a generous pinch of white pepper, and a generous pinch of cayenne.

Ralph thought it was just right.

Hot Peppered Pecans are great before dinner with drinks.

In making large quantities of these I found that it is all right to double the recipe but not more than that. Actually, even double, the stirring became a job. I prefer to make the single recipe as many times as necessary. But if you do double it, be sure to use a large enough saucepan to stir the syrup and the nuts together.

Alfred A. Knopf Peanut Butter Candy

My editor, Nancy Nicholas, sent this to me. The recipe comes from Nicholas Latimer, who works in the Knopf publicity department. His aunt makes them. Thank you all. Too good—and too easy. (Nancy's recipe had this note: "Amazing but true.") The taste will remind you of Reese's peanut butter cups.

32 PIECES

8 ounces (2 sticks) unsalted butter, melted
2 cups graham cracker crumbs
2½ cups confectioners sugar

1 cup chunky peanut butter
8 ounces milk chocolate

Line an 8-inch square cake pan as follows. Turn the pan over, cover with a 12-inch square of aluminum foil shiny side down, fold down the sides and corners to shape the foil, remove the foil, turn the pan over again, and place the foil into the pan, pressing it carefully to fit smooth. Set aside.

In the large bowl of an electric mixer (or any large bowl, with a wooden spatula) mix the butter with the graham cracker crumbs, sugar, and peanut butter.

Turn into the lined pan. With the bottom of a teaspoon smooth the mixture to make an even layer. Let stand at room temperature.

Break up the chocolate and place it in the top of a small double boiler over hot water on low heat. Cover with a folded paper towel (to absorb steam) and the pot cover. Let stand for a few minutes until partly melted. Then uncover and stir until completely melted and smooth.

Remove the top of the double boiler (dry its underside), and pour the chocolate onto the peanut butter layer.

With the bottom of a teaspoon smooth the chocolate all over the bottom layer, touching the sides of the foil.

Refrigerate for an hour (or longer, if you wish) until firm.

Lift the candy from the pan by lifting the aluminum foil. Place the candy, still on the foil, on a cutting board. Fold down the sides of the foil and let stand. If you cut this into squares while it is cold it will crumble. Let it stand for about an hour, then cut into 32 small bars.

Serve at room temperature.

Sauces

Top Secret

While I was working on the recipe for Lemon Cream Cheese Pie (see page 256) I experimented with several different types of cottage cheese: large curd, small curd, high fat, low fat—whatever. After the recipe was written I had several containers of cottage cheese that I had processed left over in the refrigerator. One day for lunch I put some fresh strawberries on a plate and spooned some of the processed cheese over the top. I swooned. I said that nobody would guess that it was cottage cheese. I tried it out on friends. They said sour cream, crème fraîche, yogurt, cream cheese and heavy cream, food of the gods, and whatnot. Nobody guessed cottage cheese, just plain cottage cheese. (Incidentally, ½ cup of cottage cheese has from 80 to 110 calories, depending on its fat content; ½ cup of sour cream has about 400 calories.)

I was in some new kind of heaven and vowed that I would eat nothing but strawberries and processed cottage cheese as long as berries were in season; then I would switch to some other fruit. I loved each bite of the pure, simple, natural, bland, maybe-a-bit-sour-but-not-really-sour flavor.

I also tried it with a bit of sweetening and flavoring. For each ½ cup of cheese I mixed in 1 teaspoon of granulated sugar—or 1 teaspoon of mild honey—and a few drops (very little) of vanilla extract. I can't tell you which is better, sweetened or not, because they are equally divine. (The small amount of sweetening really only cuts the slight sourness of the cheese; add more, if you wish.)

This may be served immediately after it is prepared, but if it is refrigerated for a few hours the mixture will thicken slightly and become even better. Prepare as much or as little as you want. Plan on ½ to 1 cup per person if you are serving this with strawberries or sliced fresh peaches. If you serve it with apple pie or baked apples or with peach or blueberry cobbler or something filling like that, you might not need so much. But when someone knows what this is—how low in calories—they will eat twice as much.

Place the cottage cheese (see Note), 1 to 2 cups at a time, in the bowl of a food processor fitted with the metal chopping blade. Process for 1 full minute (no less) until as smooth as honey. You will think it is ready sooner, but please do process for the full minute, at least. Stop the machine once to scrape down the sides during processing. When you think it is done, process still a few seconds longer. The sugar or honey and vanilla may be added before, during, or after the processing.

Transfer to a covered container and refrigerate for several hours or longer.

This Top Secret or the following Ricotta Cream can be made in a blender. It is possible, but just barely. In my Waring blender I have to do it in many very small additions, stop and start the machine frequently, and use low speed at first for each addition. It is a hassle. It is really best to use a food processor.

NOTE: *I like this best made with large-curd 4 percent milk fat cottage cheese (Sealtest). If you use 1 percent milk fat cottage cheese it will be a thinner, airier mixture without the depth and grandeur of the 4 percent milk fat cheese. (The 1 percent cheese has about 80 calories to a ½-cup portion, and the 4 percent cheese has 100 to 110 calories for the same amount. Not much difference in the numbers but a big difference in the taste and texture.)*

Ricotta Cream

This recipe is the same as the preceding Top Secret, but it is made with ricotta cheese instead of cottage cheese; this is a little blander and lighter—cottage cheese has more of a tart flavor and is denser after it is processed. I like both cheeses equally for these recipes. I use any all-natural whole-milk ricotta cheese. This totally bland flavor is sensational with tart foods, most especially Cranberry Upside-Down Cake (see page 103).

Honey Ricotta Cream

This is a sweetened and flavored version of the preceding recipe. Serve it as a thick sauce with any fresh or cooked fruit (it is wonderful with raw pears) or with fruit cobbler, fruit pie, baked apples, et cetera.

1 15- or 16-ounce container ricotta cheese
¼ cup unflavored yogurt

¼ cup honey

Process the cheese in a food processor for 1 minute, scraping down the sides after about ½ a minute. Then add the yogurt and honey and process again only to mix.

Refrigerate in a covered container for a few hours or overnight.

White Custard Cream

Serve this divine sauce with almost any fresh fruit; or serve it with bread pudding, baked apples, apple pie, et cetera. It is similar to a soft custard but is lighter since it is made with egg whites only, no yolks. It is about as thick as soft whipped cream—almost the consistency of sour cream—extraordinary.

2½ CUPS

2 cups whipping cream
2 tablespoons granulated sugar
4 egg whites from eggs graded "large" (to make ½ cup of whites; they may be whites that were frozen and then thawed)

1 teaspoon vanilla extract
Few drops almond extract

Place 1 cup of the cream (reserve the remaining 1 cup of cream) in the top of a large double boiler over hot water on moderate heat, uncovered, to scald. When you see a thin skin over the top or small bubbles around the edge, stir in the sugar and temporarily remove the top of the double boiler.

In the small bowl of an electric mixer beat the remaining cup of cream with the (unbeaten) egg whites for about a minute only to mix very well; the mixture will not increase or thicken.

Stir a little of the beaten mixture into the hot cream, stir in a little more, and then stir in all of it.

Replace the top of the double boiler over hot water on moderate heat. Cook, stirring and scraping the sides and bottom of the pan constantly for 5 or 6 minutes until the mixture registers 170 to 175 degrees on a sugar or candy thermometer and thickens enough to coat a spoon. (This will thicken more as it chills; do not overcook now or the mixture will lose its smoothness.)

Remove the top of the double boiler and strain the sauce through a fine strainer set over a bowl. Stir frequently until completely cool. Then stir in the vanilla and almond extracts. (To add only a few drops of the almond extract it is best to pour a few drops slowly into a spoon; pouring directly into the sauce is dangerous—use very very little.)

When cool, refrigerate. This may be refrigerated for a day or two. To cover for the refrigerator, first place a paper napkin or towel over the top of the bowl and then cover that with plastic wrap or foil. Otherwise, moisture forms on the underside of the plastic wrap or foil and drips back into the sauce, thinning it slightly.

Sweet Sour Cream

Serve this with cobblers, apple desserts, fresh pears, fresh figs, mangoes, melon, fresh berries; almost any time you would serve whipped cream or Crème Fraîche. There's nothing to it, everyone loves it, and it lasts for several days. For every cup of sour cream use ½ teaspoon of vanilla extract and 1½ teaspoons of granulated sugar. Place the cream in a bowl, whisk it until soft, whisk in the vanilla and sugar, and then either serve right away while it is a rather thin mixture, or refrigerate it until it thickens again, or longer. I like it thick, but for some desserts it might be better a bit thinner; just whisk it briskly to thin it.

Crème Fraîche

Only a few years ago this was practically unheard of in America. Now, many people make their own, or buy it in fancy food stores.

There is nothing to making your own, but it must be made ahead of time. It takes from 1 to 3 days; then it can be kept for about 4 weeks.

1 cup whipping cream

It is divine with fresh berries, fresh figs, baked apples, fresh peaches, fruit pie, fruit pudding, et cetera, et cetera.

When this is served with fruit as a dessert, it is best to plan on 1 cup of cream for every 3 portions. Multiply the recipe as you wish.

1 teaspoon buttermilk

Pour the cream into a jar with a cover. Add the buttermilk and stir to mix. Cover the jar and let stand at room temperature for from 1 to 3 days until it is as thick as commercial sour cream.

Refrigerate for at least 24 hours or up to 4 weeks, or for as long as it still tastes good. In the refrigerator, after a day or so, it will thicken quite a bit more and will become very firm. Use it as it is (I love it thick) or whisk it a bit to soften.

The Governor's Crème Fraîche

I have tried to sweeten and flavor crème fraîche before mixing the cream with the buttermilk and before letting it stand to thicken, but it does not work. The mixture never does thicken if it has sugar. So, this is made with prepared Crème Fraîche.

1 cup Crème Fraîche (see preceding recipe)
3 tablespoons light brown sugar, firmly packed

½ teaspoon vanilla extract
Pinch of nutmeg

Stir the ingredients to mix. Taste for additional nutmeg; you should be able to taste the nutmeg but only faintly. When you mix the ingredients, the sugar will melt and will cause the crème fraîche to become thinner. Refrigerate. After a few hours it will thicken to a nice consistency for a sauce. If it stands overnight it will become almost as thick as it was before the sugar was added; delicious either way.

Brandied Butterscotch Sauce

Caramelized sugar, cream, butter, and Cognac—heaven! With fruit and ice cream this should be enough sauce for 6 generous portions.

Recently I have been using a nonstick frying pan for caramelizing sugar, and it is great. The sugar seems to melt and brown better, and there

is no hassle washing caramelized sugar off the pan —it just floats off. (Although the interior of the pan is dark, it does not interfere with judging the color of the caramelized sugar.)

1½ CUPS

1 cup whipping cream
1 cup granulated sugar
3 tablespoons unsalted butter, cut into small pieces

1 teaspoon vanilla extract
3 tablespoons Cognac

Place the cream in a small saucepan, uncovered, over moderate heat and let it come to a low boil.

Meanwhile, place the sugar in a frying pan that is about 11 inches wide and has about a 2-quart capacity (the pan may be nonstick or not). Place the frying pan over high heat and stir constantly with a long-handled wooden spatula until the sugar starts to melt and caramelize. At this point, while there are still some lumps of unmelted sugar, reduce the heat to moderate and let cook briefly until the sugar is smooth and is a rich mahogany color.

The cream should be very hot now; it should be ready to boil, if not actually boiling. Remove the frying pan from the heat; gradually add the hot cream, stirring constantly with the long-handled wooden spatula. (The mixture will bubble up furiously.)

When the cream is added to the sugar it will cause a few lumps to form in the mixture. Stir over moderate heat, again letting the mixture boil (adjust the heat as necessary to prevent boiling over), until all the lumps melt and the sauce is smooth.

Remove from the heat, stir in the butter, then the vanilla and Cognac.

Carefully pour the mixture into a bowl and whisk it briskly with a wire whisk until the butter is incorporated and the sauce is as smooth as honey (although a bit thinner).

This can be served at any temperature, but I like it best very cold; the sauce thickens when it is refrigerated to a gorgeous consistency, thicker than honey.

Butterscotch Custard Sauce

Make this ahead of time and serve it very cold with any cobbler or pandowdy, bread pudding, et cetera.

2⅓ CUPS

1 cup milk
1 cup whipping cream
4 egg yolks

⅓ cup dark brown sugar, firmly packed
Pinch of salt
1 teaspoon vanilla extract

Place the milk and cream in a heavy saucepan, uncovered, over moderate heat to scald, or until you see a slightly wrinkled skin on the top.

Meanwhile, in the top of a large double boiler, off the heat, whisk the yolks lightly just to mix. Gradually mix in the sugar and salt and whisk briskly for about a minute.

Slowly add the scalded milk and cream, whisking steadily.

Place over hot water on moderate heat. Scrape the bottom and sides constantly with a rubber spatula and cook until the mixture thickens slightly and will coat a metal spoon; it might take about 10 minutes. When it is ready it will register 180 degrees on a sugar or candy thermometer.

Remove from the heat immediately and without waiting pour the sauce through a fine strainer set over a bowl. Stir in the vanilla.

Cool, uncovered, stirring frequently and gently. Then cover and refrigerate.

Serve very cold (you might place it in the freezer for about 15 minutes before serving). Stir briefly before serving.

This amount should serve 8 to 10 people.

Cranberry Topping

Cranberries have been on American menus since the Pilgrims' first Thanksgiving. The sauce is spectacular on vanilla ice cream or custard or bread pudding or anything bland and creamy (cheesecake) or on baked apples, apple pie, or on sliced bananas or sliced or sectioned oranges (the fruit may be drizzled with Grand Marnier first)—or just on a teaspoon. This may be made with fresh or frozen cranberries. It can be served at room temperature, or only slightly warm (when it is very cold the flavor seems weaker, and when it is very hot it is still delicious but thin). A jar of this makes a gorgeous Christmas present.

Just read the ingredients—what a combination!

3 CUPS

1 12-ounce package (3 cups) fresh or frozen
    cranberries
4 ounces (1 stick) unsalted butter

1 cup light brown sugar (see Note)
½ cup Grand Marnier
½ cup whipping cream

(If you use frozen berries do not thaw them first.) Pour the berries into a large bowl of cold water and swoosh them around; loose stems will settle to the bottom, so, with your hands, lift the berries from the top and drain them in a strainer.

Place the butter and brown sugar in a covered saucepan with about a 2-quart capacity. Stir occasionally over moderate heat until the butter melts. Add the cranberries and Grand Marnier. Cover and cook until the mixture comes to a boil. Then adjust the heat so that the mixture simmers and cook, covered, until the berries pop and/or soften. You may press some of them against the side to mash them slightly. Do not cook too long; some berries should remain whole and the others should be coarse. Stir in the cream.

Remove from the heat and let cool.

Transfer to a covered container or two. Let stand or refrigerate.

To serve, this may be warmed slightly in a pan over low heat.

NOTE: *Although this tastes just as delicious with dark brown sugar the color will not be as bright and pretty.*

Raisin Blueberry Sauce

We had this in Maine, on pancakes. There it was made with small wild blueberries. Here I make it with large, silvery, commercial berries. It is terrific on vanilla ice cream, on cheesecake, bread pudding, sliced fresh peaches, or sliced oranges.

1½ CUPS

¼ cup raisins
⅓ cup granulated sugar
1 tablespoon cornstarch
⅛ teaspoon cinnamon
Pinch of salt

2 tablespoons cold water
1½ teaspoons lemon juice
2 cups fresh blueberries or frozen (not thawed)
    dry-packed blueberries

Place the raisins in a vegetable steamer or a strainer over shallow hot water on moderate heat. Cover, bring to a boil, and let simmer for 10 to 15 minutes. The raisins should be very soft and moist. Uncover and set aside.

In a 4- to 5-cup heavy saucepan mix the sugar, cornstarch, cinnamon, and salt; stir well. Add the water and lemon juice and continue to stir with a rubber spatula until the dry ingredients are thoroughly moistened and there are no lumps. Add the berries.

Place over moderate heat and stir occasionally until the mixture begins to simmer. Reduce the heat slightly and simmer gently for 2 minutes, stirring a bit with a rubber spatula. (Cornstarch thins out if it is overcooked or overbeaten.)

Some of the berries will be broken, some will remain whole; the liquid will be deep purple, slightly thickened—wonderful. Add the raisins. Remove from the heat.

Transfer to a wide bowl to cool. Then refrigerate.

Serve cold.

This should be enough for 4 portions.

Strawberry-Strawberry Sauce

This is a thin sauce with no thickening; it is light and fresh and has a delicate flavor. Perfect over vanilla ice cream and/or cooked or uncooked peaches, or seedless grapes, fresh pineapple, fresh raspberries, or fresh strawberries.

This amount will possibly be enough for 3 or 4 portions. The sauce may be refrigerated for several days.

1¼ CUPS

2 cups (generous ½ pound) fresh strawberries
3 tablespoons water
3 tablespoons strawberry preserves

2 tablespoons granulated sugar
½ teaspoon lemon juice
2 teaspoons kirsch

Wash, hull, and drain the berries (see page 14) and set them aside on paper towels.

Place the water, preserves, and sugar in a small saucepan over low heat. Stir occasionally and bring to a low boil.

Place the berries in a food processor bowl fitted with the metal chopping blade and process them to a smooth purée. (Or purée them in several batches in a blender.) Add the warm strawberry preserve mixture and process (or blend) again briefly.

Place a wide but fine strainer over a wide bowl. Pour the purée into the strainer. Press down on the purée with a ladle to push it through the strainer. Discard the seeds that remain in the strainer.

Stir the juice and kirsch into the sauce.

Transfer to a covered container and refrigerate.

Serve very cold.

Peanut Butter Sauce

Smooth and creamy. Kids love this served over vanilla ice cream and sliced bananas. Not only kids.

1¼ CUPS

¾ cup light corn syrup
¼ cup water
Tiny pinch of salt
⅓ cup smooth peanut butter

1 tablespoon unsalted butter
1 egg
1 teaspoon vanilla extract
⅓ cup whipping cream

In a heavy saucepan with about a 1½-quart capacity stir the corn syrup with the water and salt. Bring to a boil, uncovered, over moderate heat. Then reduce the heat slightly and let the sauce simmer for 5 minutes. Add the peanut butter and stir well with a small wire whisk (if it appears curdled, don't worry—it is OK). Remove from the heat, add the butter, and stir gently to melt.

In a small bowl beat the egg with a whisk just to mix. Very gradually stir about half of the warm peanut butter mixture into the egg; then stir the egg mixture into the remaining warm peanut butter mixture.

Place over very low heat and cook, scraping the bottom and sides constantly and gently with a rubber spatula, for 1½ minutes (to cook the egg).

Remove from the heat and cool to room temperature.

Stir in the vanilla and (unwhipped) cream.

Refrigerate. (I like this best very cold, right out of the refrigerator. It will be thick and creamy.)

Goldrush Sauce

EUREKA!!! *We struck gold. And this is the mother lode. When this is served slightly warm on ice cream it is a Goldrush Sundae (a.k.a. Gold Brick Sundae—it is most popular in the Midwest, where it is traditionally served with vanilla ice cream). The sauce is the kind that turns chewy-gooey on ice cream, and it is loaded with crunchy chunks of chopped Almond Roca, Heath Bars, or any other hard toffee candy either chocolate-coated or not, and toasted pecans. With ice cream, the dessert is both warm and cold, thick and chewy caramel-like, both smooth and crunchy-chunky, dark dark chocolate, pure 14 karat.*

The sauce can be made ahead of time, if you wish.

2 CUPS

2½ ounces unsweetened chocolate
1 tablespoon unsalted butter
⅓ cup boiling water
2 tablespoons light corn syrup
1 cup granulated sugar
1 teaspoon vanilla extract

About 1 scant cup Almond Roca (see page 41) or Heath Bars (see Note), cut into ½- to ⅓-inch pieces
½ cup pecans, toasted (see To Toast Pecans, page 7), either halves or large pieces

Place the chocolate, butter, and boiling water in a 1½-quart heavy saucepan. Cook over low heat, stirring, until the chocolate is melted. Whisk the mixture with a small whisk until it is smooth. Stir in the corn syrup and sugar.

Raise the heat to moderate and stir until the mixture comes to a boil. Then stop stirring, reduce the heat as necessary, and let boil moderately for exactly 8 minutes.

Remove the pan from the heat. Place the bottom of the pan briefly in a bowl of cold water in order to stop the boiling.

Stir in the vanilla. Let cool a few minutes until the sauce is only warm, not hot. Stir in the candy and the pecans.

Serve the sauce slightly warm. It may be refrigerated and then reheated over low heat. If it is too thick after it is refrigerated and then reheated, add hot water, 1 teaspoonful at a time.

If the sauce becomes slightly granular when it has cooled, don't worry; it will become as smooth as satin again when it is warmed.

When this is refrigerated it becomes too firm to be spooned or cut out of its container. Therefore, it is best to store it in something with straight or flared sides. Then, to remove it, place the container in hot water until the firm sauce loosens and will slide out. It can then be reheated in the top of a double boiler over warm water on low heat.

NOTE: *If you use Health Bars, you need five $1\frac{1}{16}$-ounce bars.*

Bittersweet Chocolate Sauce

This is especially delicious over Caramel (see page 339) or Coconut (see page 340) Ice Cream, or any other. It is really bittersweet—add a bit more sugar, if you wish—but for bittersweet lovers this is just right.

1¼ CUPS

½ cup milk
½ cup whipping cream
3 ounces unsweetened chocolate

2 tablespoons (or up to a total of 3 tablespoons) granulated sugar
1 tablespoon unsalted butter

Place the milk, cream, and chocolate in a heavy saucepan, uncovered, over low heat. Let cook, stirring occasionally, until the chocolate is melted. Then use a whisk, an eggbeater, or an electric mixer and whisk or beat until perfectly smooth. At first the chocolate will form tiny specks in the liquid, but as you continue to whisk or beat it will become smooth.

Stir in 2 tablespoons of the sugar. Taste it. Now it is extra-bittersweet. Add a bit more sugar, if you wish, until the sweetness/bitterness seems just right to you; remember that with cold/smooth/sweet ice cream, the bitter sauce is a great combination. Do not make the sauce too sweet. (I use 2 tablespoons but a total of 3 tablespoons is not too sweet.)

Add the butter and stir to melt.

Let stand until room temperature. The sauce will thicken slightly as it cools. It should be served at room temperature.

If you make this ahead of time and refrigerate it, reheat it slightly before serving.

Devil's Food Chocolate Sauce

Elegant; rich and buttery, dark and delicious chocolate. Serve warm or at room temperature; it may be reheated. Or serve it cold (it is great refrigerated —it becomes very thick when it is cold) over coffee ice cream.

This wants desperately to burn on the bottom of the pan while you are making it; use an enameled cast-iron pan (Le Creuset or any other equally heavy).

1⅔ CUPS

4 ounces (1 stick) unsalted butter
1 ounce unsweetened chocolate
⅔ cup granulated sugar
¼ cup unsweetened cocoa powder (preferably Dutch-process)

½ cup heavy whipping cream
1 teaspoon vanilla extract

In a 1- to 2-quart saucepan over low heat melt the butter and chocolate, stirring occasionally. Add the sugar, cocoa, and cream. Stir with a wire whisk until thoroughly incorporated. Increase the heat a bit to low-medium. Stir with a wire whisk occasionally and also scrape the bottom with a rubber spatula occasionally until the mixture comes to a low boil. (If you are impatient and if you use medium heat, scrape the bottom constantly with a rubber spatula.) Watch carefully for burning and adjust the heat as necessary.

When the mixture comes to a low boil, remove the pan from the heat and stir or whisk in the vanilla.

Serve hot or cooled. Reheat carefully to prevent burning (a double boiler is the safest way). Refrigerate up to two weeks if you wish.

NOTE: *I like to double the recipe and have an extra jar for our guests to take home.*

Index

for Cream Cheese Coffee
Cake, 155
for Fresh Apricot Pie, 29
for Frozen Peanut Butter Pie,
39
for Individual Maple Pecan
Tarts, 48
Lemon
Coconut, for Kansas
Cookies, 319
for Rancho Santa Fe
Lemon Tart, 51
for Lemon Cream Cheese
Pie, 256
for Pennsylvania Dutch
Peach Cobbler, 198
Prune and Apricot, for Prune
and Apricot Turnovers, 54
Raisin, for Raisin Pillows, 312
Salted Almond Chocolate, for
Salted Almond Chocolate
Pie, 44
for Savannah Banana Pie, 41
for Shoofly Pie, 35
for Sour Cream Apple Tart, 32
for Surprise Cakes, 182
for Tassies, 179
Whipped Cream, for Dione's
Chocolate Roll, 120
Flan, Cream Cheese (Flan de
Queso Crema), 225
Flour
notes on, 3
to sift, 3
Flowers, as cake decorations, 15
Fluffy Chocolate Icing, for Red
Beet Cake, 81
Folding, as technique, 13–14
Freezer thermometers, notes on,
10
Freezing techniques
for cakes, 17, 117
for cookies, 17
for egg whites and yolks, 6–7
for unbaked pie shells, 24
French Toast, Cinnamon Bun,
162
Fresh Apricot Pie, 28
Fresh ginger
in Chocolate Gingersnaps, 282
in Ginger Ginger Cake, 137
to grate, 8–9

notes on, 8
in 100 Percent Whole Wheat
Ginger Cookies, 302
Fried Bread Pudding, 218
Frozen Fudge Cake, 116
Frozen Peanut Butter Pie, 39
Fruit
Bars, California, 207
Layer, for Cranberry Grunt,
202
see also Names of fruits
Fruitcakes, to cut, 18
Frying thermometers, notes on,
10
Fudge
Cake, Frozen, 116
Caramel, Pecan Brownies, 274
Chocolate
Candy-Cookies, 294
Cookies (Chocolate
Miracles), 292
Everybody's Favorite, 353

Gelatin mixtures, to fold into,
13–14
Georgia Peach Cobbler, 196
Ginger
Cakes, Miniature, 180
candied
in Apple Cream Cheese Pie,
252
in Chocolate Gingersnaps,
282
in My Mother's
Gingersnaps, 300
in Scones, 149
Carrot Cake, 89
Cookies, 100 Percent Whole
Wheat, 302
fresh
in Chocolate Gingersnaps,
282
in Ginger Ginger Cake, 137
to grate, 8–9
notes on, 8
in 100 Percent Whole
Wheat Ginger Cookies,
302
in Gingerbread Muffins, 173
Ginger Cake, 137

White Pepper and, Lemon
Cake, 138
Gingerbread Muffins, 173
Gingersnaps
Chocolate, 282
My Mother's, 300
Glaze(s)
Apricot, for Rancho Santa Fe
Lemon Tart, 51
Big Daddy's, for Big Daddy's
Cake, 110
Bittersweet, for Miniature
Ginger Cakes, 181
for Blueberry Surprise Cake,
103
Chocolate, for Boston Cream
Pie, 72
for Cinnamon Buns, 161
for Doughnuts, 159
Lemon, for White Pepper and
Ginger Lemon Cake, 139
Orange, for Miami Beach
Sour Cream Cake, 126
for Oreo Cookie Cake, 124
for Washington State Cherry
Cobbler, 192
see also Icings; Sauces; Top-
pings
Goldrush Sauce, 366
Governor's, The, Crème
Fraîche, 362
Grand Marnier Strawberry
Soufflé, 236
Granny's Old-Fashioned Sugar
Cookies, 303
Grapefruit
to peel, 15
to section, 15
Grunt, Cranberry, 201

Half moon–shaped cookies, to
make, 304
Hard Sauce, for Indian
Pudding, 214
Heath Bars, in Candy Cookies,
290
Hershey's Brownies, 270
Hollywood Honey Cake, 147
Honey Cake, Hollywood, 147
Hot Chocolate Mousse, 228
Hot Peppered Pecans, 354

378

A Note About the Author

Maida Heatter, author of Maida Heatter's Book of Great Desserts, Maida Heatter's Book of Great Cookies, Maida Heatter's Book of Great Chocolate Desserts, and Maida Heatter's New Book of Great Desserts, is the daughter of Gabriel Heatter, the radio commentator. She studied fashion illustration at Pratt Institute and has done fashion illustrating and designing, made jewelry, and painted. But her first love has always been cooking. She taught it in classes in her home, in department stores, and at cooking schools across the country. For many years she made all the desserts for a popular Miami Beach restaurant owned by her husband, Ralph Daniels.

She prepared desserts for the 1983 Summit of Industrialized Nations at Colonial Williamsburg, Virginia, for President Reagan and six other heads of state.

Ms. Heatter has one daughter, Toni Evins, a painter and illustrator, who did the drawings for all of Ms. Heatter's books.

A Note on the Type

The text of this book was set in Electra, a typeface designed by William Addison Dwiggins for the Mergenthaler Linotype Company and first made available in 1935. Electra cannot be classified as either "modern" or "old-style." It is not based on any historical model, and hence does not echo any particular period or style of type design. It avoids the extreme contrast between thick and thin elements that marks most modern faces, and is without eccentricities that catch the eye and interfere with reading. In general, Electra is a simple, readable typeface that attempts to give a feeling of fluidity, power, and speed.

W. A. Dwiggins (1880–1956) began an association with the Mergenthaler Linotype Company in 1929 and over the next twenty-seven years designed a number of book types which include the Metro series, Electra, Caledonia, Eldorado, and Falcon.

Composed by Maryland Linotype Composition
Company, Inc., Baltimore, Maryland.
Printed and bound by Murray Printing Company,
Westford, Massachusetts.

Typography and binding design by Virginia Tan.

Jacket photograph credits: food stylist, Andrea Swinson; prop stylist, Linda Cheverton; Marseilles table spreads (foreground), from Laura Fisher; white-on-white trapunto quilt (background), 1825, from Thomas K. Woodard.